Black Collectibles
Sold In America

P.J. Gibbs

Photographs by P.J. Gibbs/Decorative Images

COLLECTOR BOOKS

A Division of Schroeder Publishing Co., Inc.

The current values in this book should be used only as a guide. They are not intended to set prices, which vary from one section of the country to another. Auction prices as well as dealer prices vary greatly and are affected by condition as well as demand. Neither the Author nor the Publisher assumes responsibility for any losses that might be incurred as a result of consulting this guide.

Additional copies of this book may be ordered from:

Collector Books
P.O. Box 3009
Paducah, KY 42002-3009

@ $19.95 Add $2.00 for postage and handling.

Copyright: P.J. Gibbs, 1987
Values updated: 1993

This book or any part thereof may not be reproduced without the written consent of the Author and Publisher.

Printed by IMAGE GRAPHICS, INC., Paducah, Kentucky

Dedication

The dedication of this book is to my very good friends Lynne D. and Dr. J. Lynne. Thank you for your relentless nudging and tenacity when I lost my direction with my writing, and to you, my dear Dr. J., for providing me with the main ingredient needed to get me back to my typewriter. The Summer of '89 will always have a special place in my heart and memory as a time for living life to its fullest.

Special Acknowledgment

This book could not have been written without the patience, cooperation and support of many people. In the buying, selling and trading world of Black collectibles, prices fluctuate as the market attempts to stabilize levels for many high-priced items. Those individuals and organizations that have contributed photographs, lists of Black collectibles, and auction catalogues are not responsible for the final prices or price ranges listed. We are extremely grateful, however, for their contributions. This book and the many listings would not be possible without the generosity of the following companies and individuals:

American Coins and Stamps Exchange
Madison, Tennessee

R. Carr Collection
California

Christie's East
New York, New York

M. Davern Collection
Pennsylvania

Elam Collection
Whiteway Antique Mall
Nashville, Tennessee

M. Falls Collection
Tennessee

Buck Froman Collection
Oregon

The Great Escape
Nashville, Tennessee

Harris Auction Galleries
Baltimore, Maryland

Lost & Found Antiques
Kensington, Maryland

V. Mackemull Collection
Maryland

Mannings Books & Prints
San Francisco, California

Mountain Manner (Ghost) Antiques
Hamburg, Pennsylvania

Museum of Tobacco Art and History
U.S. Tobacco Company
Nashville, Tennessee

John C. Newcomer – Americana
Keedysville, Maryland

The Paper Pile
San Anselmo, California

Phillips Collection
Maryland

Pineapple Door Antiques
Chattanooga, Tennessee

Public Library of Nashville/
Davidson County
Nashville, Tennessee

Ron Rooks
Baltimore, Maryland

Rossman Collection
California

Saad and Sharpe Collection
Nashville Antique Mall
Nashville, Tennessee

Sotheby's
New York, New York

Tennessee State Museum
Nashville, Tennessee

Charlene Upham – Antiques
Mardela Springs, Maryland

Village Antiques, Inc.
Tampa, Florida

Whiteway Antique Mall
Nashville, Tennessee

References

Christie's East. *Christie's Collectibles*, (1975–1979). New York, New York: Christie's East.

Foulke, Jan and Howard. *4th, 5th, and 6th Blue Book/Dolls & Values*, Cumberland, Maryland: Hobby House Press, Inc.

Harris Auction Galleries, Inc. "Collector's Auction – Black Americana," (July, 1983, 1981 & March, 1984). Baltimore, Maryland: Harris Auction Galleries.

Ketchum, Jr., William C. *The Catalog of American Collectibles*, New York, New York: Rutledge Books.

The Catalog of American Antiques, New York, New York: Rutledge Books.

Kovel, Ralph and Terry. *Kovel's Antiques & Collectibles Price List.* New York, New York: Crown Publishers, Inc.

Rinker, Harry I. *Warman's Americana & Collectibles, 1st Edition.* Elkins Park, Pennsylvania: Warman Publishing Company, Inc.

Table of Contents

Preface

This book has been written in an attempt to organize and to supply information about a large group of antiques that are becoming very popular in today's collectibles market. Black items have been collected in America since the beginning of the 18th century. There is a wide range of collectible Black items which reflect both the changing times of our country and the change of attitudes toward the Black people which these items represent. These rather unique and somewhat controversial items have intrigued collectors for centuries. It was not until the late 1800s that a noticeable interest in Black collectibles became apparent. Advertisers and manufacturers began to turn out items bearing the images of Black Americans and African people by the millions. These items were geared mainly toward the souvenir market and thus became widespread in America and abroad. Most of the items were of a comical nature and impelled many buyers to mail them as gifts of novelty to friends and family. The range of the Black memorabilia was from ceramic figurines of varying sizes to postcards of varying materials such as silk, linen, leather, and ordinary paper types.

Prior to the 1930s, one may safely assume that there was a great demand for Black memorabilia since there are still literally thousands of these items on the market today from that era. Between the 1930s and the 1950s, there was a gradual change in the number of Black artisans, directly related to the WPA (Work Projects Administration) created by the federal government which put Black artisans to work on a number of cultural projects. Black items consist of both the "exaggerated" and "naturalistic" images. Also Black collectibles consist of those items made in the image of Black people and those items made by Black artisans. As one might expect, there was not a great demand for items that could not be readily utilized between the 1930s and the 1950s, since the Depression, World War II, and the Korean Conflict all had an impact on the personal economy of most Americans. There is, however, a great demand today for items from this time period because they not only reflect the Art Deco style, WPA work projects by Black artisans, and the Impressionistic-Surrealistic art styles of the 1940s and early 1950s, but Black memorabilia from this period is also rare and highly collectible.

After the 1950s and into the 1960s–early 1970s, there was an increase in the amount and variety of Black material culture. This increase reflects the improved economy, the increase in the number of Black artisans and novelty and toy manufacturers, and the gradual change in the image which Americans had of Blacks. The Civil Rights Movement during the 1960s and 1970s spawned a great deal of new artistic products not only about Blacks but also by Black artisans. These items include, but are not limited to: (1) protest posters; (2) stamps of famous Blacks; (3) busts and statues; (4) paintings and prints; (5) stationery and postcards; (6) ethnically correct dolls and toys and (7) ceramics and sculptures. Ironically, although these items are of recent vintage, very few can be found on the collectibles market. Most probably, because such items were heavily utilized and subsequently destroyed during the mid-1970s, very few remain today.

This book will discuss the Black collectibles market, focusing on the controversy, Black collectibles trend and development, prices of Black collectibles, where to find Black collectibles, collecting and classification of Black collectibles. A number of selected color photographs and a list of museums with Black memorabilia have been included. The intent of this book is not to present information about every company, individual and country that made Black collectibles, rather the attempt is to give the reader enough general information to gain some understanding about the different types of Black material culture that he or she will encounter.

Let us hear from you! For information about our monthly guide to buyers, sellers, and traders of Black collectibles and to tell us about your collection, write to:

CGL
Box 158472
Nashville, Tennessee 37215

Introduction

Black memorabilia has been, and is still being made today, by both Black and White artisans. In order for an item to be considered a Black collectible, it must be made in the imagery of a Black person or it must be directly attributed to a Black artisan. The first of these items usually depicted slaves of an unusual beauty, those exhibiting a particular physical oddity, or those working at their appointed tasks. Many White artists were intrigued by the Black people and produced some paintings and carvings representing Blacks. The slaves also created not only art depicting their own people, but other subjects as well, such as iron fences, pottery, furniture, and folk-carvings. Since slaves were not taught to write for many years, their works usually were not signed, with some few exceptions. Not all White artists signed their works either, thus the problem of maker identification is common in earlier material culture created by both Blacks and Whites.

It is our opinion, after much observation, that unless a signature or identifying mark is found on a piece of art, one can only determine its origin by the process of elimination and comparison with other styles of the same period. When researching early Black memorabilia which was not mass produced, the process of elimination becomes a tedious task and one has to rely not only on written data but on a certain amount of insight along with a working knowledge of historical events. For example, if a piece of furniture found in an old Charleston, South Carolina home has been attributed to a slave but lacks readily available documentation, one would have to do a piece of investigative work.

After purchasing the piece from the dealer, one would first identify the home out of which the piece originated, through simply asking the dealer the origin of the estate. Once the name of the estate had been established, then one would have to locate old records identifying the contents of the estate. One might find them in the hands of the family, a museum (not necessarily locally), state archives, or some other private collector. A search of the records would be made to establish that the item in question did exist among the household effects. If this is found to be true, the next step is to determine whether the furnishings were made on the premises or purchased elsewhere. To accomplish this, one has to locate some documentation, usually a diary or family history which indicates that such articles were indeed created on the estate's premises. After all of the above steps have been taken, it has to be further established that slaves in this household were trained to make the article in question, thus giving more credibility to the idea that the article was made by a slave. Information pertaining to slave-holdings of a household were usually filed with local city government and stated the occupation or training of the slaves. After extensive investigative work, the only conclusion that can be drawn is, "This article from the said estate may possibly have been made by a slave." We have cited this example to illustrate the difficulty in positively identifying the unsigned and undocumented works often attributed to slaves.

It has been the trend for most folk-styled works of art of Black people to be instantly attributed to a Black artisan. Along with this attribution, a collector may also expect an increase in the cost of the piece. If indeed the piece can be accurately attributed to a Black artisan, the value of such a piece should be greatly escalated due to its rarity.

The collector should buy any collectible, and especially a Black collectible, because he or she likes it, not for the long stories which usually accompany the hand made pieces. If the item is made in the image of a Black person without exaggerated features and it pre-dates 1850, it is already a rare piece. Most items made after 1850 were made in large quantities and will usually bear a manufacturer's name. The mass-produced items can sometimes be as costly as the earlier handmade items if they are well executed and unique. Due to the variety of execution methods and quality of Black memorabilia, we have devised a classification system. Our classification system is based on two things – the technique used to produce the items and the quality of their execution. In order to simplify our classification system we have assigned the letters A to G for determining the technique of execution and the numbers 1 to 3 to denote the quality of execution. It is our hope that the classification system put forth in this book will become a standard measurement for all Black collectibles of the past as well as the future.

As mentioned earlier, handmade articles were mostly made prior to the early 1900s. Folk art pieces dominated the earlier years, including such items as wooden dolls and toys, furnishings, single portraits, paintings of slaves and Black farm workers in the fields, nannies caring for the children of White families, on occasion, a Black family in front of a small cabin, and a large quantity of Black rag dolls, commonly called "mammy" and "pickaninny" dolls. All of the items mentioned above are rare and usually expensive if they are found in good to fair condition. After the industries of our country became highly mechanized, all consumable goods experienced an increase in production. The techniques used to create Black items changed but the subject matter did not. Millions of cloth dolls were produced along with "mammy" type ceramic cookie jars, small figurines of Blacks with alligators chasing them, metal banks, tin toys, prints advertising tobacco and whiskey, other paper goods ranging from soap powder boxes (Gold Dust) with widely smiling Black children with untidy hair and bulging eyes to dainty etchings of beautiful Black ladies and distinguished Black gentlemen. The American market had fully opened up! Between the early 1900s and 1950s, the bulk of the Black collectibles being made was comparable with those made earlier, with a tremendous increase in production. In addition to the more common objects being produced, there were decorative silver and pewter spoons with Black images as their theme, coins bearing the faces of Blacks of importance, movie posters, sheet music, lamp bases, an occasional beverage pitcher and tumblers, photographs and prints (hand tinted), wooden shaving brushes and clothes brushes, hair combs plus accompanying paper labels showcasing hairstyles achieved by using certain advertised products, and an increase in the number of non-cloth Black dolls (made of popular materials of which White dolls were being made) appearing in trendy outfits.

The items discussed above were those objects depicting Black images. We have not, however, considered the numerous talented Black artisans of the early 19th and 20th centuries. These artisans were working to create furniture, paintings, pottery, ceramics, photographs, and dolls. Unfortunately, many of these items are unsigned or they are often indistinguishable from works by non-Black artists of the same time period. In earlier works by Black artisans, some vestiges of an "African Heritage" can be detected. Over the years, many Black artisans' works exhibiting this influence were rejected by White art critics and collectors. Their works were harshly judged and called unskillful. As a direct result, many Black artists discontinued the use of their African stylization and incorporated more European styles. The integrating of European styles into Black art has made if difficult to distinguish Black art from non-Black art. Many of the late 19th century and early-to-mid 20th century Black art works are considered "sleepers" as collectible memorabilia.

To this point, we have only talked about American-made Black memorabilia. There is, however, a large quantity of items on the market that were made in other countries such as England, Germany, France, China, Japan, and on the continents of Africa and Australia. Some of these countries had Black populations that would fashion items in their image, usually immigrants from Africa, West Indies, or Australia (Aborigines). Some of the collectibles found from these foreign countries are considerably older than American Black collectibles. An old Black collectible of American origin is considered to be rare but not necessarily more valuable than a foreign object. Foreign Black collectibles are often thought of as examples from Japan during the 20th century. Although the market is abundant with 1920–1940 Japanese imports, there is still an equally large number of quality foreign Black memorabilia available today.

During the period from 1950 to 1970, the images of Black-related material changed from caricature to more naturalistic figures. The creation of the many toys, ceramics, mammy dolls, and caricature advertising prints slowed in most industries. This period in America marked a change in our history. Whites in America began to respond to the new image which Black Americans exhibited. A civil rights movement was launched full scale in this country by the 1960s. A growing concern for the negative imagery affecting Black children became a national issue. The market for derogatory items, as described above, dropped drastically. A new demand for more naturalistic material was created and the industries supplied this new demand full scale. More Black people began to earn competitive salaries and they too participated in the buying market. Black-owned toy companies began to open; art galleries, ceramic shops, and many other types of traditionally White-only businesses thrived.

The Controversy

The controversy over the existence of Black collectibles is one which divides the collectors into two major camps. One camp feels items which depict Blacks in a negative light should not be sold. On the other side, individuals feel that Black collectibles are an artifact of history, and as such, should be sold in the same manner that other artifacts are sold. In this instance, there is no right or wrong. Both sides have valid reasons for their acceptance or rejection of different types of Black collectibles.

What is left beyond the controversy are some observations. First, Black collectibles of all types have been increasing in popularity in recent years. The evidence for this movement is quite clear and noticeable. For years, dealers hid the Black collectibles for fear that the patrons would be offended. Over the past 15 years (since the early 1970s), the attitude of the dealer has changed a burgeoning marketplace. These changes are reflected in the liquidation of large Black collections, a special auction devoted exclusively to Black collectibles, shows which have only dealers in Black collectibles, at least two major conferences on Black memorabilia, the creation of Black collectibles museums, the setting aside of special places on the shelves of shops, flea markets and shows, mail order dealers for selected customers, and the publication of several articles and pamphlets on Black antiquities. Quite obviously, the buying, selling and trading area for Black memorabilia is changing as it establishes a place in the collectibles market.

Second, their existence cannot be denied in spite of the controversy over their aesthetic presentation. Although not considered to be collectible until recent years, Black antiquities have a long history of being created in many countries around the world. Whether created in Africa or France, Black material culture reflected the feelings of the creators about their subject matter. The interesting issue is that Black collectibles are not usually thought of when one considers African artifacts. African artifacts are separated from items created especially to represent Black persons living in the United States. Although England, France, West Germany, Italy, and South Africa exported items with Blacks on them to the United States to a limited degree, the bulk of exported material came from Japan. The question arises, "Which Blacks were these countries representing?"

Third and last, the range of Black antiquities is extremely large when items representing Blacks and material created by Blacks are both considered. Because items with Blacks as subjects are easily identified as Black memorabilia, the materials created by Black artisans such as pottery, furniture, ceramics, dolls, prints, paintings, or books are usually not looked upon as Black collectibles. Most assuredly they are Black collectibles, and as stated earlier, represent rare items, extremely collectible and sleepers (not currently sought after, but may be in demand in the coming years.) This book makes no attempt to illustrate each type of Black collectible but rather gives a broad background and shows representative samples of Black material culture.

Black Collectibles – Trend and Development

This trend toward collecting Black-related memorabilia is not as recent as the antiques market might indicate. During the early 1900s, toys with Blacks as subjects were popular, as evidenced by the many varieties which have survived to this date. In addition, although not always naturalistic in their representation, small ceramic figurines, mammy dolls, composition dolls, and folk art were popular. No one can predict how long this trend will last. The expectation is that Black collectibles will follow the route of other types of antiquities. The following is the expected trend:

LEVEL I:
The item is sold at an auction house, antique shop, or antique show. It is introduced to the public as a collectible and random prices prevail. Market for this item is not yet established.

LEVEL II:
After introduction, item begins to circulate among dealers and demand increases as public awareness increases. Market price not yet set. Items become available as public sells to dealer. Item becomes collectible.

LEVEL III:
Item gains popularity as information about it appears in collectible publications. Dealers increase stock, and auction houses continue sales to meet public interest. Poorly executed items sell rapidly. Quality items sell at auctions, usually bringing higher prices and beginning to set the price of related items.

LEVEL IV:
Marketplace is saturated with item and prices reach regionally stable levels. Demand levels off. Publications continue, and turning point for item is reached in market.

LEVEL V:
As item stabilization point is reached, several things can occur. (A) Item demand decreases while antique dealers' shelves increase with stock. Prices decrease and public loses interest. (B) Item demand stabilizes, prices remain constant regionally, stock remains stable, and public interest is constant. (C) Item demand increases while prices rise for quality items. Poor quality items stockpile. Public interest increases and publications increase.

Black collectibles are presently at the Level II stage of the collectible development – the public demand is beginning. Prices are unstable, auction sales are developing, and shows specializing in Black collectibles are increasing. The time involved in Black collectibles moving from Level I to Level V is unpredictable. If they follow the route of other collectible trends, a few years is expected for the full transition of Black collectible development. With a collectible as highly demanded as is the Black collectible, it may experience a trend of prolonged "price instability," as the doll market in America has seen. Once the price is stabilized regionally, one may settle in for a long and interesting collecting experience. The variety of these collectibles can be a constant amazement and delight to even the avid collectors.

Prices of Black Collectibles

Determining the amount to pay for a particular Black collectible depends on two major things – demand and quality of the item in question. The demand is measured by the number of persons who seek Black collectibles and the number of dealers who seek to find and sell these items. Mammy dolls, composition and vinyl Black dolls, ceramic figurines, inexpensive Cream of Wheat prints, Black banks and tins are in the greatest demand. Most of these items tend to be readily accessible. Other things such as folk art, primitive paintings, paintings from the 1930s–1950s, Black wooden dolls, bisque and china dolls, large original posters, and documented furniture, sculpture, pottery, and artwork by Black artisans are more expensive. For Black memorabilia, inexpensive items which were originally cheap tend to remain inexpensive. Items which are either handmade by Black or non-Black artisans or well-executed manufactured pieces are expensive.

No one can guarantee the investment quality of a Black collectible although such claims are often made. One often hears dealers speak of "investment quality Black collectibles" as if there is some method for insuring that prices will increase. Moreover, the terms *rare* and *unusual* are used to add an increased price to a particular item. Unless the item in question is handmade, unusual, or unique as determined by the classification system – A through G – the high price tags often presented are not justifiable. Quality is the often intangible judgment made about a collectible and is usually attributed to the item by consensus of the dealer and buyer in the marketplace. Such consensus has not yet been reached about the many different types of Black memorabilia, and therefore, prices fluctuate locally and regionally. Black collectibles generally run 10% to 30% higher than non-Black comparable items. Although popular, the collectibles in which Blacks were subjects or those made by Black artisans are less available than similar items within a given category but ceramic figures, plastic salt and pepper shakers, plastic syrup dispensers, Cream of Wheat prints, sheet music, record albums, and other such items are easy to find. The prices of Black collectibles will be determined by eventual marketplace demand and the quality of the items which eventually are for sale.

Where To Find Black Collectibles

Finding Black collectibles can prove to be an interesting but often difficult task if you do not know where to look. It has been the belief of many dealers and collectors that large quantities of Black collectibles are in the Black community. While this is the case in some instances, Whites have equal quantities of Black collectibles. In fact, both Blacks and Whites have been buying these pieces for many years.

Black collectibles can also be found at estate sales, yard sales, auctions, flea markets, and junk shops. Estate sales and flea markets are the best places to begin your search. It has been our experience that if you do not ask for the Black-related items, you may miss out. Many times we have been ready to depart from a "searching ground" and have decided to inquire about Black collectibles. You may have guessed it – several treasures were produced. We have yet to figure out why the collectibles are pulled out from what appear to be hiding places or keepsake areas. If you are a serious collector, *look everywhere and ask everyone.*

When buying your treasures, try to buy them in groups, even if you already have duplicates. This buying behavior will help ensure you the first phone call when more of the merchandise is available through your source. Duplicates can prove to be "gems." You can trade your duplicates for others items or sell them for cash. Buying, selling, and trading are always good courses of action when you are trying to build a collection. By participating in all three of the above activities, you are in contact with a larger group of people that can help develop your collection. On occasion, you may want to run an ad in a national or regional trade paper for collectors, advertising your desires or your sell items. You will be surprised at the response. Our collection has been amassed mainly by mail purchases. In one year, we managed to collect over 1,000 Black postcards all by mail.

Collecting

Collectors are offered a wide variety of items when beginning their Black collections. Some people choose to develop a diverse collection of paintings, prints, ceramics, toys, etc., to exhibit the realm of the collectibles. Others may choose to concentrate on ceramic goods or any of the many other media available. The selective collectors often concentrate their efforts on amassing large collections of all media from a single time period, for example circa 1850–1900.

The important thing to remember when collecting is to buy the very best for your money. If you decide to collect only decorative Black spoons, buy the best. Do not be tempted by the low cost of inferior quality items. You may have only a few items at the end of a year's search, but your collectibles will be of a higher quality. Should you ever want to liquidate your collection, you can do so more easily than if you had a larger number of poor quality items. Since the prices have not been set regionally for Black collectibles, you will be wise to try to buy as low as possible. Upon the release of this book and future written material, it is our belief that prices will begin to stabilize regionally.

Collecting Black collectibles can be fun, educational, and exciting. Enjoy!!

Classification of Black Collectibles

Because Black collectibles vary in quality, there has to be a method for grading them. Below is a classification system which accounts for quality of the collectible:
1. Handmade or manufactured
2. Black or non-Black artisan
3. Mass produced or not
4. Unique or common
5. Signed or unsigned

It also accounts for the various grades of Black collectibles:
1. Excellent execution
2. Average execution
3. Poor execution

CLASS A – Black artisan, handmade, not mass-produced, unique, documented and/or signed.
1. Excellent execution
2. Average execution
3. Poor execution

CLASS B – Non-Black artisan, handmade, not mass-produced, unique, documented and/or signed.
1. Excellent execution
2. Average execution
3. Poor execution

CLASS C – Handmade, unique, not mass-produced, undocumented and/or unsigned.
1. Excellent execution
2. Average execution
3. Poor execution

CLASS D – Manufactured, mass-produced, unique, documented and/or signed.
1. Excellent execution
2. Average execution
3. Poor execution

CLASS E – Manufactured, mass-produced, not unique, documented and/or signed.
1. Excellent execution
2. Average execution
3. Poor execution

CLASS F – Undocumented and/or unsigned, mass-produced, manufactured, unique.
1. Excellent execution
2. Average execution
3. Poor execution

CLASS G – Undocumented and/or unsigned, manufactured, mass-produced, not unique.
1. Excellent execution
2. Average execution
3. Poor execution

Guide To Using This Book

The remainder of this book has both color photographs and over 1,000 additional listings of other Black collectibles not shown. The photographs are divided into broad categories covering many smaller subject headings. Please read the introductory paragraph which explains each section.

You will also find the classification system in use under each photograph. The classification system is made available to help you organize the quality of varying types of Black collectibles. Following the color plate section are additional listings of Black collectibles not represented in photos.

SELECTED PHOTOGRAPHS

Pictorial Images

Novelties and Souvenirs, and Pictorial Images are the largest areas of Black collectibles. In this book, "Pictorial Images" covers all of the topics under the following categories: (1) paintings, (2) photographs, (3) postcards, and (4) prints. These four categories have been placed under this one heading because they all are two-dimensional images in various media. Paintings can represent both Blacks as the subject and Blacks as the artisan. As subjects, paintings of Blacks can date back as far as the arrival of Blacks in America. Painting of Blacks which pre-date the 1820s are very rare. For the most part, paintings found after the 1820s show Blacks working or in portraiture style. Black artists in America were rare and did not become recognized until the first half of the 20th century. Because there are so many artists, we recommend that persons study this category carefully and research other written materials on the topic before purchasing large quantities of paintings. Paintings of Blacks by noted artists can cost thousands of dollars. To date, however, very few paintings by Black artists are costly because few were able to exhibit their works in major galleries prior to the 1950s.

Some rare photographs depicting slaves during the 1860s represent only a small portion of this vast field of collecting. Most collectible photographs found today date between the late 1880s and the 1920s and feature different types of photographic techniques (i.e. ambrotypes, daguerreotypes, tin types, and photogravures.) Common images on photographs are Black men and women. The rare images are children, with the rarest being babies. Common photographs are usually less than $100.00. Rare photographs illustrating Black cowboys, Confederate soldiers, famous personalities (prior to the 1930s) are often expensive – $100.00 plus.

Postcards are the most common of the pictorial images. Postcards with Black images are found in a variety of materials, i.e. silk, leather, linen, and paper. Plentiful are those cards with sterotypical images on them. Rare are those cards with famous Blacks, Black history scenes, and cards with moveable parts. The average cost of a card is $3.00 to $10.00 with the rarer ones costing considerably more.

Prints cover the following areas: (1) prints made from paintings, (2) woodcuts, (3) steel engravings, (4) lithographs. Such areas illustrate the variety of published material found with Black images: newspapers such as *Harper's Weekly* and *Frank Leslie's Illustrated,* magazines such as *Judge, Puck,* and *Post,* encyclopedias with illustrated stories of Blacks, Currier and Ives prints, and all books with articles about Blacks accompanied by illustrations. Generally, prints which were originally made to be prints, such as Currier and Ives, are expensive and highly collectible. Illustrations taken from books or magazines are usually less than $50.00 each and are not as much in demand.

Category: Pictorial Images
Item Type: Photograph
Classification: G-3
Dimensions: 5½" h x 3½" w
Description: Photographic postcard, semi-glossy. No postmark. Fair condition with some fading.
Artisan/Manufacturer: Unmarked
Date: ca. 1915–1940
Price range: $20.00–30.00
Note of Interest: Scarce

Category: Pictorial Images
Item Type: Photograph
Classification: F-2
Dimensions: 5½" h x 3½" w
Description: Photographic postcard, semi-glossy. No postmark. Good condition.
Artisan/Manufacturer: Unmarked
Date: ca. 1915–1940
Price range: $20.00–35.00
Note of Interest: Scarce

Category: Pictorial Images
Item Type: Photograph
Classification: F-2
Dimensions: 5½" h x 3½" w
Description: Photographic postcard, semi-glossy. No postmark. Good condition.
Artisan/Manufacturer: Unmarked
Date: ca. 1915–1940
Price range: $25.00–35.00
Note of Interest: Scarce

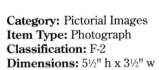

Category: Pictorial Images
Item Type: Photograph
Classification: F-2
Dimensions: 5½" h x 3½" w
Description: Photographic postcard, no postmark.
Artisan/Manufacturer: Unmarked
Date: ca. 1915–1940
Price range: $25.00–35.00
Note of Interest: Scarce

Category: Pictorial Images
Item Type: Photograph
Classification: G-2
Dimensions: 14" h x 11" w
Description: Charcoal-enhanced photograph. The edges have been crudely cut down to fit into a frame. White paint used to outline the lace on the subject's dress. Good condition.
Artisan/Manufacturer: Unmarked
Date: ca. 1880s–1920s
Price range: $75.00–95.00
Note of Interest: Plentiful

Category: Pictorial Images
Item Type: Photograph
Classification: E-3
Dimensions: 9¼" h x 10½" w
Description: A group photograph of "The Charleston, S.C. Orphans Brass Band." Good condition.
Artisan/Manufacturer: Unmarked, origin South Carolina.
Date: ca. 1920s–1940s
Price range: $28.00–38.00
Note of Interest: Common/plentiful. The technique used to develop the above photograph is common and can easily be found with different subject matters. However, it is not an easy task to find old photographs of Blacks with documentation unless they are celebrities.

Category: Pictorial Images
Item Type: Photograph
Classification: D-2
Dimensions: 29" h x 34" w
Description: Handpainted photograph of a Florida scene. "Southern Waters." Original frame, excellent condition.
Artisan/Manufacturer: A. Thieme U.S. Print No. 931
Date: ca. 1930s
Price range: $250.00–375.00
Note of Interest: Common

Category: Pictorial Images
Item Type: Photograph
Classification: E-2
Dimensions: 6" h x 4½" w
Description: Studio photograph of what appears to be a middle-class Black lady. Good condition.
Artisan/Manufacturer: J.B. Whatley; Marshall, Texas
Date: ca. 1880s–1890s
Price range: $20.00–25.00
Note of Interest: Common

Category: Pictorial Images
Item Type: Photograph
Classification: F-1
Dimensions: 20½" h x 26½" w
Description: Charcoal enhanced photograph with handbrushed outlines on the babies' gowns. Original oak frame. Some water damage on the edges of the photograph. Good condition.
Artisan/Manufacturer: Unmarked
Date: ca. 1875–1890s
Price range: $250.00–375.00
Note of Interest: Scarce

Painting (Crayon)

Category: Pictorial Images
Item Type: Painting, watercolor
Classification: B-2
Dimensions: 8" h x 6½" w
Description: An original watercolor rendered in caricature form. Signed and dated, excellent condition. Taken from the artist's sketch pad (perforated edges still visible.)
Artisan/Manufacturer: Gregor Duncan
Date: ca. 1937
Price range: $300.00–450.00
Credits: The Paper Pile; San Anselmo, California
Note of Interest: Scarce. The artist of the above watercolor is noted for his works in various magazines.

Category: Pictorial Images
Item Type: Painting, crayon
Classification: B-2
Dimensions: 17" h x 13" w
Description: Framed crayon skillfully done. Linear in form with hard and soft lines to create shadows and distinct separation of images while maintaining a harmonious balance of complimentary colors with some gradations of certain hues. Excellent condition, signed.
Artisan/Manufacturer: Davenport Griffin
Date: ca. 1930s
Price range: $2,500.00–3,000.00
Credits: Village Antiques Inc.; Tampa, Florida
Note of Interest: Scarce. Davenport Griffin was a painter, teacher, and lithographer.

Category: Pictorial Images
Item Type: Painting
Classification: B-2
Dimensions: 16" h x 19½" w
Description: Well-executed street scene done on paper. Excellent condition, signed.
Artisan/Manufacturer: Ann Hunter
Date: ca. 1900–1930
Price range: $450.00–600.00
Credits: Village Antiques Inc.; Tampa, Florida
Note of Interest: Scarce

Category: Pictorial Images
Item Type: Drawing/Etching
Classification: B-3
Dimensions: 17" h x 19" w
Description: Sailboat with men active in the foreground. Black and white rendering. Excellent condition. Signed and numbered.
Artisan/Manufacturer: George Pearse Ennis. Marked Ennis #11, name signed in script.
Date: ca. 1920s
Price range: $1,800.00–2,800.00
Credits: Village Antiques Inc.; Tampa, Florida
Note of Interest: Scarce

Postcards

Category: Pictorial Images
Item Type: Postcard
Classification: D-2
Dimensions: 5½" h x 3½" w
Description: Black and white gravure of a small Black child done in caricature. Signed by the artist, Dennis Ton. "Some Folks Made Me Tir'd." Postmark on the back 1912, U.S. postage green 1¢ stamp. Good condition.
Artisan/Manufacturer: Gravure series No. #283
Date: ca. 1912
Price range: $20.00–30.00
Note of Interest: Common

Category: Pictorial Images
Item Type: Postcard
Classification: D-2
Dimensions: 7¾" h x 5" w
Description: "Where is dat Valentine at ob mine." A caricature, linen postcard.
Artisan/Manufacturer: Tuck
Date: ca. 1910
Price range: $18.00–30.00
Credits: The Paper Pile; San Anselmo, California
Note of Interest: Common

Category: Pictorial Images
Item Type: Stereo-optic view card, "Down in Dixie."
Classification: D-2
Dimensions: 3½" h x 7" w
Description: Low gloss pressed paper card with subtle coloring. Good condition.

Artisan/Manufacturer: Griffith & Griffith; The World Wide View Co., 200 Monroe Street, Chicago, Illinois
Date: ca. 1915–1930
Price range: $15.00–20.00
Note of Interest: Common

Category: Pictorial Images
Item Type: Stereo-optic view card, "95. Mrs. Newlywed's New Wench Cook."
Classification: D-2
Dimensions: 3½" h x 7" w
Description: Low gloss pressed paper card with subtle coloring. Good condition.

Artisan/Manufacturer: Griffith & Griffith; The World Wide View Co., 200 Monroe Street, Chicago, Illinois
Date: ca. 1915–1930
Price range: $15.00–20.00
Note of Interest: Common

Category: Pictorial Images
Item Type: Stereo-optic view card, "91. Tell Me Dat You Lub Me Darlin' Dina."
Classification: D-2
Dimensions: 3½" h x 7" w
Description: Low gloss pressed paper card with subtle coloring. Good condition.

Artisan/Manufacturer: Griffith & Griffith; The World Wide View Co., 200 Monroe Street, Chicago, Illinois
Date: ca. 1915–1930
Price range: $25.00–30.00
Note of Interest: Common

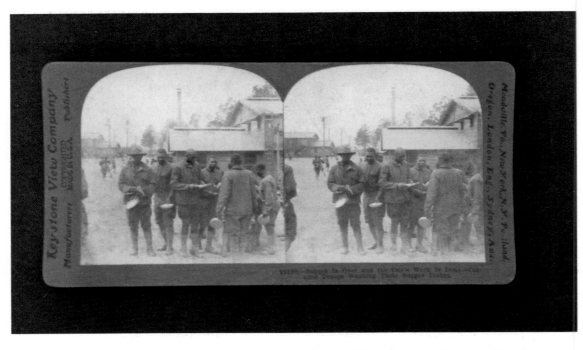

Category: Pictorial Images
Item Type: Stereo-optic view card, "19108. Supper Is Over and the Day's Work Is Done – Colored Troops Washing Their Supper Dishes."
Classification: D-2
Dimensions: 3½" h x 7" w
Description: Low gloss arch-shaped photographs mounted on a pressed paper card. Good condition.

Artisan/Manufacturer: Keystone View Company, copyrighted. Made in U.S.A. Meadville, Pa.; New York, N.Y.; Portland, Oregon; London, England; Sydney Australia.
Date: ca. 1915–1940
Price range: $25.00–30.00
Note of Interest: Common. Old photographs of Black soldiers are in demand.

Category: Pictorial Images
Item Type: Sunday School card (enrollment card), postcard
Classification: G-3
Dimensions: 5½" h x 3½" w
Description: Tinted photograph with small children seated, displaying an empty chair for the new enrollee. Photo on the top half of a paper card with the bottom half available for information. Postcard on the back.
Artisan/Manufacturer: Unknown
Date: ca. 1940s–1950s
Price range: $8.00–18.00
Note of Interest: Plentiful

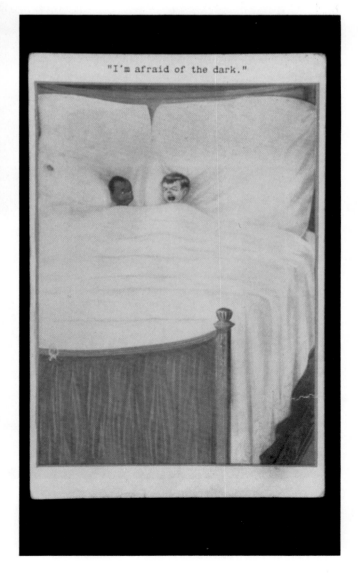

Category: Pictorial Images
Item Type: Postcard
Classification: D-3
Dimensions: 5½" h x 3½" w
Description: Linen postcard, making commentary on the Black/White issue, light-heartedly done, "I'm afraid of the dark." Postmaked "Tompkins Sq. Station, New York 1914" with 1¢ green stamp. Good condition.
Artisan/Manufacturer: Quaint Kid Series
Date: ca. 1914
Price range: $25.00–35.00
Note of Interest: Common

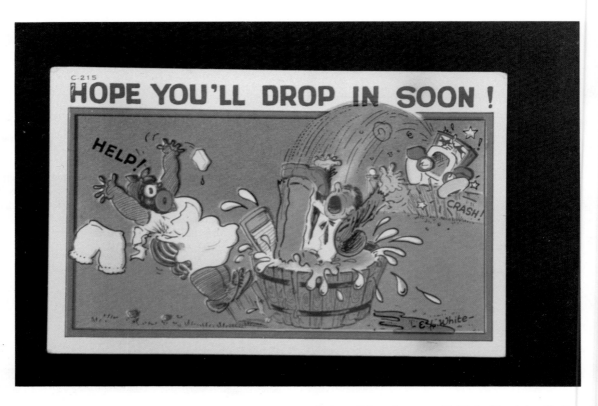

Category: Pictorial Images
Item Type: Postcard
Classification: E-3
Dimensions: 3½" h x 5½" w
Description: Caricature line postcard, "Hope You'll Drop In Soon!" No postmark on the back. Good condition.

Artisan/Manufacturer: Published by Asheville Post Card Co., Asheville, North Carolina
Date: ca. 1910–1930s
Price range: $8.00–12.00
Note of Interest: Plentiful

Category: Pictorial Images
Item Type: Postcard
Classification: G-3
Dimensions: 3½" h x 5½" w
Description: Linen postcard, comical caricature, "Shut Yo'

Mouth and Mammy Will Have You White As Snow In A Minute!" No postmark. Colorful.
Artisan/Manufacturer: Unmarked
Date: ca. 1930s–1950s
Price range: $8.00–12.00
Note of Interest: Plentiful

Category: Pictorial Images
Item Type: Postcard
Classification: G-2
Dimensions: 3½" h x 5½" w
Description: Embossed image, brightly colored on a beige background. "New Year Wishin, I'se heap happy an' I wants yu to be happy too." Satin finish on linen. 1919 postmark.
Artisan/Manufacturer: © (with "S. BERGMAN – 1913 – N–Y–) surrounding the circle. Lower left corner on back.
Date: ca. 1913
Price range: $15.00–20.00
Note of Interest: Common

Category: Pictorial Images
Item Type: Postcard
Classification: D-1
Dimensions: 5½" h x 3½" w
Description: Low gloss photograph. "I'm so lonesome, awful lonesome, Gee! I wish I had a beau!" Signed by the artist and dated.
Artisan/Manufacturer: Copyright 1908 by E.G. Harris, Denver, Colorado, No. 6.
Date: ca. 1908
Price range: $25.00–35.00
Note of Interest: Scarce

Category: Pictorial Images
Item Type: Postcard
Classification: E-3
Dimensions: 3½" h x 5½" w
Description: Linen, comical caricature, "I May Be A 'Little Shaver' – But I Got Mah Eye On Somethin' BIG!" No postmark.

Artisan/Manufacturer: Published for Asheville Post Card Co., Asheville, North Carolina. A "Colourpicture" publication.
Date: ca. 1930s–1950s
Price range: $8.00–12.00
Note of Interest: Plentiful

Category: Pictorial Images
Item Type: Postcard
Classification: E-3
Dimensions: 3½" h x 5½" w
Description: Glossy paper postcard, comical caricature, "What Would You Have Done?" No postmark.

Artisan/Manufacturer: Published by Asheville Post Card Co., Asheville, North Carolina 28802. K-828
Date: ca. 1950s–1960s
Price range: $8.00–12.00
Note of Interest: Plentiful

Category: Pictorial Images
Item Type: Postcard
Classification: E-3
Dimensions: 5½″ h x 3½″ w
Description: Vibrantly colored linen postcard, comical caricature, "Two Loving Hearts." Good condition.
Artisan/Manufacturer: Published by Asheville Post Card Co., Asheville, North Carolina.
Date: ca. 1930s–1950s
Price range: $9.00–15.00
Note of Interest: Plentiful

Category: Pictorial Images
Item Type: Postcard
Classification: E-3
Dimensions: 3½″ h x 5½″ w
Description: Paper, comical caricature, "Who's In There? Why Don't You Answer Him!–Wish I Could Get An Answer From You!" 523 (right bottom corner) No postmark. Good condition.
Artisan/Manufacturer: Published for Asheville Post Card Co., Asheville, North Carolina. A "Colourpicture" publication.
Date: ca. 1930s–1950s
Price range: $8.00–12.00
Note of Interest: Plentiful

Category: Pictorial Images
Item Type: Postcard
Classification: E-3
Dimensions: 5½" h x 3½" w
Description: Colorful postcard on high gloss paper. Comical, "Oh – I Is Not! … It Must Be Sumthin' I Et!" Good condition, no postmark.
Artisan/Manufacturer: Natural color reproduction. Curteichcolor ® Art Creation Reg. U.S. Pat. Off. P-178.
Date: ca. 1930s–1950s
Price range: $9.00–15.00
Note of Interest: Plentiful

Category: Pictorial Images
Item Type: Postcard
Classification: D-3
Dimensions: 5½" h x 3½" w
Description: German-made low gloss paper postcard making a statement about the Black/White issue – "Ein dunkler Punkt." (Which translates "A Dark Point.") "Eine Studie in schwarz and weiss!"
Artisan/Manufacturer: J. Harrap & Son, Holborn Bldgs., London, England
Date: ca. 1910s–1920s
Price range: $30.00–45.00
Note of Interest: Scarce

Category: Pictorial Images
Item Type: Postcard
Classification: D-2
Dimensions: 5½" h x 3½" w
Description: Embossed colorful image of a young man playing a banjo. "To My Valentine." Signed by the artist, Ellen H. Clapsaddle. Postmarked "1911 Sylvania, Pa., Feb. 13 PM" with 1¢ green stamp. Good condition.
Artisan/Manufacturer: International Art Publishing Co., New York, Berlin. Printed in Germany. Series No. 780.
Date: ca. 1911
Price range: $25.00–35.00
Note of Interest: Scarce

Category: Pictorial Images
Item Type: Postcard
Classification: D-2
Dimensions: 3½" h x 5½" w
Description: Historical brown-tinted postcard on linen. Dr. Booker T. Washington & Emmet J. Scott, Executive Secretary, Tuskegee Institute, Ala. Good condition.
Artisan/Manufacturer: The Albertype Co.; Brooklyn, New York.
Date: Early 20th century
Price range: $35.00–50.00
Note of Interest: Scarce

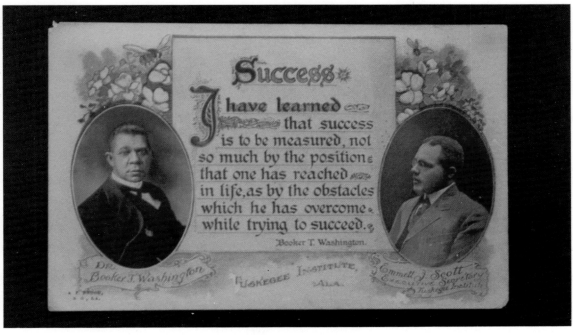

Category: Pictorial Images
Item Type: Postcard
Classification: E-3
Dimensions: 3½" h x 5½" w
Description: Linen, comical caricature, colorful.

Artisan/Manufacturer: Published by the Asheville Post Card Co., Asheville, North Carolina
Date: ca. 1930s–1950s
Price range: $8.00–12.00
Note of Interest: Plentiful

Category: Pictorial Images
Item Type: Postcard
Classification: E-3
Dimensions: 3½" h x 5½" w
Description: Linen, comical caricature, colorful. No postmark.

Artisan/Manufacturer: Published for Asheville Post Card Co., Asheville, North Carolina. A "Colourpicture" Publication.
Date: ca. 1930s–1950s
Price range: $8.00–18.00
Note of Interest: Plentiful

WAITING AT THE CHURCH

Category: Pictorial Images
Item Type: Postcard
Classification: E-3
Dimensions: 5½" h x 3½" w
Description: Comical caricature paper postcard. Colorful and in good condition. "Waiting At The Church."
Artisan/Manufacturer: "American Post Card. 'Happy Day.' Serial Number 81. Published by the Ullman Manufacturing Co., New York 1914 (on front of card).
Date: ca. 1910s–1920s
Price range: $8.00–12.00
Credit: M. Davern Collection
Note of Interest: Plentiful

Category: Pictorial Images
Item Type: Greeting card
Classification: E-2
Dimensions: 5½" h x 7¼" w
Description: Moveable hinged card done in caricature form. Brightly colored heavy paper.

Artisan/Manufacturer: Apple (mark on the back) – "Printed in Germany."
Date: ca. 1930–1955
Price range: $30.00–40.00
Credit: M. Davern Collection
Note of Interest: Common

29

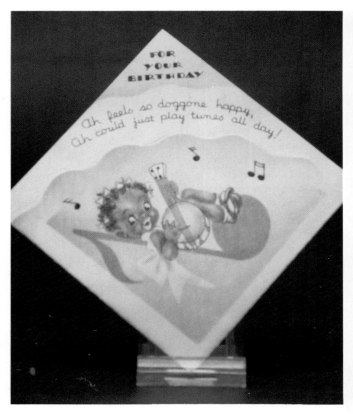

Category: Pictorial Images
Item Type: Greeting card (birthday card).
Classification: E-3
Dimensions: 4" h x 4" w
Description: Comical birthday card, double folding. Good condition.
Artisan/Manufacturer: Hallmark
Date: ca. 1935–1945
Price range: $7.00–10.00
Credits: M. Davern Collection
Note of Interest: Common

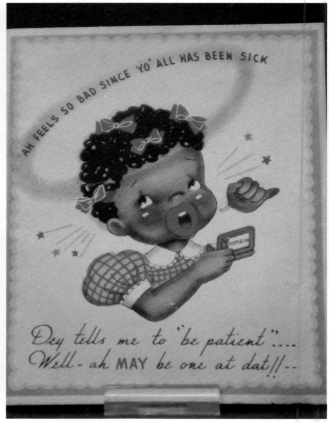

Category: Pictorial Images
Item Type: Greeting card
Classification: E-3
Dimensions: 5¾" h x 4¾" w
Description: Paper fold-out card, comical image done in subtle colors with a soft beige background and soft-tone trim. Excellent condition.
Artisan/Manufacturer: American Greeting Card
Date: ca. 1935–1955
Price range: $9.00–12.00
Credits: M. Davern Collection
Note of Interest: Plentiful

Category: Pictorial Images
Item Type: Postcard
Classification: E-3
Dimensions: 3½" h x 5½" w
Description: Paper half-tone card. Good condition
Artisan/Manufacturer: Marked "954"
Date: ca. 1890–1915
Price range: $8.00–15.00
Credits: M. Davern Collection
Note of Interest: Plentiful

Category: Pictorial Images
Item Type: Postcard
Classification: E-2
Dimensions: 5⅜" h x 3½" w
Description: Paper, colorful embossed images. "Thanksgiving Day." Good condition.
Artisan/Manufacturer: Marked: "Ser. 608." Design copyright by H.W. Taggert, New York.
Date: ca. 1900–1920
Price range: $10.00–15.00
Credits: M. Davern Collection
Note of Interest: Plentiful

Category: Pictorial Images
Item Type: Postcard
Classification: E-2
Dimensions: 3½" h x 5½" w
Description: Colorful paper card done in caricature. Good condition, postmarked 1910.
Artisan/Manufacturer: Marked: C$^{ard}_{karte}$ $_{arte}$
Date: ca. 1910–1920
Price range: $10.00–15.00
Credits: M. Davern Collection
Note of Interest: Plentiful

Category: Pictorial Images
Item Type: Postcard
Classification: E-3
Dimensions: 3½" h x 5½" w
Description: Glossy paper card of Blacks at work. "Negro Scene in South Carolina." Good condition.
Artisan/Manufacturer: "Carte Postage Universelle"

Date: ca. 1890–1915
Price range: $10.00–12.00
Credits: M. Davern Collection
Note of Interest: Plentiful. This is a typical "work scene" card. Many can be found depicting Blacks in various regions of the United States performing various tasks (i.e., sugar cane cutting, cotton picking, turpentine tapping, etc.)

Category: Pictorial Images
Item Type: Postcard
Classification: E-3
Dimensions: 3½" h x 5⅝" w
Description: Glossy paper card of a "genre scene" (everyday life). "An Old Kentucky Home."

Artisan/Manufacturer: Marked "S.S. Kirk"
Date: ca. 1890–1910
Price range: $10.00–12.00
Credits: M. Davern Collection
Note of Interest: Plentiful

Category: Pictorial Images
Item Type: Postcard
Classification: D-2
Dimensions: 3¼" h x 5½" w
Description: Leather-stamped card with brown and green dyes to enhance the images. Excellent condition. "I've got a feeling for you." (Writing done in script.) Decorative border.

Artisan/Manufacturer: Marked "K copyrighted - 105"
Date: ca. 1890–1910
Price range: $20.00–30.00
Credits: M. Davern Collection
Note of Interest: Common. Leather cards proved not to be very practical and thus were made as a novelty for a short time period, ca. 1890–1940.

Category: Pictorial Images
Item Type: Postcard
Classification: D-2
Dimensions: 3½" h x 5⅛" w
Description: Leather-stamped card with brown and red dyes to enhance the images. Excellent condition. "Here Am Where I Gets Off At."

Artisan/Manufacturer: Unmarked
Date: ca. 1890–1920
Price range: $20.00–30.00
Credits: M. Davern Collection
Note of Interest: Common

Category: Pictorial Images
Item Type: Print
Classification: D-2
Dimensions: 6" h x 4" w
Description: Print of a painting. Medium quality paper. Detailing of the imagery is good. Signed in pencil, not numbered. Quantity produced unknown. Excellent condition.
Artisan/Manufacturer: Eugene E. White
Date: ca. 1969
Price range: $60.00–70.00
Note of Interest: Scare. The artist of the work above still resides in the California area.

Category: Pictorial Images
Item Type: Calendar
Classification: G-2
Dimensions: 20" h x 11" w
Description: A very vividly colored/tinted print attached to a full year calendar. Excellent condition. "Smiling Thru."
Artisan/Manufacturer: Unmarked
Date: ca. 1937
Price range: $28.00–35.00
Note of Interest: Plentiful

Category: Pictorial Images
Item Type: Print
Classification: D-2
Dimensions: 25" h x 21" w
Description: A print of a painting, "Saturday." Paper is of medium quality. Printing process also of medium quality. Excellent condition. Signed in pencil by the artist, number printed not available.
Artisan/Manufacturer: Eugene E. White
Date: ca. 1960s (painting – 1953)
Price range: $145.00–165.00
Note of Interest: Scarce

34

THE OLD BARN FLOOR.

Category: Pictorial Images
Item Type: Print
Classification: F-3
Dimensions: 13" h x 16" w (unframed)
Description: Reprint of an original. Possibly from a calendar.
Artisan/Manufacturer: Currier & Ives
Date: ca. 1950s
Price range: $65.00–80.00
Note of Interest: Plentiful

Category: Pictorial Images
Item Type: Serigraph/Print
Classification: D-1
Dimensions: 28" h x 23" w
Description: Original serigraph done in abstract form. "Home Sweet Home" Ap. Samella Lewis, "69" written in pencil on bottom.
Artisan/Manufacturer: Samella Lewis
Date: 1969
Price range: $550.00–700.00
Note of Interest: Scarce. Samella Lewis is a Black-American artist born in New Orleans, Louisiana. Permanent collections at Baltimore Museum of Fine Arts, High Museum of Atlanta, Virginia Museum of Fine Arts.

Category: Pictorial Images
Item Type: Print
Classification: D-1
Dimensions: 15" h x 12" w (unframed)
Description: Original print honoring "First Bishop of the National Haitien Church. Consecrated in Grace Church, New York City, November 8th, 1874. Copyright 1875 by Currier & Ives, 125 Nassau St., N.Y. (Right Rev. James T. Holly, D.D.)" Good condition, fine detailing of the image.
Artisan/Manufacturer: Currier & Ives
Date: 1875
Price range: $350.00–550.00
Note of Interest: Scarce. The above print was probably a special commission by the church.

Category: Pictorial Images
Item Type: Color lithograph
Classification: E-3
Dimensions: 10" h x 12" w
Description: A color lithograph from *Truth* magazine. Caricature of a painting by Kenyan Cox. Good condition.
Artisan/Manufacturer: Litho by J.M. Flagg
Date: ca. 1895 (June 22, 1895 issue of *Truth*)
Price range: $135.00–215.00
Credits: The Paper Pile, San Anselmo, California
Note of Interest: Common

Category: Pictorial Images
Item Type: Print, lithograph
Classification: D-2
Dimensions: 14¼" h x 10½" w
Description: Cartoons of a political and social statement.
Artisan/Manufacturer: Puck Press
Date: Early 20th century.
Price range: $35.00–40.00
Credits: Manning's Books & Prints
Note of Interest: Common. *Puck,* the Democratic-oriented magazine, illustrated the political issues and social issues during the onset of the 20th century. Its contemporary counterpart is believed to be *Judge* (Republican-oriented magazine.)

Category: Pictorial Images
Item Type: Print, lithograph
Classification: D-2
Dimensions: 10⅜" h x 13½" w
Description: Original colored cartoons, satiric of conditions in society, both social and political. Good condition. "The Worm Turned."
Artisan/Manufacturer: Sackett & Wilhelms Litho & Print Co., New York. Copyright: 1901 by the Judge Co. of New York.
Date: ca. 1901
Price range: $30.00–40.00
Credits: Manning's Books & Prints
Note of Interest: Common. Literally thousands of magazine covers were produced but only a small number of them have survived time. *Judge* was believed to be a Republican-oriented magazine often times making comments about the Democratic policies and the party itself. The counterpart to this magazine and its competitor is believed to be *Puck*.

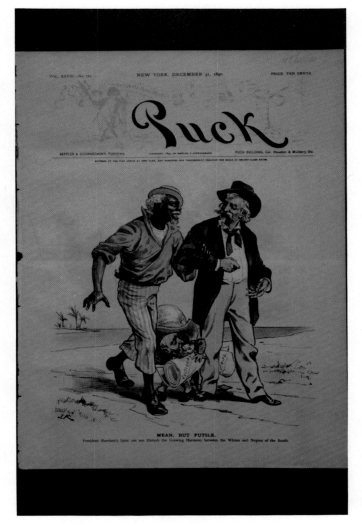

Category: Pictorial Images
Item Type: Print, lithograph
Classification: D-2
Dimensions: 13½" h x 10½" w
Description: Color lithograph cover of a magazine. Low gloss paper. Good condition. "Mean But Futile."
Artisan/Manufacturer: *Puck* Magazine, copyright 1890 by Keppler & Schwarzmann Publishers. Litho by J.K.
Date: Dec. 31, 1890
Price range: $35.00–45.00
Credits: Manning's Books & Prints
Note of Interest: Common

Category: Pictorial Images
Item Type: Print
Classification: E-2
Dimensions: 11" h x 16" w
Description: Black and white paper engraving. Good condition. "Virginia Tenth Annual Convention of the Knights of LABOR…"
Artisan/Manufacturer: Frank Leslie's Illustrated Newspaper
Date: Oct. 16, 1886
Price range: $25.00–35.00

Credits: Manning's Books & Prints
Note of Interest: Plentiful. Most prints from illustrated newspapers are plentiful and usually of mundane subjects. On occasion, however, a rare print can be found either by a well-known engraver or of a popular or interesting subject matter. Only the very rare prints can command a higher price than the above price range. Many dealers hand-tinted the old prints to enhance their desirability but the additional coloring should only raise the price slightly, if at all, because the prints were originally done in black and white or a neutral color.

Category: Pictorial Images
Item Type: Print
Classification: E-2
Dimensions: 11" h x 16" w
Description: Engraving of a genre scene (everyday life). "Their Pride" from the painting by Thomas Hovenden.

Artisan/Manufacturer: *Harper's Weekly*
Date: Dec. 8, 1888
Price range: $25.00–35.00
Credits: Manning's Books & Prints
Note of Interest: Plentiful

Category: Pictorial Images
Item Type: Print
Classification: E-2
Dimensions: 11" h x 16" w
Description: Engraving making a political statement about the conditions of Blacks in America. "The Bloody Shirt" reformed. Good condition

Artisan/Manufacturer: *Harper's Weekly/* TH: NAST ARTIST
Date: August 12, 1876
Price range: $25.00–35.00
Credits: Manning's Books & Prints
Note of Interest: Plentiful

Category: Pictorial Images
Item Type: Print
Classification: E-2
Dimensions: 11" h x 16" w
Description: Engraving. Good condition. Soft neutral tones. "The Soup Kitchen Charity." Drawn by S.G. McCutchen.

Artisan/Manufacturer: *Harper's Weekly*
Date: April 12, 1879
Price range: $25.00–35.00
Credits: Manning's Books & Prints
Note of Interest: Plentiful

Category: Pictorial Images
Item Type: Print, lithograph
Classification: D-2
Dimensions: 13⅜" h x 19¾" w
Description: Color lithograph, double size (2 page). "JOHN A. LOGAN IN 1859."
Artisan/Manufacturer: *Puck/*painted by Gillam
Date: 1859
Price range: $45.00–65.00
Credits: Manning's Books & Prints
Note of Interest: Common

Category: Pictorial Images
Item Type: Print
Classification: E-2
Dimensions: 15¾" h x 10¼" w
Description: Engraving, cover page. "A Memory of Emancipation Day." Fair condition.
Artisan/Manufacturer: *Harper's Weekly,* New York
Date: Jan. 4, 1902
Price range: $35.00–45.00
Note of Interest: Plentiful. Front cover prints of interest as described above tend to cost slightly more than inside issue prints.

Category: Pictorial Images
Item Type: Print
Classification: E-2
Dimensions: 15¾" h x 10¼" w
Description: Engraving, tinted warm tones of neutral colors. Typical animal hunt scene with a Black male in a landscape setting. Good condition. "Christmas Morning – Comin' From De Store."
Artisan/Manufacturer: *Harper's Weekly* (A.B. Frost, artist)
Date: Dec. 1883
Price range: $30.00–40.00
Credits: Manning's Books & Prints
Note of Interest: Plentiful. Well-known artist, A.B. Frost, will increase the price somewhat.

Category: Pictorial Images
Item Type: Print
Classification: E-2
Dimensions: 16" h x 11" w
Description: Engraving of a political nature. "Is This A Republican Form of Government?" Excellent condition.
Artisan/Manufacturer: *Harper's Weekly,* TH: NAST artist
Date: September 2, 1876
Price range: $20.00–35.00
Credits: Manning's Books & Prints
Note of Interest: Plentiful

Category: Pictorial Images
Item Type: Print
Classification: E-2
Dimensions: 11" h x 16" w
Description: Engraving, good condition. Comical/light humor. "Parade Day."
Artisan/Manufacturer: *Harper's Weekly,* drawing by H.P. Wolcott
Date: August 14, 1880
Price range: $25.00–35.00
Credits: Manning's Books & Prints
Note of Interest: Plentiful

Category: Pictorial Images
Item Type: Print
Classification: E-3
Dimensions: 16" h x 11" w
Description: Engraving, good condition. "Christmas Morning – The Challenge."
Artisan/Manufacturer: *Harper's Weekly,* drawing by Peter S. Newell
Date: ca. 1880s–1890s
Price range: $15.00–25.00
Note of Interest: Plentiful

THE JUG BAND, OF PALATKA, FLA.; PHOTO BY J. G. MANGOLD.

Category: Pictorial Images
Item Type: Print
Classification: D-3
Dimensions: 11" h x 16" w
Description: Engraving of a local photo in Palatka, Florida. Printed paper in good condition. "The Jug Band, of Palatka, Fla.: Photo by J.G. Mangold."
Artisan/Manufacturer: *Frank Leslie's Illustrated Newspaper.*
Date: March 28, 1891
Price range: $20.00–30.00
Credits: Manning's Books & Prints
Note of Interest: Common

Category: Pictorial Images
Item Type: Print
Classification: E-3
Dimensions: 16" h x 11" w
Description: Engraving of a photograph, good condition. "The Ku-Klux-Klan." Photo by Mr. John O. Johnson.
Artisan/Manufacturer: *Frank Leslie's Illustrated Newspaper.*
Date: October 7, 1871
Price range: $20.00–30.00
Credits: Manning's Books & Prints
Note of Interest: Plentiful

Category: Pictorial Images
Item Type: Print
Classification: E-2
Dimensions: 11" h x 16" w
Description: Engraving making a bold political statement. "State Rights 1866."

Artisan/Manufacturer: *Harper's Weekly* (no artist name)
Date: Jan. 12, 1867
Price range: $25.00–35.00
Credits: Manning's Books & Prints
Note of Interest: Plentiful

Category: Pictorial Images
Item Type: Print
Classification: E-2
Dimensions: 11" h x 16" w
Description: Engraving done in warm neutral tones. "The Ute War – The Colored Troops Fighting Their Way Into The Beleaguered Camp." Drawn by C.S. Remhart.

Artisan/Manufacturer: *Harper's Weekly*
Date: Nov. 1, 1879
Price range: $35.00–50.00
Credits: Manning's Books & Prints
Note of Interest: Common

Category: Pictorial Images
Item Type: Print
Classification: E-3
Dimensions: 11" h x 16" w
Description: Engraving done in caricature. "Scene On A Mississippi River Steamer." Sketched by A.R. Ward.
Artisan/Manufacturer: *Harper's Weekly*
Date: Nov. 9, 1867
Price range: $20.00–30.00
Credits: Manning's Books & Prints
Note of Interest: Plentiful

THE CHRISTMAS 'POSSUM.

Drawn by A. B. Frost.

Category: Pictorial Images
Item Type: Print
Classification: E-3
Dimensions: 16" h x 11" w
Description: Engraving of a return from the hunt scene. "The Christmas Possum." Drawn by A.B. Frost. Excellent condition.
Artisan/Manufacturer: *Harper's Weekly*
Date: ca. 1880s–1890s
Price range: $35.00–50.00
Credits: Manning's Books & Prints
Note of Interest: Plentiful

Category: Pictorial Images
Item Type: Print
Classification: D-2
Dimensions: 16" h x 11" w
Description: A cover page engraving of a historical event in America. "The First Vote." Drawn by A.R. Ward. Excellent condition.
Artisan/Manufacturer: *Harper's Weekly*.
Date: November 16, 1867
Price range: $25.00–35.00
Credits: Manning's Books & Prints
Note of Interest: Plentiful

Category: Pictorial Images
Item Type: Print
Classification: E-3
Dimensions: 16" h x 11" w
Description: Engraving done in neutral tones. "The Civil War In America…" A commentary about American politics as interpreted by England.
Artisan/Manufacturer: *The Illustrated London News*
Date: June 29, 1861
Price range: $20.00–25.00
Credits: Manning's Books & Prints
Note of Interest: Plentiful

Category: Pictorial Images
Item Type: Print
Classification: E-2
Dimensions: 10¾" h x 14½" w
Description: Engraving, good condition. "Merry
Christmas and Christmas Gift, Ole Massa."
Artisan/Manufacturer: *Every Saturday.* Illustrated by
W.L. Sheppard, Delaware
Date: Dec. 31, 1870
Price range: $25.00–30.00
Credits: Manning's Books & Prints
Note of Interest: Plentiful

Category: Pictorial Images
Item Type: Print
Classification: G-3
Dimensions: 12¾" h x 9½" w
Description: Engraving, good condition. Taken from the
book *Picturesque America,* p. 202.
Artisan/Manufacturer: *Picturesque America*
Date: ca. 1920s–1930s
Price range: $15.00–25.00
Credits: Manning's Books & Prints
Note of Interest: Plentiful

Category: Pictorial Images
Item Type: Prints (The Buffalo Soldiers)
Classification: D-3
Dimensions: 9¾" h x 7" w
Description: A series of prints on heavy paper – off-white color from a brown book entitled *The Century Illustrated Monthly Magazine,* November 1888 to April 1889. The Century Co., New York. T. Fisher Unwin, London. Vol. XXXVII. New Series Vol. XV. Pages 899-912. Illustrator Frederic Remington. Excellent condition.
Artisan/Manufacturer: *The Century Illustrated Monthly Magazine*
Date: 1888–1889
Price range: $50.00–70.00
Credits: Manning's Books & Prints
Note of Interest: Common

veillance and countersigned by the secret police in-
pector of the district, and then handed over to the
Department for the Preservation of Order and Public
afety.

It would seem to the lay mind that such a
eport as this, made out and submitted monthly,
hould enable the chief of police to write the
atural history of a suspect with considerable
ccuracy; but, after all, it does not attain the
esults expected from it. The subterranean
nine in the Little Garden Street in St. Peters-
urg, which contained eighty pounds of dyna-
ite, was excavated, loaded, and equipped
ith batteries, wires, and a Ruhmkorf coil by
wo terrorists disguised as cheese merchants,
ho were under precisely this sort of supervis-
n. Their shop was even visited and inspected
ree days before the late Tsar's assassination,
d yet the mine was not discovered. It is my
pinion that the abilities of the Russian secret
olice are greatly overrated. I have had as
uch experience as most foreigners in evading
d misleading them, and I have heard the
perience of three or four hundred revolution-
ts who have carried on a contest of wits with
em for years. In every city in the Empire
ere are hundreds of revolutionists whom the
lice have not been able to discover; hekto-
aphed and lithographed copies of forbidden
ritings — including this very series of articles
-circulate from hand to hand throughout the
mpire; and I do not think there is a prison in
uropean Russia or in Siberia, with the single

exception of the Castle of Schlüsselburg, where
the imprisoned revolutionists do not have written communication with their friends outside.

A well-informed St. Petersburg correspond-
ent of the "New York Tribune" recently said,
with reference to the Russian police, "I do not
believe there is another department in the Empire about which such erroneous impressions
exist, and which, especially abroad, is so terribly
overrated. There is not another police department in Europe which is so badly organized, so
ill-informed, and so utterly incapable as that of
the Tsar."

This statement is perhaps too strongly ex-
pressed, but I believe it to be essentially true.
The Russian secret police are by no means up
to their reputation.

And what, after all, is the use of such a system,
and such a police? An observer who regards
the Russian situation from an American point of
view can hardly help thinking that the Tsar, who
is a well-meaning man, would have a happier
life and a more useful life if he would abandon
his policy of repression; call for the resigna-
tion of his despotic Minister of the Interior,
Count Dmitri Tolstoi; discharge five-sixths of
his police and gendarmes, and admit his people
to a share in the government of the state. The
condition of things could hardly be worse than
it is, and a liberal policy, steadily and consist-
ently followed, might make Russia a prosper-
ous and happy country as well as a mighty
Empire.

George Kennan.

A SCOUT WITH THE BUFFALO-SOLDIERS.

WRITTEN AND ILLUSTRATED BY FREDERIC REMINGTON.

I SAT smoking in
the quarters of an
army friend at
Fort Grant, and
through a green
lattice - work was
watching the dusty
parade and congratulat-
ing myself on the pos-
session of this spot of comfort
in such a disagreeably hot
climate as Arizona Territory
offers in the summer, when
strode my friend the lieutenant, who threw
cap on the table and began to roll a
arette.

Carlos way, and I'm off in the morning. Would
you like to go with me?" He lighted the cigarette and paused for my reply.

I was very comfortable at that moment, and
knew from some past experiences that marching under the summer sun of Arizona was
real suffering and not to be considered by one
on pleasure bent; and I was also aware that
my friend the lieutenant had a reputation as a
hard rider, and would in this case select a few
picked and seasoned cavalrymen and rush
over the worst possible country in the least
possible time. I had no reputation as a hard
rider to sustain, and, moreover, had not backed
a horse for the year past. I knew too that
Uncle Sam's beans, black coffee, and the bacon

WHY PARSON JOHNSON VETOED THE ENTERTAINMENT FOR THE BENEFIT OF THE CUBAN PATRIOTS.

Category: Pictorial Images
Item Type: Print, lithograph
Classification: D-2
Dimensions: 10¼" h x 13¾" w
Description: A cartoon page from a magazine. Full color lithographs of a political nature. "Why Parson Johnson Vetoed The Entertainment For the Benefit Of The Cuban Patriots."
Artisan/Manufacturer: *The Puck Press*
Date: ca. 1890s–1925
Price range: $25.00–40.00
Credits: Manning's Books & Prints
Note of Interest: Common

A HEAD-ON COLLISION.
OR, HE BUMPS BEST WHO BUMPS LAST.

Category: Pictorial Images
Item Type: Print, lithograph
Classification: D-2
Dimensions: 13¾" h x 10¼" w
Description: A cartoon page, full-color lithograph from a magazine. "A Head-On Collision/or He Bumps Best Who Bumps Last." Good condition.
Artisan/Manufacturer: *The Puck Press* (Leighton Budd, artist)
Date: ca. 1890s–1925
Price range: $20.00–35.00
Credits: Manning's Books & Prints
Note of Interest: Common

Category: Pictorial Images
Item Type: Print
Classification: E-3
Dimensions: 9½" h x 6¼" w
Description: Engraving on off-white paper, taken from the book, *Eminent Opponents of the Slave Power.* Good condition.
Artisan/Manufacturer: Engraved by J.C. Buttre
Date: ca. 1860s
Price range: $20.00–30.00
Credits: Manning's Books & Prints
Note of Interest: Plentiful

Category: Pictorial Images
Item Type: Print
Classification: E-2
Dimensions: 6" h x 8" w
Description: Engraving tinted with greens and blues on off-white paper. "Eva Pointing Out The Happy Land." Painted by A. Hunt.
Artisan/Manufacturer: Engraved by F.E. Jones
Date: ca. 1859
Price range: $125.00–150.00
Credits: Manning's Books & Prints
Note of Interest: Common

Category: Pictorial Images
Item Type: Print
Classification: E-3
Dimensions: 11" h x 8" w
Description: A print from the book, *A Treasury of Stephen Foster*. Tinted scenes on paper, sheet music on the reverse side (pg. 99 "Massa's in de Cold Ground").
Artisan/Manufacturer: John Tasker Howard, author; William Sharp, illustrator.
Date: ca. 1920–1940
Price range: $15.00–25.00
Credits: M. Davern Collection
Note of Interest: Plentiful

Category: Pictorial Images
Item Type: Print
Classification: E-3
Dimensions: 11" h x 8" w
Description: A print from the book, *A Treasury of Stephen Foster*. Tinted scenes on paper, sheet music on the reverse side (pg. 51 "My Brudder Gone").
Artisan/Manufacturer: John Tasker Howard, author; William Sharp, illustrator.
Date: ca. 1920–1940
Price range: $15.00–25.00
Credits: M. Davern Collection
Note of Interest: Plentiful

Category: Pictorial Images
Item Type: Print
Classification: E-3
Dimensions: 11" h x 8" w
Description: A print from the book, *A Treasury of Stephen Foster*. Tinted scenes on paper, sheet music on the reverse side (pg. 59 "Oh! Lemuel").
Artisan/Manufacturer: John Tasker Howard, author; William Sharp, illustrator.
Date: ca. 1920–1940
Price range: $15.00–25.00
Credits: M. Davern Collection
Note of Interest: Plentiful

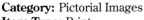

Category: Pictorial Images
Item Type: Print
Classification: E-3
Dimensions: 11" h x 8" w
Description: A print from the book, *A Treasury of Stephen Foster*. Tinted scenes on paper, sheet music on the reverse side (pg. 71 "Nelly Bly").
Artisan/Manufacturer: John Tasker Howard, author; William Sharp, illustrator.
Date: ca. 1920–1940
Price range: $15.00–25.00
Credits: M. Davern Collection
Note of Interest: Plentiful

Category: Pictorial Images
Item Type: Print
Classification: E-3
Dimensions: 11" h x 8" w
Description: A print from the book, *A Treasury of Stephen Foster.* Tinted scenes on paper, sheet music on the reverse side (pg. 87 "Old Folks At Home").
Artisan/Manufacturer: John Tasker Howard, author; William Sharp, illustrator.
Date: ca. 1920–1940
Price range: $15.00–25.00
Credits: M. Davern Collection
Note of Interest: Plentiful

Category: Pictorial Images
Item Type: Print
Classification: E-3
Dimensions: 11" h x 8" w
Description: A print from the book, *A Treasury of Stephen Foster.* Tinted scenes on paper, sheet music on the reverse side (pg. 39 "Lou'siana Belle").
Artisan/Manufacturer: John Tasker Howard, author; William Sharp, illustrator.
Date: ca. 1920–1940
Price range: $15.00–25.00
Credits: M. Davern Collection
Note of Interest: Plentiful

Category: Pictorial Images
Item Type: Print
Classification: E-3
Dimensions: 11" h x 8" w
Description: A print from the book, *A Treasury of Stephen Foster.* Tinted scenes on paper, sheet music on the reverse side (pg. 35 "Away Down Souf").
Artisan/Manufacturer: John Tasker Howard, author; William Sharp, illustrator.
Date: ca. 1920–1940
Price range: $15.00–25.00
Credits: M. Davern Collection
Note of Interest: Plentiful

Category: Pictorial Images
Item Type: Print
Classification: E-3
Dimensions: 11" h x 8" w
Description: A print from the book, *A Treasury of Stephen Foster.* Tinted scenes on paper, sheet music on the reverse side (pg. 43 "Old Uncle Ned").
Artisan/Manufacturer: John Tasker Howard, author; William Sharp, illustrator.
Date: ca. 1920–1940
Price range: $15.00–25.00
Credits: M. Davern Collection
Note of Interest: Plentiful

Category: Pictorial Images
Item Type: Print
Classification: E-3
Dimensions: 11" h x 8" w
Description: A print from the book, *A Treasury of Stephen Foster.* Tinted scenes on paper, sheet music on the reverse side (pg. 131 "Glendy Bunk").
Artisan/Manufacturer: John Tasker Howard, author; William Sharp, illustrator.
Date: ca. 1920–1940
Price range: $15.00–25.00
Credits: M. Davern Collection
Note of Interest: Plentiful

Category: Pictorial Images
Item Type: Print
Classification: E-3
Dimensions: 11" h x 8" w
Description: A print from the book, *A Treasury of Stephen Foster.* Tinted scenes on paper, sheet music on the reverse side (pg. 139 "Down Among the Cane Brakes").
Artisan/Manufacturer: John Tasker Howard, author; William Sharp, illustrator.
Date: ca. 1920–1940
Price range: $15.00–25.00
Credits: M. Davern Collection
Note of Interest: Plentiful

Category: Pictorial Images
Item Type: Etching
Classification: E-3
Dimensions: 10" h x 8" w
Description: Etching of a musician playing an instrument, framed
Artisan/Manufacturer: Barcena
Date: ca. 1930
Price range: $495.00–800.00
Credits: Village Antiques Inc., Tampa, Florida
Note of Interest: Plentiful

Category: Pictorial Images
Item Type: Print
Classification: D-2
Dimensions: 16" h x 11" w
Description: Historical engraving, cover page. Neutral tones. "Fredrick Douglass."
Artisan/Manufacturer: *Harper's Weekly* (N.Y.)
Date: Nov. 24, 1883
Price range: $25.00–35.00
Credits: Manning's Books & Prints
Note of Interest: Plentiful

Category: Pictorial Images
Item Type: Print
Classification: E-3
Dimensions: 11" h x 8" w
Description: A print from *A Treasury of Stephen Foster*. Tinted scenes on paper, sheet music on reverse side (pg. 195, "Some Folks").
Artisan/Manufacturer: John Tasker Howard, author; William Sharp, illustrator.
Date: ca. 1920–1940
Price range: $15.00–20.00
Credits: M. Davern Collection
Note of Interest: Plentiful

Category: Pictorial Images
Item Type: Print
Classification: D-2
Dimensions: 16" h x 11" w
Description: Engraving done in neutral tones on off-white
    paper in a naturalistic manner. "A Brown Study."
Artisan/Manufacturer: *Harper's Weekly,* by late William Hunt
Date: March 5, 1870
Price range: $20.00–30.00
Credits: Manning's Books & Prints
Note of Interest: Plentiful

Category: Pictorial Images
Item Type: Print
Classification: E-3
Dimensions: 11" h x 16" w
Description: Engraving of a comical nature done in neutral
    tones on off-white paper. "A String of Blackberries."
    Good condition.
Artisan/Manufacturer: *Harper's Weekly*
Date: August 29, 1874
Price range: $15.00–25.00
Credits: Manning's Books & Prints
Note of Interest: Plentiful

Category: Pictorial Images
Item Type: Print
Classification: E-2
Dimensions: 16" h x 11" w
Description: Engraving done in neutral tones on paper. Makes a plea for freedom. "Franchise. And Not This Man?"
Artisan/Manufacturer: *Harper's Weekly*
Date: August 5, 1865
Price range: $25.00–45.00
Credits: Manning's Books & Prints
Note of Interest: Plentiful

Category: Pictorial Images
Item Type: Print
Classification: E-2
Dimensions: 11" h x 16" w
Description: Engraving, good condition. "The Massacre At Fort Pillow." Sketched on site with the aid of a telescope by a field artist during the climax of an attack.
Artisan/Manufacturer: *Harper's Weekly*
Date: April 30, 1864
Price range: $25.00–35.00
Credits: Manning's Books & Prints
Note of Interest: Plentiful. The article on the attack at Fort Pillow is included at the end of the Print Section under "Articles."

Category: Pictorial Images
Item Type: Print
Classification: E-3
Dimensions: 11" h x 16" w
Description: Engraving, good condition. (1 of 3 scenes) "Negroes Building Stockades Under The Recent Act of Congress."

Artisan/Manufacturer: *Harper's Weekly*
Date: August 30, 1862
Price range: $25.00–35.00
Credits: Manning's Books & Prints
Note of Interest: Plentiful

Category: Pictorial Images
Item Type: Print
Classification: E-2
Dimensions: 11" h x 21" w
Description: Engraving of an action scene done in neutral tones on paper. Good condition. "A Negro Regiment In Action."

Artisan/Manufacturer: *Harper's Weekly*
Date: March 14, 1863
Price range: $35.00–55.00
Credits: Public Library of Nashville and Davidson County
Note of Interest: Plentiful. An article on "Negroes As Soldiers" is included at the end of the Print Section under "Articles."

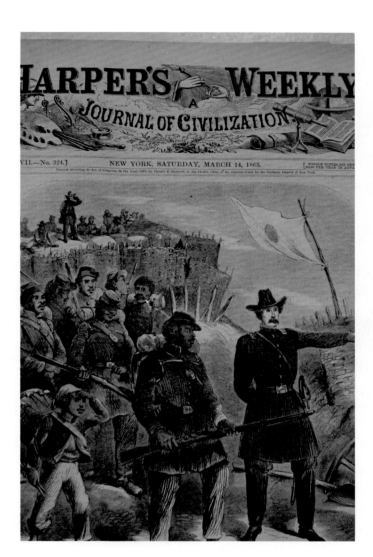

Category: Pictorial Images
Item Type: Print
Classification: D-2
Dimensions: 16" h x 11" w
Description: Engraved cover page illustrating the progress of the war. "Teaching The Negro Recruits The Use of the Minié Rifle."
Artisan/Manufacturer: *Harper's Weekly,* Saturday Vol. VII, No. 324, New York
Date: March 14, 1863
Price range: $25.00–45.00
Credits: Public Library of Nashville and Davidson County
Note of Interest: Plentiful

Category: Pictorial Images
Item Type: Print
Classification: E-2
Dimensions: 11" h x 16" w
Description: Engraving of a comical and caricature nature. "The Behemoth Club of Blackville." Good condition.
Artisan/Manufacturer: *Harper's Weekly,* drawn by Sol Eytinge, Jun.
Date: Nov. 9, 1878
Price range: $20.00–30.00
Credits: Public Library of Nashville and Davidson County
Note of Interest: Plentiful. This print is one of a long series of "Blackville" characters, including the "Twins" from their courtship to marriage. The artist's name, Sol Eytinge, Jun., can be found on most of the "Blackville" prints. After the 1860's, the imagery of many Blacks appearing in newspapers similar to *Harper's Weekly* were of a comical nature and often done in a caricature style. Often strong social statements can be read in the captions of such prints.

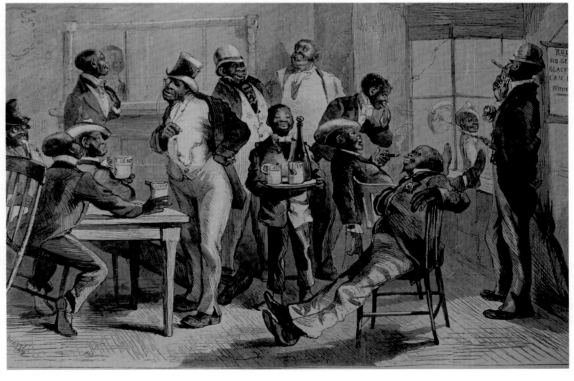

Category: Pictorial Images
Item Type: Print
Classification: E-2
Dimensions: 11" h x 16" w
Description: Engraving done in a comical and caricature nature. "Decorative Art At Last Reached Blackville, Dat Small Japan Jug Cum Frum De Ruins of Pompy."

Artisan/Manufacturer: *Harper's Weekly,* drawn by Sol Eytinge, Jun.
Date: Nov. 23, 1878
Price range: $25.00–35.00
Credits: Public Library of Nashville and Davidson County
Note of Interest: Plentiful. Part of the "Blackville" series.

Category: Pictorial Images
Item Type: Print
Classification: E-3
Dimensions: 11" h x 16" w
Description: Engraving, good condition. "Negroes Leaving Their Homes."

Artisan/Manufacturer: *Harper's Weekly*
Date: April 9, 1864
Price range: $25.00–35.00
Credits: Public Library of Nashville and Davidson County
Note of Interest: Plentiful

Category: Pictorial Images
Item Type: Print
Classification: E-3
Dimensions: 11" h x 16" w
Description: Engraving, "Blackville" series. Good condition. "The Coaching Season In Blackville – The Grand Start."

Artisan/Manufacturer: *Harper's Weekly*
Date: September 28, 1878
Price range: $25.00–35.00
Credits: Public Library of Nashville and Davidson County
Note of Interest: Plentiful

Category: Pictorial Images
Item Type: Print
Classification: E-3
Dimensions: 11" h x 16" w
Description: Engraving, "Blackville" series. Good condition. "After Doing Paris and The Rest of Europe, The Bridal Party Return To Blackville."

Artisan/Manufacturer: *Harper's Weekly*
Date: Oct. 26, 1878
Price range: $25.00–35.00
Credits: Public Libraray of Nashville and Davidson County
Note of Interest: Plentiful

Category: Pictorial Images
Item Type: Print
Classification: E-2
Dimensions: 11" h x 16" w
Description: Engraving, good condition. Naturalistic rendering of life's toll on an elderly gentleman. A contrast of the young and the old in imagery. "Old and Weary."

Artisan/Manufacturer: *Harper's Weekly,* drawn by S.G. McCutcheon
Date: Nov. 2, 1878
Price range: $25.00–35.00
Credits: Public Library of Nashville and Davidson County
Note of Interest: Plentiful

Category: Pictorial Images
Item Type: Print
Classification: E-2
Dimensions: 11" h x 16" w
Description: Caricature engraving from the "Blackville" series. "Baseball at Blackville – The White Stockings Against the Black Legs – First Blood For The Black Legs."

Artisan/Manufacturer: *Harper's Weekly,* drawn by Sol Eytinge, Jun.
Date: July 27, 1878
Price range: $25.00–35.00
Credits: Public Library of Nashville and Davidson County
Note of Interest: Plentiful

Category: Pictorial Images
Item Type: Print
Classification: E-2
Dimensions: 11" h x 16" w
Description: Engraving, "Blackville" series caricature. "Wedding Trip of the Blackville Twins – Off For Europe."

Artisan/Manufacturer: *Harper's Weekly*
Date: 1878
Price range: $25.00–35.00
Credits: Public Library of Nashville and Davidson County
Note of Interest: Plentiful

Category: Pictorial Images
Item Type: Print
Classification: E-2
Dimensions: 11" h x 16" w
Description: Engraving, "Blackville" series. "New Year's Day In Blackville – The Twins Receive." Good condition.

Artisan/Manufacturer: *Harper's Weekly,* drawn by Sol Eytinge, Jun. ® corner W.H. Redding Yc.
Date: Jan. 12, 1878
Price range: $25.00–35.00
Credits: Public Library of Nashville and Davidson County
Note of Interest: Plentiful

HARPER'S WEEKLY.

INJURED INNOCENCE.—[Drawn by C. M. Coolidge.]

Category: Pictorial Images
Item Type: Print
Classification: E-3
Dimensions: 11" h x 16" w
Description: Engraving, caricature, "Blackville" series. "Private Theatricals At Blackville, I Hang Upon De Honey O Doze Lips!"
Artisan/Manufacturer: *Harper's Weekly,* drawing by Sol Eytinge, Jun.
Date: April 20, 1878
Price range: $25.00–35.00
Credits: Public Library of Nashville and Davidson County
Note of Interest: Plentiful

Category: Pictorial Images
Item Type: Print
Classification: E-3
Dimensions: 11" h x 9" w
Description: Engraving. Social mockery of Blacks stealing chickens. Good condition. "Injured Innocence."
Artisan/Manufacturer: *Harper's Weekly,* drawn by C.M. Coolidge
Date: Feb. 9, 1878
Price range: $12.00–20.00
Credits: Public Library of Nashville and Davidson County
Note of Interest: Plentiful. Many caricatures and novelty items show an ongoing mythical love of Blacks for chickens. These items were popular and many are on today's collectible market.

66

Category: Pictorial Images
Item Type: Print
Classification: E-2
Dimensions: 11" h x 16" w
Description: Engraving, "Blackville" series, caricature. Good condition. "The Duello In Blackville."

Artisan/Manufacturer: *Harper's Weekly,* drawn by Sol Eytinge, Jun.
Date: June 8, 1878
Price range: $25.00–35.00
Credits: Public Library of Nashville and Davidson County
Note of Interest: Plentiful

Category: Pictorial Images
Item Type: Print
Classification: E-3
Dimensions: 11" h x 16" w
Description: Engraving, "Blackville" series, caricature. Good condition. "Love In Blackville – The Wooing of the Twins."

Artisan/Manufacturer: *Harper's Weekly,* drawn by Sol Eytinge, Jun.
Date: May 11, 1878
Price range: $25.00–35.00
Credits: Public Library of Nashville and Davidson County
Note of Interest: Plentiful

Category: Pictorial Images
Item Type: Print
Classification: E-2
Dimensions: 16" h x 11" w
Description: Engraving done in soft tones. Good condition. "Done Brown."
Artisan/Manufacturer: *Harper's Weekly*, drawn by J.W. Alexander
Date: Nov. 1881
Price range: $25.00–35.00
Credits: Public Library of Nashville and Davidson County
Note of Interest: Plentiful

Category: Pictorial Images
Item Type: Print
Classification: E-3
Dimensions: 11" h x 16" w
Description: Engraving of a common scene during the end of slavery in America. "Camp of Negro Refugees." The print is rendered in a naturalistic style. The dark and light gray tones give the illusion of a shadowy night. Good condition.
Artisan/Manufacturer: *Harper's Weekly,* sketched by Theodore R. Davis
Date: July 1, 1865
Price range: $25.00–35.00
Credits: Public Library of Nashville and Davidson County
Note of Interest: Plentiful

Category: Pictorial Images
Item Type: Print
Classification: E-2
Dimensions: 11" h x 16" w
Description: Engraving, caricature, "Blackville" series. "The Great Social Event At Blackville – The Wedding of the Twins." Good condition.

Artisan/Manufacturer: *Harper's Weekly*, drawn by Sol Eytinge, Jun.
Date: July 13, 1878
Price range: $25.00–35.00
Credits: Public Library of Nashville and Davidson County
Note of Interest: Plentiful

Category: Pictorial Images
Item Type: Print
Classification: E-3
Dimensions: 11" h x 16" w
Description: Engraving, good condition. "A Rebel Captain Forcing Negroes To Load Cannon Under Fire of Berdan's Sharpshooters."

Artisan/Manufacturer: *Harper's Weekly*, sketched by M. Mead
Date: May 10, 1862
Price range: $25.00–35.00
Credits: Public Library of Nashville and Davidson County
Note of Interest: Plentiful. The above print was sketched by Mr. Mead from behind the line of fire while observing through a telescope, according to a short by-line in an original *Harper's Weekly* (May 10, 1862).

Political Memorabilia

Blacks have played an important role in American politics for many years, but political memorabilia such as pamphlets about Black socialists in the 1930s and 1940s or Black candidates for local, state, and national offices prior to the 1950s and 1960s are very scarce. Therefore, the posters and buttons presented here represent a very narrow segment of these collectibles.

Most of these items come from the 1960s, which marked a time of political upheaval in the United States for Blacks and Whites. Although these items are of recent vintage, they are extremely scarce and expensive, particularly the posters with famous Blacks such as Shirley Chisolm, Dick Gregory, Malcolm X, Huey Newton, and Martin Luther King. Often such posters can be found in the attics and basements of individuals who were politically active during this time. Also, because these posters were "used" as props or wall hangings, few are found in mint condition. Many of the companies that produced these items were small and are now out of business. The price range is generally high if purchased from a dealer or collector – approximately $35.00 to $1,000.00. Generally, the surface is poster board, paper, or linen. The printing processes most often used were offset printing or serigraphy. This field is one of the newest in Black collectibles and very little research has been accomplished in this area.

1925   Malcolm X   1965

Category: Political Memorabilia
Item Type: Poster
Classification: D-2
Dimensions: 22" h x 17" w
Description: Commemorative serigraph of Malcom X.
Artisan/Manufacturer: Julian Richardson Associates
Date: Copyright, 1967, by Benjin
Price range: $350.00–550.00
Credits: Michael Rossman; Oakland, California

Category: Political Memorabilia
Item Type: Poster
Classification: D-3
Dimensions: 22" h x 17" w
Description: Poster. Muhammad Ali, political statement
Artisan/Manufacturer: Unmarked
Date: 1967–1971
Price range: $55.00–75.00
Credits: Michael Rossman; Oakland, California

Category: Political Memorabilia
Item Type: Poster
Classification: D-3
Dimensions: 17" h x 22" w
Description: Poster, tribute remembering Malcom X
Artisan/Manufacturer: Unmarked
Date: 1967–1970
Price range: $75.00–135.00
Credits: Michael Rossman; Oakland, California

Category: Political Memorabilia
Item Type: Poster
Classification: D-3
Dimensions: 22" h x 17" w
Description: Poster. Possibly Stokley Carmichael, political statement
Artisan/Manufacturer: Unmarked
Date: 1967–1970
Price range: $75.00–135.00
Credits: Michael Rossman; Oakland, California

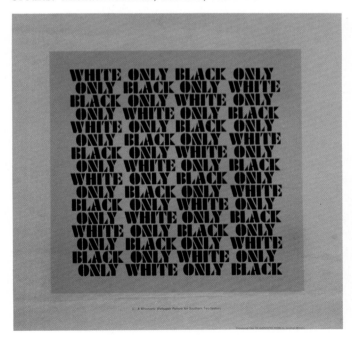

Category: Political Memorabilia
Item Type: Poster
Classification: D-3
Dimensions: 17¾" h x 17¾" w
Description: Political statement poster
Artisan/Manufacturer: Reproduced from *Six Rusticated Poems* by Johnathan Williams
Date: 1968
Price range: $80.00–125.00
Credits: Michael Rossman; Oakland, California

BLACK IS ALSO A CONSCIOUSNESS

Category: Political Memorabilia
Item Type: Poster
Classification: D-2
Dimensions: 22" h x 16¾" w
Description: Positive poster, Blacks in America
Artisan/Manufacturer: Unmarked
Date: 1967–1970
Price range: $100.00–165.00
Credits: Michael Rossman; Oakland, California

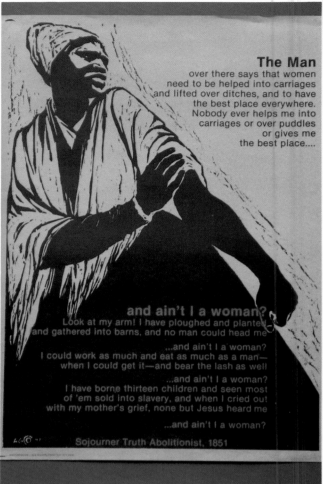

The Man
over there says that women
need to be helped into carriages
and lifted over ditches, and to have
the best place everywhere.
Nobody ever helps me into
carriages or over puddles
or gives me
the best place....

and ain't I a woman?
Look at my arm! I have ploughed and planted
and gathered into barns, and no man could head me

...and ain't I a woman?
I could work as much and eat as much as a man—
when I could get it—and bear the lash as well

...and ain't I a woman?
I have borne thirteen children and seen most
of 'em sold into slavery, and when I cried out
with my mother's grief, none but Jesus heard me

...and ain't I a woman?

Sojourner Truth Abolitionist, 1851

Category: Political Memorabilia
Item Type: Poster
Classification: D-3
Dimensions: 23½" h x 17¼" w
Description: Poster, Sojourner Truth, Abolitionist. Political statement.
Artisan/Manufacturer: LG Co.
Date: 1971
Price range: $95.00–155.00
Credits: Michael Rossman; Oakland, California

Category: Political Memorabilia
Item Type: Poster
Classification: D-3
Dimensions: 17½" h x 23" w
Description: Malcolm X poster. As with other famous Blacks, many items of memorabilia were created about Malcolm X. Items from this time period are not generally available.
Artisan/Manufacturer: Ernest W. Chambers
Date: Copyright, Belinda Burton, 1968
Price range: $300.00–450.00
Credits: Michael Rossman; Oakland, California

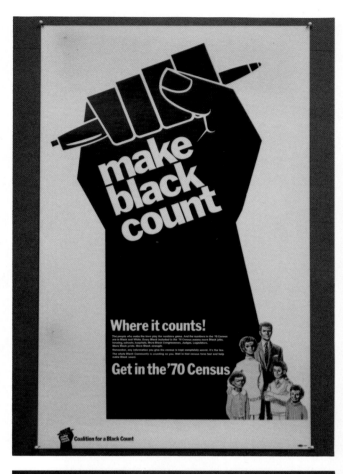

Category: Political Memorabilia
Item Type: Poster
Classification: D-3
Dimensions: 22½" h x 14" w
Description: Poster exhorting Black participation in the 1970 census.
Artisan/Manufacturer: Coalition for a Black Count
Date: 1969–1970
Price range: $75.00–125.00
Credits: Michael Rossman; Oakland, California

Category: Political Memorabilia
Item Type: Poster
Classification: D-2
Dimensions: 19¼" h x 12¾" w
Description: Medgar Evers, remembrance poster
Artisan/Manufacturer: Unmarked
Date: 1967–1970
Price range: $75.00–125.00
Credits: Michael Rossman; Oakland, California

Category: Political Memorabilia
Item Type: Poster
Classification: D-2
Dimensions: 22⅝" h x 17⅞" w
Description: Political statement poster
Artisan/Manufacturer: By Hugo Gallert
Date: 1969–1970
Price range: $75.00–135.00
Credits: Michael Rossman; Oakland, California

Category: Political Memorabilia
Item Type: Poster
Classification: D-3
Dimensions: 22⅛" h x 14¼" w
Description: Solicitation to encourage voting. Scarce.
Artisan/Manufacturer: Bay Area Urban League
Date: 1968–1970
Price range: $60.00–95.00
Credits: Michael Rossman; Oakland, California

Category: Political Memorabilia
Item Type: Poster
Classification: E-3
Dimensions: 21¾" h x 17" w
Description: Advertisement poster. Political statement. Scarce for specific individuals.
Artisan/Manufacturer: C A L
Date: 1970
Price range: $65.00–100.00
Credits: Michael Rossman; Oakland, California

Category: Political Memorabilia
Item Type: Poster
Classification: E-3
Dimensions: 17" h x 14" w
Description: Caption "Black is Beautiful When Black Respect Black." Political state poster, common
Artisan/Manufacturer: Unmarked
Date: 1968–1971
Price range: $65.00–100.00
Credits: Michael Rossman; Oakland, California

Category: Political Memorabilia
Item Type: Poster
Classification: E-3
Dimensions: 22⅝" h x 17¾" w
Description: Political statement poster, common.
Artisan/Manufacturer: Charles Bible
Date: 1970
Price range: $95.00–150.00
Credits: Michael Rossman; Oakland, California

Category: Political Memorabilia
Item Type: Poster
Classification: E-3
Dimensions: 22½" h x 17" w
Description: Common, positive statement poster
Artisan/Manufacturer: Morris-Greene
Date: 1967–1969
Price range: $65.00–100.00
Credits: Michael Rossman; Oakland, California

Category: Political Memorabilia
Item Type: Poster
Classification: D-2
Dimensions: 22½" h x 17¾" w
Description: Caption, "Rev. Martin Luther King, Jr." Scarce;
a great deal of memorabilia has been created honoring
Martin Luther King, Jr. Pieces from this time period are
not numerous
Artisan/Manufacturer: Erwin H. Cobb
Date: Copyright 1967
Price range: $275.00–350.00
Credits: Michael Rossman; Oakland, California

JOURNAL OF BLACK POETRY PRESS—COPYWRITE 1970 — BEN CALDWELL

Category: Political Memorabilia
Item Type: Poster
Classification: E-3
Dimensions: 22½" h x 17¼" w
Description: Caption "Journal of Black Poetry Press – Ben Caldwell." Scarce; advertisement for the journal.
Artisan/Manufacturer: By BNJN
Date: 1970
Price range: $75.00–125.00
Credits: Michael Rossman; Oakland, California

Category: Political Memorabilia
Item Type: Poster
Classification: D-2
Dimensions: 24¼" h x 18" w
Description: Political statement poster; scarce
Artisan/Manufacturer: Copi Syess
Date: 1970
Price range: $225.00–385.00
Credits: Michael Rossman; Oakland, California

On August 25, 1969 the United States Government broke its promise to the children of Mississippi.

Legal Defense Fund

Category: Political Memorabilia
Item Type: Poster
Classification: E-3
Dimensions: 22" h x 15½" w
Description: Fundraising poster, common
Artisan/Manufacturer: Legal Defense Fund
Date: 1969
Price range: $60.00–80.00
Credits: Michael Rossman; Oakland, California

Category: Political Memorabilia
Item Type: Poster
Classification: E-3
Dimensions: 17⅛" h x 11" w
Description: Caption "Hallelujah, Hallelujah…" Celebration of Life poster, common.
Artisan/Manufacturer: Black Panther Party Central Headquarters
Date: 1969–1971
Price range: $75.00–125.00
Credits: Michael Rossman; Oakland, California

Category: Political Memorabilia
Item Type: Poster
Classification: D-3
Dimensions: 22⅝" h x 17½" w
Description: Political statement poster, common.
Artisan/Manufacturer: Charles Stroud
Date: Copyright 1968
Price range: $65.00–110.00
Credits: Michael Rossman; Oakland, California

Category: Political Memorabilia
Item Type: Poster
Classification: E-3
Dimensions: 16⅝" h x 11⅜" w
Description: Caption "Smash the State." Political statement poster
Artisan/Manufacturer: Tribe/5
Date: 1969–1971
Price range: $65.00–95.00
Credits: Michael Rossman; Oakland, California

Category: Political Memorabilia
Item Type: Poster
Classification: E-3
Dimensions: 22⅝" h x 17¼" w
Description: Unity poster. Black African – Black America. Scarce.
Artisan/Manufacturer: Charles Bible
Date: 1969–1971
Price range: $100.00–165.00
Credits: Michael Rossman; Oakland, California

Category: Political Memorabilia
Item Type: Poster
Classification: E-3
Dimensions: 23" h x 17¼" w
Description: Eldridge Cleaver wanted poster, political statement
Artisan/Manufacturer: Unmarked
Date: 1970
Price range: $125.00–200.00
Credits: Michael Rossman; Oakland, California

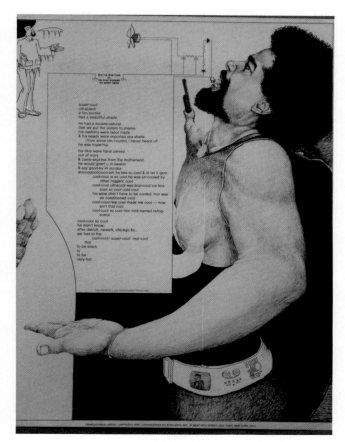

Category: Political Memorabilia
Item Type: Poster
Classification: E-3
Dimensions: 22⅝" h x 17¾" w
Description: Political statement poem, scarce
Artisan/Manufacturer: Charles Bible, artist
Date: 1969–1971
Price range: $115.00–175.00
Credits: Michael Rossman; Oakland, California

Category: Political Memorabilia
Item Type: Poster
Classification: E-3
Dimensions: 22⅝" h x 17¼" w
Description: Political statement poster, scarce
Artisan/Manufacturer: Charles Bible
Date: 1969–1970
Price range: $95.00–145.00
Credits: Michael Rossman; Oakland, California

Category: Political Memorabilia
Item Type: Poster
Classification: D-3
Dimensions: 17" h x 13" w
Description: "Black Man with Stripe Shirt," political statement poster.
Artisan/Manufacturer: Emory
Date: 1965–1969
Price range: $115.00–175.00
Credits: Michael Rossman; Oakland, California

Category: Political Memorabilia
Item Type: Poster
Classification: D-2
Dimensions: 20" h x 13" w
Description: Black Panther Party fundraising poster. Huey P. Newton. Common.
Artisan/Manufacturer: Black Panther Party
Date: 1968–1971
Price range: $115.00–175.00
Credits: Michael Rossman; Oakland, California

Category: Political Memorabilia
Item Type: Poster
Classification: D-2
Dimensions: 22⅛" h x 16¼" w
Description: Angela Davis. Scarce. Caption "Angela."
Artisan/Manufacturer: Barry Sharpiro
Date: 1971
Price range: $300.00–400.00
Credits: Michael Rossman; Oakland, California

Category: Political Memorabilia
Item Type: Poster
Classification: D-2
Dimensions: 17" h x 13" w
Description: Stokley Carmichael, scarce.
Artisan/Manufacturer: Emory
Date: 1965–1967
Price range: $200.00–300.00
Credits: Michael Rossman; Oakland, California

Category: Political Memorabilia
Item Type: Poster
Classification: D-2
Dimensions: 20" h x 14" w
Description: Black Panther Party, political statement. Common.
Artisan/Manufacturer: Emory
Date: 1969
Price range: $100.00–150.00
Credits: Michael Rossman; Oakland, California

Category: Political Memorabilia
Item Type: Poster
Classification: D-2
Dimensions: 19½" h x 12" w
Description: "Free Huey Newton" political statement poster, common.
Artisan/Manufacturer: Emory
Date: 1969–1970
Price range: $100.00–150.00
Credits: Michael Rossman; Oakland, California

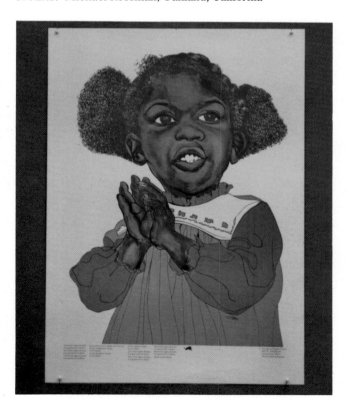

Category: Political Memorabilia
Item Type: Poster
Classification: D-2
Dimensions: 20" h x 14" w
Description: Scarce. Posters of children, reflecting positive images, were common in the late 1960s and early 1970s. Such posters are now sought after by collectors.
Artisan/Manufacturer: Emory
Date: 1969–1970
Price range: $145.00–225.00
Credits: Michael Rossman; Oakland, California

Category: Political Memorabilia
Item Type: Poster
Classification: D-3
Dimensions: 20⅝" h x 14" w
Description: Black Panther Party political statement poster, common.
Artisan/Manufacturer: Emory
Date: 1969
Price range: $85.00 – 125.00
Credits: Michael Rossman; Oakland, California

Category: Political Memorabilia
Item Type: Poster
Classification: D-3
Dimensions: 20⅝" h x 14" w
Description: "The Lumpen." Black Panther Party political statement poster, common.
Artisan/Manufacturer: Emory
Date: 1969 – 1970
Price range: $85.00 – 125.00
Credits: Michael Rossman; Oakland, California

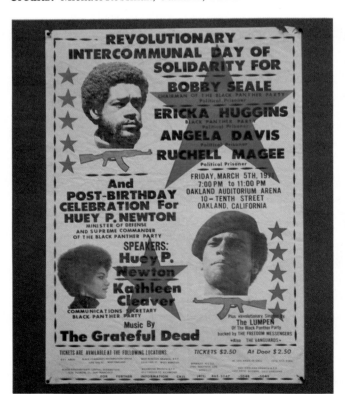

Category: Political Memorabilia
Item Type: Poster
Classification: D-3
Dimensions: 20" h x 14" w
Description: Fundraising poster, Black Panther Party
Artisan/Manufacturer: Black Panther Party
Date: 1969
Price range: $75.00 – 125.00
Credits: Michael Rossman; Oakland, California

Category: Political Memorabilia
Item Type: Poster
Classification: D-2
Dimensions: 22¼" h x 14¼" w
Description: Caption "By lifting their hands against Lil Bobby, they lifted their hands against the best that humanity possesses." Scarce.
Artisan/Manufacturer: Black Panther Party Central Headquarters
Date: 1968
Price range: $75.00–125.00
Credits: Michael Rossman; Oakland, California

Category: Political Memorabilia
Item Type: Poster
Classification: D-2
Dimensions: 17⅝" h x 11" w
Description: Caption "WHY MUST BLACK PEOPLE LOOK AT EACH OTHER THROUGH PRISON BARS?" Common.
Artisan/Manufacturer: Black Panther Party Central Headquarters
Date: 1969
Price range: $75.00–125.00
Credits: Michael Rossman; Oakland, California

Category: Political Memorabilia
Item Type: Poster
Classification: D-1
Dimensions: 22" h x 17" w
Description: Political statement. Black woman with child, common.
Artisan/Manufacturer: Emory
Date: 1967
Price range: $75.00–125.00
Credits: Michael Rossman; Oakland, California

Category: Political Memorabilia
Item Type: Poster
Classification: D-2
Dimensions: 22" h x 17" w
Description: Stokley CarMichael. "Prime Minister of Colonized Afro-America." Scarce.
Artisan/Manufacturer: Emory
Date: 1969–1970
Price range: $125.00–225.00
Credits: Michael Rossman; Oakland, California

Category: Political Memorabilia
Item Type: Poster
Classification: D-2
Dimensions: 23¼" h x 17¼" w
Description: Black Panther Party poster, scarce.
Artisan/Manufacturer: Distributed by the Hubert Brown Elliot League
Date: 1969
Price range: $85.00–150.00
Credits: Michael Rossman; Oakland, California

Category: Political Memorabilia
Item Type: Poster
Classification: D-3
Dimensions: 22¾" h x 17¼" w
Description: Eldridge Cleaver. Photo-poster. Black Panther Party.
Artisan/Manufacturer: Black Panther Party
Date: 1970
Price range: $115.00–165.00
Credits: Michael Rossman; Oakland, California

Category: Political Memorabilia
Item Type: Poster
Classification: D-2
Dimensions: 18⅝" h x 17⅝" w
Description: Poster paying tribute to Malcolm X, scarce.
Artisan/Manufacturer: Unmarked
Date: 1967, copyright ovoidplanet 1968, second printing.
Price range: $85.00–125.00
Credits: Michael Rossman; Oakland, California

Category: Political Memorabilia
Item Type: Poster
Classification: D-2
Dimensions: 17⅛" h x 11" w
Description: Black Panther Party poster statement, scarce.
Artisan/Manufacturer: Black Panther Party Central Headquarters
Date: 1968–1969
Price range: $85.00–125.00
Credits: Michael Rossman; Oakland, California

Category: Political Memorabilia
Item Type: Poster
Classification: D-2
Dimensions: 22¾" h x 17¼" w
Description: Poster of Angela Davis, scarce.
Artisan/Manufacturer: Tribune Times
Date: 1971
Price range: $90.00–150.00
Credits: Michael Rossman; Oakland, California

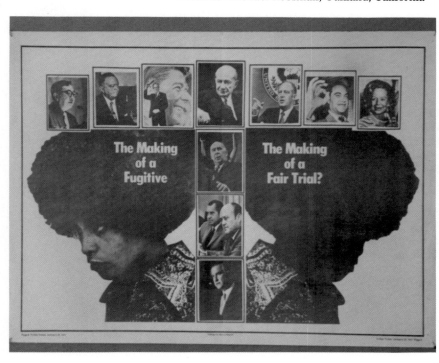

Category: Political Memorabilia
Item Type: Poster
Classification: D-2
Dimensions: 22½" h x 17¼" w
Description: Page from newspaper, "Right On."
Artisan/Manufacturer: Unmarked
Date: ca. 1969
Price range: $75.00–125.00
Credits: Michael Rossman; Oakland, California

Category: Political Memorabilia
Item Type: Poster
Classification: D-3
Dimensions: 22⅝" h x 17" w
Description: Southern Christian Leadership Conference poster. Typical, illustrating their support for the plight of low-income persons.
Artisan/Manufacturer: SCLC
Date: Copyright 1968
Price range: $85.00–125.00
Credits: Michael Rossman; Oakland, California

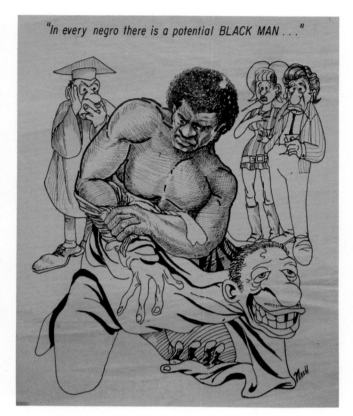

Category: Political Memorabilia
Item Type: Poster
Classification: D-2
Dimensions: 22" h x 17" w
Description: H. Rap Brown, political activist, 1960s. Scarce.
Artisan/Manufacturer: Ervin H. Cobb
Date: 1967
Price range: $110.00–200.00
Credits: Michael Rossman; Oakland, California

Category: Political Memorabilia
Item Type: Poster
Classification: D-1
Dimensions: 22½" h x 17½" w
Description: Poster which symbolizes the difference of opinion between persons calling themselves "Negro" and those who thought of themselves as "Black."
Artisan/Manufacturer: NASH
Date: 1969
Price range: $85.00–145.00
Credits: Michael Rossman; Oakland, California

Category: Political Memorabilia
Item Type: Poster
Classification: D-2
Dimensions: 22" h x 17" w
Description: Le Roi Jones, activist, author, and poet during the 1960s and 1970s. Scarce.
Artisan/Manufacturer: Ervin H. Cobb
Date: 1967
Price range: $125.00–200.00
Credits: Michael Rossman; Oakland, California

Category: Political Memorabilia
Item Type: Poster
Classification: E-3
Dimensions: 22¼" h x 17¼" w
Description: Poster promoting positive interaction between Black males and females, scarce.
Artisan/Manufacturer: Drawing by Jack Thoat
Date: 1971
Price range: $85.00–145.00
Credits: Michael Rossman; Oakland, California

Category: Political Memorabilia
Item Type: Poster
Classification: D-2
Dimensions: 22⅛" h x 17" w
Description: Poster board material, print. Malcolm X poster, scarce.
Artisan/Manufacturer: Afro-Am Publishing Co., Chicago, Ill.
Date: 1966
Price range: $200.00–300.00
Credits: Michael Rossman; Oakland, California

Category: Political Memorabilia
Item Type: Button
Classification: D-3
Dimensions: 1½"
Description: Metal button, scarce. (Black Student Unions were fixtures on college campuses in the late 1960s and early 1970s. Buttons such as this one were usually thrown out or lost in college dorm rooms.)
Artisan/Manufacturer: San Francisco College
Date: 1960s–1970s
Price range: $25.00–35.00
Credits: The Paper Pile/San Anselmo, California

Category: Political Memorabilia
Item Type: Button
Classification: D-2
Dimensions: 1¾"
Description: Metal button, Black Panther Party. Scarce.
Artisan/Manufacturer: Unmarked
Date: 1960–1970
Price range: $25.00–35.00
Credits: The Paper Pile/San Anselmo, California

Category: Political Memorabilia
Item Type: Button
Classification: D-2
Dimensions: 1¾"
Description: Metal button typical of the Black Panther Party. Scarce.
Artisan/Manufacturer: Unmarked
Date: 1960–1970, plus
Price range: $15.00–25.00
Credits: The Paper Pile/San Anselmo, California

Category: Political Memorabilia
Item Type: Button
Classification: D-2
Dimensions: 1⅜"
Description: Metal button with plastic coating. All original memorabilia with Malcolm X on it is collectible. Such buttons are scarce and usually date from the late 1960s to early 1970s.
Artisan/Manufacturer: Unmarked
Date: 1960–1970, plus
Price range: $30.00–45.00
Credits: The Paper Pile/San Anselmo, California

Category: Political Memorabilia
Item Type: Button
Classification: D-2
Dimensions: 1⅝"
Description: Metal button with plastic coating. Adam Clayton Powell, Congressman from New York, was a prominent political figure during the 1960s. Scarce.
Artisan/Manufacturer: Unmarked
Date: 1960s
Price range: $45.00–55.00
Credits: The Paper Pile/San Anselmo, California

Category: Political Memorabilia
Item Type: Button
Classification: D-2
Dimensions: 1⅝"
Description: Metal button typical of the late 1960s period of Black protest. "Black Is Beautiful"
Artisan/Manufacturer: Houston, Texas on side
Date: 1960s
Price range: $15.00–25.00
Credits: The Paper Pile/San Anselmo, California

Category: Political Memorabilia
Item Type: Button
Classification: D-2
Dimensions: 1½"
Description: Metal button, Eldridge Cleaver on front. Political statement of 1960s Black Equality Movement. "It's Time To Intensify The Struggle"
Artisan/Manufacturer: 20
Date: 1960s
Price range: $15.00–25.00
Credits: The Paper Pile/San Anselmo, California

Category: Political Memorabilia
Item Type: Button
Classification: D-2
Dimensions: ¾"
Description: Metal with plastic coating. The Student Nonviolent Coordinating Committee (SNCC) flourished in the 1960s and early 1970s. Like other material from this period, it is scarce.
Artisan/Manufacturer: Unmarked
Date: 1960–1970
Price range: $25.00–35.00
Credits: The Paper Pile/San Anselmo, California

Category: Political Memorabilia
Item Type: Button
Classification: D-2
Dimensions: 1¾"
Description: Metal button with plastic coating. Scarce are the buttons which show Eldridge Cleaver running for president. Such items were usually discarded.
Artisan/Manufacturer: Symbol on back
Date: 1960–1970
Price range: $45.00–55.00
Credits: The Paper Pile/San Anselmo, California

Category: Political Memorabilia
Item Type: Button
Classification: D-2
Dimensions: 1½"
Description: Metal button with plastic coating. Although of recent vintage, buttons of this type are scarce.
Artisan/Manufacturer: Unmarked
Date: Late 1960s
Price range: $30.00–40.00
Credits: The Paper Pile/San Anselmo, California

Category: Political Memorabilia
Item Type: Button
Classification: D-2
Dimensions: 1¾"
Description: Metal button with plastic coating. These two athletes who participated in the 1968 Olympics created quite a controversy when they raised their fist as they stood to receive their medals.
Artisan/Manufacturer: Unmarked
Date: ca. 1968
Price range: $35.00–45.00
Credits: The Paper Pile/San Anselmo, California

Money – Stamps

Money and stamps are two of the biggest areas of collectibles, if separated from Black collectibles. In the Black collectibles arena, there are Blacks on coins, paper money and commemorative tokens. The coins are the silver half-dollars made in the late 1940s and early 1950s with Booker T. Washington and George Washington Carver on them. During the late 1800s, many of the Confederate States that were printing paper dollars used images of blacks in different scenes. Most were depicted working at some farm trade (picking cotton, harvesting crops, working with farm animals, etc.) Although not plentiful, these Confederate dollars are not very expensive. The images are often not very clear and some have been called Black but are poorly executed images of Whites. The commemorative tokens depicting Blacks date between the 18th and 19th centuries. They are called "slave tokens" and can be seen at the American Numismatic Museum in New York City. Prices for these items range in the high teens for the silver coins; single digits to the hundreds for the Confederate bills. Although most are expensive, the commemorative tokens are rare and market value is difficult to compute. There are very few reproductions in the half-dollars but fake Confederate dollars abound. One should be wary of the Confederate dollars and study them before purchasing or buy from a reputable dealer. The novice collector should be careful when purchasing older coins. Many were counterfeited during the time in which they were made.

Stamps, on the other hand, are not in the same category as money. Of the hundreds of different types of stamps printed, very few have Blacks on them. Although they are not considered rare collectible stamps, as Black collectibles, they are unusual. Prices are generally below $50.00 per short block (four stamps). These stamps are readily available through most stamp dealers. (As a point of interest, there are over 100 stamps made by foreign countries of Dr. Martin Luther King, Jr.) As Black collectibles, stamps and money may rise slightly faster than expected.

Category: Money/stamps
Item Type: Money
Classification: D-1
Dimensions: 1¼" diameter
Description: Booker T. Washington. Philadelphia mint, half-dollar. Front – image of Mr. Washington, 1946. Back – Washington's birthplace, Franklin County, Virginia. Cabin embossed on bottom.
Date: 1946
Price range: $30.00–45.00
Credits: American Coin & Exchange; Madison, Tennessee.
Note of Interest: Common. Other dates of mint are 1947, 1948, 1949, 1950, 1951. The small letter (P, D or S) found on coins represent the mint location. (i.e. Philadelphia, Denver, San Francisco. Philadelphia was the largest mint, then Denver; San Francisco was the smallest and minted the least coins.)

Category: Money/stamps
Item Type: Money
Classification: D-1
Dimensions: 1¼" diameter
Description: George W. Carver/Booker T. Washington half-dollar, "Washington-Carver coin." Image of both men.

Mint mark on reverse. "Freedom and Opportunity For All **Americanism.**" "U.S.A." inside shape of US map.
Date: 1952
Price range: $35.00–45.00
Note of Interest: Common. Other dates of mint are 1951, 1953, 1954.

Category: Money/stamps
Item Type: Money
Classification: D-3
Dimensions: 3" h x 7" w
Description: "Confederate States of America/$10.00." Poor condition. Scene of black man at a table.

Date: 1861
Price range: $20.00–30.00
Credits: American Coin & Stamp Exchange; Madison, Tennessee
Note of Interest: Common

Category: Money/stamps
Item Type: Money
Classification: D-3
Dimensions: 3" h x 7" w
Description: "Bank of Lexington/State of North Carolina" $5.00 Confederate bill. Faded tan paper with red/orange decoration. Good condition. Left bottom corner has scene of a Black man picking cotton.
Date: 1860
Price range: $30.00–45.00
Note of Interest: Common

Category: Money/stamps
Item Type: Money
Classification: D-3
Dimensions:
Description: "Kentinge and Ball, Columbia, S.C./Confederate States America – $100.00." Top scene of Black men hoeing crops. Very good condition. Uneven edges. Stamped on the back "Issued by John Boston Def…Savannah Nov. 12, 1862." Other stamps of interest paid are also present.
Date: 1862
Price range: $30.00–45.00
Note of Interest: Scarce

94

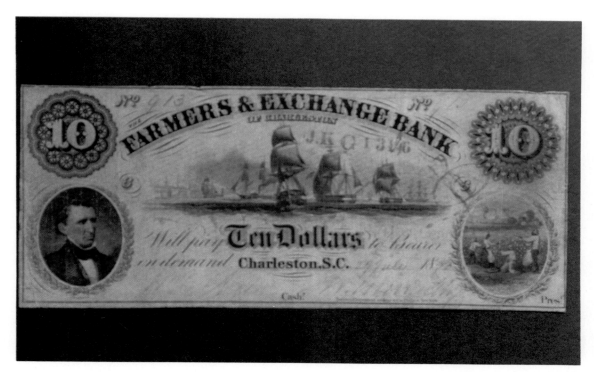

Category: Money/stamps
Item Type: Money
Classification: D-3
Dimensions: 3" h x 7" w
Description: "Farmers & Exchange Bank of Charleston" $10.00 Confederate bill. Bottom right corner displays a cotton scene with a family of four working, enclosed by a wreath. Very good condition
Date: 1853
Price range: $30.00–45.00
Note of Interest: Scarce. Paper is thin and ink is visible from the back.

Category: Money/stamps
Item Type: Money
Classification: D-3
Dimensions: 2⅞" h x 7⅛" w
Description: "The Bank of Hamburg" South Carolina, $5.00 Confederate bill. An off-white paper with orange/red decorative markings. Attractively arranged images. Upper-middle section displays a White gentleman using a stone wheel while being assisted by a young Black man. Other Black men are working in the background. Paper is thin with some ink visible from the back side of bill.
Date: 1860
Price range: $30.00–45.00
Note of Interest: Scarce

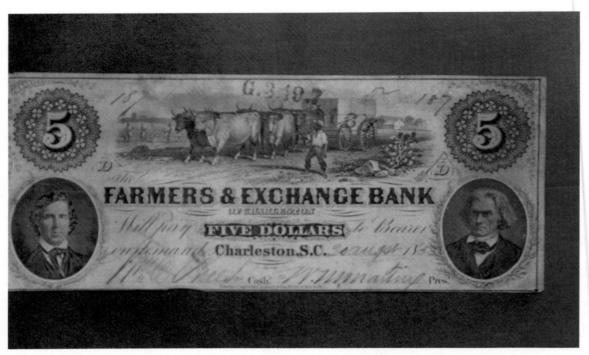

Category: Money/stamps
Item Type: Money
Classification: D-3
Dimensions: 2⅞" h x 7" w
Description: "Farmers & Exchange Bank" of Charleston, S.C. $5.00 Confederate bill. The top middle scene is of a Black man guiding a team of oxen. Other Blacks can be seen in a distant cotton field. Uneven edges due to crude cutting when the bill was produced. Good condition. Color is faded tan with black ink.
Date: 1853
Price range: $30.00–45.00
Note of Interest: Scarce. Paper is thin and translucent; ink visible from the back.

Category: Money/stamps
Item Type: Money
Classification: D-3
Dimensions: 3" h x 7⅞" w
Description: Thin $5.00 confederate bill from Winnsboro, S.C., Planters Bank of Fairfield. The scene at the very top, middle section is depicting Blacks working in the cotton fields with a white male mounted on his horse. The edges of the bill are uneven probably due to the crude techniques used to make the bill. Color is pale tan with black and a faded red "FIVE" (bottom). Good condition.
Date: 1855
Price range: $30.00–45.00
Note of Interest: Scarce. Paper is thin and translucent; ink visible from the back.

Category: Money/stamps
Item Type: Stamps
Classification: D-2
Dimensions: 2¼" h x 2" w
Description: George Washington Carver stamp (4-block). Excellent condition (no cancellation).
Date: 1948
Price range: $8.00–12.00 each
Credits: American Coin & Stamp Exchange; Madison, Tennessee
Note of Interest: Common. Carver was an educator and inventor.

Category: Money/stamps
Item Type: Stamps
Classification: D-2
Dimensions: 2⅛" h x 2½" w
Description: Frederick Douglass stamp (4-block). Excellent condition (no cancellation).
Date: Feb. 1967
Price range: $8.00–12.00 each
Credits: American Coin & Stamp Exchange; Madison, Tennessee
Note of Interest: Common. Douglass was an author and educator.

Category: Money/stamps
Item Type: Stamps
Classification: D-3
Dimensions: 2" h x 4⅛" w
Description: A 4-block stamp plate honoring W.C. Handy.
Excellent condition (no cancellation).
Date: May 1969
Price range: $3.00–5.00 each
Credits: American Coin & Stamp Exchange; Madison, Tennessee
Note of Interest: Common

Category: Money/stamps
Item Type: Stamps
Classification: D-2
Dimensions: 4⅛" h x 2⅛" w
Description: A 4-block stamp plate of Martin Luther King, Jr. Excellent condition (no cancellation).
Date: Jan. 1979
Price range: $35.00–45.00 each
Credits: American Coin & Stamp Exchange; Madison, Tennessee
Note of Interest: Plentiful, future collectible.

Category: Money/stamps
Item Type: Stamps
Classification: D-2
Dimensions: 2" h x 3¼" w
Description: 4-block 1980 USA Olympics stamp. Excellent condition (no cancellation).
Date: 1980
Price range: $35.00–45.00 each
Credits: American Coin & Stamp Exchange; Madison, Tennessee
Note of Interest: Plentiful, future collectible.

Category: Money/stamps
Item Type: Stamps
Classification: D-2
Dimensions: 4¼" h x 3" w
Description: Paul Laurence Dunbar stamp. Dunbar was an American poet. Excellent condition (no cancellation).
Date: May 1975
Price range: $35.00–45.00
Credits: American Coin & Stamp Exchange; Madison, Tennessee
Note of Interest: Common, future collectible.

Category: Money/stamps
Item Type: Stamps
Classification: D-2
Dimensions: 2⅝" h x 1" w
Description: Benjamin Banneker stamp. Excellent condition (no cancellation).
Date: Feb. 1980
Price range: $3.00–5.00 each
Credits: American Coin & Stamp Exchange; Madison, Tennessee
Note of Interest: Plentiful. Banneker was an inventor.

Category: Money/stamps
Item Type: Stamps
Classification: D-2
Dimensions: 1¼" h x 1" w
Description: Booker T. Washington stamp. Excellent condition (no cancellation).
Date: April 1940
Price range: $8.00–10.00 each
Credits: American Coin & Stamp Exchange; Madison, Tennessee
Note of Interest: Common. Washington was an educator and author.

Category: Money/stamps
Item Type: Stamps
Classification: D-2
Dimensions: 1½" h x 1" w
Description: Scott Joplin stamp, honoring him for his great musical talent. Excellent condition (no cancellation).
Date: May 1983
Price range: $3.00–5.00 each
Credits: American Coin & Stamp Exchange; Madison, Tennessee
Note of Interest: Plentiful, future collectible.

Category: Money/stamps
Item Type: Stamps
Classification: D-2
Dimensions: 1½" h x 1" w
Description: Carter G. Woodson. A part of the "Black Hertiage Series." Excellent condition (no cancellation).
Date: Feb. 1984
Price range: $3.00–5.00 each
Credits: American Coin & Stamp Exchange; Madison, Tennessee
Note of Interest: Plentiful. Woodson was an educator.

Category: Money/stamps
Item Type: Stamps
Classification: D-2
Dimensions: 1½" h x 1" w (single); 4¼" h x 3" w (6-block)
Description: Harriet Tubman stamp. A part of the "Black Heritage" Series. Excellent condition (no cancellation).
Date: Feb. 1978
Price range: $3.00–5.00 each; 25.00–30.00 (6-block)
Credits: American Coin & Stamp Exchange; Madison, Tennessee
Note of Interest: Common. Tubman was an early activist. Future collectible stamp.

Literary Collectibles

The material which falls under this category covers any printed matter that focuses on Blacks or is written by Blacks. The range of material is large and includes many types of items – pamplets, booklets, articles, magazines, and books.

During the early 19th and 20th centuries, published Black authors were rare. Therefore, original books by such persons as Benjamin Bannecker, Sojourner Truth, Booker T. Washington, and W.E.B. DuBois will sell in the medium-to-high price range. There are those books which do not depict Blacks in a positive manner, concentrating on the more stereotypical image of Blacks being chased by alligators, holding onto chickens, or eating watermelon. The dialogue in these books is often stilted, with the Blacks often appearing not to understand various situations in which they find themselves in the book. For example, Little Black Sambo, which started out as a book about a boy from India, often was rewritten to depict an African or American Black child.

Other books fall into the magazines category such as *Jet, Opportunity,* or the two or three comic books from the 1940s which focused on "Negroes." Not all of the literary collectibles will be books or booklets but may be an article about a famous Black person which uses photographs or prints to illustrate the point of the story. The method for determining the quality of the product encompasses both an assessment of the subject covered, condition of the material, author of the piece, number of illustrations, age, country of origin, and status in the art world.

Literary collectibles such as *Harper's Magazine* often fall into two categories – an article on W.E.B. DuBois might be considered literary where a lithograph of him in the magazine might be cut out and sold as a print. Popular items are the stereotypical early books, historical books, pamphlets of socialist workers from the 1930s and 1940s, early *Jet* magazines, booklets from such organizations as NAACP, or the Urban League, magazines such as *Ramparts* or *Avant-Garde* (late 1960s and early 1970s) and original writings on slaves or famous Blacks. Prices vary widely because very little consensus has been reached in this area.

Category: Literary Collectibles
Item Type: Magazine
Classification: D-2
Dimensions: 12⅞" h x 11½" w
Description: Horse-drawn setter with 3 Black men, cover story
Artisan/Manufacturer: Southern Agriculturist (May 15, 1929)
Price range: $8.00–12.00
Credits: The Great Escape; Nashville, Tennessee

Category: Literary Collectibles
Item Type: Book
Classification: D-2
Description: *Epaminondas and His Auntie*
Artisan/Manufacturer: Written by Sara Cone Bryant. Illustrated by Inez Hogan. Houghton Mifflin Company, Boston and New York.
Date: ca. 1930s
Price range: $50.00–80.00
Credits: M. Davern Collection

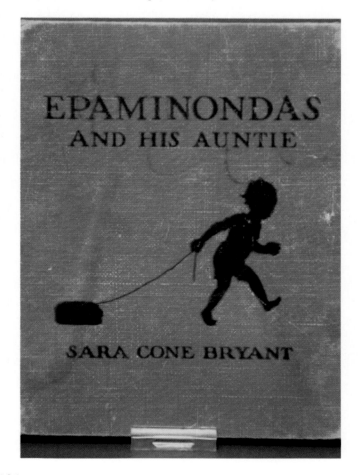

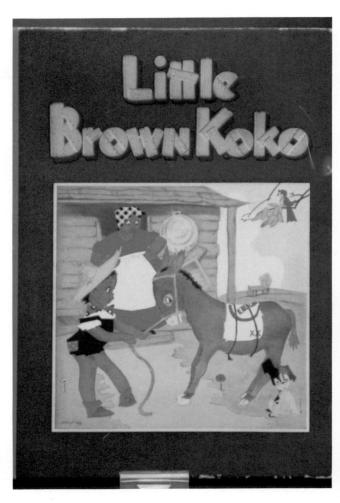

Category: Literary Collectibles
Item Type: Book
Classification: D-1
Dimensions: 10¾" h x 7¾" w
Description: *Little Brown Koko*
Artisan/Manufacturer: Written by Blanche Seale Hunt. Illustrated by Dorothy Wagstaff. Published by American Colortype Company, Chicago and New York.
Date: 1940
Price range: $65.00–85.00
Credits: M. Davern Collection

Category: Literary Collectibles
Item Type: Book
Classification: E-2
Dimensions: 6¾" h x 5½" w
Description: Paper, *Little Black Sambo*
Artisan/Manufacturer: Rand McNally & Company
Date: 1934 edition
Price range: $55.00–75.00
Credits: M. Davern Collection

Category: Literary Collectibles
Item Type: Magazine
Classification: D-2
Dimensions: 12⅞" h x 11½" w
Description: Black man watering a horse with rider mounted
Artisan/Manufacturer: Southern Agriculturist. Photo by James Speed; Nashville, Tenn., Louisville, Ky.
Date: August 15, 1929
Price range: $8.00–12.00
Credits: The Great Escape; Nashville, Tennessee

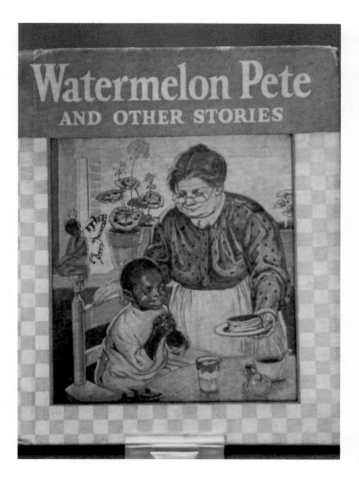

Category: Literary Collectibles
Item Type: Book
Classification: E-2
Dimensions: 6¾" h x 5½" w
Description: Paper, *Watermelon Pete and Other Stories*
Artisan/Manufacturer: Rand McNally & Company
Date: 1927 edition
Price range: $35.00–50.00
Credits: M. Davern Collection

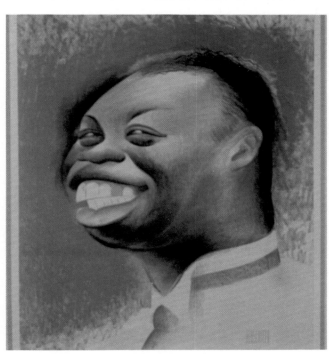

Category: Literary Collectibles
Item Type: Book
Classification: D-1
Description: *Harlem As Seen By Hirschfeld,* 1,000 copies printed.
Artisan/Manufacturer: Text by William Saroyan, Hyperion Press of New York, No. 759
Date: 1941
Price range: $950.00–1,500.00
Credits: Ron Carr; Capitola, California

Category: Literary Collectibles
Item Type: Book
Classification: E-3
Dimensions: 7⅜" h x 5¼" w
Description: Paper, *Diamond Cookbook Compiled From Tested Recipes.*
Artisan/Manufacturer: Cream of Wheat Company, Minneapolis, Minnesota
Date: 1910–1940
Price range: $35.00–45.00
Credits: M. Davern Collection

Category: Literary Collectibles
Item Type: Book
Classification: D-2
Description: *Little Brown Koko Has Fun*
Artisan/Manufacturer: Written by Blanche Seale Hunt. Illustrated by Dorothy Wagstaff. Published by American Colortype Co., Chicago and New York
Date: Copyright 1945 (USA)
Price range: $55.00–85.00
Credits: Ron Carr; Capitola, California

Category: Literary Collectibles
Item Type: Book
Classification: D-2
Description: *The Story Book of Clothes*
Artisan/Manufacturer: Written by Maud and Miska Petersham
Date: Copyright 1933 (Great Britain)
Price range: $55.00–85.00
Credits: Ron Carr; Capitola, California

Category: Literary Collectibles
Item Type: Book
Classification: D-2
Description: *Turkey Trott*
Artisan/Manufacturer: Written by Kate Gambold Dyer. Illustrated by Janet Robson, published by The Platt & Munk Co., Inc., NY, NY
Date: 1942
Price range: $65.00–85.00
Credits: Ron Carr; Capitola, California

Category: Literary Collectibles
Item Type: Book
Classification: D-2
Description: *Nicodemus Helps Uncle Sam*
Artisan/Manufacturer: Written by Inez Hogan
Date: Copyright 1943 (USA)
Price range: $60.00–95.00
Credits: Ron Carr; Capitola, California

Category: Literary Collectibles
Item Type: Book
Classification: D-3
Description: *Frawg*
Artisan/Manufacturer: Written by Annie Vaughan Weaver. Published by Frederick A. Stokes Company
Date: MCMXXX (1930)
Price range: $95.00–145.00
Credits: Ron Carr; Capitola, California

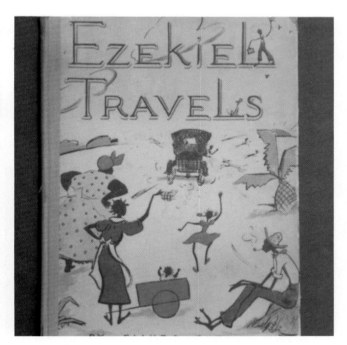

Category: Literary Collectibles
Item Type: Book
Classification: D-3
Description: *Ezekiel Travels*
Artisan/Manufacturer: Written by Elvira Garner. Published by Henry Holt and Company; New York, New York
Date: 1938 (USA)
Price range: $80.00–125.00
Credits: Ron Carr; Capitola, California

Category: Literary Collectibles
Item Type: Book
Classification: D-2
Description: *Unkle Rastus' Christmas Tree*
Artisan/Manufacturer: Designed and written by S. Herbert
  Voorhees. Illustrated by Mildred C. Hayes.
Date: Copyright 1921, Peckville, Pa.
Price range: $300.00 – 400.00
Credits: Ron Carr; Capitola, California

Category: Literary Collectibles
Item Type: Book
Classification: D-2
Description: *Pore Lil Mose, His Letters to his Mammy*
Artisan/Manufacturer: R.F. Outcault 1902, New York Herald
  (NY) Published by The Grand Union Tea Co., Brooklyn
  Burrough, New York
Date: 1902
Price range: $500.00 – 650.00
Credits: Ron Carr; Capitola, California

Category: Literary Collectibles
Item Type: Book
Classification: D-1
Description: *The Camptown Races*
Artisan/Manufacturer: McLoughlin Brothers, N.Y., N.Y.
Date: 1880
Price range: $375.00 – 550.00
Credits: Ron Carr; Capitola, California

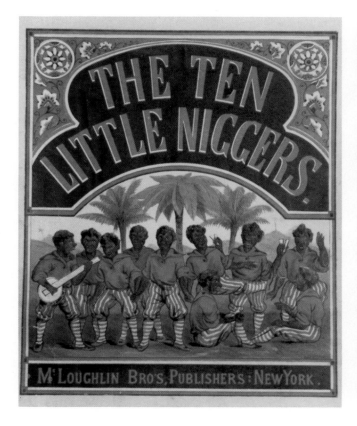

Category: Literary Collectibles
Item Type: Book
Classification: E-2
Description: *The Ten Little Niggers*
Artisan/Manufacturer: McLoughlin Brothers, New York, New York
Date: 1897
Price range: $350.00–475.00
Credits: Ron Carr; Capitola, California

Category: Literary Collectibles
Item Type: Book
Classification: E-2
Description: The Bo-Peep Series, *Ten Little Niggers*
Artisan/Manufacturer: Unmarked
Date: ca. 1920
Price range: $225.00–350.00
Credits: Ron Carr; Capitola, California

Category: Literary Collectibles
Item Type: Book
Classification: E-2
Description: *The Ten Little Niggers,* litho on linen
Artisan/Manufacturer: Charles Graham Company, New York, New York
Date: ca. 1920
Price range: $225.00–350.00
Credits: Ron Carr; Capitola, California

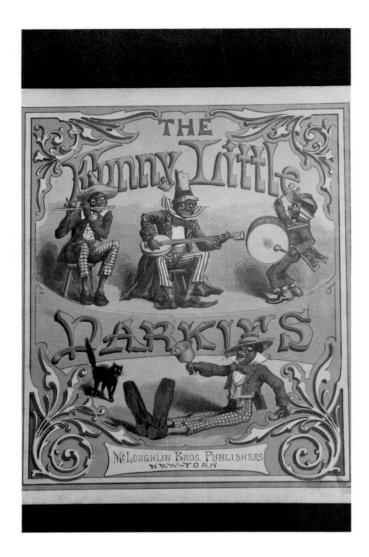

Category: Literary Collectibles
Item Type: Book
Classification: E-2
Description: *The Funny Little Darkies*
Artisan/Manufacturer: McLouglin Brothers Publisher; New York, New York
Date: ca. 1890
Price range: $325.00 – 475.00
Credits: Ron Carr; Capitola, California

Category: Literary Collectibles
Item Type: Book
Classification: D-2
Description: *The Kentucky Twins*
Artisan/Manufacturer: Raphael Tuck & Sons, Ltd., (England) M. Tayler, artist
Date: ca. 1910
Price range: $375.00 – 475.00
Credits: Ron Carr; Capitola, California

Category: Literary Collectibles
Item Type: Magazine
Classification: E-2
Dimensions: 6" h x 4" w
Description: "How Connecticut Mixed Family Faces Bigotry" cover story
Artisan/Manufacturer: Johnson Publishing Company
Date: November 7, 1963
Price range: $8.00–12.00
Note of Interest: *Jet* magazine is one of a few journals which chronicle Black history; it survives to date.

Category: Literary Collectibles
Item Type: Magazine
Classification: E-2
Dimensions: 6" h x 4" w
Description: "Should Negro Stars Join Freedom Fight" cover story
Artisan/Manufacturer: Johnson Publishing Company
Date: May 9, 1963
Price range: $8.00–12.00
Credits: The Paper Pile, San Anselmo, California

Category: Literary Collectibles
Item Type: Magazine
Classification: E-2
Dimensions: 6" h x 4" w
Description: "What President Johnson thinks about Negroes" cover story
Artisan/Manufacturer: Johnson Publishing Company
Date: Dec. 26, 1963
Price range: $8.00–12.00
Credits: The Paper Pile, San Anselmo, California

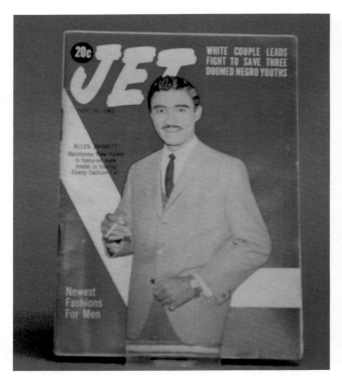

Category: Literary Collectibles
Item Type: Magazine
Classification: E-2
Dimensions: 6" h x 4" w
Description: "White Couple Leads Fight to Save Three Doomed Negro Youths" cover story
Artisan/Manufacturer: Johnson Publishing Company
Date: November 14, 1963
Price range: $8.00–12.00
Credits: The Paper Pile, San Anselmo, California

Category: Literary Collectibles
Item Type: Magazine
Classification: E-2
Dimensions: 6" h x 4" w
Description: "Preacher Who Uses Jazz to Attract Teens" cover story
Artisan/Manufacturer: Johnson Publishing Company
Date: January 10, 1963
Price range: $8.00–12.00
Credits: The Paper Pile, San Anselmo, California

Category: Literary Collectibles
Item Type: Magazine
Classification: E-2
Dimensions: 6" h x 4" w
Description: "Should Negros Boycott Santa Claus" cover article
Artisan/Manufacturer: Johnson Publishing Company
Date: October 17, 1963
Price range: $8.00–12.00
Credits: The Paper Pile, San Anselmo, California

Category: Literary Collectibles
Item Type: Magazine
Classification: E-2
Dimensions: 6" h x 4" w
Description: "The Astonishing Widow Medgar Evers Left Behind" cover plus inside story
Artisan/Manufacturer: Johnson Publishing Company
Date: July 11, 1963
Price range: $8.00–12.00
Credits: The Paper Pile, San Anselmo, California

Category: Literary Collectibles
Item Type: Magazine
Classification: E-2
Dimensions: 6" h x 4" w
Description: "North Carolina's Bias-Battling McKissick Clan" cover plus inside story
Artisan/Manufacturer: Johnson Publishing Company
Date: August 1, 1963
Price range: $8.00–12.00
Credits: The Paper Pile, San Anselmo, California

Category: Literary Collectibles
Item Type: Magazine
Classification: E-2
Dimensions: 6" h x 4" w
Description: "Inside The March on Washington" cover story
Artisan/Manufacturer: Johnson Publishing Company
Date: September 12, 1963
Price range: $6.00–10.00
Credits: The Paper Pile, San Anselmo, California

Category: Literary Collectibles
Item Type: Magazine
Classification: E-2
Dimensions: 6" h x 4" w
Description: "Dallas Today, City of Pride and Prejudice" cover story
Artisan/Manufacturer: Johnson Publishing Company
Date: December 19, 1963
Price range: $10.00–15.00
Credits: The Paper Pile, San Anselmo, California

Category: Literary Collectibles
Item Type: Magazine
Classification: E-2
Dimensions: 6" h x 4" w
Description: "Negro Campaigns For Governor of Mississippi"
Artisan/Manufacturer: Johnson Publishing Company
Date: October 31, 1963
Price range: $8.00 – 12.00
Credits: The Paper Pile, San Anselmo, California

Category: Literary Collectibles
Item Type: Magazine
Classification: E-2
Dimensions: 6" h x 4" w
Description: "Ku Klux Klan's Daylight Flogging of Louisiana Principal"
Artisan/Manufacturer: Johnson Publishing Company
Date: July 4, 1963
Price range: $8.00 – 12.00
Credits: The Paper Pile, San Anselmo, California

Category: Literary Collectibles
Item Type: Magazine
Classification: E-2
Dimensions: 6" h x 4" w
Description: "The Negro Town with Florida's Lowest Crime Rate"
Artisan/Manufacturer: Johnson Publishing Company
Date: August 15, 1963
Price range: $8.00 – 10.00
Credits: The Paper Pile, San Anselmo, California

Category: Literary Collectibles
Item Type: Magazine
Classification: E-2
Dimensions: 6" h x 4" w
Description: "Sad Plight of Negro Mother and Her Quads" inside story
Artisan/Manufacturer: Johnson Publishing Company
Date: October 10, 1963
Price range: $8.00 – 12.00
Credits: The Paper Pile, San Anselmo, California

Category: Literary Collectibles
Item Type: Magazine
Classification: E-2
Dimensions: 6" h x 4" w
Description: "Negro Girl Only Graduate of Va. $1 Million School" cover, inside story
Artisan/Manufacturer: Johnson Publishing Company
Date: May 28, 1959
Price range: $8.00–10.00
Credits: The Paper Pile, San Anselmo, California

Category: Literary Collectibles
Item Type: Magazine
Classification: E-2
Dimensions: 6" h x 4" w
Description: "Tragedy of 2,000 Children of Negro Soldiers Who Are Without a Country" cover story
Artisan/Manufacturer: Johnson Publishing Company
Date: August 8, 1963
Price range: $8.00–12.00
Credits: The Paper Pile, San Anselmo, California

Category: Literary Collectibles
Item Type: Magazine
Classification: E-2
Dimensions: 6" h x 4" w
Description: "Inside Report on Birmingham" inside story
Artisan/Manufacturer: Johnson Publishing Company
Date: October 3, 1963
Price range: $8.00–12.00
Credits: The Paper Pile, San Anselmo, California

Category: Literary Collectibles
Item Type: Magazine
Classification: E-2
Dimensions: 6" h x 4" w
Description: "Tragic Case of Louisiana Negro Who Tried to Vote" cover, inside story
Artisan/Manufacturer: Johnson Publishing Company
Date: April 15, 1963
Price range: $8.00–12.00
Credits: The Paper Pile, San Anselmo, California

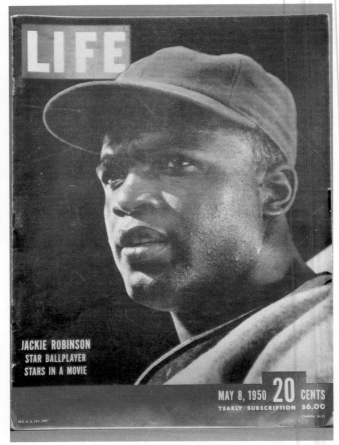

Category: Literary Collectibles
Item Type: Magazine
Classification: E-2
Dimensions: 14" h x 11" w
Description: Coretta Scott King, cover plus inside story
Artisan/Manufacturer: Time, Inc.
Date: September 12, 1969
Price range: $25.00–40.00
Credits: The Paper Pile, San Anselmo, California

Category: Literary Collectibles
Item Type: Magazine
Classification: E-2
Dimensions: 14" h x 11" w
Description: Jackie Robinson, cover plus inside story
Artisan/Manufacturer: Time, Inc.
Date: May 8, 1950
Price range: $25.00–40.00
Credits: The Paper Pile, San Anselmo, California

Category: Literary Collectibles
Item Type: Magazine
Classification: E-2
Dimensions: 14" h x 11" w
Description: Martin Luther King, cover plus inside article. Issue on his death.
Artisan/Manufacturer: Time, Inc.
Date: April 12, 1968
Price range: $55.00–75.00
Credits: The Paper Pile, San Anselmo, California

Category: Literary Collectibles
Item Type: Magazine
Classification: D-2
Dimensions: 11" h x 9" w
Description: Muhammad Ali, cover plus story
Artisan/Manufacturer: Ramparts Magazine, Inc.
Date: June 1967
Price range: $25.00–40.00
Credits: The Paper Pile, San Anselmo, California

Category: Literary Collectibles
Item Type: Magazine
Classification: E-2
Dimensions: 14" h x 11" w
Description: Black models, cover plus inside story
Artisan/Manufacturer: Time, Inc.
Date: October 17, 1969
Price range: $15.00–25.00
Credits: The Paper Pile, San Anselmo, California

Category: Literary Collectibles
Item Type: Magazine
Classification: D-2
Dimensions: 11" h x 9" w
Description: Bobby Seale, cover story
Artisan/Manufacturer: Ramparts Magazine, Inc.
Date: January 1970
Price range: $20.00–30.00
Credits: The Paper Pile, San Anselmo, California

Category: Literary Collectibles
Item Type: Magazine
Classification: D-2
Dimensions: 11" h x 8½" w
Description: James Baldwin, cover story; "The Negro's Push For Equality" inside story
Artisan/Manufacturer: Time, Inc.
Date: May 17, 1963
Price range: $25.00–45.00
Credits: The Paper Pile, San Anselmo, California

Category: Literary Collectibles
Item Type: Magazine
Classification: D-2
Dimensions: 11" h x 8½" w
Description: "Thelonious Monk, Jazzman," cover story; "Jazz: BeBop and Beyond," inside story
Artisan/Manufacturer: Time, Inc.
Date: February 28, 1964
Price range: $20.00–30.00
Credits: The Paper Pile, San Anselmo, California

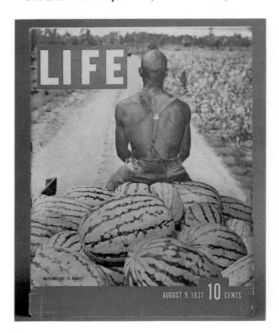

Category: Literary Collectibles
Item Type: Magazine
Classification: E-3
Description: *Life* Magazine
Artisan/Manufacturer: *Life* Magazine; Time, Inc.
Date: August 9, 1937
Price range: $20.00–30.00
Credits: The Paper Pile, San Anselmo, California

Category: Literary Collectibles
Item Type: Magazine
Classification: D-1
Dimensions: 11" h x 8½" w
Description: "Death On The Yard" cover story
Artisan/Manufacturer: Ramparts Corporation
Date: April 1973
Price range: $15.00–25.00
Credits: The Paper Pile, San Anselmo, California

Category: Literary Collectibles
Item Type: Magazine
Classification: D-1
Description: Huey P. Newton, cover story plus article
Artisan/Manufacturer: Ramparts Corporation
Date: October 26, 1968
Price range: $20.00–30.00
Credits: The Paper Pile, San Anselmo, California

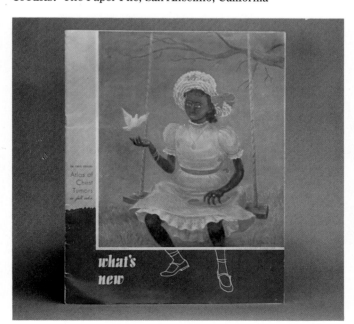

Category: Literary Collectibles
Item Type: Magazine
Classification: D-2
Dimensions: 12" h x 9½" w
Description: Paper. *What's New* cover story; "The Dove" by
Doris Lee
Artisan/Manufacturer: Abbott Laboratories, North Chicago,
Illinois
Date: July 1950
Price range: $25.00–30.00
Credits: The Paper Pile, San Anselmo, California

Category: Literary Collectibles
Item Type: Magazine
Classification: D-1
Description: Martin Luther King, Jr. cover story
Artisan/Manufacturer: Time, Inc.
Date: January 3, 1964
Price range: $25.00–45.00
Credits: The Paper Pile, San Anselmo, California

Category: Literary Collectibles
Item Type: Magazine
Classification: D-1
Description: Martin Luther King, Jr. cover and inside story
Artisan/Manufacturer: Time, Inc.
Date: February 18, 1957
Price range: $35.00–45.00
Credits: The Paper Pile, San Anselmo, California

Category: Literary Collectibles
Item Type: Magazine
Classification: E-2
Dimensions: 14" h x 10" w
Description: Paper, *Life* Magazine
Artisan/Manufacturer: Time-Life Inc.
Date: March 6, 1964
Price range: $25.00–45.00
Credits: The Paper Pile, San Anselmo, California

Category: Literary Collectibles
Item Type: Magazine
Classification: D-2
Dimensions: 14" h x 10" w
Description: Paper, *Life* Magazine, Louis Armstrong cover
Artisan/Manufacturer: Time, Inc.
Date: April 15, 1966
Price range: $25.00–45.00
Credits: The Paper Pile, San Anselmo, California
Note of Interest: Common. A fold-out full image is a part of the front cover, artistically done.

Category: Literary Collectibles
Item Type: Magazine
Classification: E-2
Dimensions: 14" h x 10" w
Description: Paper, *Life* Magazine; Dorothy Dandridge on front.
Artisan/Manufacturer: Time, Inc.
Date: November 1, 1954
Price range: $35.00–45.00
Credits: The Paper Pile, San Anselmo, California

Advertisements

The range of products in the marketplace using Black images are as varied as the products themselves – notably, the tradecard ads, Cream of Wheat ads, canned products (beans, peaches, etc.); any product which was black or had the word *black* in the title, or a product which was white (paint, whitewash, etc.) or with the word *white* in the title in which a Black image could be used to create a color contrast. Blacks were used in all manners – as subjects (cooks, "mammys," wide-eyed children, etc), in stereotypical roles (Blacks chasing chickens, eating watermelons, or as butlers, servants, or maids) and as statues holding signs, or in rare cases, as mannequins. Questions are often raised about the conflict between the image of Blacks in America between 1800 and 1950 and their use in the promotional activities of major companies. One must remember that manufacturers and companies used promotional gimmicks to sell their wares and Blacks provided the instant visibility needed to position their products in the marketplace.

The range of advertising subject matter is vast and covers everything from sewing machines to shoe polish; from tobacco to whiskey. The prices of such collectibles are determined by the material from which they are made.

Category: Advertisement
Item Type: Fans
Classification: F-2
Dimensions: 9¼" h x 8⅝" w
Description: Fans such as these were used quite often to advertise churches, car companies, and mechanic's garages.
Artisan/Manufacturer: Unmarked
Date: 1930–1950
Price range: $15.00–25.00 each
Credits: Lost & Found Antiques; Kensington, Maryland

Category: Advertisement
Item Type: Label
Classification: E-3
Dimensions: 4" h x 5½" w
Description: Butter beans lable from can "Old Black Joe." Common in South
Artisan/Manufacturer: Old Black Joe Co.; Hohenwald, Tennessee
Date: 1920–1945
Price range: $8.00–18.00 each

Category: Advertisement
Item Type: Trade card
Classification: E-2
Dimensions: 5⅜" h x 3½" w
Description: Flour advertisement. Trade card, common.
Artisan/Manufacturer: Washburn's 196 Best Hungarian Process, Minneapolis, Minnesota
Date: 1920–1935
Price range: $15.00–25.00 each
Credits: M. Davern Collection

Category: Advertisement
Item Type: Trade card
Classification: E-2
Dimensions: 6⅞" h x 4⅛" w
Description: No product specified, common. Caption – "Who's Dar."
Artisan/Manufacturer: Unmarked
Date: 1914–1935
Price range: $25.00–30.00 each
Credits: M. Davern Collection
Note of Interest: Common, part of a set of three.

Category: Advertisement
Item Type: Trade card
Classification: E-2
Dimensions: 2¾" h x 4⅞" w
Description: Shoe advertisement, common card
Artisan/Manufacturer: Edwin C. Burt
Date: 1910–1930
Price range: $15.00–25.00 each
Credits: M. Davern Collection

Category: Advertisement
Item Type: Trade card
Classification: E-2
Dimensions: 5" h x 3½" w
Description: Coffee company, common card
Artisan/Manufacturer: Arbuck E. Brothers Coffee Company
Date: 1915–1935
Price range: $10.00–25.00 each
Credits: M. Davern Collection

Category: Advertisement
Item Type: Trade card
Classification: E-2
Dimensions: 5¼" h x 3¼" w
Description: Bone meal advertising card, common
Artisan/Manufacturer: Walker, Stratman & Co., Pittsburgh, Pennsylvania
Date: 1920–1945
Price range: $15.00–25.00 each
Credits: M. Davern Collection

Category: Advertisement
Item Type: Trade card
Classification: E-2
Dimensions: 3" h x 4¾" w
Description: Typical trade card using Black subject to make product "stand out," common.
Artisan/Manufacturer: Jas. S. Kirk & Co., soapmaker, Chicago
Date: 1920–1945
Price range: $10.00–15.00 each
Credits: M. Davern Collection

Category: Advertisement
Item Type: Recipe card
Classification: D-2
Dimensions: 3¾" h
Description: Recipe for Burnham's Clam Chowder, common
Artisan/Manufacturer: David W. Young Co.
Date: 1926–1940
Price range: $25.00–30.00 each
Credits: M. Davern Collection

Category: Advertisement
Item Type: Trade card
Classification: E-3
Dimensions: 2⅝" h x 1½" w
Description: Small trade stamps, advertising decorative color paints
Artisan/Manufacturer: Marked, W.P. Fuller & Co. Manufacturers
Date: 1920–1935
Price range: $15.00–25.00 each
Credits: M. Davern Collection

Category: Advertisement
Item Type: Trade card
Classification: E-2
Dimensions: 6⅛" h x 3¾" w
Description: Recipe card, common
Artisan/Manufacturer: Mother's Coupon Dept., Chicago, Illinois
Date: 1925–1940
Price range: $25.00–30.00 each
Credits: M. Davern Collection

Category: Advertisement
Item Type: Bank, glass
Classification: E-2
Dimensions: 4½" h
Description: Mustard jar with Joe Lewis image. Items of this type were often sold because they gave the manufacturers instant recognition when using a celebrity to advertise a product.
Artisan/Manufacturer: Nash-Underwood, Inc.; Chicago, Illinois
Date: 1930–1950
Price range: $30.00–65.00
Credits: Manning's Books and Prints
Note of Interest: Red paper lips missing.

Category: Advertisement
Item Type: Tobacco tin
Classification: D-1
Dimensions: 7½" h x 18½" d (at widest part)
Description: Mammy Roly Poly. Comes in 4 different tobacco tins – (1) Dixie Queen Plug Cut, (2) Mayo's, (3) Red Indian, and (4) US Marine. Scarce.
Artisan/Manufacturer: Mayo's Tobacco Company
Date: ca. 1900
Price range: $725.00–1,000.00
Credits: Ron Carr; Capitola, California

Category: Advertisement
Item Type: Print
Classification: E-3
Dimensions: 16½" h x 11¼" w
Description: Magazine page, origin unknown. Gold Medal Flour advertising. Common.
Artisan/Manufacturer: Washburn-Crosby Co., Minneapolis, Minnesota
Date: Copyright 1911
Price range: $35.00–50.00
Credits: Manning's Books and Prints

Category: Advertisement
Item Type: Print
Classification: E-3
Dimensions: 16" h x 11" w
Description: Book page, origin unknown. Gold Medal Flour advertising. Common.
Artisan/Manufacturer: Copyright 1906, Washburn-Crosby Co., Minneapolis, Minnesota
Date: 1906
Price range: $35.00–50.00
Credits: Manning's Books and Prints

Category: Advertisement
Item Type: Print
Classification: E-3
Dimensions: 3½" h x 9" w
Description: Fruit label for oranges, common.
Artisan/Manufacturer: A.S. Herlong Packing Company, Leesburg, Florida
Date: 1910–1940
Price range: $8.00–15.00
Credits: The Paper Pile, San Anselmo, California

Category: Advertisement
Item Type: Trade card
Classification: E-3
Dimensions: 4¼" h x 12½" w
Description: Grape label trade card. Cards of this type were used to illustrate a product whose color was black.
Artisan/Manufacturer: Victor Fruit Growers; Escalon, California
Date: 1920–1945
Price range: $8.00–15.00
Credits: The Paper Pile, San Anselmo, California

Category: Advertisement
Item Type: Trade card
Classification: E-2
Dimensions: 4¾" h x 3" w
Description: Color lithograph. A.L. Foster, clothing manufacturer
Artisan/Manufacturer: Frank Vernon
Date: ca. 1890–1920
Price range: $15.00–25.00
Credits: The Paper Pile, San Anselmo, California

Category: Advertisement
Item Type: Trade card
Classification: E-2
Dimensions: 4" h x 3" w
Description: Color trade card for biscuits. Common.
Artisan/Manufacturer: Biscuit Manufacturing, Rumpler
Date: ca. 1880–1920
Price range: $25.00–30.00
Credits: The Paper Pile, San Anselmo, California

Category: Advertisement
Item Type: Trade card
Classification: E-2
Dimensions: 3" h x 5" w
Description: Typical trade card using Black subjects to advertise a product, common.
Artisan/Manufacturer: Domestic Sewing Machine Company
Date: 1880–1920
Price range: $15.00–25.00
Credits: The Paper Pile, San Anselmo, California

Category: Advertisement
Item Type: Trade card
Classification: E-3
Dimensions: 4¼" h x 3" w
Description: Advertising for soap, common.
Artisan/Manufacturer: Higgins Soap
Date: ca. 1886–1920
Price range: $25.00–35.00
Credits: The Paper Pile, San Anselmo, California

Category: Advertisement
Item Type: Menu
Classification: E-3
Dimensions: 6½" h x 3½" w
Description: Topsy's Roost Restaurant, six pages.
Artisan/Manufacturer: Topsy's Roost, San Francisco, California
Date: 1929
Price range: $25.00–35.00
Credits: The Paper Pile, San Anselmo, California

Category: Advertisement
Item Type: Trade card
Classification: E-2
Dimensions: 4¼" h x 3½" w
Description: Advertising for soap. Often cards with illustrations such as this one were used to demonstrate the effectiveness of the product.
Artisan/Manufacturer: Lautz Brothers
Date: ca. 1880–1920
Price range: $25.00–35.00
Credits: The Paper Pile, San Anselmo, California

Category: Advertisement
Item Type: Trade card
Classification: E-2
Dimensions: 4½" h x 3" w
Description: Advertising trade card. No specific product, illustrated.
Artisan/Manufacturer: Unmarked
Date: ca. 1880–1920
Price range: $20.00–25.00
Credits: The Paper Pile, Oakland, California

Category: Advertisement
Item Type: Label
Classification: E-3
Dimensions: 3¾" h x 8½" w
Description: Advertising label for fruit, common.
Artisan/Manufacturer: A.S. Herlong Packing Company, Leesburg, Florida
Date: 1910–1940
Price range: $8.00–15.00
Credits: The Paper Pile, San Anselmo, California

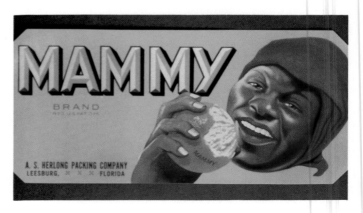

"AUNTY FAT, ANL AUNTIE LEAN."

Category: Advertisement
Item Type: Trade card
Classification: E-3
Dimensions: 4½" h x 3½" w
Description: Advertising cough cherries, common.
Artisan/Manufacturer: Unmarked
Date: ca. 1880–1920
Price range: $25.00–35.00
Credits: The Paper Pile, San Anselmo, California

Category: Advertisement
Item Type: Trade card
Classification: E-2
Dimensions: 5" h x 3" w
Description: No advertisement on card. This medium was used quite frequently by companies during late 1800s and early 1900s to illustrate various products.
Artisan/Manufacturer: Bufford-Poston
Date: ca. 1890–1920
Price range: $15.00–20.00
Credits: The Paper Pile, San Anselmo, California

Category: Advertisement
Item Type: Product label
Classification: E-3
Dimensions: 9" h x 9" w
Description: Citrus label. Typical product advertisement item, common.
Artisan/Manufacturer: Waverly Growers Cooperative
Date: ca. 1930
Price range: $8.00–15.00
Credits: The Paper Pile, San Anselmo, California

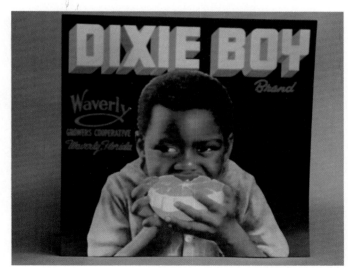

Category: Advertisement
Item Type: Page, Cream of Wheat
Classification: E-3
Dimensions: 12" h x 10" w
Description: Edward V. Beewer for Cream of Wheat. Taken from *Needlecraft* magazine. "Uncle Tom's Cabin."
Artisan/Manufacturer: Cream of Wheat Company
Date: May 1921
Price range: $25.00–35.00
Credits: The Paper Pile, San Anselmo, California

Category: Advertisement
Item Type: Page, Cream of Wheat
Classification: E-3
Dimensions: 12" h x 10" w
Description: Taken from *Literary Digest,* September 9, 1922. Caption - "An Old Friend."
Artisan/Manufacturer: Cream of Wheat Company
Date: September 9, 1922
Price range: $35.00–50.00
Credits: The Paper Pile, San Anselmo, California

Category: Advertisement
Item Type: Sales, poster
Classification: E-2
Dimensions: 14" h x 22" w
Description: Advertisement poster. Typical, late 1800s.

Artisan/Manufacturer: Worth Navy Union Made
Date: ca. 1890–1900
Price range: $200.00–350.00
Credits: The Paper Pile, San Anselmo, California

Figural Images

Although figurals are common, not many collectibles come under this category without a great deal of confusion. Most of the true busts/statues are of males – very few women were depicted. In many cases, they were made as banks, humidors or matchholders. Because these objects were often used in the household, they were attractively decorated. Today, many collectors will not use these items for their original purpose for fear of breaking or staining the collectible. In most cases, these objects are now used as statues/busts.

Objects which were originally made as decorative items are usually small ceramic pieces from Germany, Japan, and the United States. Bronze, iron, bisque, and wood are not common and generally expensive. The most desirable collectibles were made between 1880 and 1930. There are occasionally rare tobacco advertisement statues from England and the United States. Most of the busts on today's market are of considerable quality with the exception of some Japanese mass-produced pieces.

Category: Figural Images
Item Type: Figurine
Classification: D-2
Dimensions: 3¾" h x 4" w
Description: A light-hearted figure of a young woman with a light brown complexion. All bisque. Rendered in a naturalistic manner. Excellent condition.
Artisan/Manufacturer: Germany
Date: ca. 1920s
Price range: $175.00–225.00
Credits: V. Mackemull Collection
Note of Interest: Scarce

Category: Figural Images
Item Type: Figurine
Classification: D-2
Dimensions: 3½" h x 2½" w
Description: All bisque delicately executed figurine of a man seated. Well dressed, with monocle. Slightly exaggerated features, face painted black. Excellent condition.
Artisan/Manufacturer: Germany
Date: ca. 1890s–1920s
Price range: $150.00–200.00
Credits: V. Mackemull Collection
Note of Interest: Common

Category: Figural Images
Item Type: Figurine
Classification: D-2
Dimensions: 2¹³/₁₆" h x 2½" w
Description: Well executed, fine example of an early 20th century bisque figurine rendered in a naturalistic manner. Young boy in a clown's outfit holding an accordion, delicately painted. Face, hands, ankles painted black. Excellent condition.
Artisan/Manufacturer: Germany
Date: ca. 1900s–1920s
Price range: $95.00–145.00
Credits: V. Mackemull Collection
Note of Interest: Common

Category: Figural Images
Item Type: Figurine
Classification: E-2
Dimensions: 2" h
Description: Very light brown painted clown image delicately executed, made of a fine quality bisque. Naturalistic features.
Artisan/Manufacturer: Germany
Date: ca. 1880s–1920s
Price range: $75.00–110.00
Credits: V. Mackemull Collection
Note of Interest: Common

Category: Figural Images
Item Type: Figurine
Classification: E-2
Dimensions: 1½" h x 3½" w
Description: Naturalistic rendering of a young girl lying down, propped on one elbow. Executed in fine quality bisque with the girl's face, arms and legs painted dark brown. Molded painted clothing.
Artisan/Manufacturer: Germany
Date: ca. 1890s–1920s
Price range: $125.00–210.00
Credits: V. Mackemull Collection
Note of Interest: Common

Category: Figural Images
Item Type: Bust
Classification: E-2
Dimensions: 2¹³⁄₁₆" h x 1¼" w
Description: Glazed bisque bust of a brown-faced female figure. Simply yet well executed. Figure is rendered in a naturalistic manner. Half-statue terminating at the hips. Matronly figure in molded domestic clothing. Excellent condition.
Artisan/Manufacturer: Germany
Date: ca. 1900s–1920s
Price range: $75.00–125.00
Credits: V. Mackemull Collection
Note of Interest: Common

Category: Figural Images
Item Type: Figurine
Classification: E-2
Dimensions: 8¼" h
Description: All bisque, well-executed figure of a young man well dressed with hat and cane in hand. Bare feet and poised on a base of vegetation form. Features slightly exaggerated (red oversize lips), face, arms, legs painted black.
Artisan/Manufacturer: Germany No. 482
Date: ca. 1890s–1920s
Price range: $165.00–255.00
Credits: V. Mackemull Collection
Note of Interest: Common

Category: Figural Images
Item Type: Figurine (double figure)
Classification: E-2
Dimensions: 6¼" h
Description: "A Dark Secret." One boy gesturing to another. The young boys are made of fine painted bisque and rendered in a naturalistic manner. Excellent condition.
Artisan/Manufacturer: Heubach, Germany
Date: ca. 1900s–1920s
Price range: $175.00–250.00
Credits: V. Mackemull Collection
Note of Interest: Common

Category: Figural Images
Item Type: Figurines
Classification: E-2
Dimensions: 2⁷⁄₁₆" h x 2" w
Description: Three all bisque girls, well executed and hand painted with fine clothing. Each wearing a bonnet. Faces and hands painted black, legs covered with white stockings. Each figure seated. Excellent condition.
Artisan/Manufacturer: Germany
Date: ca. 1900s–1920s
Price range: $100.00–150.00
Credits: V. Mackemull Collection
Note of Interest: Common

Category: Figural Images
Item Type: Figurine
Classification: E-2
Dimensions: 5¾" h
Description: All bisque girl in molded painted bonnet, dress with apron, and matching shoes. Basket on arm. Face and hands of figure are painted black and executed in caricature. Excellent condition.
Artisan/Manufacturer: Germany 5612 98
Date: ca. 1890s–1920s
Price range: $250.00–325.00
Credits: V. Mackemull Collection
Note of Interest: Common

Category: Figural Images
Item Type: Statue
Classification: F-2
Dimensions: 17" h
Description: Chalk statue with a fired brown finish. Molded clothing with sculptured features. Surface damage to left leg. Good condition. Naturalistic features.
Artisan/Manufacturer: Unmarked
Date: ca. 1880s–1920
Price range: $225.00–375.00
Credits: Charlene Upham Antiques

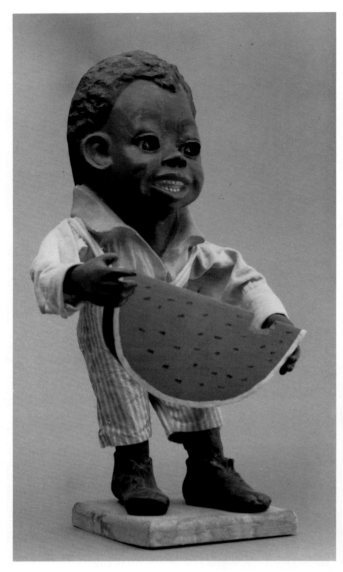

Category: Figural Images
Item Type: Statue
Classification: D-2
Dimensions: 23" h
Description: Brown, with a clockwork mechanism in the head which enables the eyes to move from side to side. Painted cast iron, wood arms hinged to the body by wire, and plaster legs, boots, and head. Clothing partially molded and painted with cloth clothing over the areas that are not molded. Iron rods anchor the figure to its base. Watermelon is removable; arms adjustable. Display item.
Artisan/Manufacturer: Regent Manufacturing Co., Chicago
Date: ca. 1890–1910
Price range: $2,800.00–3,500.00
Credits: Ron Carr; Capitola, California

Category: Figural Images
Item Type: Statue/clock
Classification: D-1
Dimensions: 16" h
Description: Cast iron, Sambo Winker with a Waterbury clock in the form of a banjo. Color of clothing may vary. Eyes move up and down.
Artisan/Manufacturer: Bradley/Hubbard
Date: ca. 1880–1890s
Price range: $2,950.00–3,500.00
Credits: Ron Carr; Capitola, California
Note of Interest: Scarce

Category: Figural Images
Item Type: Statue
Classification: D-2
Dimensions: 7¼" h
Description: French Art Deco figure of a musician, glossy finish. Caricature.
Artisan/Manufacturer: Robj; Paris, France
Date: ca. 1920s
Price range: $2,200.00–2,800.00
Credits: Ron Carr; Capitola, California
Note of Interest: Scarce. This figure is one of a set.

Category: Figural Images
Item Type: Statue
Classification: G-2
Dimensions: 10⅜" h
Description: Molded features and clothing, painted and fired ceramic. Naturalistic features with painted lips.
Artisan/Manufacturer: Unmarked
Date: ca. 1960–1970
Price range: $75.00–90.00
Credits: M. Davern Collection
Note of Interest: Plentiful

135

Category: Figural Images
Item Type: Statue
Classification: F-1
Dimensions: 25½" h
Description: Tobacco figure made of painted plaster, advertising a new product "The New Pipe." A Black boy holding a pipe made in his image.
Artisan/Manufacturer: American or English made, unmarked
Date: ca. 1880s–1920s
Price range: Not available
Credits: Museum of Tobacco Art and History, U.S. Tobacco Company
Note of Interest: Scarce

Category: Figural Images
Item Type: Statue, cigar/pipe lighter
Classification: D-1
Dimensions: 8½" h
Description: Black male, posed flamboyantly with an impish expression. Made of pewter with a brass base. Molded clothing and features.
Artisan/Manufacturer: English origin, unmarked
Date: ca. 1900
Price range: Not available
Credits: Museum of Tobacco Art and History, U.S. Tobacco Company
Note of Interest: Scarce

Category: Figural Images
Item Type: Statue, pipe tamper
Classification: F-2
Dimensions: 2½" h
Description: All brass pipe tamper molded into the figure of 2 boxers on a platform which terminates into the tamper. Facial features still distinguishable. Excellent condition.
Artisan/Manufacturer: Unmarked
Date: ca. 1750–1790
Price range: Not available
Credits: Museum of Tobacco Art and History, U.S. Tobacco Company
Note of Interest: Scarce

Category: Figural Images
Item Type: Figurine
Classification: E-1
Dimensions: 3¹¹⁄₁₆" h x 3½" w
Description: Small boy executed in a naturalistic style with molded, painted features and clothing. Medium brown bisque with articulated fingers on the left hand. Open mouth.
Artisan/Manufacturer: Germany No. 14
Date: ca. 1880s–1920s
Price range: $110.00–145.00
Credits: V. Mackemull Collection
Note of Interest: Common

Category: Figural Images
Item Type: Figurine
Classification: E-2
Dimensions: 3¼" h x 2" w
Description: Small boy rendered in a naturalistic style with molded features and clothing. Medium brown bisque.
Artisan/Manufacturer: Germany
Date: ca. 1900s–1920s
Price range: $95.00–145.00
Credits: V. Mackemull Collection
Note of Interest: Common

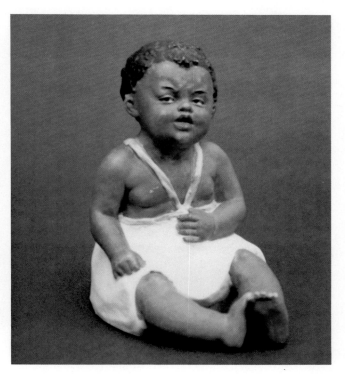

Category: Figural Images
Item Type: Figurine
Classification: D-2
Dimensions: 6" h
Description: Female dressed in a lavish dress complete with underskirt and gloves. Naturalistic features, molded and painted with molded clothing. No shoes, bare feet visible. Medium brown bisque with upswept hair and open mouth.
Artisan/Manufacturer: Germany (origin), sunburst symbol attributed to the Heubach company.
Date: ca. 1890s–1920s
Price range: $210.00–325.00
Credits: V. Mackemull Collection
Note of Interest: Common

Category: Figural Images
Item Type: Figurine
Classification: E-2
Dimensions: 4⅞" h x 4½" w
Description: Small boy of light brown bisque. Molded painted features and clothing. Articulated fingers on the left hand.
Artisan/Manufacturer: Germany
Date: ca. 1900s–1920s
Price range: $175.00–225.00
Credits: V. Mackemull Collection
Note of Interest: Common

Category: Figural Images
Item Type: Figurine
Classification: D-2
Dimensions: 8½" h
Description: Black-brown molded bisque figure of a young girl holding a white doll in her right hand. Both figures have molded painted features and clothing. Both are smartly dressed. Larger figure wearing a bonnet. Mounted on a bisque base.
Artisan/Manufacturer: Germany No. 27
Price range: $210.00–285.00
Credits: V. Mackemull Collection
Note of Interest: Common

Category: Figural Images
Item Type: Figurine
Classification: D-2
Dimensions: Female - 5¾" h; Male - 5½" h
Description: Caricatured male and female figures with molded painted features and clothing. Male holding a banjo; female holding a fan in her right hand, has bare feet, and wearing a hat. Both figures are rendered in medium brown bisque.
Artisan/Manufacturer: Made in Germany, D17 Heubach
Date: ca. 1890s–1920s
Price range: $375.00–550.00 (pair)
Credits: V. Mackemull Collection
Note of Interest: Common

Category: Figural Images
Item Type: Figurine
Classification: D-2
Dimensions: 5" h x 1½" w
Description: Small boy with molded painted features and clothing, jointed arms. Dark brown bisque.
Artisan/Manufacturer: Germany
Date: ca. 1900–1920s
Price range: $110.00–150.00
Credits: V. Mackemull Collection
Note of Interest: Common

Containers

This title covers all of the containers which hold other objects. Included are string holders, humidors, salt and pepper shakers, and cookie, tobacco, and syrup jars. These objects are made of wood, ceramics, tin, and chalk. Blacks are presented as adults and children. For the most part, women are presented as "mammy," children in pairs – male and female – and black men as cooks, waiters, or other "flashy" characters. Containers were made in all of the countries that shipped into the United States (England, Germany, Japan, France, and Italy.) Most of the containers were either the entire body or the bust (head, neck, and chest). Some reproduction cookie jars are being made. Prices for objects in this category can range in the hundreds.

Category: Figural Images
Item Type: Container, humidor
Classification: D-2
Dimensions: 6¼" h
Description: Terra cotta humidor with the image of a man holding a short cigar between his teeth. Slightly exaggerated, molded painted features nestled in the middle section of an avocado-shaped container. Excellent condition.
Artisan/Manufacturer: Germany, unmarked
Date: ca. 1920
Price range: $600.00–725.00
Credits: Ron Carr; Capitola, California
Note of Interest: Scarce

Category: Figural Images
Item Type: Busts, humidors
Classification: D-1
Dimensions: 4¾" h, 5½" h, 6" h
Description: Bisque busts of men with bibbed caps and bow ties. Naturalistic molded painted features and clothing accessories. (2 largest figures unglazed) Excellent condition.

Artisan/Manufacturer: Germany, unmarked
Date: ca. 1920
Price range: $275.00, $375.00, $475.00
Credits: Ron Carr; Capitola, California
Note of Interest: Common

Category: Figural Images
Item Type: Statue, bust humidor
Classification: F-1
Dimensions: 8" h (man with baskets), 7" (bust)
Description: Metal male figure sitting between two metal baskets. Metal male bust. Both figures are well-dressed with top hats and bearing naturalistic molded, painted features and painted clothing.
Artisan/Manufacturer: USA, unmarked
Date: ca. 1900–1920s
Price range: Not available
Credits: Museum of Tobacco Art and History, US Tobacco Company
Note of Interest: Scarce, style borrowed from Germany.

Category: Figural Images
Item Type: Bust humidor
Classification: D-1
Dimensions: 7" h
Description: Molded painted naturalistic rendering of a male image with molded cap and shirt. Mouth open, teeth showing. Medium brown image. Excellent condition. All bisque.
Artisan/Manufacturer: Germany
Date: ca. 1920s
Price range: $450.00–625.00
Credits: Ron Carr; Capitola, California
Note of Interest: Common

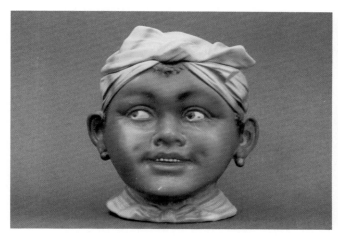

Category: Figural Images
Item Type: Container, humidor
Classification: D-2
Dimensions: 5" h x 4½" w
Description: Medium brown faced container with molded
   painted features and head turban. Mouth open with teeth
   showing. Porcelain, excellent condition.
Artisan/Manufacturer: Germany, unmarked.
Date: ca. 1870–1890
Price range: $185.00–225.00
Note of Interest: Common

Category: Figural Images
Item Type: Container, humidor
Classification: D-2
Dimensions: 8¼" h
Description: Terra cotta barrel-shaped container with a head of
   a boy with molded painted features wearing a nightcap. The
   boy's head, which is medium brown, serves as a top to the
   barrel. Excellent condition.
Artisan/Manufacturer: Germany, unmarked.
Date: ca. 1920
Price range: $295.00–475.00
Credit: Ron Carr; Capitola, California
Note of Interest: Common

Category: Figural Images
Item Type: Container, humidor
Classification: D-2
Dimensions: 7" h
Description: Terra cotta barrel-shaped container with a young
   boy's head serving as the top. The boy's medium brown face
   is rendered in a naturalistic fashion, boasting a nightcap. The
   container is molded and painted with the facial features
   accented.
Artisan/Manufacturer: Germany
Date: ca. 1920
Price range: $225.00–285.00
Credit: Ron Carr; Capitola, California
Note of Interest: Common

Category: Figural Images
Item Type: Figurine container, cigarette holder
Classification: D-1
Dimensions: 7½" h
Description: All bisque, molded and painted figure of a boy sitting on a bale of cotton. Naturalistic rendering of the boy's medium brown face. Excellent condition.
Artisan/Manufacturer: Germany (F.B. on right corner of the cotton bale.)
Date: ca. 1920s
Price range: $450.00–625.00
Credits: Ron Carr; Capitola, California

Note of Interest: Common

Category: Figural Images
Item Type: Container, humidor
Classification: D-1
Dimensions: 4¾" h
Description: All bisque head of a man with a pipe between his teeth, the collar of his shirt serves as a base. Naturalistic. Molded, painted medium brown features. Excellent condition.
Artisan/Manufacturer: Germany
Date: ca. 1920s
Price range: $250.00–295.00
Credits: Ron Carr; Capitola, California
Note of Interest: Common

Category: Figural Images
Item Type: Container, humidor
Classification: D-1
Dimensions: 3¾" h
Description: Black-brown all bisque image of a young man, rendered in a naturalistic fashion. Molded, painted features with a faint impression of a bow tie. Open mouth with teeth showing. Excellent condition.
Artisan/Manufacturer: Germany
Date: ca. 1920s
Price range: $250.00–295.00
Note of Interest: Common

Category: Figural Images
Item Type: Statue, humidor
Classification: D-1
Dimensions: 8½" h
Description: Terra cotta figure of an older gentleman smoking a pipe while sitting on a bale of cotton. The entire piece is molded and painted with a naturalistic rendering of the male image, black-brown tone for complexion. Top of the body lifts off for access to the container. Excellent condition.
Artisan/Manufacturer: Austria made (JM Co)
Date: ca. 1920s
Price range: $750.00–1,000.00
Credits: Ron Carr; Capitola, California
Note of Interest: Scarce

Category: Figural Images
Item Type: Figurine, container/humidor
Classification: D-1
Dimensions: 8½" h
Description: Terra cotta container in the shape of a squash with a full male figure on top. The figure is sitting, holding his right ankle, with a pipe in his left hand. The young man's face is of a naturalistic style with only slight exaggeration of the lips. The upper torso of the figure serves as a handle.
Artisan/Manufacturer: Austria made (JM Co)
Date: ca. 1920s
Price range: $850.00–1,200.00
Note of Interest: Scarce

Category: Figural Images
Item Type: Statue, humidor
Classification: D-1
Dimensions: 7½" h
Description: Terra cotta molded, painted container in a log shape with a young boy on top holding an ear of corn. The boy has dark brown naturalistic features. The log is well-executed with an uncanny likeness to real bark. Excellent condition.
Artisan/Manufacturer: Austria made (JM Co)
Date: ca. 1920s
Price range: $750.00–1,000.00
Credits: Ron Carr; Capitola, California
Note of Interest: Scarce

Category: Figural Images
Item Type: Figurine, humidor
Classification: D-2
Dimensions: 10" h
Description: All-bisque male figure seated in a chair. The top portion of the chair and the figure lift off. A naturalistic serene look has been captured in the young man's face. He is of a black-brown color, wearing light shades of pink and beige to give a striking contrast. Facial features and clothing are molded and painted. Excellent condition.
Artisan/Manufacturer: Germany, unmarked
Date: ca. 1920s
Price range: $875.00–1,200.00
Credits: Ron Carr; Capitola, California
Note of Interest: Scarce

Category: Figural Images
Item Type: Container, humidor
Classification: D-1
Dimensions: 8¼" h
Description: Both pieces are made entirely of terra cotta. Molded painted features, clothing and cotton sacks. The male figure is rendered in a naturalistic manner with the female image slightly exaggereated. Each character's body fits into the cotton sacks leaving only their upper torsos visible. Mouths open with teeth showing. Cotton sacks are very realistic. Black-brown color used for the faces. Excellent condition.
Artisan/Manufacturer: Austria (JM Co)
Date: ca. 1920s
Price range: $375.00–450.00 each
Credits: Ron Carr; Capitola, California
Note of Interest: Scarce

Category: Figural Images
Item Type: Container, humidor
Classification: D-1
Dimensions: 9½" h
Description: All-bisque male figure seated and holding a whole watermelon. The figure bears strong Negroid naturalistic features which are molded and painted medium brown. Also with molded, painted clothing and shoes. The upper portion of the melon which is attached to the man's body lifts off to open the container. Excellent condition.
Artisan/Manufacturer: Marked "Austria."
Date: ca. 1880s–1890s
Price range: $1,200.00–1,600.00
Credits: Ron Carr; Capitola, California
Note of Interest: Scarce

Category: Figural Images
Item Type: Container, humidor
Classification: D-2
Dimensions: 8¼" h
Description: Terra cotta molded, painted bust of a man smoking a cigar, complete with ascot and top hat. The bust of the man is merged into a barrel shape. Black-brown color is used on the facial area. Excellent condition.
Artisan/Manufacturer: Austria (JM Co)
Date: ca. 1900–1920s
Price range: $475.00–600.00
Credits: Ron Carr; Capitola, California
Note of Interest: Common. This style of tobacoo jar or humidor was also copied in the United States.

Category: Figural Images
Item Type: Statue, nodder
Classification: F-2
Dimensions: 22¼" h
Description: Imposing male figure with brown painted composition head and hands. Fabric used for clothing and cloth body which appears to have been dipped into a hardening liquid to stiffen the material. The hat is removable and the image is affixed to a wooden painted base. Excellent condition.
Artisan/Manufacturer: Unmarked
Date: ca. 1920–1930s
Price range: $800.00–1,000.00
Credits: Ron Carr; Capitola, California
Note of Interest: Scarce

Category: Figural Images
Item Type: Container, cruet set
Classification: E-3
Dimensions: Larger figures - 6" h; smaller figures - 4¼" h
Description: Painted, highly glazed ceramic cruet set in its original metal rack. Caricature in nature with red lips and exaggerated eyes. Painted, molded clothing and hats/caps.
Artisan/Manufacturer: Japan
Date: ca. 1930–1940
Price range: $110.00–185.00 set
Credits: M. Davern Collection
Note of Interest: Plentiful

Category: Figural Images
Item Type: Containers, bust/holders
Classification: G-3
Dimensions: 7¾" h and 5¼" h
Description: Highly glazed painted ceramic figures of Black persons in domestic attire. The largest is a string holder; the smallest, a spoon holder. Excellent condtion.
Artisan/Manufacturer: Unmarked
Date: ca. 1940–1950
Price range: Large - $85.00–110.00; small - $45.00–65.00
Credits: M. Davern Collection
Note of Interest: Plentiful. Items of this type were made in the United States and abroad. The string fits in the under side of the large figure.

Category: Figural Images
Item Type: Containers, salt & pepper
Classification: E-3
Dimensions: 4" h
Description: Highly glazed painted ceramic salt & pepper shakers. Molded, painted features and clothing. Both with spoons in opposite hands. Holes for condiments in the heads of the figures. Brown faces and hands. Excellent condition.
Artisan/Manufacturer: Japan
Date: ca. 1930
Price range: $55.00–75.00 pair
Credits: Pineapple Door Antiques, Chattanooga, Tennessee
Note of Interest: Plentiful. Many of the above items may be unmarked. When examining salt & pepper sets, observe coloring, styling, size and size of the holes in the top of the items to ensure that they are a matched pair. Usually the holes of a pepper shaker will be smaller than those of a salt shaker.

Category: Figural Images
Item Type: Containers, spice set
Classification: E-3
Dimensions: 4" h each
Description: Aunt Jemima-style spice containers made of hard plastic and painted. Black painted faces and arms with spice names painted in script on each apron (paprika, ginger, nutmeg, cinnamon, cloves, allspice.) The set of 6 containers is in the original gold tinted aluminum hood-shaped rack with scalloped edges. Background scene on rack done in black silhouette. Excellent condition. NO FLAKING.
Artisan/Manufacturer: F & F Mold & Die Works, Dayton, Ohio, Made in U.S.A.
Date: ca. 1930s
Price range: $275.00–375.00 complete set with rack
Credits: M. Davern Collection
Note of Interest: Plentiful

Category: Figural Images
Item Type: Containers, string holders
Classification: E-3
Dimensions: Black - 7¼" h; brown - 6¾" h
Description: Painted highly glazed ceramic string holders done in caricature style of "Mammy" type. One with a painted black face and the other brown. Good condition.
Artisan/Manufacturer: Black, unmarked; brown marked "USA."
Date: ca. 1920–1940
Price range: $165.00–210.00 each
Credits: M. Davern Collection
Note of Interest: Plentiful

Category: Figural Images
Item Type: Containers, cookie jar and salt & pepper sets
Classification: E-2
Dimensions: Large male cookie jar - 10¼" h; medium male pepper shaker - 7½" h; medium female salt shaker - 6¾"; small female salt - 4" h; small male pepper - 4½" h.
Description: Highly glazed bright yellow ceramic pieces. Painted black face. Caricature. Molded spoons in the male pepper shakers' hands. Excellent condition.
Artisan/Manufacturer: Pearl china/hand-decorated/22 kt. gold/USA/635
Date: ca. 1935–1945
Price range: Large male cookie jar - $195.00–250.00; large salt & pepper set - $175.00–200.00; small salt & pepper set - $75.00–95.00
Credits: M. Davern Collection
Note of Interest: Plentiful. Also found in green and pink.

Category: Figural Images
Item Type: Containers, cookie jars
Classification: Black – G-2; Brown – E-3
Dimensions: Large – 11⅛" h; small – 10¼" h
Description: Cookie jars with lift-off upper torsos. Painted, molded, high glazed ceramic figures of matronly women often referred to as "Mammy" figures. Brown-faced figure has the word "cookies" embossed on the front of the jar. Both figures have been made in caricature form with large eyes and large red lips. Black face – excellent condition. Brown face – good condition with some discoloration on head scarf.
Artisan/Manufacturer: Black - unmarked; brown - McCoy decal
Date: ca. 1930–1945
Price range: Brown (w/decal) – $175.00–250.00; black – $155.00–225.00
Credits: M. Davern Collection
Note of Interest: Plentiful. Beware of reproductions, especially McCoy.

Category: Figural Images
Item Type: Containers - cookie jars
Classification: G-2
Dimensions: Male - 9¾" h; female - 9½" h
Description: Both containers have painted brown faces and hands. The female has brown shoes; the male has black shoes. The imagery of these jars is not caricature but rather slightly exaggerated. Both pieces are highly glazed and painted ceramic. Excellent condition. (Not a set.)
Artisan/Manufacturer: Both unmarked
Date: Both ca. 1930–1950
Price range: $255.00–325.00 each
Credits: M. Davern Collection
Note of Interest: Plentiful

Category: Figural Images
Item Type: Containers, humidor
Classification: D-2
Dimensions: 6¾" h x 4½" w
Description: A copper trimmed brass container with a lead head and terminating with lead feet. The head has molded features, low luster. Each seam of the 8-sided container is trimmed with copper. Excellent condition.
Artisan/Manufacturer: English origin
Date: ca. 1790–1820
Price range: Not available
Credits: Museum of Tobacco Art and History, US Tobacco Company
Note of Interest: Scarce

Category: Figural Images
Item Type: Container, cookie jar
Classification: E-3
Dimensions: 12¼" h
Description: Hard plastic molded figure with brown painted features. Molded, painted clothing. Excellent condition. Slightly exaggerated features.
Artisan/Manufacturer: F & F Mold & Die Works/Made USA, Dayton, Ohio
Date: ca. 1930–1940
Price range: $200.00–275.00
Credits: M. Davern Collection
Note of Interest: Plentiful

Category: Figural Images
Item Type: Containers - salt & pepper, creamer, sugar
Classification: E-3
Dimensions: Large male pepper, large female salt - 5¼"; medium male pepper and medium female salt - 3½"; small male creamer and small female sugar - 2⅛" h
Description: Molded hard plastic images rendered in a caricature nature. Painted black faces and hands. Dressed in molded domestic clothing. The smallest figures are attached to the yellow containers (sugar and creamer) serving as handles. Excellent condition – salt/pepper sets; good condition – sugar and creamer (some flaking).
Artisan/Manufacturer: F & F Mold & Die Works/Made USA, Dayton, Ohio
Date: ca. 1930–1940s
Price range: Salt & pepper (large set) - $75.00–125.00; salt & pepper (medium set) - $65.00–95.00; sugar & creamer - $65.00–95.00.
Credits: M. Davern Collection
Note of Interest: Plentiful. May be brown or black.

Novelties/Souvenirs

Novelties is one of the single largest categories of Black collectibles. These objects provide a wide variety of memorabilia. This category evokes the most controversy because the objects often present unflattering and biased images of Blacks. Every conceivable novelty company, toy company, southern and northern state tourist bureau, doll company and other retailer created novelties with Blacks as the main subject. All types of materials were used – paper, ceramic, tin, iron, other metals, wood, plastic, vinyls, and chalk. Most of these objects were created purely for the purpose of amusement, although some objects served as toys, functional objects, and "art objects." Surprisingly, many of these objects were cheap but have survived to date. Although often caricature in nature, the "quality" of the objects varied as did the materials and categories. The title "novelty" has been given to this material because, for the most part, they are not very useful. Many countries shipped collectibles into the United States. The objects from Germany, particularly the ceramics, were of the highest quality, while those from Japan were usually of very poor quality. Those made in the United States are of mixed condition. Common objects are those illustrating kids on alligators, outdoor privies, eating watermelon, and kissing, touching, or comparing themselves. Uncommon are the bisque objects, French Art Deco pieces, Blacks on plates, silver or brass objects and wooden pieces. Common objects are often expensive and the demand for this category is high. Although quite plentiful, there are modern reproductions.

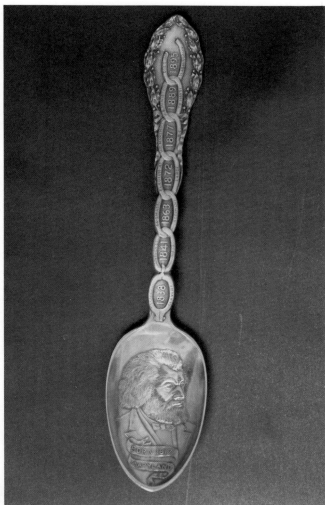

Category: Novelty
Item Type: Souvenir spoon
Classification: D-2
Dimensions: 6" h
Description: Sterling silver spoon with the image of Frederick Douglass in the bottom portion. Top and stem decorated with the dates 1838, 1841, 1863, 1872, 1877, 1889, 1895. Excellent condition.
Date: ca. 1890s–1920s
Price range: $150.00–200.00
Credits: Glenn & Ingrid Phillips Collection
Note of Interest: Common

Category: Novelty
Item Type: Souvenir spoons
Classification: D-1
Dimensions: All are 5¾"
Description: Enamel spoons with embossed/molded tops with enamel bottoms. Left - "Cutting Cane, New Orleans, La." (scene of Blacks in the cane fields); middle - "The Real Thing, Norfolk, Virginia" (man eating watermelon); right - "The Real Thing, Atlanta" (man eating watermelon).
Date: ca. 1890s–1920s
Price range: $225.00–275.00
Credits: Glenn & Ingrid Phillips Collection
Note of Interest: Collection

Category: Novelty
Item Type: Souvenir spoon
Classification: D-2
Dimensions: 6"
Description: Sterling silver spoon, embossed top with female images and a shallow relief scene of "Uncle Tom's Cabin" in the bottom. Excellent condition.
Date: ca. 1890s–1930s
Price range: $150.00–200.00
Credits: Glenn & Ingrid Phillips Collection
Note of Interest: Common

Category: Novelty
Item Type: Souvenir spoon
Classification: D-2
Dimensions: 4¼"
Description: Twisted stem sterling silver spoon with a male bust adorned by small lizard-like creatures on the top portion and a smooth bottom. Excellent condition.
Date: ca. 1900–1930s
Price range: $150.00–200.00
Credits: Glenn & Ingrid Phillips Collection
Note of Interest: Common

Category: Novelty
Item Type: Souvenir spoon
Classification: D-1
Dimensions: 5¾"
Description: The enamel scene depicts Blacks picking cotton. "Georgia" on the stem; "State Capitol" on back.

Excellent condition. Colors - green, red, and blue.
Date: ca. 1900–1930
Price range: $225.00–275.00
Credits: Glenn & Ingrid Phillips Collection
Note of Interest: Common

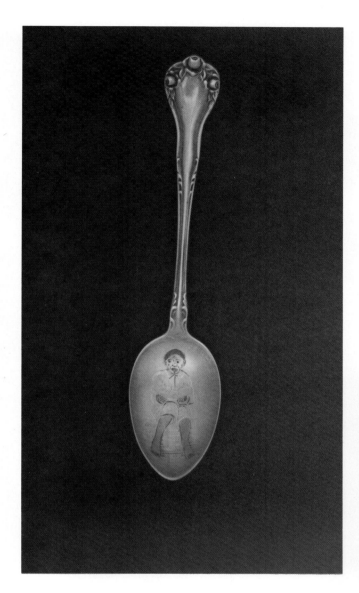

Category: Novelty
Item Type: Souvenir spoon
Classification: D-3
Dimensions: 5½"
Description: Sterling silver spoon with a molded design on the top and stem. A shallow relief design of a child sitting, holding a slice of watermelon. "Stolen Sweets, Cordele, Ga." Excellent condition.
Date: ca. 1900–1930s
Price range: $155.00–225.00
Credits: Glenn & Ingrid Phillips Collection
Note of Interest: Common

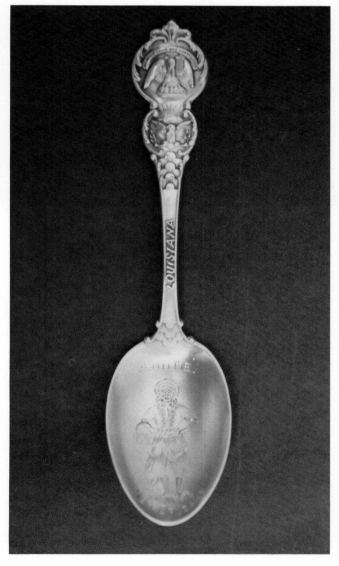

Category: Novelty
Item Type: Souvenir spoon
Classification: D-1
Dimensions: 5"
Description: New Orleans sterling spoon "AUNTIE (image) New Orleans" in the lower portion. "Louisiana" on the stem with an eagle and "JUSTICE UNION and Confidence." Excellent condition.
Date: ca. 1900–1930s
Price range: $175.00–250.00
Credits: Glenn & Ingrid Phillips Collection
Note of Interest: Common

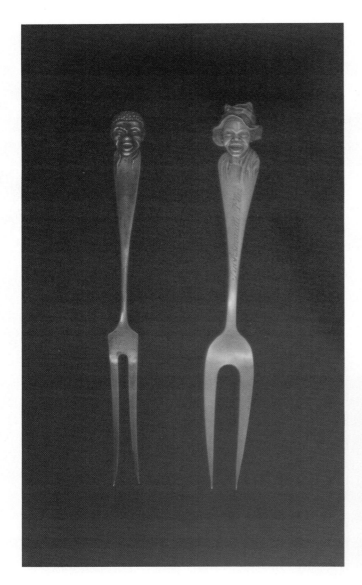

Category: Novelty
Item Type: Souvenir fork (2)
Classification: D-3
Dimensions: 4½" each
Description: Sterling silver forks. Left – image of a man, "Clearwater Harbor, La." on the back. Right – image of man with a hat, "Jacksonville, Fla." on the front. Excellent condition.
Date: ca. 1900–1930s
Price range: $125.00–185.00
Credits: Glenn & Ingrid Phillips Collection
Note of Interest: Common

Category: Novelty
Item Type: Souvenir spoons, letter opener
Classification: D-3
Dimensions: Left to right – 6", 5¼", 6"
Description: All sterling silver images on the upper portion of the items are molded in the "Sunny South" character style. "Jacksonville, Fla."
Date: ca. 1900–1930s
Price range: $125.00–185.00 each
Credits: Glenn & Ingrid Phillips Collection
Note of Interest: Common. The "Sunny South" character is a common image.

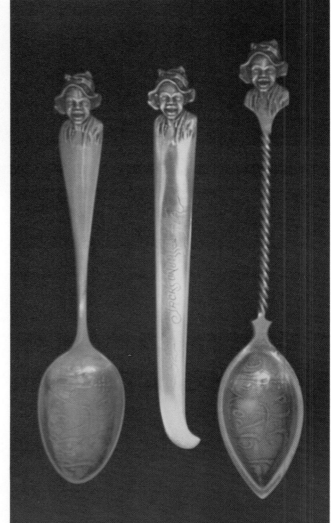

Category: Novelty
Item Type: Souvenir spoons
Classification: D-3 (embossed), D-1 (enamel bottom), D-2 (enamel top)
Dimensions: 5", 5¼", 5½"
Description: Left – "Your Milk Maid, New Orleans, La." Embossed image of a woman smoking a pipe on the upper portion. Lower portion has an embossed shallow relief image of a milk wagon. Middle – "Oraline Seller." Embossed top with an enamel scene in the lower portion, Black older lady seated. Right – "Hygelia Hotel." Enamel top with the image of female. (Old Point; Comford, Va.) All spoons are made of sterling silver and in excellent condition.
Date: ca. 1880–1920s
Price range: Left - $175.00–275.00; middle - $225.00–325.00; right - $175.00–275.00.
Credits: Glenn & Ingrid Phillips Collection
Note of Interest: Common. Enamel spoons generally cost more.

Category: Novelty
Item Type: Souvenir spoons (3)
Classification: D-3
Dimensions: 5¾", 5", 4¼"
Description: Left – "Jacksonville, Fla./Sunny South," male image in upper portion; boy eating melon with legs crossed in the lower portion. Middle – "Old City Gate/St. Augustine, Fla.," male image on the upper portion with an alligator wrapped around his neck. The gates of the city are embossed on the lower portion. Right – Male image in upper portion, engraved inscription in lower portion. All of the spoons are made of sterling silver and in excellent condition.
Date: ca. 1900–1930s
Price range: $125.00–185.00 each
Credits: Glenn & Ingrid Phillips Collection
Note of Interest: Common.

Category: Novelty
Item Type: Broom label
Classification: E-3
Dimensions: 5" h x 3½" w
Description: Colorful paper label once used to adorn a broom. The printed image of the man playing a banjo is executed in a naturalistic yet somewhat abstract form. Unused, excellent condition.
Artisan/Manufacturer: Made in U.S.A./Dixie
Date: ca. 1920s
Price range: $8.00–12.00
Credits: The Paper Pile, San Anselmo, California
Note of Interest: Plentiful

Category: Novelty
Item Type: Australian bronzes
Classification: E-2 (outhouse), D-1 (man with pipe)
Dimensions: Man with pipe - 2½" h. Outhouse - 2" h x 1³⁄₁₆" w
Description: Australian painted bronzes. Molded features, slightly exaggerated. Excellent condition.
Artisan/Manufacturer: Australia
Date: ca. 1880–1930
Price range: Man with pipe - $125.00–175.00. Boy in outhouse - $115.00–165.00.
Credits: V. Mackemull Collection
Note of Interest: Common

Category: Novelty
Item Type: Pencil sharpener
Classification: F-2
Dimensions: 1⁷⁄₁₆" h x 1⁵⁄₁₆" w
Description: Metal pencil sharpener molded in the shape of a man with exaggerated features wearing a top hat and bowtie. Face painted medium brown. Sharpener in the underside of the head. Excellent condition.
Artisan/Manufacturer: Unmarked, Germany
Date: ca. 1900–1920
Price range: $125.00–175.00
Credits: Lost & Found Antiques, Kensington, Maryland
Note of Interest: Common

Category: Novelty
Item Type: Figurine
Classification: G-2
Dimensions: 5½" h
Description: Ceramic painted glazed figure with slightly exaggerated features holding a bowl. Excellent condition.
Artisan/Manufacturer: Unmarked
Date: ca. 1930–1940
Price range: $55.00–65.00
Credits: M. Davern Collection
Note of Interest: Plentiful

Category: Novelty
Item Type: Spoon rest
Classification: E-2
Dimensions: 4¼" h x 5¼" w
Description: Glazed ceramic spoon rest with the head and bust of a medium brown man with a large white chef's hat. Head attached by a wire, and applied ceramic feet. Excellent condition.
Artisan/Manufacturer: Serio Lefton © SU413 J.C
Date: ca. 1920s–1940s
Price range: $75.00–110.00
Credits: M. Davern Collection
Note of Interest: Plentiful

Category: Novelty
Item Type: Figurine, toothpick holder
Classification: E-3
Dimensions: 4" h x 3¼" w
Description: Small boy with a cello made of molded painted glazed ceramic. Toothpick holder attached to the figure's back. Face and hands painted black. Excellent condition.
Artisan/Manufacturer: Japan
Date: ca. 1930–1940
Price range: $55.00–65.00
Credits: M. Davern Collection
Note of Interest: Plentiful

Category: Novelty
Item Type: Cup
Classification: G-3
Dimensions: 4" h
Description: A glazed ceramic cup with Black figures of girl and
  boy done in caricature style. "Ooo! There is a difference."
  Excellent condition.
Artisan/Manufacturer: Unmarked
Date: ca. 1940s–1950s
Price range: $45.00–60.00
Credits: M. Davern Collection
Note of Interest: Plentiful

Category: Novelty
Item Type: Figurine, toothpick holder
Classification: G-3
Dimensions: 4⅜" h x 4½" w
Description: Painted brown figure of a young girl with bare feet and
  painted molded dress, holding a slice of melon. Attached to a
  barrel motif container which holds toothpicks. Entire piece is
  painted glazed ceramic. Excellent condition. Caricature style.
Artisan/Manufacturer: Unmarked
Date: ca. 1930–1950
Price range: $55.00–65.00
Credits: M. Davern Collection
Note of Interest: Plentiful

Category: Novelty
Item Type: Pincushion
Classification: E-3
Dimensions: 2½" h
Description: Unfired ceramic boy with straw-stuffed pincushion
  on a paper box label over wood. Cushion tied with green
  string. Black painted face and hands, holding a natural
  cotton ball. Good condition. "Education Souvenir of Hot
  Springs, Arkansas, Watch The Cotton Grow."
Artisan/Manufacturer: Made by Baton Rouge Turtle Co.,
  Baton Rouge, La., Pat Pend.
Date: ca. 1920s–1930s
Price range: $35.00–45.00
Credits: M. Davern Collection
Note of Interest: Plentiful

Category: Novelty
Item Type: Pincushion
Classification: E-3
Dimensions: 2¾" h
Description: Figural pincushion done in caricature style with
  the character's hat serving as a pincushion. The face and
  hands of the seated figure are a black/grey color – painted
  and glazed. Excellent condition.
Artisan/Manufacturer: Made in Japan
Date: ca. 1930–1940
Price range: $45.00–55.00
Credits: M. Davern Collection
Note of Interest: Plentiful

Category: Novelty
Item Type: Teapot
Classification: E-3
Dimensions: 3¾" h x 5⅞" w
Description: Brown-faced glancing eyed teapot. Molded and painted. Exaggerated features. Excellent condition.

Artisan/Manufacturer: Made in Japan, hand painted
Date: ca. 1930s–1940s
Price range: $75.00–125.00
Credits: M. Davern Collection
Note of Interest: Plentiful

Category: Novelty
Item Type: Teapot
Classification: E-3
Dimensions: Elephant with bamboo handle, 7" h x 8½" w. Elephant with tail as handle, 6½" x 10" w.
Description: Ceramic glazed elephants with small painted men atop them. Figures painted black with bright colored turbans and loin cloths. Bamboo handle on one with the other's tail functioning as a handle. Figures lift off as top of the pots with the trunks serving as the spouts. Excellent condition.

Artisan/Manufacturer: Japan, marked Made in Japan/Hand Painted.
Date: ca. 1920s–1930s
Price range: $175.00–255.00 each
Credits: M. Davern Collection
Note of Interest: Plentiful

Category: Novelty
Item Type: Figurine, toothpick holder
Classification: G-3
Dimensions: 5¾" h x 6" w
Description: Painted, glazed ceramic double figure, male/female children. Medium brown faces and hands. Boy holding a slice of melon; girl holding an ear of corn. Corn motif container between the figures. Excellent condition.
Artisan/Manufacturer: Unmarked
Date: ca. 1930–1940
Price range: $55.00–75.00
Credits: M. Davern Collection
Note of Interest: Plentiful

Category: Novelty
Item Type: Mug
Classification: E-2
Dimensions: 5½" h
Description: Painted, glazed ceramic mug with the face of a jovial gentleman. Naturalistic features with exaggeration of the eyes. A ceramic arm extends upward grasping a half rolling pin which forms the handle of the cup. Excellent condition.
Artisan/Manufacturer: Stern
Date: ca. 1930s–1940s
Price range: $110.00–145.00
Credits: M. Davern Collection
Note of Interest: Common

Category: Novelty
Item Type: Figurine, toothpick holder
Classification: G-3
Dimensions: 5½" h
Description: Painted, glazed figure with a brown face and arms carrying a small container affixed to her back. The all ceramic figure is rendered with exaggerated features. Excellent condition.
Artisan/Manufacturer: Unmarked
Date: ca. 1930–1940
Price range: $45.00–65.00
Credits: M. Davern Collection
Note of Interest: Plentiful

Category: Novelty
Item Type: Figurine
Classification: F-1
Dimensions: 5½" h
Description: Painted, glazed ceramic male figure with a ceramic fish on the end of a wooden pole and string. The seated figure has a basket on each side of his seat. Pipe in mouth. Brown face and hands. Excellent condition.
Artisan/Manufacturer: Unmarked
Date: ca. 1930s–1960
Price range: $95.00–125.00 (complete with fish)
Credits: M. Davern Collection
Note of Interest: Plentiful. Often the fish and pole are missing.

Category: Novelty
Item Type: Figurine
Classification: F-3
Dimensions: 4½" h x 8½" w
Description: Molded, painted, glazed ceramic seated figure rendered with strong negroid features. Bare brown feet, arms, and face. Figure is holding a container in his right arm with a pineapple in the left hand. Excellent condition.
Artisan/Manufacturer: Mill Hunter '59
Date: ca. 1959
Price range: $55.00–75.00
Credits: M. Davern Collection
Note of Interest: Scare

Category: Novelty
Item Type: Figurine
Classification: D-1
Dimensions: 7½" h x 6" w
Description: Well-executed figure of a young boy standing on a platform with a vegetable and flower motif. The figure's face, hands and feet are done in medium brown. All ceramic, glazed. Excellent condition.
Artisan/Manufacturer: 7072 65
Date: ca. 1900–1930s
Price range: $125.00–175.00 complete
Credits: M. Davern Collection
Note of Interest: Common

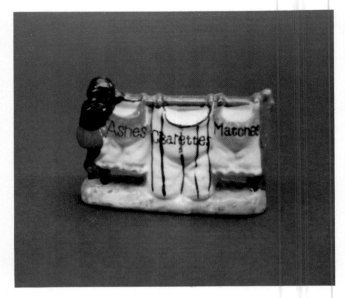

Category: Novelty
Item Type: Souvenir figurine
Classification: E-3
Dimensions: 5" h
Description: Small figural piece with a container attached. Figure painted black. "Souvenir of Canada." Good condition. Caricature.
Artisan/Manufacturer: Japan
Date: ca. 1930–1940
Price range: $35.00–45.00
Credits: Pineapple Door Antiques, Chattanooga, Tennessee
Note of Interest: Plentiful

Category: Novelty
Item Type: Cigarette caddy
Classification: E-3
Dimensions: 2½" h x 3¼" w
Description: All ceramic painted, glazed caddy with a small black-painted boy to the side of the "Ashes" container. Caricature features. Good condition.
Artisan/Manufacturer: Japan
Date: ca. 1920s–1940s
Price range: $35.00–45.00
Credits: Lost & Found Antiques, Kensington, Maryland
Note of Interest: Plentiful

Category: Novelty
Item Type: Cigarette holder
Classification: E-3
Dimensions: 5½"
Description: Inexpensively made cigarette holder/ashtray with a molded brown painted figure of a small boy posed in a sitting position on the "Ashes" container. The cigarette container has a wooden moveable lid hinged with wire. All ceramic and glazed with the exception of the wooden lid. Good condition.
Artisan/Manufacturer: Japan
Date: ca. 1920s–1940s
Price range: $35.00–45.00
Note of Interest: Plentiful

Category: Novelty
Item Type: Figurine, toothpick holder
Classification: E-3
Dimensions: 3½" h x 2¾" w
Description: All bisque painted brown boy posing next to a pig. The character is rendered in caricature form. Holes for toothpicks are molded into the back of the pig. Excellent condition.
Artisan/Manufacturer: No. 1119
Date: ca. 1920s–1930s
Price range: $95.00–125.00
Credits: V. Mackemull Collection
Note of Interest: Common

Category: Novelty
Item Type: Figurine
Classification: D-3
Dimensions: 2" h x 4" w
Description: All bisque boy painted black, tickling a white hippo with a feather. The image of the boy is rendered in caricature form. Excellent condition.
Artisan/Manufacturer: Germany
Date: ca. 1900s–1920s
Price range: $95.00–125.00
Credits: V. Mackemull Collection
Note of Interest: Common

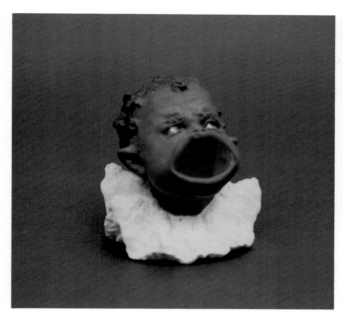

Category: Novelty
Item Type: Bust, night light
Classification: D-1
Dimensions: 3½" h
Description: All bisque piece with exaggerated features. Very delicately done. Ruffled collar of a clothing article used as the base. Excellent condition.
Artisan/Manufacturer: Germany No. 96
Date: ca. 1900–1920
Price range: $95.00–150.00
Credits: V. Mackemull Collection
Note of Interest: Common

Category: Novelty
Item Type: Figurine
Classification: E-3
Dimensions: 2" h x 1" w
Description: Small boy on a potty with his moth open and large lips painted red. The figure is painted black and glazed all ceramic. "Mat de mer." Good condition.
Artisan/Manufacturer: Japan
Date: ca. 1920s–1940s
Price range: $25.00–35.00
Credits: Lost & Found Antiques, Kensington, Maryland
Note of Interest: Plentiful

Category: Novelty
Item Type: Figurine, night light
Classification: E-2, E-2, E-3
Dimensions: Boys on potty (E-2) - 3" h x 2" w; Night light (E-2) - 2½" h; Outhouse (E-3) - 2¾" h.
Description: Boys on potty are all bisque, well executed, hand painted and mounted on a base. Faces painted black. Outhouse has one figure on a pot and the other peeking in the door. Both figures are painted black and the entire piece is made of bisque mounted on a platform. The night light figure is styled in caricature form, his mouth is used for the candle. All three pieces are in excellent condition.
Artisan/Manufacturer: Boys on potty - Germany, No. 57060; Outhouse and night light - Germany, unmarked.
Date: ca. 1900s–1920s
Price range: Boys on potty - $110.00–150.00; Night light - $75.00–110.00; Outhouse - $75.00–110.00
Credits: V. Mackemull Collection
Note of Interest: Night light - common; Potty - plentiful.

Category: Novelty
Item Type: Figurine
Classification: E-3
Dimensions: 4¼" h x 2½" w
Description: Small bisque boy sitting inside of a shell fashioned to resemble a chair. Boy painted black with molded, painted clothing, bare feet. Excellent condition.
Artisan/Manufacturer: Germany
Date: ca. 1900–1930s
Price range: $95.00–125.00
Credits: V. Mackemull Collection
Note of Interest: Plentiful (style), common (origin of manufacture)

Category: Novelty
Item Type: Figurine
Classification: E-2
Dimensions: 4" h
Description: Well-executed all bisque figure straddling an alligator. The figure is rendered in caricature form with large eyes and red lips. Molded, painted Black features with painted clothing and bare feet. Excellent condition.
Artisan/Manufacturer: Germany
Date: ca. 1900–1930s
Price range: $125.00–150.00
Credits: V. Mackemull Collection
Note of Interest: Plentiful

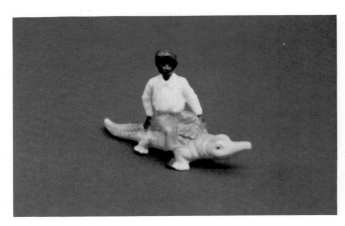

Category: Novelty
Item Type: Figurine
Classification: E-3
Dimensions: 1¾" h x 3¼" w
Description: Delicately executed fine bisque. Young boy riding an alligator dressed in molded clothing. Bare feet and facial features rendered in a naturalistic manner. Subtle colors used to paint the alligator and clothing. Boy's face, hands, and feet painted black. Excellent condition.
Artisan/Manufacturer: Germany
Date: ca. 1900–1920s
Price range: $95.00–110.00
Credits: V. Mackemull Collection
Note of Interest: Plentiful

Category: Novelty
Item Type: Figurine
Classification: E-2
Dimensions: 6" h
Description: Young boy dressed from the waist down in molded pants, attempting to retrieve a melon from the jaws of an alligator. All bisque with painted, molded features. Caricature style. Gator molded and painted. Figure painted black. Excellent condtion.
Artisan/Manufacturer: Germany
Date: ca. 1900–1930s
Price range: $125.00–150.00
Credits: V. Mackemull Collection
Note of Interest: Plentiful

Category: Novelty
Item Type: Figurine
Classification: E-2
Dimensions: 4½" h x 4¾" w
Description: A comical all bisque piece done in a caricature manner. The young boy is shown in an odd predicament with the goose apparently looking for food. The boy's molded, painted face bears an expression of dismay. Face painted black-brown. Excellent condition.
Artisan/Manufacturer: Germany
Date: ca. 1900–1930s
Price range: $110.00–125.00
Credits: V. Mackemull Collection

Category: Novelty
Item Type: Figurine
Classification: E-3
Dimensions: Small boy - 1¼" h x 1¼" w. Large boy - 2¼" x 1¹⁵⁄₁₆" w.
Description: Fine quality bisque figures of young boys holding chickens. Each is painted black with molded, painted features and clothing. Bare feet, caricature in style. Excellent condition.
Artisan/Manufacturer: Germany
Date: ca. 1910–1940s
Price range: Small - $55.00–75.00; Large - $95.00–110.00
Credits: V. Mackemull Collection
Note of Interest: Plentiful

Category: Novelty
Item Type: Figurine (double image)
Classification: E-1
Dimensions: 4¼" h x 2½" w
Description: Well-executed double bisque figurine. Beautifully molded features and clothing on both characters. Black image with naturalistic features. Delicately fashioned poses of both attempting to sit on one potty. Excellent condition.
Artisan/Manufacturer: Made in Germany
Date: ca. 1880s–1920s
Price range: $175.00–265.00
Credits: V. Mackemull Collection
Note of Interest: Common

Category: Novelty
Item Type: Figurines (3)
Classification: E-2
Dimensions: Boy sitting - 2¼"; Boy in melon - 4" h x 4" w; Boy lying on cotton - 3¾"
Description: Fine quality bisque figures with exaggerated features. All eating watermelon in various poses. Molded and painted features, all painted dark brown. (1) Boy with a cone-shaped hat emerging out of a bisque melon. (2) Small boy seated on a block holding a large slice of melon. (3) A small boy lying on his stomach atop a burlap cotton bale, up on his elbows, eating a slice of melon All in excellent condition.
Artisan/Manufacturer: Germany
Date: ca. 1900–1930s
Price range: Sitting - $75.00–95.00; Inside melon - $95.00–110.00; Laying - $75.00–125.00.
Credits: V. Mackemull Collection
Note of Interest: Plentiful

Category: Novelty
Item Type: Figurine (double image)
Classification: D-2
Dimensions: 3½" h x 3½" w
Description: Bisque piece done in both a comical and caricature manner. Molded and painted with the woman's features rendered in a medium brown. The figural image is of a Black woman seated on a non-Black sailor's lap. Excellent condition.
Artisan/Manufacturer: Heubach (Germany) #211
Date: ca. 1900–1920
Price range: $145.00–210.00.
Credits: V. Mackemull Collection
Note of Interest: Common

Category: Novelty
Item Type: Bust, cork
Classification: E-2
Dimensions: 3¼" h
Description: All bisque cork with paper on the head area molded in the shape of a hat (bisque hat missing). Caricature, brown painted molded face. Good condition. "Sunny South" type character.
Artisan/Manufacturer: Germany
Date: ca. 1920s–1940s
Price range: $110.00–145.00.
Credits: V. Mackemull Collection
Note of Interest: Common

Category: Novelty
Item Type: Figurines (3)
Classification: D-1
Dimensions: Girl sitting - 2" h x 2½" w; Boy sitting - 2" h x 3" w; Boy standing - 3" h
Description: Well executed figures of small children. Painted, molded bisque of a fine quality. (1) Girl sitting painted black; (2) Boy standing is dark brown; (3) Boy seated is light brown and is pouring flour or sugar over his legs. All figures have naturalistic features and are in excellent condition.
Artisan/Manufacturer: Germany (origin of the 3 figures). Seated girl marked #378–5.
Date: ca. 1880s–1920s
Price range: $125.00–275.00 each
Credits: V. Mackemull Collection
Note of Interest: Common

Category: Novelty
Item Type: Figurine
Classification: D-1
Dimensions: 4¼" h
Description: All bisque delicately painted figure done in a naturalistic manner of a boy seated, eating an ear of corn. The figure is rendered in a medium brown color with painted, molded clothing. Excellent condition.
Artisan/Manufacturer: Germany
Date: ca. 1900–1920s
Price range: $145.00–225.00.
Credits: V. Mackemull Collection
Note of Interest: Common

Category: Novelty
Item Type: Figurine (double image)
Classification: E-3
Dimensions: 7" h x 4" w
Description: All bisque piece molded and painted with the images of a young couple sitting on a chair, each holding a slice of melon. Well-dressed pair with caricature features, faces painted black. Excellent condition.
Artisan/Manufacturer: Germany
Date: ca. 1900–1920s
Price range: $225.00–275.00.
Credits: V. Mackemull Collection
Note of Interest: Common

Category: Novelty
Item Type: Figurines (9)
Classification: E-1 to E-3
Dimensions: Largest - 2¾" h; smallest - 1¼" h
Description: A group of seated figures glazed and unglazed of children eating watermelon. All of the figures are delicately painted, some brown and others black. All are done in a naturalistic manner with a slight exaggeration of the lips on the large figures. All are in excellent condition.

Artisan/Manufacturer: 4060 (on image measuring 1¾" h); origin is Germany on all figures.
Date: ca. 1900–1930s
Price range: $90.00–125.00 each
Credits: V. Mackemull Collection
Note of Interest: Plentiful

Category: Novelty
Item Type: Figurine
Classification: E-2
Dimensions: 4¼" h x 3½" w
Description: All bisque black painted figure of a young boy holding a slice of melon with his chest bare and a molded piece of cloth on his lower body. A naturalistic rendering of his features. Figure in a seated position. Excellent condition.
Artisan/Manufacturer: Germany #7367
Date: ca. 1900–1920s
Price range: $125.00–175.00.
Credits: V. Mackemull Collection
Note of Interest: Common

Category: Novelty
Item Type: Measuring tape
Classification: F-2
Dimensions: 1½" h x 1" w
Description: Celluloid head of a young girl, face painted brown with a pleasant expression. Rendered in a naturalistic manner. Excellent condition.
Artisan/Manufacturer: Unmarked
Date: ca. 1900–1940s
Price range: $75.00–95.00.
Credits: V. Mackemull Collection
Note of Interest: Scarce

Category: Novelty
Item Type: Figurine
Classification: E-3
Dimensions: 1½" h x 1" w
Description: All ceramic molded figure of a nude black painted small child attached to a potty. "You-R-Next." Entire piece glzed. Caricature in style. Excellent condition.
Artisan/Manufacturer: Unmarked
Date: ca. 1920s–1940s
Price range: $45.00–55.00.
Credits: Pineapple Door Antiques; Chattanooga, Tennessee
Note of Interest: Plentiful

Category: Novelty
Item Type: Figurine
Classification: E-3
Dimensions: 1½" h x 1" w
Description: Bisque figurine atop a cotton mass with oats attached to a burlap bundle. The figure has a cloth hat, holding a slice of melon. Caricature style with brown painted features. Good condition.
Artisan/Manufacturer: Japan
Date: ca. 1920s–1940s
Price range: $45.00–55.00.
Credits: Pineapple Door Antiques; Chattanooga, Tennessee
Note of Interest: Plentiful

Category: Novelty
Item Type: Figurines (2)
Classification: E-3
Dimensions: 5¼" h
Description: All ceramic glazed figures in the form of black painted angels adorned in white robes. Slight exaggeration of the eyes. Excellent condition.
Artisan/Manufacturer: Paper label, Japan
Date: ca. 1940–1955
Price range: $55.00–75.00 pair.
Credits: M. Davern Collection
Note of Interest: Common

Category: Novelty
Item Type: Figurines (5)
Classification: G-3
Dimensions: 5" h
Description: Brown painted features, set of 5. All ceramic with molded instruments, no moveable parts, glazed. Good condition.
Artisan/Manufacturer: Unmarked
Date: ca. 1940s–1955
Price range: $95.00–145.00 set
Credits: M. Davern Collection
Note of Interest: Plentiful

Category: Novelty
Item Type: Figurine, group image
Classification: E-3
Dimensions: 5¾" h (tallest figure) x 6½" w
Description: One-piece molded painted set of figures. One Black with a black painted face and two non-Blacks. Singing children with molded choir robes, all ceramics. Good condition.
Artisan/Manufacturer: Marked 418
Date: ca. 1950–1970
Price range: $75.00–125.00 set
Credits: M. Davern Collection
Note of Interest: Plentiful

169

Category: Novelty
Item Type: Textile, linen
Classification: G-3
Dimensions: 23" h x 16⅜" w
Description: Lithographed linen for decorative kitchen use. Mother and children are rendered in a light-hearted caricature fashion. The facial features are brown with slight exaggeration of the eyes and painted red lips. Little girl's hair is adorned with an excessive amount of bows. Excellent condition.
Artisan/Manufacturer: Unmarked
Date: ca. 1935–1940
Price range: $65.00–90.00
Credits: M. Davern Collection
Note of Interest: Common

Category: Novelty
Item Type: Bells
Classification: E-3
Dimensions: Large female - 3½" h; small female - 2¼"; male - 3¼" h
Description: The matched pair of bells, male & female, have ceramic brown painted, molded faces, molded clothing with the bell in their hollow lower bodies. The smallest bell has a black painted wooden face and upper body of painted wood. Lower hollow skirt made of metal. All of the characters are done in a caricature style. All in good to excellent condition.
Artisan/Manufacturer: Ceramic pair (Japan); Wood/metal bell (unmarked)
Date: ca. 1920–1945
Price range: Ceramic (pair) - $55.00–75.00. Wood/metal - $45.00–55.00
Credits: M. Davern Collection
Note of Interest: Plentiful

Category: Novelty
Item Type: Figurines (3)
Classification: G-3
Dimensions: Large female - 2¼" h; small female - 1½" h; male - 1½" h
Description: Iron painted characters with Black faces. Some paint flaking on all of the figures, no breakage. Fair condition. Caricature in style.
Artisan/Manufacturer: Unmarked
Date: ca. 1910–1930
Price range: $95.00–125.00 each (Condition varies price)
Credits: M. Davern Collection
Note of Interest: Common

Category: Novelty
Item Type: Figurines (2)
Classification: Female – G-3; Male – G-2
Dimensions: Female - 3⅛" h; Male - 3" h
Description: Iron figurines with dark brown painted faces. Matronly female standing. Elderly male seated with his ankles crossed holding a large slice of melon. Good condition.
Artisan/Manufacturer: Female - unmarked. Male - marked 41/14 Made in USA M
Date: ca. 1910–1930
Price range: $150.00–195.00 each
Credits: M. Davern Collection
Note of Interest: Common

Category: Novelty
Item Type: Figurines (2)
Classification: F-3
Dimensions: Male sitting - 2½" h, Male standing - 2⅝" h
Description: Iron figures with instruments. Molded, painted features. Sitting figure has brown face; standing figure has black face. Caricature in style, fair condition.
Artisan/Manufacturer: Unmarked
Date: ca. 1910–1940
Price range: $150.00–195.00 each
Credits: M. Davern Collection
Note of Interest: Common

Category: Novelty
Item Type: Figurines (2)
Classification: G-3
Dimensions: 2" h
Description: All wood carved figures attached to a platform. Carved instruments. Caricature in style. Excellent condition.
Artisan/Manufacturer: Unmarked
Date: ca. 1930–1950
Price range: $65.00–85.00
Credits: M. Davern Collection
Note of Interest: Plentiful

Category: Novelty
Item Type: Figurines (2)
Classification: G-3
Dimensions: Female - 3⅛" h; male - 3" h
Description: All bisque female with painted features is in a cotton boll (natural unbleached cotton). Figure is painted black. Male is a ceramic pincushion in the mold of a young man kneeling, holding two oversized dice. Pincushion is nestled in the figure's back. Both figurines are done in caricature style. Excellent condition.
Artisan/Manufacturer: Unmarked
Date: ca. 1920–1940s
Price range: $25.00–35.00 each
Credits: M. Davern Collection
Note of Interest: Plentiful

Category: Novelty
Item Type: Figurine
Classification: G-3
Dimensions: 5½" h
Description: Ceramic top with cloth bottom. Molded, brown painted features. Caricature in style. Excellent condition.
Artisan/Manufacturer: Unmarked
Date: ca. 1930–1940
Price range: $35.00–50.00
Credits: M. Davern Collection
Note of Interest: Plentiful

Category: Novelty
Item Type: Figurines (2)
Classification: E-3
Dimensions: Large - 6⅛" h; small - 4¼" h
Description: Plastic souvenir figures. Heads are attached by a wire causing them to nod, thus referred to as "nodders." Good condition.
Artisan/Manufacturer: Large - Florida; small - Puerto Rico
Date: ca. 1940–1950s
Price range: $35.00–45.00
Credits: M. Davern Collection
Note of Interest: Plentiful

Category: Novelty
Item Type: Figurine
Classification: F-3
Dimensions: 5" h
Description: Celluloid, molded, brown-painted young lady. Jointed strung arms. Good condition.
Artisan/Manufacturer: Unmarked
Date: ca. 1910–1930
Price range: $30.00–40.00
Credits: M. Davern Collection
Note of Interest: Plentiful

Category: Novelty
Item Type: Figurines (6)
Classification: E-3
Dimensions: Large male & female – 7¼" h; medium male & female – 4⅞" h; male & female sitting on a bench (back row) – 6¼" h
Description: All bisque "nodders" painted black. Front row nodders have magnets in their mouths (known as "kissers"). Good condition.

Artisan/Manufacturer: Kenmar, Japan
Date: ca. 1940–1955
Price range: $65.00–95.00 per set
Credits: M. Davern Collection
Note of Interest: Plentiful

Category: Novelty
Item Type: Figurine
Classification: E-3
Dimensions: 6⅝" h
Description: Cloth black face doll in a cotton ball placed in a basket. Good condition.
Artisan/Manufacturer: "Cotton Souvenir" – Memphis, Tennessee
Date: ca. 1930s–1940s
Price range: $45.00–65.00
Credits: M. Davern Collection
Note of Interest: Plentiful

Category: Novelty
Item Type: Figural, cigarette box
Classification: D-1
Dimensions: 6⅝" h
Description: Wooden carved cigarette box with the image of a male. Cigarettes eject from hole in his mouth. The head lifts off as a lid. Music box on the underside. Excellent condition.
Artisan/Manufacturer: Marked "The Blue Daune's Old Black Joe"
Date: ca. 1910–1920s
Price range: $375.00–500.00
Credits: M. Davern Collection
Note of Interest: Scarce

Category: Novelty
Item Type: Figural, brushes
Classification: G-3
Dimensions: Large – 8⅛" h, medium – 7" h, small – 4½" h
Description: Wooden top brushes with painted caricature male and female images on them. The brushes range from clothing to shaving items. All in excellent condition.
Artisan/Manufacturer: Unmarked
Date: ca. 1910–1940
Price range: $45.00–65.00 each
Credits: M. Davern Collection
Note of Interest: Plentiful

Category: Novelty
Item Type: Bells (6)
Classification: E-3
Dimensions: Back row (left to right): 5¾" h, 4¼" h, 5⅜" h. Front row (left to right): 4", 3¾", 4".
Description: All of the bells have black faces. The 3 large figures have cloth tops; the 3 small ones are made of wood. All caricature in style. Cloth dresses and head scarves. Metal bells covered by colorful printed dresses. Excellent condition.
Artisan/Manufacturer: Front left "New Orleans" (others unmarked)
Date: ca. 1910–1940s
Price range: $45.00–65.00 each
Credits: M. Davern Collection
Note of Interest: Plentiful

Category: Novelty
Item Type: Figurine, bookends
Classification: F-3
Dimensions: 5⅝" h
Description: All ceramic bookends with clowns molded and painted on each block form. Excellent condition.
Artisan/Manufacturer: Unmarked
Date: ca. 1935–1945
Price range: $75.00–90.00 each
Credits: M. Davern Collection
Note of Interest: Plentiful

Entertainment

The collectibles in this category are most often found among record albums, sheet music, photographs, handbills, programs, and posters. Black people in the United States and abroad have played a large part in the entertainment field, thus collectibles in the category are widespread and plentiful.

Prior to the 1940s, many Black images did not appear on the record album covers. Record manufacturers felt that the images might inhibit their sale. These albums are highly collectible as are the albums of the 1950s. Prices are generally less than $100.00.

Sheet music abounds! The bulk of Black-related sheet music found today shows images of the South or commentaries about Black life-styles. The images depicted are usually exaggerated in their presentation but some can be found with naturalistic features. Many artists were commissioned to create the covers for sheet music and song books. In fact, collectors of Black memorabilia sheet music collect these items for their imagery rather than the songs. Generally, sheet music is inexpensive and can be purchased easily.

Photographs, as part of Black entertainment memorabilia, are usually of famous or unusual Black entertainers in all fields (actors, musicians, theater, etc.) These items are not plentiful, yet they remain relatively inexpensive. Of course, photographs with autographs by the entertainers are more valuable, but beware of forgeries. Famous people's signatures can be easily checked through books of autographs or autograph societies but obscure signatures are difficult to authenticate.

Handbills, programs, and posters are items from plays, musicals, or movies. Of these three, handbills are rare, programs are common, and posters are most plentiful. The most expensive handbills and programs will be those in which famous Blacks appeared as stars or those which had all Black casts prior to the 1930s. The most expensive movie posters will be those with Blacks as the main image that were printed prior to 1940, particularly if Blacks were in unusual roles (i.e. cowboys, detectives, or gangsters). The cost of these items range from double digits to hundreds of dollars.

Category: Entertainment
Item Type: Sheet music
Classification: E-1
Dimensions: 9¾" h x 7¼" w
Description: Popular play during the 1940s and 1950s. The cast was usually Black. Main song "Summertime" from play.
Artisan/Manufacturer: Gershwin Publishing Corp.
Date: ca. 1935–1945
Price range: $20.00–35.00
Credits: Lost & Found Antiques; Kensington, Maryland

Category: Entertainment
Item Type: Handbill
Classification: E-2
Dimensions: 9½" h x 6¾" w
Description: Minstrel show, Black representation
Artisan/Manufacturer: YMCA
Date: ca. 1920–1940
Price range: $20.00–30.00
Credits: Lost & Found Antiques; Kensington, Maryland
Note of Interest: Common

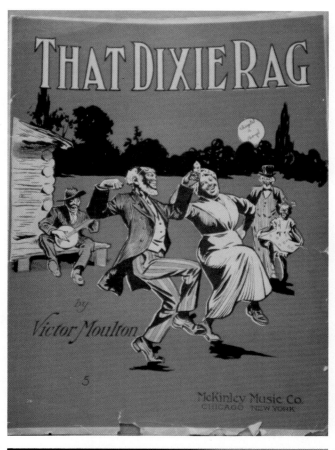

Category: Entertainment
Item Type: Sheet music
Classification: E-2
Dimensions: 13¾" h x 10⅜" w
Description: Blacks on cover dancing a jig. Illustration depicts song title's meaning – "Happy Times."
Artisan/Manufacturer: McKinley Music Co.
Date: ca. 1890–1910
Price range: $20.00–30.00
Credits: Lost & Found Antiques; Kensington, Maryland
Note of Interest: Common

Category: Entertainment
Item Type: Record
Classification: E-1
Dimensions: 13¼" h x 12½" w
Description: Fats Domino, singer and musician. LP – "When I'm Walking."
Artisan/Manufacturer: Columbia Records
Date: ca. 1969
Price range: $15.00–30.00
Credits: The Great Escape; Nashville, Tennessee
Note of Interest: Common

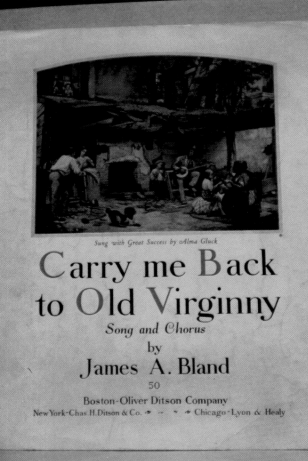

Category: Entertainment
Item Type: Sheet music
Classification: E-2
Dimensions: 13¾" h x 10⅜" w
Description: Blacks shown on cover of sheet music in relaxed positions. Song title is meant to evoke nostalgic moments.
Artisan/Manufacturer: Oliver Dotson Company, Boston
Date: ca. 1900
Price range: $20.00–30.00
Credits: Lost & Found Antiques; Kensington, Maryland

Category: Entertainment
Item Type: LP Record
Classification: E-1
Dimensions: 13¼" h x 12¼" w
Description: Ray Charles, singer and musician, playing the keyboard.
Artisan/Manufacturer: ABC Paramount
Date: ca. 1964
Price range: $30.00–45.00
Credits: The Great Escape; Nashville, Tennessee
Note of Interest: Common

Category: Entertainment
Item Type: LP Record
Classification: E-1
Dimensions: 13¼" h x 12½" w
Description: Ray Charles, singer and musician. All photos on front of album cover are of Ray Charles.
Artisan/Manufacturer: ABC Paramount
Date: ca. 1960
Price range: $20.00–35.00
Credits: The Great Escape; Nashville, Tennessee
Note of Interest: Common

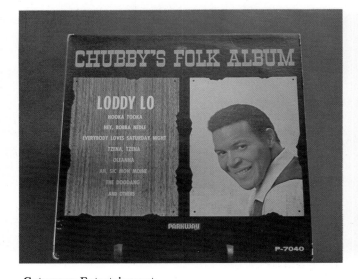

Category: Entertainment
Item Type: LP Record
Classification: E-1
Dimensions: 13¼" h x 12½" w
Description: Wood grain with song listings on left side of cover and photo of Chubby Checker on right side.
Artisan/Manufacturer: Paramount Records
Date: ca. 1963
Price range: $15.00–25.00
Credits: The Great Escape; Nashville, Tennessee

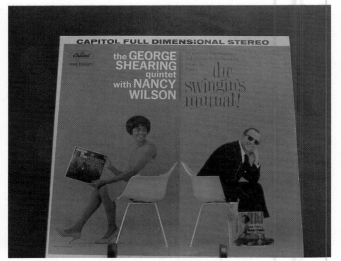

Category: Entertainment
Item Type: LP Record
Classification: E-1
Dimensions: 13¼" h x 12½" w
Description: Nancy Wilson, popular jazz/blues singer
Artisan/Manufacturer: Capitol Records
Date: ca. 1960s
Price range: $15.00–20.00
Credits: The Great Escape; Nashville, Tennessee
Note of Interest: Common

Category: Entertainment
Item Type: LP Record
Classification: E-1
Dimensions: 13¼" h x 12½" w
Description: Cecil Taylor, musician. The Cecil Taylor Quartet, featuring Archie Shepp. Demo album.
Artisan/Manufacturer: Barnaby Candid Series
Date: ca. 1970
Price range: $8.00–15.00
Credits: The Great Escape; Nashville, Tennessee
Note of Interest: Common

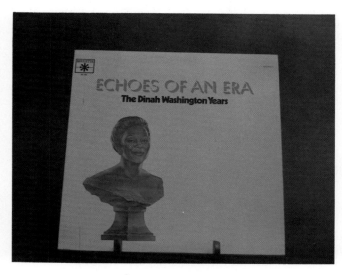

Category: Entertainment
Item Type: LP Record
Classification: E-1
Dimensions: 13¼" h x 12½" w
Description: Dinah Washington, singer. 2 record set, good condition.
Artisan/Manufacturer: Roulette Records Inc.
Date: ca. 1965–1970
Price range: $20.00–25.00
Credits: The Great Escape; Nashville, Tennessee
Note of Interest: Common

Category: Entertainment
Item Type: LP Record
Classification: E-1
Dimensions: 12¼" h x 12¼" w
Description: Dinah Washington, singer. "The Dinah Washington Years." 2 record set, good condition.
Artisan/Manufacturer: Roulette Records, Inc.
Date: ca. 1965–1970
Price range: $20.00–25.00
Credits: The Great Escape; Nashville, Tennessee
Note of Interest: Common

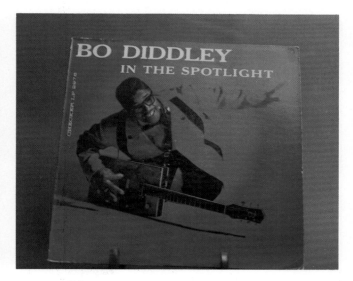

Category: Entertainment
Item Type: LP Record
Classification: E-1
Dimensions: 12¼" h x 12¼" w
Description: Bo Diddley, musician.
Artisan/Manufacturer: Checker LP, hi-fidelity sound
Date: ca. 1958–1965
Price range: $15.00–25.00
Credits: The Great Escape; Nashville, Tennessee

Category: Entertainment
Item Type: Record - 78 rpm
Classification: E-1
Dimensions: 10½" h x 12" w
Description: Art Tatum, musician. 4 record set. "Piano Impressions." Album – A-1
Artisan/Manufacturer: American Recording Artists
Date: ca. 1940s
Price range: $70.00–95.00
Credits: The Great Escape; Nashville, Tennessee

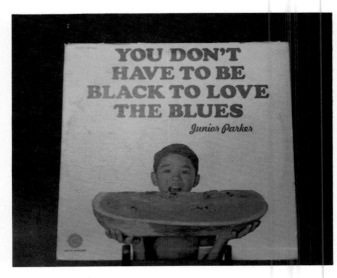

Category: Entertainment
Item Type: LP Record
Classification: E-2
Dimensions: 12¼" h x 12¼" w
Description: Junior Parker, musician. Sonny Lester, producer. Photo by Berry Berenson
Artisan/Manufacturer: Groove Merchant International Inc., N.Y., N.Y.
Date: ca. 1965
Price range: $25.00–30.00
Credits: The Great Escape; Nashville, Tennessee

Category: Entertainment
Item Type: LP Record
Classification: E-1
Dimensions: 11½" h x 12" w
Description: Billie Holiday, "Music For Torching." Photos by Norman Grante. Cover and liner by David Stone Martin.
Artisan/Manufacturer: Verve Records
Date: 1956 issue of 1954 album
Price range: $110.00–125.00 (original)
Credits: The Great Escape; Nashville, Tennessee

Category: Entertainment
Item Type: LP Record
Classification: E-1
Dimensions: 11" h x 12" w
Description: Art Tatum, born 1910, Toledo, Ohio. Studied violin, 13 years of age. Died 1956. Supervised by Norman Grane (original music).
Artisan/Manufacturer: Verve Records
Date: ca. 1957
Price range: $55.00–65.00
Credits: The Great Escape; Nashville, Tennessee

Category: Entertainment
Item Type: LP Record
Classification: E-1
Dimensions: 12" h x 12" w
Description: Sam Cooke, popular Black singer during the early 1960's. Died at young age. "You Send Me," an extremely popular song from the time.
Artisan/Manufacturer: Radio Corp. of America
Date: 1962
Price range: $25.00–35.00
Credits: The Great Escape; Nashville, Tennessee

Category: Entertainment
Item Type: LP Record
Classification: E-1
Dimensions: 10½" h x 12" w
Description: Robert Johnson. "King of the Delta Blues Singers." Cover art: Daily/Planet; typographical design: Nick Fasciano. Robert Johnson's first records recorded in a makeshift studio in a San Antonio hotel room, Nov. 1936.
Artisan/Manufacturer: Columbia Records, NY., N.Y.
Date: ca. 1955
Price range: $35.00–45.00
Credits: The Great Escape; Nashville, Tennessee

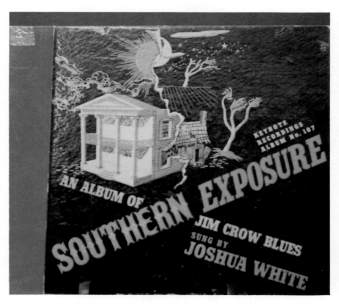

Category: Entertainment
Item Type: LP Record
Classification: E-1
Dimensions: 10¼" h x 12" w
Description: On cover, by Langston Hughes "… Josh is a Fine Folk-Singer of Anybody's Songs – Southern Negro or Southern Writing Plantation Work-Songs, or Modern Union Songs… Any Songs That Come From the Heart of People…"
Artisan/Manufacturer: Keynote Recordings, Inc., NY., N.Y.
Date: ca. 1940
Price range: $25.00–35.00
Credits: The Great Escape; Nashville, Tennessee

Category: Entertainment
Item Type: LP Record
Classification: E-1
Dimensions: 10¼" h x 12" w
Description: On cover, by Langston Hughes "… Josh is a Fine Folk-Singer of Anybody's Songs – Southern Negro or Southern Writing Plantation Work-Songs, or Modern Union Songs… Any Songs That Come From the Heart of People…"
Artisan/Manufacturer: ASCH Recordings
Date: ca. 1940s
Price range: $20.00–25.00
Credits: The Great Escape; Nashville, Tennessee

Category: Entertainment
Item Type: Sheet music
Classification: E-3
Dimensions: 14" h x 10½" w
Description: Language stereotyped for Blacks. Black male and female illustrate song title "Der'll Be Wahm Coons A Prancin'."
Artisan/Manufacturer: Music supplement of the Sunday Examiner
Date: ca. 1890–1930
Price range: $20.00–25.00
Credits: Manning's Books and Prints
Note of Interest: Common

Category: Entertainment
Item Type: Sheet music
Classification: E-3
Dimensions: 12¼" h x 9" w
Description: Small Black child holding cotton balls to illustrate association of Blacks with cotton. Song title "Cotton Fluff."
Artisan/Manufacturer: Clayton F. Summy Company
Date: Copyright 1936
Price range: $15.00–25.00
Credits: Manning's Books and Prints

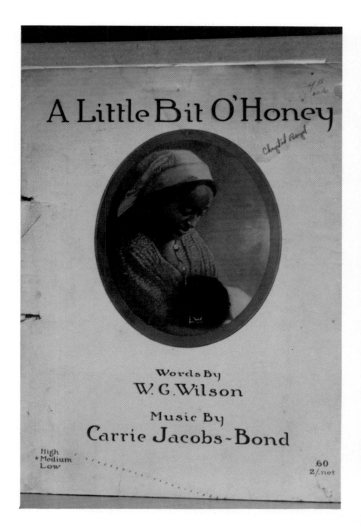

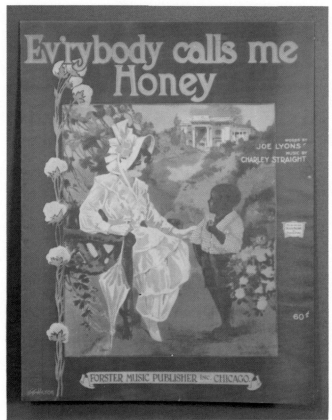

Category: Entertainment
Item Type: Sheet music
Classification: E-1
Dimensions: 13¾" h x 10½" w
Description: Sheet music in which the title expresses a
sentiment presumably used by Blacks
Artisan/Manufacturer: Forster Music Publisher
Date: Copyright 1919
Price range: $15.00–25.00 each
Credits: Manning's Books and Prints

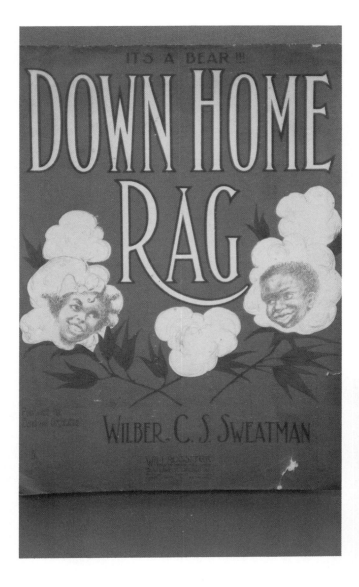

Category: Entertainment
Item Type: Sheet music
Classification: E-3
Dimensions: 13¾" h x 10⅜" w
Description: Black children in cotton balls illustrate the song title "It's A Bear!! Down Home Rag."
Artisan/Manufacturer: Will Rossiter Company
Date: Copyright 1916
Price range: $15.00–25.00
Credits: Manning's Books and Prints

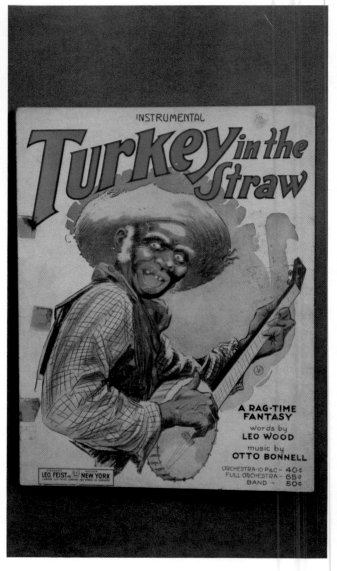

Category: Entertainment
Item Type: Sheet music
Classification: E-3
Dimensions: 12⅜" h x 9¼" w
Description: Caricature of Black man with banjo. Common theme, popular song, "Turkey in the Straw."
Artisan/Manufacturer: Music by Otto Bonnell
Date: Copyright 1921
Price range: $15.00–25.00
Credits: Manning's Books and Prints

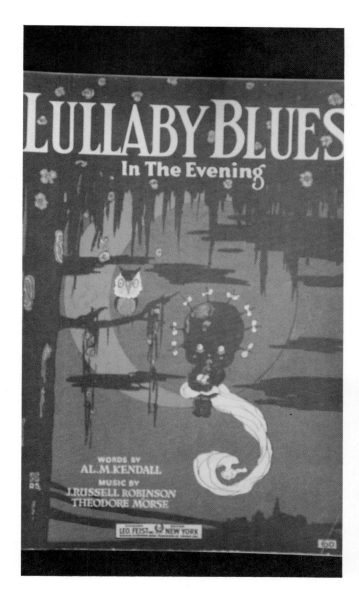

Category: Entertainment
Item Type: Sheet music
Classification: E-3
Dimensions: 12¼" h x 9¼" w
Description: Black child illustrates "Lullaby Blues." Cover illustration.
Artisan/Manufacturer: J. Russell Robinson
Date: 1919
Price range: $15.00–25.00
Credits: Manning's Books and Prints
Note of Interest: Common

Category: Entertainment
Item Type: Sheet music
Classification: E-3
Dimensions: 11¼" h x 11" w
Description: Cover illustrates the song title, "The Plantation Dance." Blacks dance on plantation.
Artisan/Manufacturer: W.F. Shaw & Co.
Price range: $15.00–25.00
Credits: Manning's Books and Prints
Note of Interest: Common

Category: Entertainment
Item Type: Sheet music
Classification: E-3
Dimensions: 16" h x 11" w
Description: Typical piece of sheet music with Blacks used to demonstrate title. "If the Man in the Moon Were a Coon."
Artisan/Manufacturer: Will Rossiter Publisher
Date: Copyright 1905
Price range: $10.00–25.00
Credits: Manning's Books and Prints

Category: Entertainment
Item Type: Theatre program
Classification: E-1
Dimensions: 9" h x 6" w
Description: "Hello Dolly" with Pearl Bailey and Cab Calloway. Playbill.
Artisan/Manufacturer: Shubert Theatre
Date: January 1, 1970
Price range: $15.00–25.00
Credits: The Paper Pile; San Anselmo, California
Note of Interest: Scarce

Category: Entertainment
Item Type: Theatre program
Classification: E-1
Dimensions: 9" h x 7" w
Description: "Brown Buddies." Blacks on cover of program, 28 pages.
Artisan/Manufacturer: New York Theatre Program Corporation
Date: October 20, 1930
Price range: $20.00–25.00
Credits: The Paper Pile; San Anselmo, California
Note of Interest: Scarce

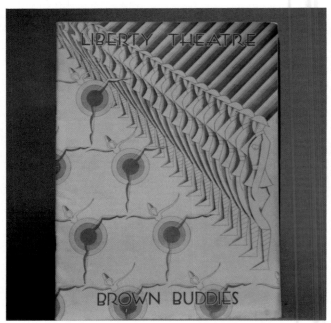

Category: Entertainment
Item Type: Theatre program
Classification: E-1
Dimensions: 9½" h x 7" w
Description: "Green Pastures," popular production for Black actors and audiences. 42 pages.
Artisan/Manufacturer: The New York Magazine Program
Date: October 13, 1930
Price range: $20.00–25.00
Credits: The Paper Pile; San Anselmo, California

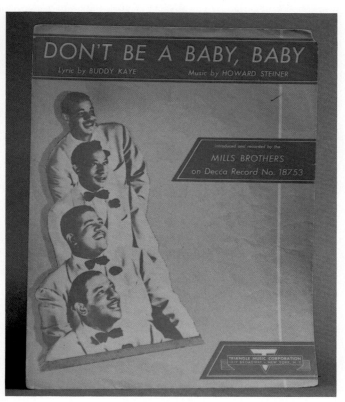

Category: Entertainment
Item Type: Sheet music
Classification: E-1
Dimensions: 12" h x 9" w
Description: Mills Brothers, very popular Black group in 1940s and 1950s. "Don't Be a Baby, Baby."
Artisan/Manufacturer: Triangle Music Corporation
Date: 1946
Price range: $15.00–25.00
Credits: The Paper Pile; San Anselmo, California
Note of Interest: Common

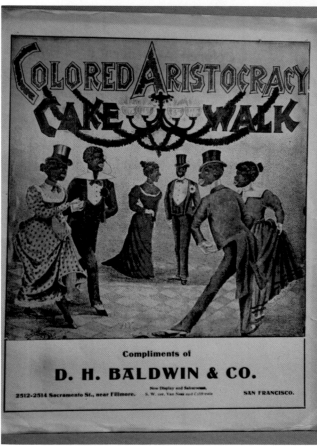

Category: Entertainment
Item Type: Sheet music
Classification: E-1
Dimensions: 14" h x 11" w
Description: "Colored Aristocracy Cake Walk." Common song type in the late 1800s and early 1900s.
Artisan/Manufacturer: Greene Music Co.
Date: 1899
Price range: $25.00–35.00
Credits: The Paper Pile; San Anselmo, California

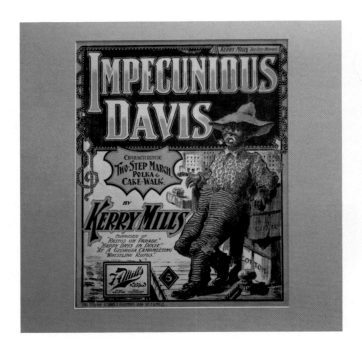

Category: Entertainment
Item Type: Sheet music
Classification: E-1
Dimensions: 10" h x 13" w
Description: "Impecunious Davis," a two-step march by Kerry Mills, framed. (Many collectors purchase sheet music as much for the cover as for the music.)
Date: 1899
Price range: $55.00–75.00 framed
Credits: The Paper Pile; San Anselmo, California

Category: Entertainment
Item Type: Movies
Classification: E-1
Dimensions: 11" h x 14" w
Description: Lobby card, framed. The Little Rascals, "Fishy Tales."
Artisan/Manufacturer: Monogram Pictures
Date: 1951
Price range: $25.00–45.00 framed
Credits: The Paper Pile; San Anselmo, California

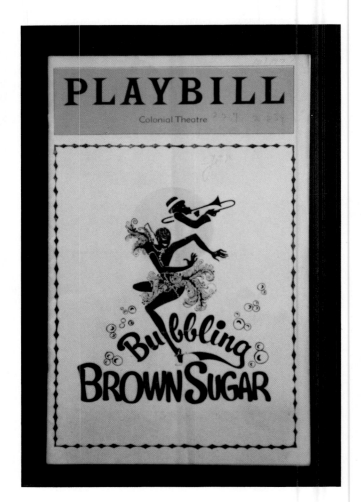

Category: Entertainment
Item Type: Playbill
Classification: E-1
Dimensions: 9" h x 6" w
Description: Announcement for the play, "Bubbling Brown Sugar."
Artisan/Manufacturer: Colonial Theatre
Date: 1925–1950
Price range: $20.00–25.00
Credits: The Paper Pile; San Anselmo, California
Note of Interest: Scarce

Toys

Toys with Black images on them were made from many materials – paper/cardboard, wire (iron), tin, and wood. It appears from all indications that the bulk were made approximately between 1890 and 1920. Most were created in tin. The range of games covers board games, target games, wind-up toys, objects which require that the individual push, pull or throw, and a few pinball games. The titles and images of the toys are often negative, focusing on images of Blacks that were popular at the time. Finding these toys with all the parts is extremely rare. Because these are toys, children played with them, often losing pieces and destroying parts of the wind-up toys or automated objects. Mint pieces are expensive, in demand, and difficult to find. Black-related toys were not made in bulk. In many cases, they were designed but never executed. Contrary to popular belief, most of the Black toys, whether negative or positive, originated in the North.

Old toys are generally expensive. Black toys, because of their rarity and collectibility, are very expensive, difficult to find, and usually in poor condition. The variety is wide ranging and thus offers the collector a real choice and opportunity to specialize within this area. Toys were imported from many foreign countries, especially Germany.

Category: Toys
Item Type: Plastic, clown
Classification: G-3
Dimensions: 12" h
Description: Marionette, plastic. Black clown with painted features. Original clothes and box.
Artisan/Manufacturer: Unmarked
Date: 1945–1955
Price range: $95.00–115.00
Credits: M. Davern Collection

Category: Toys
Item Type: Tin, noisemaker
Classification: G-2
Dimensions: 4" h
Description: Painted tin noisemaker. When twirled by handle on back, noise is created.
Artisan/Manufacturer: Unmarked
Date: 1920–1940
Price range: $45.00–65.00
Credits: Lost & Found Antiques; Kensington, Maryland

Category: Toys
Item Type: Tin, bank
Classification: D-2
Dimensions: 3¼" h
Description: "Log Cabin Bank" written on side of roof.
Artisan/Manufacturer: J. Chenin (USA)
Date: ca. 1920
Price range: $550.00–700.00
Credits: Ron Carr; Capitola, California

Category: Toys
Item Type: Tin, bank
Classification: D-2
Dimensions: 6" h, expands to 9½" h
Description: Tin with litho. When bank fills as coins are inserted, legs grow.
Artisan/Manufacturer: Made in England
Date: ca. 1950
Price range: $400.00–500.00
Credits: Ron Carr; Capitola, California

Category: Toys
Item Type: Tin, bank
Classification: D-2
Dimensions: 5¾" h
Description: Tin mechanical bank. Man dances while woman plays banjo.
Artisan/Manufacturer: Weeden Manf., New Bedford, Massachusetts
Date: ca. 1988
Price range: $2,200.00–2,800.00
Credits: Ron Carr; Capitola, California

Category: Toys
Item Type: Music box
Classification: D-1
Dimensions: 8¼" h
Description: Tin , music box
Artisan/Manufacturer: German
Date: ca. 1920
Price range: $550.00–700.00
Credits: Ron Carr; Capitola, California

Category: Toys
Item Type: Wind-up toy
Classification: D-1
Dimensions: 8½" h
Description: Tin , wind-up toy. Trademark "Rollo Chair."
Artisan/Manufacturer: Stock & Co. (German) Distributed by Ferdinand Strauss Corp. (N.Y., N.Y.)
Date: ca. 1921
Price range: $650.00–800.00
Credits: Ron Carr; Capitola, California

Category: Toys
Item Type: Push toy
Classification: D-1
Dimensions: 3¾" h
Description: Tin litho push toy
Artisan/Manufacturer: German KC Company
Date: ca. 1926
Price range: $375.00–475.00
Credits: Ron Carr; Capitola, California

Category: Toys
Item Type: Dancing figures
Classification: D-1
Dimensions: 6" h figures (Base: 7" long x 2¾" w)
Description: Happy Jack and Happy James. Tin, animated. Steam operated.
Artisan/Manufacturer: German, marked W.K.
Date: ca. 1920
Price range: $1,100.00–1,500.00
Credits: Ron Carr; Capitola, California

Category: Toys
Item Type: Game
Classification: D-1
Dimensions: 9" h x 21" w
Description: "Cake Walk" made of paper
Artisan/Manufacturer: Anglo-American Game Co., Montreal, Canada; Parker Brothers, Salem, Massachusetts (USA)
Date: ca. 1920
Price range: $350.00–450.00
Credits: Ron Carr; Capitola, California

Category: Toys
Item Type: Tin bank
Classification: D-2
Dimensions: 6¾" h
Description: Tin, man's head applied. Press lever in front, tongue sticks out, coin goes in mouth and eyes close.
Artisan/Manufacturer: Unmarked
Date: ca. 1930
Price range: $300.00–425.00
Credits: Ron Carr; Capitola, California

Category: Toys
Item Type: Cast iron bank
Classification: D-1
Dimensions: 6¼" h
Description: Coin is placed in hand. When lever behind left shoulder is pressed, she raises hand, eyes roll back, and tongue flips out as she swallows coin. "Dinah."
Artisan/Manufacturer: John Harper & Company, Ltd. Willenhall, England
Date: ca. 1911
Price range: $1,100.00–1,500.00
Credits: Ron Carr; Capitola, California

Category: Toys
Item Type: Cast iron bank
Classification: D-1
Dimensions: 5" h x 4" w
Description: Painted cast iron. Man on bail of cotton, mouth is slot for pennies. (Known in various color combinations.)
Artisan/Manufacturer: Unmarked
Date: ca. 1900
Price range: $3,900.00–4,800.00
Credits: Ron Carr; Capitola, California

Category: Toys
Item Type: Pot metal bank
Classification: E-2
Dimensions: 5½" h
Description: Painted pot metal. Coin goes in back. (Comes in various color combinations.)
Artisan/Manufacturer: Unmarked
Date: ca. 1930
Price range: $375.00–475.00
Credits: Ron Carr; Capitola, California

Category: Toys
Item Type: Toy bank
Classification: D-2
Dimensions: 7¼" h
Description: Tin litho. Insert coin in man's chest, press lever on lower left side. Coin enters bank with dipsy-do action from wrist.
Artisan/Manufacturer: J. Levey Co., London; bank made in Germany
Date: Marked June 4th, 1909
Price range: $2,200.00–2,800.00
Credits: Ron Carr; Capitola, California

Category: Toys
Item Type: Toy bank
Classification: D-2
Dimensions: 5" h
Description: Tin, clock-type bank with original key. Tongue sticks out to receive coin. When coin is pushed in mouth, eyes move.
Artisan/Manufacturer: Chad Valley, England
Date: ca. 1950
Price range: $500.00–600.00
Credits: Ron Carr; Capitola, California

Category: Toys
Item Type: Animated toy
Classification: D-2
Dimensions: 3" h x 4" (base)
Description: Wire, tin. Acrobat tumbles when pushed.
Artisan/Manufacturer: German
Date: ca. 1921
Price range: $225.00–275.00
Credits: Ron Carr; Capitola, California

Category: Toys
Item Type: Wind-up
Classification: D-1
Dimensions: 8¾" h
Description: Tin litho wind-up. Man with chicken in right hand, bulldog bites posterior (bounces back and forth.) "Hey-Hey, the Chicken Snatcher."
Artisan/Manufacturer: Louis Marx, New York
Date: ca. 1924
Price range: $1,100.00–1,500.00
Credits: Ron Carr; Capitola, California

Category: Toys
Item Type: Wind-up
Classification: D-1
Dimensions: Small man - 5¼" h; large man - 7" h; base - 3" w x 4¼" h x 2" d
Description: Tin, litho. Faces and hands hand painted. Animated, one plays violin, other one jigs. Possible prototype, not mass produced.
Artisan/Manufacturer: Line Mar Toys, imported by Louis Marx
Date: ca. 1953
Price range: $1,200.00–1,700.00
Credits: Ron Carr; Capitola, California

195

Category: Toys
Item Type: Automaton
Classification: D-1
Dimensions: 10½" h
Description: Wood and cast iron. Preacher (comes in a variety of types) has original key, Bible in left hand. Clockwork mechanism. Body moves and right hand goes up/down.
Artisan/Manufacturer: Ives & Company, Bridgeport, Connecticut
Date: ca. 1875
Price range: $2,500.00–3,000.00
Credits: Ron Carr; Capitola, California

Category: Toys
Item Type: Aluminum bank
Classification: D-2
Dimensions: 9" h
Description: Mechanical, aluminum and wood. Coin is placed in hand, lever is pressed, coin flips in mouth.
Artisan/Manufacturer: Unmarked
Date: ca. 1931
Price range: $1,500.00–2,000.00 (scarce)
Credits: Ron Carr; Capitola, California

Category: Toys
Item Type: Bank
Classification: D-1
Dimensions: 4" h
Description: Terra cotta. Two faces when flipped. Coin slot in one hat.
Artisan/Manufacturer: Austria (J.M. Co)
Date: ca. 1920
Price range: $500.00–600.00
Credits: Ron Carr; Capitola, California

Category: Toys
Item Type: Wind-up
Classification: D-2
Dimensions: 8" h
Description: Tin litho wind-up. Black woman, "Mammy" written under apron.
Artisan/Manufacturer: Lindstrom Toys, United States
Date: ca. 1939
Price range: $275.00–350.00
Credits: Ron Carr; Capitola, California

Category: Toys
Item Type: Wind-up
Classification: D-1
Dimensions: 7½" h
Description: Tin litho wind-up. He walks with suitcases.
Artisan/Manufacturer: Made in Germany
Date: ca. 1921
Price range: $550.00–675.00
Credits: Ron Carr; Capitola, California

Category: Toys
Item Type: Wind-up
Classification: D-2
Dimensions: 7" h
Description: Tin litho wind-up. Man with sunflower in lapel. Often called "The Dude."
Artisan/Manufacturer: Germany
Date: ca. 1928
Price range: $400.00–550.00
Credits: Ron Carr; Capitola, California

Category: Toys
Item Type: Wind-up
Classification: D-1
Dimensions: 6½" h
Description: Seated man plays drum when wound-up. Tin, hand painted.
Artisan/Manufacturer: Germany
Date: ca. 1921
Price range: $1,800.00–2,200.00
Credits: Ron Carr; Capitola, California

Category: Toys
Item Type: Mechanical toy
Classification: D-2
Dimensions: 4¾" h
Description: Tin, litho. Clown hits man on head, head goes in barrel.
Artisan/Manufacturer: Germany, K 20
Date: ca. 1927
Price range: $225.00–300.00
Credits: Ron Carr; Capitola, California

Category: Toys
Item Type: Mechanical toy
Classification: D-1
Dimensions: 15" h
Description: Tin animated Black and Irishman. Irishman hits cymbals with right foot, head moves from side to side. Black man shakes bells up and down, head goes back and forth.
Date: ca. 1920
Price range: $2,500.00–3,000.00
Credits: Ron Carr; Capitola, California

Category: Toys
Item Type: Wind-up
Classification: D-1
Dimensions: 6" h
Description: Man seated, dog bites posterior when wound up. Tin litho.
Artisan/Manufacturer: German
Date: ca. 1920
Price range: $1,100.00–1,500.00
Credits: Ron Carr; Capitola, California

Category: Toys
Item Type: Mechanical toy
Classification: D-2
Dimensions: Top of hat to top of base - 5" h. Base - 5" h x 2½" w
Description: Twist crank and chicken goes in mouth from basket. Papier maché man on wood base.
Artisan/Manufacturer: German
Date: ca. 1890–1910
Price range: $1,200.00–1,500.00
Credits: Ron Carr; Capitola, California

Category: Toys
Item Type: Toy
Classification: D-1
Dimensions: 8½" h
Description: Black Dopey. Unique, original prototype. Painted features (blue eyes), watermelon in hand, painted coveralls. Tin.
Artisan/Manufacturer: Louis Marx; Erie, Pennsylvania
Date: April 3, 1939
Price range: $1,700.00–2,000.00 (scarce)
Credits: Ron Carr; Capitola, California

Category: Toys
Item Type: Mechanical toy
Classification: D-1
Dimensions: 9¾" h
Description: Triple animation of Charleston trio – violin player, jig dancer, dog with cane. Tin.
Artisan/Manufacturer: Louis Marx & Company (New York, New York)
Date: 1921
Price range: $600.00–775.00
Credits: Ron Carr; Capitola, California

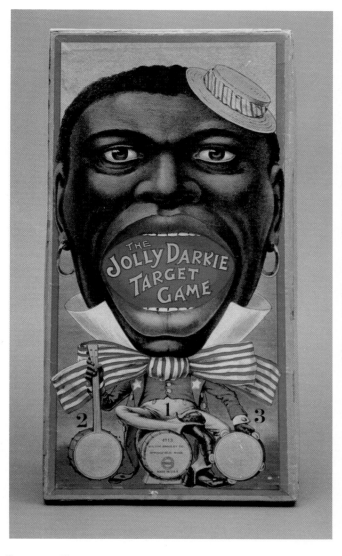

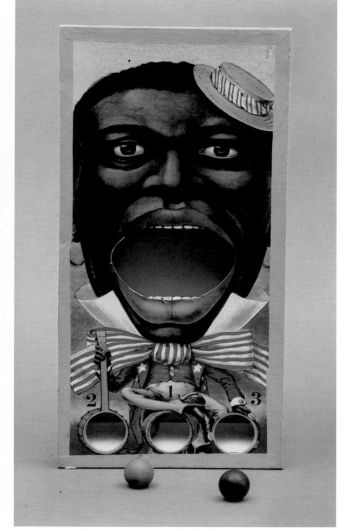

Category: Toys
Item Type: Games (2 games, similar playing models)
Classification: D-1
Dimensions: 15½" h x 12" w
Description: "The Jolly Darkie Target Game"

Artisan/Manufacturer: Milton Bradley Co., Springfield, Massachusetts
Date: 1915–1917
Price range: $225.00–325.00
Credits: Ron Carr; Capitola, California

Category: Toys
Item Type: Animated music box
Classification: D-1
Dimensions: 8" h, central figure
Description: Tin animated music box. Punch and Judy with Mammy.
Artisan/Manufacturer: Marked Germany (Western Zone). Painted D.R.G.M.
Date: 1947–1948
Price range: $1,100.00–1,500.00
Credits: Ron Carr; Capitola, California

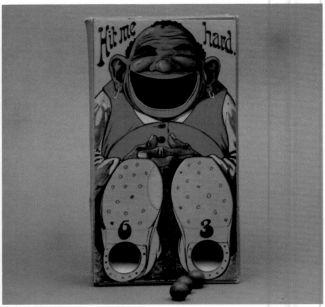

Category: Toys
Item Type: Game
Classification: D-2
Dimensions: 13" h x 13" w
Description: "Twin Target"
Artisan/Manufacturer: Milton Bradley, Springfield, Massachusetts
Date: 1920–1925
Price range: $225.00–350.00
Credits: Ron Carr; Capitola, California

Category: Toys
Item Type: Game
Classification: D-2
Dimensions: 11½" h x 9" w
Description: "Hit Me Hard"
Artisan/Manufacturer: Made in Germany, Klesfeld Works, Fuerth (Bavaria)
Date: ca. 1920
Price range: $125.00–175.00
Credits: Ron Carr; Capitola, California

Category: Toys
Item Type: Game
Classification: D-3
Dimensions: 15" h x 13" w
Description: "The Piccaninny Bowling Game"
Artisan/Manufacturer: Registered, Spear's Games in Great Britain; manufactured at the Spears Works, Bavaria, made in England
Date: 1928
Price range: $375.00–425.00
Credits: Ron Carr; Capitola, California

Category: Toys
Item Type: Game
Classification: D-3
Dimensions: 19" h x 10" w
Description: "Bean-em" with caricatures of "Mose," "Sambo," "Rastus."

Artisan/Manufacturer: All Fair, Inc., Churchville, NY (USA)
Date: Copyright 1931, Game No. 376
Price range: $475.00–650.00
Credits: Ron Carr; Capitola, California

Category: Toys
Item Type: Game
Classification: D-2
Dimensions: 9" h x 21" w
Description: "The Coon Hunt Game"
Artisan/Manufacturer: Parker Brothers, Inc., Salem Massachusetts
Date: 1920
Price range: $475.00–550.00
Credits: Ron Carr; Capitola, California

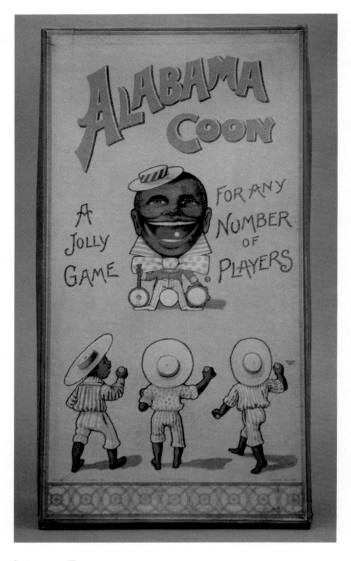

Category: Toys
Item Type: Game (comes in various sizes)
Classification: D-2
Dimensions: 21" h x 13" w
Description: "Alabama Coon, A Jolly Game For Any Number of Players."

Artisan/Manufacturer: Copyrighted, United Kingdom; designed in England; J.W.S. and S. Bavaria, Company
Date: ca. 1920
Price range: Large size: $325.00–450.00. Smaller size: $225.00–375.00.
Credits: Ron Carr; Capitola, California

Category: Toys
Item Type: Game
Classification: E-2
Dimensions: 11½" h x 11½" w
Description: "Watch on De Rind"
Artisan/Manufacturer: All-Fair, Churchville, NY
Date: Copyright 1931
Price range: $250.00–345.00
Credits: Ron Carr; Capitola, California

Category: Toys
Item Type: Game
Classification: E-2
Dimensions: 12½" h x 12½" w
Description: "Little Black Sambo – Who Gets the Most Pancakes?"
Artisan/Manufacturer: Einson Freeman Co., Inc., Book and Game Division (Long Island, NY)
Date: 1934
Price range: $125.00–215.00
Credits: Ron Carr; Capitola, California

Category: Toys
Item Type: Game
Classification: E-2
Dimensions: 15½" h x 10" w
Description: "Old Barn Door Target with Harmless Air Rifle." Rifle and cork inside of box.
Artisan/Manufacturer: Parker Brothers, Inc., Flatiron Building, Salem, NY.
Date: ca. 1920–1930
Price range: $350.00–450.00
Credits: Ron Carr; Capitola, California

Category: Toys
Item Type: Game
Classification: E-2
Dimensions: 13" h x 17¾" w
Description: "Game of Black Sambo"
Artisan/Manufacturer: Saml-Gabriel Sons & Company (NY), Made in USA
Date: ca. 1920
Price range: $125.00–250.00 (mint condition)
Credits: Ron Carr; Capitola, California

Black Dolls

Highly collectible Black dolls are generally those made between 1850 and 1970 with the bulk of them made in the years 1920–1950. Cloth or folk dolls, made all over the country, continue to be produced to date. Buyers should be wary of cloth dolls, checking when possible the material and age. Doll companies during the early 1900s often did not identify their Black dolls in advertisements and trade magazines nor did they produce very many. Many American doll manufacturers would not take the extra effort to make Black dolls with Negroid features but were content to paint white dolls brown or black. This is not so with the German or French doll companies. Of course, Black dolls were manufactured in all media – wood (rare), cloth (plentiful), china (scarce), composition (common), plastic (common), vinyl (common), and modern materials (common). Black dolls were created by doll artists and small and large companies. As with many other collectibles, not all dolls can be identified by creator, artist or manufacturer. Attributions will be made particularly to older wooden dolls, frequently called "slave creations." Such claims are hard to prove and only serve to drive prices up for the doll in question. The same claims will be made for cloth dolls. Unusual Black dolls are jointed, wooden, or automated dolls, the older wind-ups or clockwork mechanisms, French and German bisque fashion dolls, and miniatures of soap, china, wood, or wax. Because of their scarcity, Black dolls run higher than comparable white or other ethnic dolls. As with other collectibles, prices vary by region and individual.

Category: Dolls
Item Type: Paper (2)
Classification: G-3
Dimensions: 10" h each
Description: Paper dolls from the Aunt Jemima family – "Wade" (boy) and "Diana" (girl). Original and in excellent condition. Placed in modern frames to display front and back images.
Artisan/Manufacturer: Unmarked
Date: ca. 1920–1930s
Price range: $45.00–60.00 (each doll only)
Credits: The Paper Pile; San Anselmo, California

Category: Dolls
Item Type: Rubber nipple doll
Classification: C-3
Dimensions: 4" h
Description: Doll made from an old brown baby bottle nipple with painted features and dressed. The nipple doll is holding a white celluloid doll. Good condition.
Artisan/Manufacturer: Unmarked
Date: ca. 1910–1920s
Price range: $75.00–95.00
Credits: The Paper Pile; San Anselmo, California
Note of Interest: Common

Category: Dolls
Item Type: Wooden
Classification: C-1
Dimensions: 8¾" h each
Description: All hand-made wooden, articulated doll. Arms are hinged with wire. Mortise and tenon joints at the knees, curved elbows, pelt skull cap (animal fur wig), moveable feet attached by metal pins. Carved features, mother of pearl inset eyes, carved teeth. Original clothing. Excellent condition.
Artisan/Manufacturer: Unmarked
Date: ca. 1840s–1860s
Price range: $650.00–900.00
Credits: Ron Carr; Capitola, California
Note of Interest: Scarce

Category: Dolls
Item Type: Bisque
Classification: D-2
Dimensions: 5¾" h
Description: Bisque head, papier maché doll with glass eyes, painted blue boots, red painted lips, and mohair wig. Excellent condition. Naturalistic features, entire body and face painted black.
Artisan/Manufacturer: Unmarked
Date: ca. 1890–1910
Price range: $275.00–395.00
Credits: Ron Carr; Capitola, California
Note of Interest: Common

Category: Dolls
Item Type: Cloth
Classification: C-2
Dimensions: 4½" h
Description: Delicately executed cloth doll with painted molded features, mohair wig, black sewn boots, and original clothing. Excellent condition.
Artisan/Manufacturer: Unmarked
Date: ca. 1910–1930s
Price range: $95.00–150.00
Credits: Ron Carr; Capitola, California
Note of Interest: Common. Dolls less than 5" and well executed in cloth are rare.

Category: Dolls
Item Type: Bisque
Classification: E-3
Dimensions: 7¾" h
Description: All bisque, black painted doll with painted features and applied earrings. Original clothing. Jointed at the shoulders and hips. Excellent condition.
Artisan/Manufacturer: Unmarked
Date: ca. 1920–1940s
Price range: $175.00–215.00
Credits: Ron Carr; Capitola, California
Note of Interest: Plentiful

Category: Dolls
Item Type: Papier maché
Classification: F-3
Dimensions: 5¼" h
Description: All papier maché doll with molded painted features, jointed arms and legs, mohair wig. Originally nude. Excellent condition.
Artisan/Manufacturer: Unmarked
Date: ca. 1880–1900
Price range: $245.00–300.00
Credits: Ron Carr; Capitola, California
Note of Interest: Common

Category: Dolls
Item Type: Papier maché/wood
Classification: F-2
Dimensions: 10¾" h
Description: Male doll dressed as a musical performer. Squeeze the tummy and doll sticks out his tongue out and claps the cymbals. Doll has a papier maché head, wooden arms and legs, white eyes with painted black pupils. Excellent condition.
Artisan/Manufacturer: Unmarked
Date: ca. 1880–1900
Price range: $700.00–950.00
Credits: Ron Carr; Capitola, California
Note of Interest: Common

Category: Dolls
Item Type: Gourd head (2)
Classification: E-3
Dimensions: 12" h each
Description: Gourd head "Sambo" and "Mammy" dolls with soft bodies, wooden hands and feet, and painted features. Heads painted black. All original. Excellent condition.
Artisan/Manufacturer: Florida Souvenirs
Date: ca. 1941
Price range: $400.00–550.00 pair
Credits: Ron Carr; Capitola, California
Note of Interest: Common

Category: Dolls
Item Type: Bisque
Classification: D-1
Dimensions: 17" h
Description: Bisque head with composition body painted a medium brown. Human hair wig, open mouth with 4 upper teeth, dark brown sleep eyes with multi-stroke brows, deep dimple in the chin, 15-piece ball-jointed body. Redressed. Excellent condition.
Artisan/Manufacturer: Simon & Halbig
Date: ca. 1900–1920s
Price range: $450.00–550.00
Note of Interest: Common

Category: Dolls
Item Type: Bisque/papier maché
Classification: D-2
Dimensions: 21½" h
Description: Bisque head doll with a rough textured papier maché body painted medium brown. Brown stationary glass eyes with multi-stroke brows, faint dimple in the chin, open mouth with 5 teeth. Wooden painted arms and legs, ball jointed. Redressed. Excellent condition.
Artisan/Manufacturer: Lanternier Black
Date: ca. 1900–1920s
Price range: $450.00–600.00
Note of Interest: Common

Category: Dolls
Item Type: Bisque/composition
Classification: D-2
Dimensions: 20" h
Description: Bisque dome head baby with a brown painted composition body. Sleep brown glass eyes, open mouth with 2 lower teeth, fully jointed with bent legs, 5-piece body. Redressed. Excellent condition.
Artisan/Manufacturer: Armand Marseille (Germany), marked A.M. Germany 351/8K.
Date: ca. 1900–1920s
Price range: $425.00–600.00
Note of Interest: Common

Category: Dolls
Item Type: Papier maché (left - male, right - female)
Classification: F-2
Dimensions: 13" h (both)
Description: Papier maché shoulder plate dolls with maché arms and legs. Stuffed cloth bodies. Painted boots. Male has paper hat; female has papier maché hat. Glass inset eyes. Painted, molded features. Each doll squeaks when tummy is pressed. Redressed. Excellent condition.
Artisan/Manufacturer: Unmarked
Date: ca. 1880–1890s
Price range: $1,100.00–1,500.00 pair
Credits: Ron Carr; Capitola, California
Note of Interest: Common

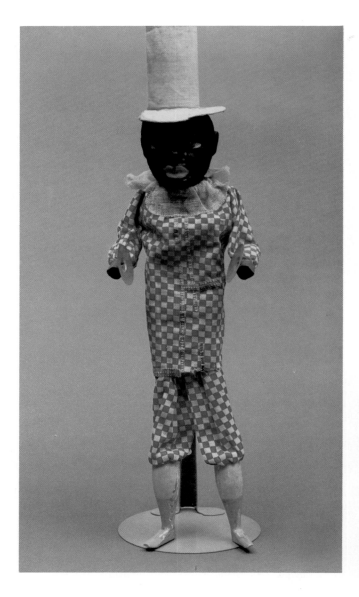

Category: Dolls
Item Type: Papier maché
Classification: F-3
Dimensions: 17" h
Description: Papier maché head, wooden arms, legs and torso. Molded, painted features. Cymbals attached to the doll's hands. Original clothing. Top hat squeaks when pressed down. Excellent condition.
Artisan/Manufacturer: Unmarked
Date: ca. 1880–1915
Price range: $850.00–1,250.00
Credits: Ron Carr; Capitola, California
Note of Interest: Scarce

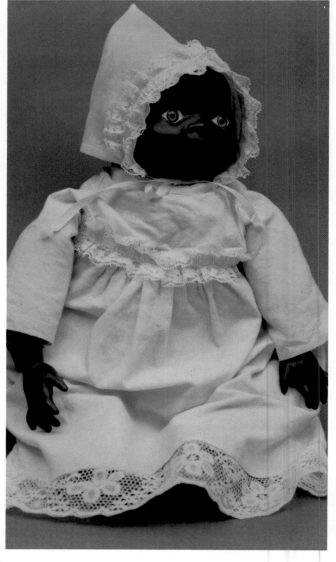

Category: Dolls
Item Type: Bisque
Classification: F-2
Dimensions: 19" h
Description: Reproduction black painted bisque doll with molded features, glassine eyes, original clothes. Excellent condition.
Artisan/Manufacturer: Putnam (mold), reproduction
Date: ca. 1960
Price range: $135.00–175.00
Credits: Ron Carr; Capitola, California
Note of Interest: Plentiful

Category: Dolls
Item Type: Composition
Classification: F-1
Dimensions: Doll - 9½" h; carriage - 7½" h
Description: Brown painted composition doll, fully jointed with wide, flat legs that are hinged at hips. Doll has painted features with naturalistic rendering. Pushing composition carriage with metal wheels. Both in excellent condition.
Artisan/Manufacturer: Unmarked
Date: ca. 1900–1930s
Price range: $375.00–425.00
Credits: Ron Carr; Capitola, California
Note of Interest: Scarce

Category: Dolls
Item Type: Hard plastic
Classification: E-2
Dimensions: 18" h
Description: Hard plastic, dark brown doll with synthetic rooted hair. Redressed. Excellent condition.
Artisan/Manufacturer: Beatrice Wright
Date: ca. 1967
Price range: $110.00–145.00
Credits: Village Antiques, Inc.; Tampa, Florida
Note of Interest: Common

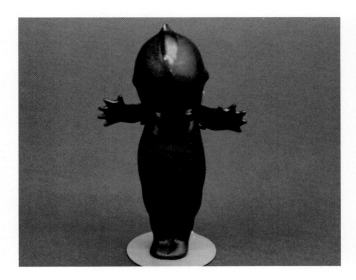

Category: Dolls
Item Type: Bisque
Classification: D-2
Dimensions: 5" h
Description: All bisque, black painted "Kewpie," referred to as a "Hottentot." Jointed arms, blue painted wings on upper back. Excellent condition.
Artisan/Manufacturer: Germany
Date: ca. 1900–1920s
Price range: $125.00–150.00
Credits: V. Mackemull Collection
Note of Interest: Common

Category: Dolls
Item Type: Bisque
Classification: F-2
Dimensions: 6½" h
Description: All bisque, black painted doll, fully jointed, glass eyes, wool wig. Original clothing. Excellent condition.
Artisan/Manufacturer: Unmarked
Date: ca. 1900–1920s
Price range: $145.00–175.00
Credits: V. Mackemull Collection
Note of Interest: Common

Category: Dolls
Item Type: Bisque (3)
Classification: G-3
Dimensions: 4½" h each
Description: All bisque, brown painted dolls with molded, painted hair and features. Jointed at shoulders, hips, and head. Ethnic features. Excellent condition.
Artisan/Manufacturer: Unmarked
Date: ca. 1920s–1930s
Price range: $45.00–65.00 each
Credits: M. Davern Collection
Note of Interest: Common

Category: Dolls
Item Type: Composition/papier maché
Classification: F-2
Dimensions: 8¼" h
Description: Papier maché "Topsy Turvey" doll with composition arms. Black doll with brown glass inset eyes, black human hair. White doll has blue glass inset eyes and blonde hair. Jointed arms, cloth stuffed bodies. Excellent condition.
Artisan/Manufacturer: Unmarked
Date: ca. 1880s–1900s
Price range: $250.00–350.00
Credits: V. Mackemull Collection
Note of Interest: Common

Category: Dolls
Item Type: Bisque (2)
Classification: D-2
Dimensions: 5½" h each
Description: All bisque dolls jointed at the shoulders. Molded, painted features with molded necklaces and skirts. One doll light brown; other painted black. Excellent condition.
Artisan/Manufacturer: Germany
Date: ca. 1890s–1920s
Price range: $300.00–350.00 pair
Credits: V. Mackemull Collection
Note of Interest: Common

Category: Dolls
Item Type: Bisque (2)
Classification: G-2
Dimensions: 5½" h (each)
Description: Brown painted bisque girl and boy dolls with jointed legs and arms and turning heads. Boy's hair molded and painted; girl has mohair wig. Both dolls have molded painted features. Excellent condition.
Artisan/Manufacturer: Unmarked
Date: ca. 1920s–1930s
Price range: $125.00–150.00 each
Credits: V. Mackemull Collection
Note of Interest: Common

Category: Dolls
Item Type: Bisque
Classification: D-1
Dimensions: 4¼" h
Description: All bisque, fully jointed doll with molded painted features, painted boots, original mohair wig, and original clothing. Figure painted medium brown. Excellent condition.
Artisan/Manufacturer: Germany
Date: ca. 1900–1915
Price range: $400.00–550.00
Credits: M. Davern Collection
Note of Interest: Scarce

Category: Dolls
Item Type: China
Classification: F-3
Dimensions: 9" h
Description: A painted black china doll fired (glazed) with molded painted features. Black pupils and red lips. China head, hands and feet with cloth body. Good condition. Redressed.
Artisan/Manufacturer: Unmarked
Date: ca. 1880–1920s
Price range: $175.00–225.00
Credits: M. Davern Collection
Note of Interest: Common

Category: Dolls
Item Type: Bisque
Classification: E-3
Dimensions: 6" h
Description: All bisque black painted doll strung with jointed arms and legs. Molded, painted features. Tufts of hair pulled through 3 holes in the doll's head to form pigtails. Dark brown painted body. Good condition.
Artisan/Manufacturer: Japan
Date: ca. 1900–1930s
Price range: $55.00–75.00
Note of Interest: Plentiful

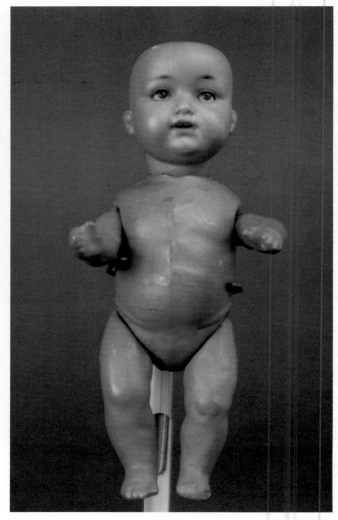

Category: Dolls
Item Type: Bisque/papier maché
Classification: D-3
Dimensions: 9" h
Description: Bisque head toddler with a papier maché body. Jointed body with a socket head. Light brown head with medium brown body. Open mouth with 2 top teeth. Open "pate" head. Good condition.
Artisan/Manufacturer: Armand Marseille (A.M.)
Date: ca. 1900–1920s
Price range: $125.00–150.00
Note of Interest: Common

Category: Dolls
Item Type: Bisque (2)
Classification: E-3
Dimensions: 2½" h each
Description: All bisque dolls painted brown with molded painted clothing and shoes. Hair is molded and has pigtails of human hair. Molded painted features. Excellent condition.
Artisan/Manufacturer: Japan
Date: ca. 1920s–1930s
Price range: $55.00–75.00 each
Credits: M. Davern Collection
Note of Interest: Common

Category: Dolls
Item Type: Cloth/stockinette
Classification: D-2
Dimensions: 6½" h (each)
Description: Brown stockinette dolls. Cotton stuffed, with stitched features and black yarn hair. Original clothing. Excellent condition.
Artisan/Manufacturer: California
Date: ca. 1930s–1950s
Price range: $110.00–125.00 pair
Credits: M. Davern Collection
Note of Interest: Common

Category: Dolls
Item Type: Cloth
Classification: C-2
Dimensions: 12" h (each)
Description: Cloth dolls with curly yarn hair, cloth applied eyes, stitched mouths. Original clothing, well dressed. Excellent condition.
Artisan/Manufacturer: Unmarked
Date: ca. 1940s–1950s
Price range: $200.00–225.00 pair
Credits: M. Davern Collection
Note of Interest: Common

Category: Dolls
Item Type: Cloth
Classification: C-3
Dimensions: 6½" h
Description: All cloth greyish-black doll with stitched features. Original clothing, good condition.
Artisan/Manufacturer: Unmarked
Date: ca. 1930–1950
Price range: $65.00–75.00
Credits: M. Davern Collection
Note of Interest: Common

Category: Dolls
Item Type: Cloth/wood
Classification: D-2
Dimensions: 15¾" h
Description: Cloth medium brown doll with stitched features, black yarn hair, and wooden arms and legs. Original clothing. Excellent condition.
Artisan/Manufacturer: Unmarked
Date: ca. 1940s–1950s
Price range: $150.00–175.00
Credits: M. Davern Collection
Note of Interest: Common. The wooden arms and legs are unusual for a doll of the 20th century.

Category: Dolls
Item Type: Cloth (2)
Classification: D-3
Dimensions: 16¼" h (each)
Description: All cloth dolls with black yarn hair, stitched and applied features. Original clothing. Medium brown coloring. Excellent condition.
Artisan/Manufacturer: Unmarked
Date: ca. 1950–1965
Price range: $150.00–175.00 pair
Credits: M. Davern Collection
Note of Interest: Common

Category: Dolls
Item Type: Cloth
Classification: C-3
Dimensions: Black doll - 5" h; white baby - 2½" h
Description: Both dolls are made of cloth and pipe cleaner wire, have cloth heads and wire bodies. The large doll is made of brown cloth. The small one represents a white baby. Stitched features. Good condition.
Artisan/Manufacturer: Unmarked
Date: ca. 1930–1945
Price range: $65.00–85.00
Credits: M. Davern Collection
Note of Interest: Common

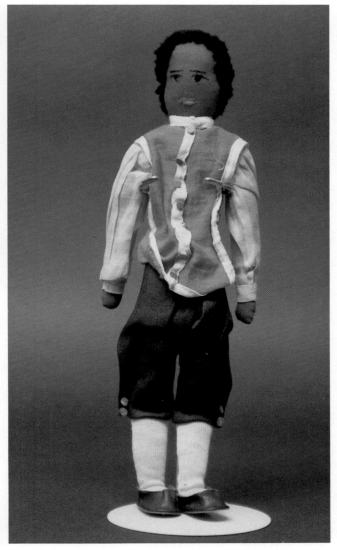

Category: Dolls
Item Type: Cloth
Classification: C-2
Dimensions: 14¼" h
Description: All cloth brown male with leather shoes and all original clothing. Well dressed. Black curly yarn hair with stitched features. Excellent condition.
Artisan/Manufacturer: Unmarked
Date: ca. 1930–1950
Price range: $110.00–125.00
Credits: M. Davern Collection
Note of Interest: Scarce

Category: Dolls
Item Type: Cloth
Classification: C-2
Dimensions: 15¾" h
Description: All cloth adult female doll. Black with stitched features, straw hat and handbag. Original clothing. Excellent condition.
Artisan/Manufacturer: Unmarked
Date: ca. 1920–1940
Price range: $175.00–200.00
Credits: M. Davern Collection
Note of Interest: Common

Category: Dolls
Item Type: Cloth
Classification: C-3
Dimensions: Male - 17½" h; Female - 19" h
Description: Brown cloth dolls with stitched features and black yarn hair. Good condition.
Artisan/Manufacturer: Unmarked
Date: ca. 1935–1945
Price range: $145.00–175.00 pair
Credits: M. Davern Collection
Note of Interest: Plentiful

Category: Dolls
Item Type: Cloth/newspaper
Classification: C-3
Dimensions: 11¼" h
Description: Stockinette male black doll with the fabric stretched over rolled newspaper. Original clothing. Stitched mouth and nose with buttons attached for eyes. Excellent condition.
Artisan/Manufacturer: Unmarked
Date: ca. 1920–1945
Price range: $120.00–145.00 pair
Credits: M. Davern Collection
Note of Interest: Scarce

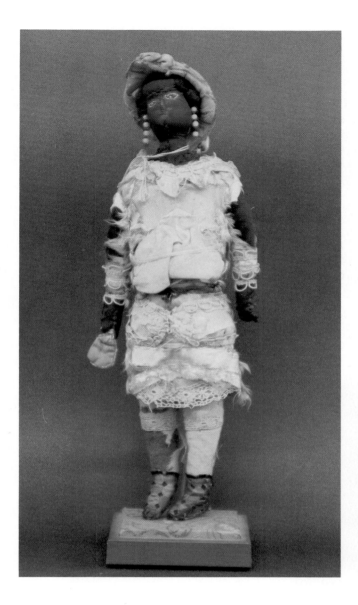

Category: Dolls
Item Type: Cloth/stockinette
Classification: C-1
Dimensions: 15¼" h
Description: Stockinette black adult doll. Silk and lace clothing. Molded and stitched features. Only remnants of the original dress and lacy undergarments remain with original leather boots. Doll's body in excellent condition.
Artisan/Manufacturer: Unmarked
Date: ca. 1920s
Price range: $300.00–400.00
Credits: Charlene Upham Antiques
Note of Interest: Scarce

Category: Dolls
Item Type: Cloth/stockinette
Classification: C-2
Dimensions: 19½" h
Description: Brown cloth/stockinette doll with stitched features. Original leather boots, redressed. Black yarn hair. Fair condition.
Artisan/Manufacturer: Unmarked
Date: ca. 1900–1930s
Price range: $145.00–225.00
Credits: Charlene Upham Antiques
Note of Interest: Common

Category: Dolls
Item Type: Cloth
Classification: C-2
Dimensions: 13½" h
Description: Black cloth doll with jointed legs. Each finger articulated with red sewn fingernails. Black yarn hair, stitched eyes. Original clothing and boots. Excellent condition.
Artisan/Manufacturer: Unmarked
Date: ca. 1900–1930
Price range: $175.00–250.00
Credits: Charlene Upham Antiques
Note of Interest: Scarce

Category: Dolls
Item Type: Cloth
Classification: C-2
Dimensions: 14½" h
Description: Black cloth doll with curly black yarn hair and blue eyes. Stitched features, sewn cloth boots. Original satin dress. Excellent condition.
Artisan/Manufacturer: Unmarked
Date: ca. 1900–1930s
Price range: $155.00–255.00
Credits: Charlene Upham Antiques
Note of Interest: Common

Folk Art

In recent years, folk art has moved from the arena of curiosity to the hotly pursued items of today. The major problem for many collectors is knowing what constitutes folk art. For some, it means anything that is made by hand or with very little machine work. Black collectible folk art is usually found in several forms – wooden toys, signs or images on wood, carved statues, cloth dolls, hand-stitched material with Blacks on cloth, hand-made quilts by Blacks, materials carved in chalk or stone with Blacks as subjects or as the artisans, and hand-painted images on tin, canvas, or other materials. Even the very small or simple items are expensive, costing hundreds or thousands of dollars. Cloth dolls, corn husk dolls, and wooden dolls are common but not inexpensive. Rare are the items which are automated by some kind of mechanism – wind-up, clockwork, or mechanical. Rarer still are those items with all parts available or with few replacement pieces. One difficulty is determining whether or not the piece was made by a Black artisan. Many pieces are attributed to Black slaves, freed men of the late 1800s, and Black artisans of the early 1900s. Unfortunately, only a few of the modern Black folk artisans have been documented. As with other Black collectibles, folk art is any item made by Black artisans or objects that depict Black images. Attribution to items with Black creators will often be used to increase the price. Baskets, pottery, quilts, cloth dolls, even furniture such as the chair from Alachua County, Florida, were made by Black craftsmen. Until studies of different folk art are made, documentation of some kind should be requested by the collector as proof that a Black person created the piece. Reproductions, fakes, made-up pieces abound in the Black folk art arena. Sometimes these are easily identifiable, such as a shiny exterior on wood. Others are more difficult to detect. Old cloth can be used to create a new piece, giving it the appearance of age. Please study the market first.

Category: Folk Art
Item Type: Figural/statue
Classification: D-1
Dimensions: 13" h
Description: All wooden hand-carved figure of a Black gentleman holding a wide brimmed hat with the other hand tucked away in his pocket. An excellent naturalistic rendering of the character. The statue has a clockwork mechanism and whistles 2 different tunes, alternating, when wound up. The character turns his head side to side while whistling. Bird-like image for the key. Excellent condition.
Artisan/Manufacturer: Germany, unmarked
Date: ca. 1920s–1930s
Price range: $2,500.00–3,200.00
Credits: Ron Carr; Capitola, California

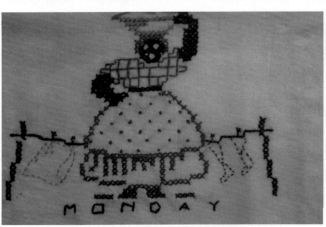

Category: Folk Art
Item Type: Textiles (7)
Classification: B-2
Dimensions: 20" h x 14" w
Description: Images for 7 days of the week embroidered on the bottom portion of white feed sacks. All hand stitched.
Artisan/Manufacturer: Tennessee origin
Date: ca. 1930s
Price range: $250.00–350.00 set
Credits: Pineapple Door Antiques; Chattanooga, Tennessee

Category: Folk Art
Item Type: Ink blotter
Classification: C-2
Dimensions: 5" h x 7" w
Description: Wooden carved image of a young man with striking features. Head is attached to an ink blotter with paper bottom. Excellent condition, well executed.
Artisan/Manufacturer: Unmarked
Date: ca. 1920s–1930s
Price range: $425.00–475.00
Credits: Ron Carr; Capitola, California
Note of Interest: Scarce

Category: Folk Art
Item Type: Whirligig
Classification: C-3
Dimensions: Body - 14" h; base - 14¼" h x 12¼" w
Description: All wood, painted features. Blades and base replaced.
Artisan/Manufacturer: Unmarked
Date: ca. 1900–1940
Price range: $200.00–250.00
Credits: Lost & Found Antiques; Kensington, Maryland
Note of Interest: Common. Wood pieces are common in folk art and many reproductions abound. New pieces are being made from old wood. Caution is suggested.

Category: Folk Art
Item Type: Textile
Classification: C-3
Dimensions: 1⅜" h x 1⅜" w
Description: White/brown/orange pillow with embroidered girl on one side; boy on other. Excellent condition.
Artisan/Manufacturer: Unmarked
Date: ca. 1930s–1950s
Price range: $45.00–60.00
Credits: M. Davern Collection
Note of Interest: Common

Category: Folk Art
Item Type: Painting
Classification: B-3
Dimensions: 13½" h x 12" w
Description: Oil on canvas
Artisan/Manufacturer: Signed Suzanne Iris, 1917.
Date: ca. 1917
Price range: $400.00–550.00
Credits: Lost & Found Antiques; Kensington, Maryland
Note of Interest: Paintings of this type are common. They are usually unsigned with undermined origins. Prices are generally high.

Category: Folk Art
Item Type: Statue
Classification: A-2
Dimensions: Unknown
Description: Carved limestone
Artisan/Manufacturer: William Edmondson
Date: ca. 1939–1950
Credits: Tennessee State Museum
Note of Interest: Scarce. William Edmondson worked in limestone material in Davidson County, Tennessee, 1934–1951. Black artist with many exhibits: Museum of Modern Art, NY (1937); Three Centuries of Art in United States (1938); Nashville Art Gallery (1941); Nashville Artist Guild (1951).

Category: Folk Art
Item Type: Doll
Classification: C-3
Dimensions: 14" h
Description: Ethnic carved features, all wood. Eyes painted white with black pupils. Open mouth with painted red lips. Carved hair, fully jointed body. Poor condition.
Artisan/Manufacturer: Unmarked
Date: 1870–1900
Price range: $225.00–275.00
Credits: Yester Year's Museum
Note of Interest: Scarce

Category: Folk Art
Item Type: Statue
Classification: A-2
Dimensions: Unknown
Description: Carved limestone
Artisan/Manufacturer: William Edmondson
Date: ca. 1939–1950
Credits: Tennessee State Museum
Note of Interest: Scarce

Category: Folk Art
Item Type: Pipe
Classification: B-1
Dimensions: 2¾" h x 6¾" l
Description: Meershaum
Artisan/Manufacturer: Gustav Fischer, Sr. (1847–1937)
Date: 1900–1930
Credits: Museum of Tobacco Art and History, US Tobacco Company
Note of Interest: Scarce. Fischer was born in Austria, educated at Vienna Arts Academy, and he immigrated to NY, finishing school. Moved to Boston in 1893 where he carved pipes in his downtown Boston shop.

Category: Folk Art
Item Type: Pipe
Classification: B-1
Dimensions: 3⅛" h x 7½" l
Description: Meershaum
Artisan/Manufacturer: Gustav Fischer, Sr. (1847–1937)
Date: 1900–1930
Credits: Museum of Tobacco Art and History, US Tobacco Company
Note of Interest: Scarce

Category: Folk Art
Item Type: Doll
Classification: C-3
Dimensions: 15¼" h
Description: Ethnic carved features. Eyes painted white with black pupils. Open mouth painted red. Carved hair, fully jointed body. Only one arm.
Artisan/Manufacturer: Unmarked
Date: 1870–1900
Price: $225.00–325.00
Credits: Yester Year's Museum
Note of Interest: Scarce

Category: Folk Art
Item Type: Tambourine
Classification: C-2
Dimensions: 9" d
Description: Sheepskin over wood.
Artisan/Manufacturer: Unmarked
Date: 1890–1920
Price: $425.00–550.00
Credits: Ron Carr; Capitola, California
Note of Interest: Items of this type are unusual and scarce.

Category: Folk Art
Item Type: Music box
Classification: C-3
Dimensions: 5½" h x 3¾" w
Description: Hand painted tin music box. Man playing banjo with music notes coming out of his mouth. Written beside his face are the words "Old Sussane, Plays-Oh Susanne."
Artisan/Manufacturer: Unmarked
Date: 1880–1900
Price: $850.00–1,100.00
Credits: Ron Carr; Capitola, California

Category: Folk Art
Item Type: Tambourine
Classification: C-3
Dimensions: 6" d
Description: Tin, printed on front "Amos' Singing Minstrells." Good condition.
Artisan/Manufacturer: Unmarked
Date: 1900–1920
Price: $750.00–900.00
Credits: Ron Carr; Capitola, California

Category: Folk Art
Item Type: Doll
Classification: C-3
Dimensions: 8" h
Description: Cornhusk doll with applied lips made of rolled cornhusk. Cloth hat, original clothes, wood base. Cane in left hand.
Artisan/Manufacturer: Unmarked
Date: 1890–1920
Price: $225.00–370.00
Credits: Ron Carr; Capitola, California
Note of Interest: Common

Category: Folk Art
Item Type: Doll
Classification: C-3
Dimensions: 9½" h
Description: Cloth wound on wire, paper hat. Wire rim glasses, mohair wig and beard. Painted red mouth. Original clothes. Bible with pages in hand. Wood cane, tar paper base.
Artisan/Manufacturer: Unmarked
Date: 1900–1940
Price: $225.00–375.00
Credits: Ron Carr; Capitola, California
Note of Interest: Common

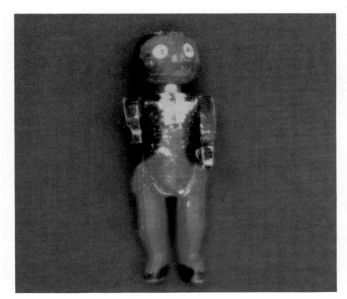

Category: Folk Art
Item Type: Doll
Classification: C-2
Dimensions: 1½" h
Description: All wood with painted features and moveable legs.
Artisan/Manufacturer: Unmarked
Date: 1890–1925
Price: $150.00–275.00
Note of Interest: Small dolls of this type are unusual. There is a possibility that it belongs with a doll house or game set.

Category: Folk Art
Item Type: Mechanical doll
Classification: C-1
Dimensions: 10½" h
Description: White metal head, hands cast iron, wood legs, cast iron feet, wood joints, clothing made of fabric, cast iron seat.
Artisan/Manufacturer: Jerome B. Secor
Date: 1880
Price: $25,000.00–30,000.00
Credits: Ron Carr; Capitola, California
Note of Interest: Instruction label attached. Clockwork mechanism. Right foot stomps; head nods or moves side to side.

Category: Folk Art
Item Type: Mr. Bones doll
Classification: B-1
Marks: Right side of box - 1¢ BANJO. Front flap - MR. BONES and a crude painting of a banjo. Left side - d/1¢.
Dimensions: Box - 26" h x 13½" w x 12½" d. Doll - 21¼".
Origin: U.S.A./Savannah Georgia
Description: An all wooden carved male with jointed hips, shoulders, knees, and elbows. The joints are mortise and tenon with specially jointed ankles. The doll is dressed in an original checkered cotton long pant suit with a red bowtie and molded wooden top hat. Carved painted features are exaggerated in caricature style. Each finger is crudely articulated. The doll comes in a large wooden case with a painted canvas flap and canvas carrying strap. The back of the box has a mechanism which makes the doll move when manipulated by hand. Excellent condition.
Date: ca. 1880–1910
Price: $10,000.00–12,000.00
Credits: John C. Newcomer - Americana
Note of Interest: Rare

Category: Folk Art
Item Type: Vessel
Classification: A-1
Description: Clay with alkaline glaze. (Not the usual salt glaze). Marked "March 31, 1858, Dave."
Artisan/Manufacturer: Dave (no last name), slave from Edgefield County, South Carolina.
Date: 1858
Credits: Photo by Louis Murdock
Note of Interest: Dave made pottery during the mid-1800s. Dave was a slave owned by Lewis Miles. It was unusual to allow a slave to sign or mark his creations. Dave pottery is signed "Dave" and the date. It is rare to find dated, fully documented signed pieces by slaves. What is just as rare is a slave being able to sign his or her name. These pieces are costly and scarce. Poetry may also be found on a piece of Dave pottery.

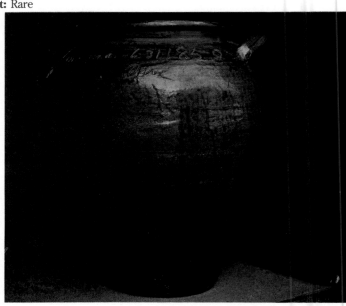

Additional Price Listings

These are additional prices on various items not pictured in the book.

Advertisement

Aunt Jemima Ad/advertising, compact nested aluminum set. Poster shows a matronly Black lady with cookware. Dated December 1919, full page 14" x 10". $195.00–225.00

Peck and Snyder Price List. Illustrated booklet with descriptions and prices of "Brudder's" Stump Speeches, Ethiopian Dramas, Darky Drama, Negro Wigs, Negro minstrel wigs and make-up. (7 pages) 5½" x 9", ca. early 1900s. $80.00–110.00

Multi-colored booklet with 16 pages; 31 verse songs and two with musical notes, five pages of various company product ads. Ca. 1930s–40s, 8¾" x 11½". $65.00–85.00

"Iron Horse Road Engine" advertisement emblem with yellow background and black lettering. Back cover has a colorful illustration of the engine. 2½" round, ca. early 1900s. Black jockey on a horse. Ritchie & Dyer Co. $55.00–65.00

"The Great American Tea Company" trade card on a blue background with black silhouetted figures on the front and the company's name on the reverse side, 4¾" x 3". $18.00–25.00

"Clark's O.N.T. Thread" trade card, colorful on the front with lettering on the reverse side. 2¾" x 3½". Black boy sitting straddle an oversized spool of thread. $18.00–25.00

"Alma Polish" trade card, colorful with the product name printed in white, plenty of lettering on the front and back of card. 3½" x 5". Black lady kneeling polishing a white lady's shoes. $18.00–25.00

"Clarence Brooks & Co. Varnishes" trade card, very colorful with two Black men dueling, reverse side blank. 4¾" x 3½". $20.00–30.00

Physician's trade card, "Dr. Henri Guillard's Persuaders," multi-colored picture on the front and lettering on the reverse side. 3¼" x 4¾". Black girl sitting on front. $18.00–25.00

"Ayer's Cathartic Pills" trade card, multi-colored. 2½" x 4½". Old Black man sitting, holding a small girl on his knee and a small boy kneeling. $18.00–25.00

"Rising Sun Stove Polish" trade card, tri-fold, multi-colored. 3½" x 5¾" closed; 6½" x 5¾" opened. $20.00–30.00

Black man in hammock, black and white card. 2½" x 4". Bed bugs on a chair and stool looking up at the man in the hammock, "Boss" Clothiers and Taylors, "Bed-Bugs Outwitted." $15.00–20.00

Young boy with a watermelon crawling through a fence. Colorful lithography. 7" x 10". Johnson & Stokes Garden and Farm Manual–1894. $195.00–225.00

Stand-up card "Great Atlantic and Pacific Tea Company." "Landlord – De rooms am airy and de place quiet. Chilun? Why bless de soul, dar ain't a chile in de neighborhood. Dinah. Yes sah, an we use de Great Atlantic & Pacific Tea Co.'s celebrated Teas and Coffees," print on reverse side, 1884. $95.00–115.00

Blotters representing the American Art Works, Inc., Coshocton, Ohio. "E.R. Bigelow" 228 Medford Road, R.R. 1, East Syracuse, N.Y. 3 different 4" x 9", with colorful lithographs depicting Blacks, 1927. $175.00–200.00 each

Insert flyer by L. Templin & Sons, Seedman & Florist, Calla, Ohio. Halftone of 4 Black children with the caption, "Say Boss, we's watchin' dem melons." Circa 1900. 3" x 5¾". $150.00–165.00

Print, representing "Becham's Patent Pills" (young woman in an apron with bill and cup in hands) circa 1900. 5" x 7", black and white. $45.00–65.00

Whiskey advertising poster, "I. W. Harper Grandfather's Whiskey, The Best the Market Affords." (A well-dressed woman with an umbrella doing her marketing with old male servant walking behind her carrying basket with bottle of I. W. Harper in basket), circa 1895, unframed, tinted halftone, 19½" x 24". $650.00–750.00

Framed, "Armour's Star Bacon" ad (Black chef displaying platter with bacon and eggs), colorful, 8" x 11". $325.00–400.00

Tin, "International Harness Soap and Ebony Oil Dressing," (Black male cleaning a harness), black and yellow lithograph. Ca. 1890. $125.00–150.00

Sample box of "Fun-To-Wash" washing powder, manufactured by the Hygienic Laboratories, Inc., Buffalo, New York, cardboard box. $75.00–85.00

Sample box of "Quick" Cream of Wheat. $75.00–95.00

Cigar box label, 6" x 10" (Black baby being stalked by an alligator) "Little African"/A Dainty Morsel, black/red with gold trim. $75.00–85.00

"Gold Dust" scouring cleanser, original used box with contents. Circa 1930. Small Black children depicted on the front of the box. $95.00–115.00

"Fun-To-Wash" washing powder manufactured only by the Hygienic Laboratories, Inc., Buffalo, N.Y., cardboard box.
$75.00–85.00

"Lucky Joe Bank," Nash's Prepared Mustard, glass face with original paper lips (which attach to the molded features of the jar), inside of this jar "only" has been painted black to add color to the image. Most jars are clear glass. Circa 1940–1960.
$30.00–65.00

Sample Box of Fairbank's "Gold Dust" scouring powder, tin bottom/top with cardboard sides.
$95.00–115.00

Paperweight, advertising "Johnson Hat Company," brightly colored lithograph of a Black man in formal attire in a red top hat.
$175.00–225.00

Cardboard color lithograph, cigar counter display (Black porter pushing a truck with travel trunk, "Redcap cigars – 5 cents"), 8½" x 9½", circa 1940.
$115.00–140.00

Cream of Wheat, framed ad "That's It – The Breakfast Food of the Nation" by Edward Brewer, 1920, 8½" x 13" in color.
$145.00–165.00

The Fisk Tire Co., beautiful magazine ad "Time to Re-tire a Fisk" (Young boy caught with a stolen watermelon which has dropped and is split in half in front of the boy) by Leslie Trasher, 8½" x 11½", 1925, matted.
$95.00–115.00

Cigar Box Labels: (2) "Lime Kiln Club" color lithograph labels depicting Blacks, framed, 1883.
$225.00–300.00 pair

"Ayer's Cathartic Pills" ad, (die-cut). (An elderly male with a baby sitting on his lap, crying because she has to take a pill which the man is about to give her. A small boy is kneeling beside the chair consoling the baby.) "The Country Doctor," 7" x 12½", framed, 1883.
$150.00–175.00

Whiskey Advertising Tin (plaque). "Paul Jones & Co., Louisville, KY" (whiskey). Left to right: woman with a slice of watermelon, a young boy on his knees and an elderly gentleman carrying a bottle of Paul Jones whiskey, with a house and chicken in the background. Color lithograph, with folded scroll corners, some wear and rust spots (good condition), "The Temptation of St. Anthony," ca. 1880.
$500.00–600.00

Whiskey Bottle: "Green River Whiskey" with a label on the back depicting a Black male with mule, b/w, clear glass bottle.
$150.00–175.00

Advertising Tin: "Mason's Original Challenge Blacking Plumber's Soil," yellow, black lithograph of Black male shining boots with dog and a young boy looking on, excellent condition, contents still intact.
$125.00–150.00

Wooden box with a paper lithograph "Mason's Challenge Blacking." Lithograph depicts a Black male shining boots with dog and young boy looking at the brilliant shine.
$150.00–175.00

"Beune Wafers" tins: Green/white round flat can with a designed top, color lithograph with yellow background. Black female cook with a basket; young boy being chased by a goose.
$125.00–150.00 each

Pepsodent, ca. 1930, "Amos & Andy," 2 stand-up die cuts.
$125.00–150.00 pair

Flashlight Crackers (firecrackers). "Dixie Boy Brand" color lithograph of a boy eating watermelon and one box has b/w label, "Cranberries - Harvest queen Early Blacks - Piccaninnies" (Three little girls with visions of cranberries and turkey), 1936.
$125.00–150.00

"The Regal Shoe" advertisement and two b/w cartoons. Brown/white with four babies. One cartoon is by Kembel. (3 items) Kembel-$175.00–185.00, others-$125.00–165.00 each

"Darkie Tooth Paste," Hawley & Hazel Chemical Co. Ltd., full tube, b/w tube with a portrait of a man in a top hat, original box.
$75.00–85.00

Tobacco Advertisement: 20" x 24", "Genuine Bull Durham Smoking Tobacco." Left to right: Boy on a railing of a fence looking at a bull in a field, pig, chicken and duck. Girl sitting on a porch eating watermelon, w/doll. Woman smoking a pipe in a rocking chair - "My! It shore am Sweet Tastum"), reproduction, 20" x 24", framed.
$750.00–850.00

"Southern Biscuit Co., Inc." tin, 10" diameter, color lithograph top of a Black butler serving tin of biscuits to three children and elderly female, 1926.
$145.00–165.00

Advertising cards: (23) cards from the 1880s and 1890s.
$15.00–25.00 each

Cream of Wheat Ads: "The Fortune Teller - You all Sh' is Gwine A Be A Great Man," color litho, and "Giddap, Uncle!", b/w lithograph, both are framed in rustic frames. (2 items)
$75.00–95.00 each

Flyer: 8½" x 11", advertising "Blome's Original ANNE RANNEL MELONS" (hard candy), black, red and brown, dated July 10, 1926, The George Blome & Son Co., Baltimore, Maryland, framed.
$125.00–145.00

Tobacco Advertisement (Poster). "Smoke Old Virginia Cheroots" Two couples out for a stroll. (The two men are possibly Bert Williams and George Walker, comedians of the early 1890's and 1900's.) 18" x 18", color lithograph, framed.
$900.00–1,000.00

Cream of Wheat Ads: "Ain't We Cute Cream of Wheat Kids?," "What do you Charge for Board, Sir?," "Sic'um, Tige," "Lest We Forget" and "The Autocrat of the Breakfast Table," unframed. (5 items)
$75.00–95.00 each

Cream of Wheat Ads: "That Settles It . . .?", "Cream of Wheat for Sail," "Jack, The Giant-Killer" and Small Girl playing with ABC blocks, (4 items) unframed.
$75.00–95.00 each

Advt. Mirrors and Pins, assortment of 4 tin-backed mirrors. 2 Fairbanks' "Gold Dust Washing Powder" (with twins), 3" x 2"; "Cotton Belt Route" with oval of child eating watermelon surrounded by frame of cotton blossoms, 3" x 2"; and "Aunt Jemima Breakfront Club," 3" dia. Also 3 asst. pins (3¼" dia.), "Trixy Coons Axle Geese/Best by Test" with picture of diapered child holding a racoon and "Natural History Series - The Blackbird-Habitat Coonland"; plus "Aunt Jemima Breakfast Club," 2¼" diameter. All repros. (8 items) $45.00–50.00 each

Advt. Packages: Gold Dust. Two products with the Gold Dust Twins. (1) "Fairbank's Gold Dust Washing Powder," cardboard carton, 2 lbs. 4 oz. size, with 16 pictures of the twins doing various household chores. (2) "Gold Dust Scouring cleanser," 14 oz. can. (2 items) $95.00–115.00 each

Advt. Poster: Green River Whiskey. Colorful ad depicting old top-hatted smiling man with his horse with demi-john of "Green River - The Whiskey Without Regrets" strapped to saddle. Old Tyme Distillers, Inc. 1919. Prints by Consolidated Lithograph Corp., Brooklyn, with Old Tyme Dist. stamp on reverse. Soiled, water damaged in margins, several tiny holes at lower right. 21" x 27½". $500.00–575.00

Advt. Print: Boot Jack Plug Tobacco. Large colorful lithographic print of two bare-bottomed little girls, seated, b/w, backs to readers in a large "Boot Jack Plug Tobacco" package reading a newspaper together titled *Tale of Two Cities*. With large column headline "Extra! War Over Boot Jack Plug." Background shows NY harbor skyline with Statue of Liberty left. N.p., n.d. (ca. 1917). 11½" x 9¼". $400.00–475.00

Advt. Print: Dukes Mixture. "Trotting Race in Blackville - The Start." Colorful comic cartoon with a jockey aboard a jerry-rigged homemade racer urging his horse on by hitting him with a jug of gin. Irregular measurement, rough cut margins - vertical from 13" to 11"; horizontal 15¾" (something apparently cut off and a name for jockey written in blue pencil lightly across right center of print). $150.00–200.00

Advt. Print: Gold Dust. The Gold Dust Twins depicted hard at work scrubbing in the bath tub with a package of "Fairbank's Gold Dust Washing Powder" shown on the stool nearby. "Kept Clean with Gold Dust." Copyright 1921 by N.K. Fairbanks Co., 12" x 21". $115.00–145.00

Advt. Print: Green River Whiskey. Colorful print depicting a top-hatted old bearded traveller with toothless grin in the stable yard holding the reins of his horse which has an umbrella and a large jug marked "Green River Wiskey Without Regrets" strapped to the saddle. Marked "Olde Tyme Distillery, Inc. 1935," printed by Consolidated Lithograph, Brooklyn. 19" x 13½" plus margins. In original frame, 24" x 19" overall. Bright and clean, lightly foxed in margins. $700.00–800.00 each

Advt. Print, Green River Whiskey. As above but in original frame with printed label on lower molding, 24" x 19" overall. Stained lower margin, marginal tears. $700.00–800.00 each

Advt. China: Shoyer's cup and saucer, heavy restaurant quality manufactured by Sterling, East Liverpool, Ohio. Pink and white decoration with inside wall of cup marked "Shoyer's" and with their waiter signature imprinted. Two Coon Chicken Inn items: B/B plate and saucer, each marked with smiling face and bell hop's cap signature. (3 items)
Shoyer's – $75.00–95.00 set
Coon Inn cup & saucer – $100.00–110.00 set
Coon Inn plate & saucer – $115.00–145.00

Advt. Egg Cup: Black plastic golliwog's open-headed top (to hold egg?) sets on blue-jacketed base with red tie and yellow vest marked with raised print name: "ROBERTSON'S GOLDEN SHRED." 2½" overall height x 1⅞" dia. top on ovoid base. 1¾" x 1¼". (Marmalade ad) $75.00–95.00

Advt. Flour Sack: Pull-over short-sleeved blouse cut out and sewn together apparently from a flour sack with a large center circle with colored print, bust length, of Jemima-type (facing slightly left) wearing a headkerchief. Sack marked "Negrita" (brand name), "Atlixco, Pueblo Mexico, Molina de San Mateo 44 Kilos." Colors quite faded. $115.00–145.00

Advt. Humidor: Stoneware. Old Green River Tobacco Co., Owensboro, Ky. Humidor in form of old whiskey jug with label depicting the famous old top-hatted man and his mule differing only from the Old Green River Whiskey in that the jug strapped to the mule is marked "Green River/Smoke Without a bite." One pound size, humidor is 8" high, 5½" diameter. $325.00–475.00

Advt. Items: (1) Dinah's Shack Menu. Large colorful printed menu with Mammy-style head of smiling woman wearing matching red and white checked neck scarf and head bandana. Ca. 1970, 19½" x 10½". (2) Cream of Wheat "CHEF" cardboard carton-end from carton originally containing 24, 14-oz. size packages. 10" x 8½". (2 items)
$55.00–70.00 each

Advt. Label: "Aunt Brand" colorful crate label with a head of a Mammy-type holding a sprig of citrus blossom (Alturas-Garfield Citrus Corp., Bartow, Polk Co., FL). 8½" x 3½".
$45.00–55.00

Advt. Labels: Three colorful advertising labels with desirable halftone prints. (a) "CAROGO BRAND/100% Pure Georgia Cane Syrup", Cane Growers Co-Operative Association, Cairo, GA, with print of large-lipped Chef holding syrup pitcher on tray before an outline of state of Georgia. 4 lb. 8 oz. can label. 5½" x 8". (b) "ZINFANDEL/SMALL BLACK BRAND" Victor Fruit Growers, Escalon, Ca. with print of small nude seated baby. 4" x 13". (c) "BLACK JOE/JUICE GRAPES" Ed Kurtz, Lodi, Cal. with print of youthful looking old "Black Joe" with bald dome and white-sided fringes and heavy white eyebrows. 4" x 13". (3 labels) $45.00–55.00 each

Advt. Label: Uncle Remus. Pictoral color lithograph label from 4 lb. 8 oz. can "Uncle Remus Brand syrup" with elderly smiling man pictured holding a can of U.R. Syrup saying "Dis

sho' am good," Robinson Syrup Co., Inc., Cairo, Georgia, copyright 1924. Litho. by H. Gamse & Bros. Baltimore, Md., 5¼" x 10½". Vertical tear across "contents" but not in picture.
$85.00–115.00

Jim Crow Sign: 4½" x 11", "Colored Seated in Rear," B&B Sign Co., August 1, 1929, framed. $125.00–150.00

Pencil Holders: Alligator with Black head sticking out of his mouth, celluloid, 5" long and 8½" long (souvenir of Atlantic City). (2 items) $65.00–75.00 each

Coke trays depicting Negros. "The Romance of Coke" series. (2 items) $150.00–175.00 each

Advertisement Tin: "Old Fashioned Molasses Kisses," Retail Stores United Candy Service, 6½" x 8" x 2¼", picture of Blacks working on the docks with cotton, paddle boat in the background. $125.00–145.00

Aluminum Cup: A collapsible cup advertising "Old Man River Pure Rye Whiskey" (Black male on bottom playing banjo, embossed). $80.00–100.00

Advt. Calendar: Clarence Brooks & Co. 2 pairs of colored lithograph cartoon prints from calendar (ca. 1900) given out by Clarence Brooks & Co. Fine Coach Varnishes, N.Y. (1) June & July - "What Dat White Trash Done Lock Dis Yer Gate Fer" & Why the Gate was Locked - As bull creates havoc. (2) Oct. & Nov. - Shooting at the Birds - but getting the laundry as the dog puts the bite on. Each pair framed together. (4 prints) $150.00–175.00 per pair

Advt. Calendar: Clarence Brooks & Co. Twelve individual advertising cards isssued by Clarence Brooks & Co. Fine Coach Varnish, N.Y. Complete for one calendar year, 12 months (ca. 1900) with colorful comic - cartoon prints (five in pairs): Mule Up (& Down) the Hill; Horse and Carriage (Racing and Breaking Up); Look Out for the Bull (at the Gate and In the Yard); Hunter and Clothes Lines; Row Boat w/ Alligators; Ephraim at the Tiller. Clean and bright, fine condition except for the three cord holes at top margin of each card. Beautifully matted with 13 openings in one large frame. (12 cards) $50.00–55.00 each; $700.00–800.00 set of 12

Advt. Cards: Domestic and comic. Three Domestic Sewing Machine Co. advertising cards: Admiring the Domestic - "Dat is the sheen Ise Yearning For," "Wes don got de Domestic, The Domestic Salesman and the goat." Together with four comic/advertising cards. (4 cards) $25.00–30.00 each

Advt. Cards: Domestic and comic. Eight colorful business and manufacturer's advertising cards including: Burdock Blood Bitters, Higgins Soap, Halsted St. Hat Store, Fellows Bros. Gent's Furnishers & Shirt Makers, Dixon's Caburet of Iron Stove Polish, Kandi Kubes, Warner's Sage Yeast and Palace Cars (R.R.). (Eight cards) $25.00–30.00 each

Advt. Cartoon: "Greedy Nigger Money Box," "Every Child

Loves the Nigger." Red, yellow and black cardboard cartoon with print of a modern version of the Jolly Nigger Mechanical Penny Bank. Mfg. by H.C. Urlwin, Ltd., Ch. Ch. 5¼" x 5¼" x 6¼"h (box only). $75.00–85.00

Trade Cards: Eight different trade cards, various sizes including two die-cuts (Mill St. Store & Dandy Jim), Maid with child, McLaughlin's XXXX Coffee, Arbuckel's Ariosa Coffee (Louisiana & Mississippi - latter torn), Sollers & Co., Shoes, Beggs' Family Medicine, Conkling & Chivvis Dry Goods (maid with baby). (8 pieces) $20.00–25.00 each

Trade Folders: Three colorful advertising folders: Oakley's Queen Soap with offer of free stereoscopic views, John L. Whiting & Son Brushes and A Tale of the Rising Sun Stove Polish. $55.00–75.00 each

Advt. Cards: "Great Atlantic & Pacific Tea Co." Set of five cards (Church Congregation being raided after misunderstanding by police.) $25.00–35.00 each

Advt. Cards: "Higgin's German Laundry Soap", set of seven cards (days of the week), few are rough. $25.00–30.00 each
$225.00–250.00 set of 7

Advt. Cards: 18 different Victorian cards. $25.00–30.00 each

Advt. Card: "Bootblack Stands," established in 1880 - Ten Chairs - No Waiting - Oldest and Best Stand in City - W.H. Gaskill - Broad and Filbert Streets, Philadelphia" (photo view of stand with 12 bootblackers working and standing around stand; reverse side lists "Places of Interest" in Philadelphia), 2⅝" x 5½". $150.00–175.00

Advt. Cards: "Dr. Thomas' Electric Oil" (Abe Johnson's Picnic; The Ride and The Wind Up) "Burdock Blood Bitters" (Abe Johnson's Pic-Nic; "The Start," 2 cups) 4¼" x 6¼", 4 items, excellent condition. $35.00–45.00 each

Advt. Cards: "Anthony and Ellis' Famous Ideal 'Uncle Tom's Cabin' Co." 7 different cards, 3½" x 5½" (one card has tear.) $25.00–35.00 each

Advt.: Two large "Cream of Wheat" ads. Common types.
$75.00–95.00 pair

Cardboard Box: "Blanket and Woolen Cleanser" Johnson Mfg. Co., Baltimore, Maryland. 1" x 3¼" x 5½". Woman holding blanket. Black, white and red, never used.
$110.00–125.00

Wooden Box: "Mason's Challenge Blacking" shoe polish. 5" x 11¼" x 7½" with two color lithographs. (Lid: 6½" dia. - man shining boots while young boy looks at image in shine with two dogs, coach in left background. Front: Logo/title very colorful.) $150.00–175.00

Candy Box: "Amos n' Andy" Williamson Candy Co., Chicago - Brooklyn - San Francisco. 3" x 8½" x 11½", lithograph, orange background, ca. 1930. $175.00–195.00

Wooden Shipping Crate: "Gold Dust Twins Washing Powder." 12½" x 19½" x 27½", stenciled on 4 sides in black ink (logo on two sides), open top. $200.00–250.00

Advt. Print: J & P Coats. Colorful print of young boy riding a large cotton spool of J&P Coats and pointing up at the large sad-faced bright sun with motto "We Never Fade." 12" x 7½". $125.00–150.00

Advt. Print: Old Virginia Cheroots. "Smoke Old Virignia Cheroots-3 for 5 cents" (The Cake Walk). Colorful lithograph depicts smiling dandy wearing green pants, red jacket, long ankle-length cream coat and green hat with a beautiful young lady on each arm. (No doubt attracted by the package of "Old Virginia" in each hand.) Another young man, not an Old Virginia customer, is left disappointed with hat in hand. (In original fine walnut Victorian frame). 17¾" x 18¼". $800.00–900.00

Advt. Print: Poster for Book/Play. Large colorful theater poster "White Slave by Bartley Campbell" depicting (foreground right) arrogant plantation owner wearing riding boots with riding crop under arm looking admiringly at octoroon (?) maiden (looking apprehensive) at foreground left, with numerous cotton field laborers at work and mansion in distance. Copyright 1911 by the Strobridge Lithograph Co., Cincinnati/N.Y. 27" x 38" plus margins. (Slightly apart at one of original folds). $800.00–900.00

Advt. Print: Regal Shoes. Colored print of kneeling bellhop holding and admiring a shoe (obviously Regal) of a number of pairs of shoes to be polished placed outside of a hotel room by the room's occupant. *Harper's Magazine*. Nov. 1921. 9½" x 6½". $75.00–95.00

Advt. Print: Sapolio. Victorian die-cut oval color lithograph advt. smiling boy's head peering from within a ripe watermelon marked "Sapolio." Reverse hand printed ad for Enoch Morgan's Sons Sapolio Scouring Soap. Lithograph by Donaldson Bros., 1882. 4" x 2¾". $55.00–65.00

Advt. Print: Winchester. Colorful "hunting" print. Young man poking a long stick into a hollow log looks aghast as a skunk emerges. The hunter jumps back and fends off the critter while the hunting dog cringes and also runs. Winchester Repeating Arms Co., 18" x 26." $700.00–800.00

Advt. Push Plate: Fine hand-printed porcelain enamel sheet metal grocery store door push plate. Gentleman dressed in colorful bright blue, yellow and red with gremlin (?) or golliwog (?) head holding a jar of Robertson's Golden Shred Marmalade (against green background). Mfg. by Dodo Designs, Ltd., Kent England. 14½" x 6½". $150.00–200.00

Advt.: Aunt Jemima White Corn Meal. 25 lb. white cloth sack with colorful paper label of the famous lady herself. With "Aunt Jemima Breakfast Club" paper hat, "Eat a Better Breakfast." Both mint. (2 pieces) $150.00–175.00 each

Advt. Trick Print: Cardboard card with colored print of smiling woman's head with closed eyes and big-lipped closed mouth. Tab at base marked "Pull." When pulled, the woman's eyes open and her mouth shows lots of teeth. Ad printed on back "Mrs. Schmidt's Bread for Husky Appetites." (Balto.) Apt. Lithograph, N.Y. ca. 1930. 4¼" x 3". $65.00–95.00

Advt. Recipe Books: 2 different Knox Gelatin recipe books, "Dainty Desserts for Dainty People." Publ. by Chas. B. Knox Co., Johnstown, N.Y. Small paperback volumes, each 40 pgs. First compiled by Janet McK. Hill, (1909); second publ. 1924. Each cover depicts b/w children dressed in chef's hats holding plates of gelatin dessert. (2 books) $65.00–75.00 each

Advt. Tins: 2 advertising tins. (1) Banner Shoe Stain Polish depicting a small boy with his portable shoe stand shining a gentleman's shoe. Banner Color Dyes Corp., New York, 3⅝" dia; 2¾ fl. oz. tin. (2) "Wow" aluminum and metal polish. ½ pt. tin, orange and black colors with little boy holding a cleaned frying pan in hand. Mfg. by A.P. & F. Co., Chicago. $75.00–95.00 each

Advt. Tins: Bixby. Two round flat tins manufactured by S.M. Bixby and Co., N.Y. (1) Bixby's "Ox Blood" Shoe Paste #10 (3¼" dia.) with cover color to match that of the Bixby Shoeshine Man at his stand polishing a gentleman's shoes (within a horseshoe outline). (2) Bixby's "Sationola" #2½ (1¾" dia.) yellow and black tin with same shoeshine man. (2 items) $75.00–95.00

Advt. Tins: International Harness Soap. Yellow and black decorated tin (sheet metal) can, 5¼" dia. x 1¼" h. with painted label depicting stable boy polishing a horse collar with a lot of tack behind him. Marked: "International Harness Soap and Ebony Oil Dressing." Manufactured by Int'l Stock Food Co., Minneapolis (ca. 1910). $95.00–115.00

Advt. Tins: Luzianne. Large lunch-pail size can marked Luzianne (ca. 1930) with the Luzianne Maid depicted (front and back) serving a tray with coffee pot and steaming cup of coffee. (Wm. B., Reily & Co., Inc., New Orleans & Baltimore.) 3 lb. can, 6" dia., 7½" h. with lid and bail for carrying. $150.00–165.00

Advt. Tins: "Mason's Original Challenge Blacking", 3½" dia. tin with transfer label of youth holding oversize boot while shoeshine man, holding a boot and brush, dances a jig (ca. 1870–1890.) Mfg. by Jas. S. Mason, Inc., Phila. $90.00–115.00

Advt. Tray: Budweiser. Tin (sheet metal) rectangular serving tray with scene entitled "St. Louis Levee in Early Seventies" depicting laborers on-loading cases and barrels of Budweiser aboard "R.E. Lee" sidewheel steamboat. Anheiser-Busch, Inc., St. Louis, 1914. Red curved margins, top marked "Budweiser" and bottom "King of Bottled Beer." Slightly marred and scarred. 13" x 17½". $210.00–250.00

Advt. Catalog: Shawknit - Shaw Stocking Co., Lowell, Mass.

"Catalogue for the Wearer - Colors Are Fast Like Mine" with 5 illustrations of children. 16 pages, in original envelope, used, but very clean, 1905. $80.00–95.00

Advt.: Cream of Wheat Chef. Two large colorful Cream of Wheat full-page magazine ads (1) Print from Leslie Wallace painting, 1916, bulldog biting seat of overalls of boy climbing chef's billboard after swiping apples from orchard. "Ah've always said and now repeat - Ma health am due to Cream of Wheat." (R) (2) Print from painting by Denman Fink, 1908–09 "A Case of Desertion" - young lad eating bowl of Cream of Wheat with back turned on half of watermelon with chef's sign in background. (R) $75.00–95.00

Advt. Fan: "Mason's Blacking" in color, depicting boy with boot and shoeshine man dancing. 6¾" dia. (lacks stick to hold card for fanning.) $65.00–75.00

Advt. Photo: Sign. V.A. Stein, Tailor (Penna.) Announcement (to the trade) "Get Your Orders in Quick - Dey Ain't going To Be None Left" based around photo of a street urchin eating a large slice of watermelon with the same words "Dey Ain't Going to be None Left." Copyright 1901, J. Austen & Co., Chicago. 10" x 13¼". $100.00–115.00

Advt. Postcard: Two "Korn Kinks" advertising postcards with comic illustrations (1907). $40.00–55.00 each

Advt. Poster: O'Baby. Store display ad for "O'Baby Chocolate Dairy Drink" titled "Ain't Dat Sumptin" depicting happy little boy licking his lips in anticipation. 22½" x 14½". $135.00–160.00

Advt. Print: Progress Beer. Colored photographic halftone print (or sign) of three men at makeshift table playing cards. The two on the left and right are cheating the third man at the table by passing an ace between them. There are 3 bottles of "Progress Beer" on the table and the men are seated on empty cases of "Progress Beer." Progress Brewing Co., Okla. City. 11" x 16½". $175.00–200.00

Advt. Products: "Go for a Smile" - Three new cartons with three large unused tubes of Darkie Toothpaste. Illustration on carton and tube is top-hatted man with bowtie and big, bright smile. Two new unused cartons of "Black Power" with erotic figure of native man wearing a shirt which when parted reveals hidden power. (Not to be sold to anyone under 18). (Five items) Top hat - $75.00–85.00 each
Erotic - $95.00–110.00

Advt. Sign: Cardboard sign, "Hylton and O'Brien Undertakers & Embalmers - Cambridge, Mass." Cambridge, Mass. - Automobile or Horse-Drawn Equipment with two photoprints at either side of the owners (ca. 1925), Creased, slight scrape. $135.00–150.00

Advt. Tin: Black & Tan. "The Original Black & Tan" sheet metal tin (cigar humidor made to hold ten cigars). Two side-by-side pictures of children. Reverse: Spriggs' Black and Tan/5c Hand Made 5C. A.E. Spriggs, Joplin, Mo., 1904, 5½" h x 3¼" x 3¼". $135.00–155.00

Advt. Tin: Glycerole. Large advertising tin representing metal trunk w/advertisement for "Glycerole for Oiling and Dressing Shoes" inside lid with four circles depicting Glycerole men with high boots. Restorff & Bettmann, Mfg., N.C. 13" x 7" x 9". Slightly battered condition. $110.00–150.00

Advt. Tin: Tobacco. "Niggerhair Smoking Tobacco" can with transfer print front and back of African's head (profile) wearing large earring and nose ring. 2 lb. tin with metal bail (use later as lunch pail). 5½" dia. x 6½" h. (B. Leidersdorf Co., Milwaukee). 1939 U.S. Int. Rev. stamp dated. $600.00–750.00

Trade Cards: 12, various sizes. Trade cards including New Home Sewing Machine Co., Hotel Nantasket, Lautz Bros. & Co. Soaps, Singer Mfg. Co., Dunham's Concentrated Coconut, Zieback Millinery Puzzle Card, Henry's Carbolic Salve, Carter's Mucilage, etc. plus Clam Bake at Melville Gardens and two Christmas cards (12 items). $15.00–25.00 each

Trade Cards: 10 different trade cards, various sizes. Mostly colorful cartoons including Wilson Reliable Yeast, Fleischmann's Yeast, Geo. E. Lane (Books), Sapolis (Reformed Burglar), Highland Brand Evaporated Cream, Obelish Pickles, etc. (10 cards) $15.00–25.00 each

Advt. Salt/Pepper: Pair "Laniappe of New Orleans" plastic Jemima-style figural shakers (marked S & P) wearing yellow blouses and red skirts with striped blue on white head kerchief and holding a blue and white coffee pot with cup and saucer. 5" H. (2 items) $75.00–110.00 pair

Advt. Sample: Maid Aid. Free sample (4 fl. oz.) bottle of "Maid Aid/Washes Anything" with label picture of maid wearing head scarf and red/white plaid dress with white apron. (An-Fo Mfg. Co., Oakland, California). $75.00–85.00

Advt. Card: Great India Tea Co. - Colorful figural flat cardboard cut-out of "mammy" serving huge turkey on platter. 11⅞" x 6¼" Reverse marked "Great India Tea Co., Utica." $15.00–25.00

Advt. Card: Leibig Co. - Color print depicting Robinson Crusoe trying to persuade group of natives to release Friday who is tied to a tree. Leibig Co. Extract of Meats, London (ca. 1890) with directions of advt. blurb on reverse. 2¾" x 4¼" (2) Bon Voyage Card - color card to friends going on journey. Cartoon of porter overladen with trunk bag, camera case and golf clubs: "Gee! Ah sho' hates to see folks lak yo' go away!' 5" x 4". (2 cards) $15.00–25.00 each

Advt. Cards: Lot of 8 colorful advt. cards, ca. 1885 including The Reformed Burglar (Sapolio); Knowles' New Photograph Studio (stubborn mule), Horse and Carriage (Domestic Sewing Machine Co.); Church Revival (Tansill's Punch - 5¢ Cigar); Keno's Chew; Kerr's Cotton. (8 cards) $15.00–25.00 each

Advt. Ornament: "Virginia Blend" 3-dimensional figure, young man seated on tree stump, left hand in pocket, right elbow on knee with hand on chin (a la "the Thinker"). Metal plate over copper (plaster-filled). 9" H. on 6¼" x 3½" base.
$175.00–225.00

Ad Booklet: Fairbank's Gold Dust Washing Powder. "Who Are We?" (die-cut Gold Dust Twins looking over book) 1907.
$75.00–95.00

Advt. Toothpick Holder: Bellhop bust figure with big wide grin and winking eye (unmarked symbol of Coon Chicken Inn). Heavy metal with copper finish painted black, red and white. Toothpicks fit into hollow pillbox hat. Rare. 3½" H.
$80.00–90.00

Advt. Vase: Tall ceramic vase with high relief figure of Chef wearing very large chef's hat with wording "Smokquee" deeply inscribed. Semi-vitreous china, marked on base "The Royal Boise, Idaho." (Vase apparently used to hold spatulas and other long-handled kitchen implements or as a celery holder.) 7½" H., mouth dia. 2½", approximately 4" at widest point. Green, brown and black on white. $95.00–110.00

Advt. Bookmark: "Dunham's Coconut" with maid holding coconut pie and printed recipes using coconut on front and reverse. $35.00–45.00

Advt. Brochure: Large full-size 8 pg. brochure for retail merchants from Hickok Belts and Buckles using cover of *Saturday Evening Post*, Jan. 4, 1921. Illustrations by Herbert Beniert of a men's room valet brushing off a customer displaying a Hickok buckle. 14" x 11". $60.00–70.00

Advt. Can: "Gold Dust Scouring Cleanser" with twins on label. Tin top and base, cardboard tube center. 14 oz. can.
$95.00–115.00

Advt. Cards: Clarence Brooks & Co. Varnishes. 5 different humorous color advt. cards series including: (1) "Who Struct De Fustest?" (2) Return of the First Born from College, (3) The First Ulster in Blackville, (4) Christmas Dinner Gone, (5) The "Fourth" in Blackville. Each 4¾" x 3⅜" from Clarence Brooks & Co. Fine Coach Varnishes, N.Y. (5 cards)
$15.00–25.00

Advt. Card: Clark's O.N.T. Spool Cotton (1 of 4) Industrial Set-Cotton Picker of the South. $15.00–25.00

Advt. Card: "Dixon's Carburet of Iron Stove Polish," colorful cartoon showing Uncle Obadiah telling his 10 little nieces and nephews about Dixon's Stove Polish. $35.00–40.00

Advt. Poster: "Green River Whiskey." Colorful ad depicting old top-hatted man with toothless smile holding reins of his horse, while it eats, with demijohn of "Green River - The Whiskey Without Regrets" strapped to saddle. Consol. lithograph 1935, in original frame with "Green River Whiskey" name on lower molding. 23" x 17". $700.00–800.00

Advt. Poster: "Peerless Hair Dressing." Peerless Beauty Supplies poster with 20 b/w halftone portraits of models showing hair styles. Photos by "The Browns," Richmond, Va. (Approx. 20" x 15", ca. 1935–1940). $145.00–170.00

Advt. Print: Cream of Wheat. "A Case of Desertion," color print from painting by Denman Fink, 1909, depicting boy seated on crate spooning from bowl, his back turned on a half-watermelon and large cut slice of watermelon left below a picture of the Cream of Wheat Chef. 15½" x 10½" (R) reverse of cover pictorial revue, July 1918; linen backed.
$75.00–95.00

Advt. Print: Cream of Wheat. "Ah Reckon As How He's De Bes' Known Man in De Worl." Colorful print from painting by Rowland M. Smith, 1913, depicting bent and bearded top-hatted old man admiring billboard picture of Cream of Wheat chef. 15½" x 10½" (R) reverse of cover of *Today's Magazine for Women,* April 1914; linen backed. $75.00–95.00

Advt. Prints: Cream of Wheat Chef. (1) "Them's My Sentiments", young boy in overalls with straw hat pointing to Cream of Wheat ad pasted to fence, from painting by James Les Wallace, copyright 1913 (appearing on reverse of *Pictoral Review* cover, April 1919) (2) "That Settles It", the chef with large question mark (copyright 1912) (appearing on reverse of *Pictorial Review* cover, Feb. 1918). (2 prints)
$75.00–95.00

Advt. Print: Cream of Wheat. "Dat's Mah Boy" print from painting by Edw. V. Brewer showing old man seated on doorstep holding a picture of the Cream of Wheat chef ad. 11" x 14". On reverse of 1918 cover. $75.00–95.00

Advt. Print: Cream of Wheat. "The Fortune Teller - You all Sho's gwine a be a great man." Full color print from painting by Edw. V. Brewer, 1914, depicting elderly man seated at Cream of Wheat crate-base table in kitchen telling the chef his fortune from a deck of cards. 15½" x 10½" (R) *Today's Magazine for Women,* Sept. 1914, linen backed.
$75.00–95.00

Advt. Print: Cream of Wheat. "Mammy's Beau" color print from painting Edw. V. Brewer, 1920, depicting a large cook in bandana and apron showing two little children a magazine picture of Cream of Wheat chef. 15½" x 10½" (R) *Companion for All the Family*, May 27, 1920; linen backed.
$75.00–95.00

Advt. Print: Cream of Wheat. "No, Sah! Ah Don't Want No 'Substitute', Ah Want Cream O' Wheat." Color print from painting by Edward V. Brewer, 1914, of top-hatted elderly man standing at grocery store counter pointing out his choice to store owner with advt. of Cream of Wheat chef tacked to counter. 15½" x 10½" (R), linen backed. $75.00–95.00

Advt. Print: Cream of Wheat chef. "Opening the Case" print from painting by Edward V. Brewer (1918) on back of *Pictorial Review,* Jan. 1918, (16" x 11"). Shows children seated and standing around the chef while he opens a wooden case of Cream of Wheat. $75.00–95.00

Advt. Print: Cream of Wheat. Print of small child almost completing building block picture of "The Chef." Painted by W.B. Cahill, copyright 1909, on reverse of *Ladies' Home Journal,* Aug. 1919 issue, 10½" x 15½". $75.00–95.00

Advt. Print: Cream of Wheat. "Putting It Down In Black & White" print from painting by Edward V. Brewer, depicting 2 children holding their bowls and licking their spoons with the chef standing behind them. 11" x 16" from Sept. 1919 issue *The Companion for All the Family.* $75.00–95.00

Advt. Print: Cream of Wheat. "Sho' Dat's De Papah Ah Wants." Color print from painting by Edward V. Brewer, 1916, of top-hatted elderly man buying newspaper/magazine with cover of Cream of Wheat Chef. 15½" x 10½" (R), reverse cover of *Pictorial Review,* Aug. 1916; linen backed. $75.00–95.00

Advt. Cards: Set of 3 "Who's Afraid?" Series, E.V. Price & Co. Chicago (Tailors) showing Afraid of - ocean waves, turkey gobbler, horse chestnut burr seed pod; Babbitt's Best Soup (election platform) and "Yes Sah I Takes Your Ordah for Van Camp's Pork & Beans." (5 pieces) $15.00–25.00 each

Advt. Cards: Printer's Samples - Set of 3 humorous cards: (1) Black and white boys about to fight egged on by Mrs. O'Toole in window. "Give it to 'em Mickey. T'was for de loikes of sich as him yer fayther got kilt in the war." (2) Nurse with triplets. Father: "Did any of them get away?" (3) Boy with watermelon under each arm on top fence rail, dog put hole in his pants. "Which will let go first, the dog or the darkey?" Blank rectangular space below each picture for retailer's advt. 4" x 2½". Black and white. (3 cards) $15.00–25.00

Advt. Cards: Sports. Set of 4 humorous cards, copyright Frank Beard (1) Croquet "Great Jerusalem"; (2) Polo on a jackass "Who, Jimmy", (3) Tennis "Sho Fly! Go Way From Dar!"; (4) Archery "Keep Your Eye on de Bull's Eye." (4 cards) $15.00–25.00 each

Advt. Carton: Cream of Wheat "Chef". On cardboard, from a carton of 24 - 14 oz. size packages. 9½" x 10¾". $75.00–95.00

Advt. Cookbooks & Recipes: (a) Mills, Mary. "Fisher's Cooky Book", Fisher Flouring Mills, Seattle (1937) with recipes for cookies, 24 pages. (b) Murray, Mary B. "Let's Enjoy Eating." Wesson Oil and Snowdrift People, 1932. 29 pp. both paperbacks. Watch with cover of interest (a) Chef Blen (b) Child Eating Watermelon. (2 books) $45.00–55.00 each

Advt. Doll: Cream of Wheat. Rare uncut cloth doll, like new, of the Cream of Wheat Chef printed in color on linen, with dotted line and directions how to sew material and stuff to create a charming 19" stuffed cloth doll. Together with original Cream of Wheat brown envelope (with 3¢ stamp) in which this advt. was mailed (ca. 1925). $125.00–145.00

Advt. Easel Card: Stand-up die-cut card from "Wm. A. Hentz & Co. Fine Old Whiskies - Philadelphia, Pa." 2 babies in basket, each holding an end of a large slice watermelon. Color lithograph. 6" x 8½", ca. 1885. $65.00–75.00

Advt. Gold Dust: "The Gold Dust Twins" grind out a reel of film from a soap powder box showing themselves making housework easier with Fairbanks Gold-Dust Washing Powder. 15½" x 10½", 1916 (R), linen backed. $75.00–95.00

Advt. Labels: "Aunty Brand" colorful crate label with a head of a "mammy"-type holding a spring of citrus blossom (Alturas-Garfield Citrus Coop. Bartow, Polk Co. Fl) 8½" x 3½" (2) "F.B. & C. Kid" magazine ad titled "Colored Kids Make a Costume Vastly More Attractive" with a boy and girl playing a trick on attractive woman, raising skirt displaying high button shoes of the manufacturer, (1920). (2 items) $35.00–45.00 each

Advt. Menu: Dinah's Shack. Large printed colorful menu with "mammy"-style head of smiling women wearing red and white checked neck and head bandanas. Ca. 1970.
$45.00–55.00

Advt. Calendar Plate: White semi-vitreous china plate, 7½" dia. with transfer print of boy eating slice of watermelon seated before a fence with prints of months of year, watermelon by his side marked "1915" and "Compliments of W.H. Rowe/Coal & Wood/Bristol, Conn." 2 age cracks.
$65.00–75.00

Advt. Carton: Coon Chicken Inn carry-out box. Cardboard carton, purple and red, print of their bellhop (mascot) with their logo on front and top of box. 3" x 4" x 7".
$65.00–75.00

Advt. Cereal Bowl: "Aunt Jemima's Kitchen" white ironstone 6⅜" dia. bowl with grey border and a signpost ad of Aunt Jemima's Kitchen. Marked on back "Made expressly for 'Aunt Jemima's Kitchens' by Wellsville China." $95.00–110.00

Advt. Comic Cards. Set of 4 cards advertising Locomotive Firemen's Old time Pic-Nic (Phila.), 1882, Lithograph by J.M. Buffords Son. (1) In Land of Cotton. (2) Going to Plantation. (3) Noon Hour on Plantation. (4) A Cabin in the Good Old Time. (4 cards) $25.00–35.00 each

Advt. Display: "Falstaff Beer" 3-dimensional display with cardboard cutout of "Marzetta Freeman/Radio & Television Star" photo holding projecting cardboard parasol with lacy edging. Approximately 21" x 15" x 5" deep at parasol. Lithograph by Falstaff Brewing Corp., St. Louis, Mo. (Cardboard creased in center). $125.00–150.00

Advt.: Tailors. Magazine *IT* (Int'l. Tailoring Co.), May, 1923. Tropical Number with cover picture of Native Man with banana leaf skirt, umbrella, barefooted but wearing hard sleeve cuffs as anklets on a tropical island beach. (2) Card from Wile, Weill & Co., Bufffalo (Tailors) used with one-cent stamp. 1905. $20.00–25.00 each

Advt. Tin: "Banner Black Shoe Stain Polish," Banner Color Dyes Corp., N.Y. Label depicts small boy with shoeshine box shining shoes. 3¾" dia. $85.00–95.00

Advt. Tin: Zeno Chewing Gum. Large tin display, 9½" L x 2¼" x 4½" manufactured by Amer. Can Co., with colored lithograph interior of lid depicting Black male lying atop wall and reaching toward the ground for pack of "Zeno Chewing Gum/Uncommonly Good!/In Every Flavor." Slight dents. $145.00–160.00

Advt. Tip Tray: Tin tip or pin tray 4¼" dia. with picture of woman with little girl in cotton field picking cotton. Marked around border: "The Source of Cottolene - Best for shortening - Best for Frying." Reverse has directions for Cottolene's use. $150.00–165.00

Advt. Print: Aunt Jemima. "Aunt Jemima Pancake Flour" color full-page advt. with partial page devoted to pictures of the "jolly family of Aunt Jemima rag dolls" - Aunt Jemima, Uncle Mose, Little Diana and Little Wade-all for 25¢ and top of package, (R) *Ladies' Home Journal,* Dec. 1924; linen backed. $95.00–110.00

Advt. Print: "Cream of Wheat Is Not Only a Dainty Dish for Little People but . . ." Color print depicting older child watching tiny tot seated in Cream of Wheat pull wagon eating Cream of Wheat while chef watches and farmer threshes wheat. (R) *McClure's Magazine,* Nov. 1901. 9¾" x 6½". $65.00–75.00

Advt. Recipe Book: Royal Baking Powder Co., N.Y., 1926. (1) "The Comical Cruises of Captain Cooky," 24 pages. Small 8 vol. self wraps, with numerous color illustrations including "The Little Blackmen." (2) Lustig, Sondheim & Rensel - The Southern Cook Book of Fine Old Recipes, Culinary Arts Press, Reading, Pa., 1939. 48 pages. Paper cover with sketch and well done little corner sketches on most pages (332 recipes). $65.00–75.00 each

Advt. Sign: Cigars. Round colorful window or light-string sign, "J.P. Alley's Hambone Sweets 5¢ Cigars" with happy smoker piloting old single-engine plane. 7" dia. (ca. 1925–1930). $55.00–65.00

Advt. Trade Cards: 15 colorful cards (ca. 1885) advertising Duluth Imperial Mills, Arbuckle's Coffee, Condell's Baking Powder, Tuttle's Shoes, various confectioners, J. Temple's Gloves, Smith's Dry Goods, Acme Soap, King's Buckwheat, Keystone Watch Cases (depicting chefs, musicians, ball games, etc.), Various sizes, various conditions (mostly excellent). (15 cards) $35.00–45.00 each

Advt. Trade Cards: 5 cards with color lithograph of woman with baby, woman in window, etc. Cards filled in with ads for Atlantic & Pacific Tea Co., I.H. Dudley & Co., C.N. Oehm & Son (Balto.), Zahm & Co. Books (Lancaster). $45.00–55.00 each

Advt. Trade Cards: Set of 4 comic trade cards of the Twin series - Introduction, Wooing, Duel & Wedding. 2" x 4¼". Lithograph by Miller and Umbdenstock, Chicago, ca. 1890. (Four cards) $150.00–175.00 set

Advt. Wooden Box: Mason's Challenge Blacking. Interior label 11" x 7" with color lithograph of shoe shine man proudly displaying large polished boot with young boy and dog admiring the brilliant shine. Exterior label parially destroyed but with circular signature as above. 11" x 7¾" x 4½". Good condition. $150.00–175.00

Advt. Print: White's Delicious Bread, colored print "Happy Days" by Henry Ihlefeld of four Black children (forefront) watching enviously as white boy and girl pass by on a wagon pulled by 2 little boys (ca. 1910). 15" x 9¾" $150.00–175.00

Advt. Misc.: (1) "Aunt Jemima Breakfast Club - Pancakes" paper hat. (2) "Stafford's Blacks" crate label picturing child wearing feathered colander, 4" x 13". (3) Comic wall card - man sitting on fence watching fox chase rabbit, 7" x 11". (4) "Dinah's Shack" match book. (4 items) $45.00–55.00 each

Advt. Sewing Kit: "Luzianne Coffee and Chicory" can-shaped folder containing needles. 4½" x 2¾". $60.00–75.00

Containers

Spice Racks: Black matronly females, full, six containers. Red and white clothing. $275.00–375.00

Salt and Pepper Shakers, ceramic Black male and female, older, 5". $65.00–85.00 pair

Cream Pitcher: Black matronly female, plastic, 5". $65.00–85.00

Cups: Ceramic, Black male and female, older, 2¾". $90.00–115.00 pair

Cookie Jar: Ceramic, Black matronly female, paint missing, 10". (as is) $135.00–165.00

Cookie Jar: Ceramic, good condition, marked "USA," 10". $175.00–250.00

Decanter: Ceramic, Gin, 12¼", marked "Japan." $125.00–150.00

Pitcher: Pitcher face of Black male and female, older, marked "Japan," pair. $145.00–165.00

Tobacco Tin: Black fat female, pipe in mouth, 7"-8", "Mayo Co." $750.00–1,050.00

Tobacco Tin: Black man with hair standing on head, "Nigger Hair." $850.00–1,200.00

Humidor/Tobacco: 4½", ceramic. Young man wearing blue/white scarf. Ca. 1890's. $275.00–325.00

Humidor/Tobacco: 8", ceramic. Young boy wearing cap, coming up from within pouch with "Good Luck" tag. Cream color, blue, red/brown, incised (JM 5467) on bottom. Ca. 1890's. $450.00–525.00

Humidor: Well-made head of a Black male with a fancy collar, wearing blue with white designed bow tie, earrings in ears, mouth open, laughing, 9½" terra cotta, ca. 1875. $700.00–850.00

Cookie Jar: "Cookies" in raised letters, McCoy. $185.00–250.00

Tobacco Humidor: 5" H., head of demonic-looking male sporting devilish goatee, wearing a hat, red, yellow, brown and black bisque. $325.00–400.00

Tobacco Humidor: 7½" H. German terra-cotta humidor of an elderly gentleman sporting a beautiful beard and wearing a well-worn hat, with his mouth open as if he is yelling, with his eyes glancing to the left. Painted blue, grey, brown, red and white, ca. 1880. $850.00–1,100.00

Tobacco Humidor: 7" H. German terra-cotta humidor of a watermelon, wearing a cap, bow and jacket, painted brown, green, yellow and red. $700.00–850.00

Condiment Set: Jemima. Plastic condiment set (5 pcs.) each 4" h. including cinnamon, cloves, nutmeg (cracked), allspice, ginger; (2) a Pair of Jemima and Uncle Mose salt and pepper shakers, 3½" h; (3) Jemima head; (4) Aunt Jemima sugar and creamer (or syrup), 5½". All F. & F. Die Works, Dayton. PLUS figural "Aunt Jemima's Cookie Jar" 10½" h., red and white plastic. (Together 11 pieces, nutmeg as is) $465.00–500.00

Cookie Jar: Yellow semi-vitreous china figural cookie jar of Chef. "Pearl China Co. Hand Dec. Dec. 22K Gold." 10½" x 6" dia. (There are two chips on lid - one center rim; other inside rim.) $195.00–250.00

Cookie Jar: Semi-vitreous china cookie jar. Lid finial is Aunt Jemima smiling head with red bandana head-wrap. Age crack on back rim of lid. Base is shaped like checked dress and dotted apron with hands on round tummy. Marked on base "Marumon Ware K. Handpainted Japan." 8" H. with woven wicker bail handle. $225.00–295.00

Souvenir: Cookie Jar. Red and white china figural cookie jar in shape of youthful Aunt Jemima-type with red head bandana and white apron over red dress with mixing bowl. Marked "New Orleans" on hem of apron. Marked "TM" in circle on reverse. 9½" H x 6" dia. base. $295.00–350.00

Candy Tin: Round candy or cookie tin with lid scene of large goose chasing a terrified, crying boy. 5¾" dia. x 3½" H. $145.00–185.00

Kitchen Aid: Grease Bowl. Ceramic (terra-cotta) tripod base, metal handled figural bowl in shape of Black-glazed clown's head with big red nose, marked "Grease" on rim of bowl. 4¾" dia., 3¼" H. $110.00–125.00

Syrup Pitcher: Aunt Jemima. Red plastic with white painted apron, neckerchief and plate in hand, 5¼" H., F & F Mold & Die Works, Dayton, Ohio. $75.00–95.00

Nutmeg Shaker: Aunt Jemima. Red plastic, 4" H., F & F Mold & Die Works, Dayton, Ohio. $45.00–55.00

Honey Pot: Figural black chef with spoon and pot in hands and open mouth (to position ladle) at the point where the head is removable. White semi-vitreous china painted black, brown, blue, red and green. Marked "Occupied Japan." 4¼" H. $55.00–75.00

Creamer: Aunt Jemima. Figural creamer, red plastic, white and black decorated, F & F Mold & Dye Works, Dayton. 5½" H. (as is) $35.00–45.00

Creamer and Sugar Breakfast Set: Yellow plastic with figural handles. Sugar has an Aunt Jemima-type woman with a red dress and white-apron. Creamer has a handle with a red-coated butler. (Both sugar and creamer repaired.) A figural salt shaker has the same butler, holding a high hat; 3½" H. All 3 items marked F & F Mold and Dye Works, Dayton, Ohio. Plus a 2¼" celluloid black baby girl doll with tiny skirt. 4 pieces. $145.00–155.00

Cookie Jar: McCoy. Ceramic figural cookie jar in form of Mammy-type woman that separates at waist (remove upper body). "Cookies" in raised letters on hem impressed in base "McCoy." Painted face (mostly worn off). $185.00–250.00

Dolls

Black doll, composition, walker, 1940–1950, standard condition, jointed. $165.00–240.00

Felt doll, Golliwog, 3", standard condition. $85.00–100.00

Felt doll, Golliwog, 4", standard condition. $85.00–100.00

Felt doll, Golliwog, 4", poor condition. $85.00–100.00

Felt doll, Golliwog, 6", excellent condition. $85.00–100.00

Felt doll, Golliwog, 10", standard condition. $85.00–100.00

Plastic, Cream of Wheat, "Rastus," no color missing, 10"-13". $70.00–90.00

Wax on wood doll, 17"-19". Wax head with wooden body and legs. Wax hands and feet. $275.00–450.00

Stockinette doll, 9"-11", mohair, female, sewn-on head, body stuffed. $150.00–200.00

Celluloid, Black female, eyes stationary, jointed arms and legs, 6"-10". $60.00–100.00

Wood, Black female, matronly, walker, 4"-6", jointed legs (place finger on head to make her walk). $125.00–150.00

"Vargas Wax Vendor Dolls." Made by the dollmaker Francisco Vargas, an emigrant from Mexico to New Orleans during the 19th century. Beeswax was used over wire to represent cotton pickers, vendors, and other tradespeople. Vargas died in the late 1890's and the family continued to produce the wax dolls until circa 1950. The early dolls made by Vargas are not marked; some of the later ones bear the family name, and the mark "Vargas/New Orleans, La." can be found on the bases to which the dolls are attached.

(A) Straw vendor, 5½", man with bundle of straw on his back/alligator on string, ca. 1890's. $450.00

(B) Stick vendor, 5½", man with bundle of sticks on his back, ca. 1890's. $465.00

(C) Potato vendor, 5½", man with bucket/sack full of potatoes, ca. 1890's. $465.00

(D) Banana vendor, 5½", (man with stalk of bananas), ca. 1890's. $525.00

(E) Pastry vendor, 5½", female with basket filled with pastries under one arm/shredded paper to swat insects under the other arm, ca. 1890's. $650.00

(F) Woman with alligator on string/small child sitting on its back, 5½", ca. 1890's. $465.00

(G) Old man smoking pipe, sitting on logs, with banjo on lap/hat in hand. 5", ca. 1920. $415.00

(H) Fish vendor, 5½", man with basket of fish/crab in hand, ca. 1890's. $465.00

(I) Vegetable vendor, 5¼", woman with basket of vegetables, ca. 1890's. $465.00

(J) Woman with tray on top of head, 5½", stamped genuine "Vargas," New Orleans, La., ca. 1900. $415.00

(K) Bamboo vendor, 5½", woman carrying sticks of bamboo, ca. 1890's. $650.00

Cloth doll - female, 15", red/green skirt with flowery top trimmed in lace, wearing jewelry/scarf on head, sewn face features, with underskirt, cloth shoes, doll in sitting position, ca. 1900. $165.00–210.00

Cloth doll - female, 17", wearing red, brown/white dress with star design, tightly curled hair, blue glass eyes, sewn mouth/nose, ca. 1920. $165.00–210.00

Bisque 4" H. baby doll in a red dress, ca. 1940.
                                                    $115.00–135.00

Bamboo stick dolls with cloth and straw top-half and bamboo stick lower body (5 dolls). $55.00–60.00

Sock doll, 23", sewn eyes, eyelashes, nose and mouth, with stitched toes and fingers in very early poplin dress of 1860's design with wool hair, good condition with slight wear on the face. $250.00–315.00

Sock doll, 22", sewn eyes, eyelashes, nose and lips, with stitched toes and fingers, bandana on head, red/white dress with apron and pinned scarf, hole in one arm (cotton exposed), good condition. $250.00–315.00

12½" doll by Horsman Dolls, Inc., plastic body with rubber head and slightly damaged celluloid carnival doll (2 items) *Horsman Doll well underpriced/updated estimate plus (celluloid doll).   Horsman – $125.00, Celluloid – $40.00

Composition. 9½", painted eyes and mouth, original clothes, damaged hands, ca. 1945. $115.00–135.00

Wax Doll. 3¾" H, with painted eyes and lips, original clothing and human hair. Ca. 1890. $220.00–255.00

Stuffed doll: 15" (mammy with arms crossed) red, brown, blue and white, with a pocket. $125.00–165.00

7¼" girl, composition, moveable joints and head, glass eyes and painted mouth and shoes, cloth hair, with hat missing.
                                                    $135.00–175.00

7" boy in his original clothes, with apron, wood arms, legs and face, and composition head with painted hair, eyes, and mouth, ca. 1870. $300.00–400.00

8⅛" male doll with original clothes and retains original paint. Painted eyes, lips and shoes, with leather ears, hands damaged/shoes. $235.00–300.00

Celluoid, 6½" girl, dressed. Made in Japan. $85.00–100.00

Rag Doll: 12", glass eyes, stitched nose and mouth, horsehair wig, with painted eyelashes, ca. 1910. $185.00–250.00

Celluloid: 10" boy, made in Japan (turtle in a diamond mark), painted eyes and lips. $115.00–150.00

Hand Puppet: Elderly man in grey suit wearing a red tie made by Child Craft. "Aunt Jemima's Pancake Flour" paper needle holder. The story "Ten Little Niggers" (taken from major text) and "Denison's Blackface Series, " a play. (Four items)
                                                    $165.00–225.00

Dolls: Clothes Brush/Dinner Bell. Turned wood head, painted face on round wood base holding clothes brush. 7" plus bell with dowel-turned handle with painted face, red dress and white lace apron/collar. 4". (2 pieces) $45.00–70.00 each

Composition. 2 composition baby dolls. 7-pc. elastic strung variety. (1) Marked "Reliable, Made in Canada" with molded hair, showing some slight scarring and a crack at crotch, 16½". (2) Unmarked doll with molded hair plus additional tufts (wool) missing from skull. Top of head with 1½" crack, loosely strung. (2 dolls) $95.00–120.00 each

Curly haired little girl doll with red ribbon in hair, moveable arms and legs. Composition with fleck on hair line and several fingers. Dressed in red print dress with lacy hem, cuffs and collar and eyelet-edged pantaloons. $95.00–115.00

Crocheted. Pair all-crocheted red, white and black wool boy and girl dolls. He has red overalls and white cap; she has red dress, white apron and bandana. (2 dolls)
$70.00–80.00 each

Cushion and Feather Duster. 2 handmade stuffed dolls (1) Jemima-styled feather duster with stuffed doll head (around handle) with painted face, and red bandana; leaf print dress with white apron/collar (around feathers), 12". (2) Pincushion elongated to form neck/head of a doll with sewn sequin eyes, nose and mouth; sewn red narrow strips representing hands and legs. Cloth overlayment to cover cushion body, 6". Both dolls with earrings. (2 pieces) $70.00–105.00 each

Dolls: Jamaican. Two stuffed dolls with painted faces. (1) Woman with colorful dress wearing long white apron marked "Minnie/Jamaican/B.W.T.," bandana head wrap, earrings and with large basket balanced on her head, 12½" to basket top. (2) Boy wearing trousers and shirt with cloth bag slung from shoulder strap, bag marked "Jamaica." He is wearing a large woven straw hat. 10" to top brim of hat (2 dolls).
$60.00–75.00 each

Dolls, Paper: Two cardboard die-cut, two-dimensional mechanical paper dolls consisting of six cut-out pieces (hands, feet, head and shoulders, body) held together by four small brass paper fasteners at shoulders and knees, making arms and legs moveable. Same girl on each lithograph, but wearing different necklaces and different color and style shoes (found years ago in an old New Orleans warehouse), 9". (2 items)
$70.00–90.00 each

Advt. Doll - Aunt Jemima Doll. Printed on checked gingham plastic (mailed flat, no doubt, as advt. gimmick. Homemaker can stuff to make inexpensive doll for child.) Stuffed, bottom sewn, 12". $165.00–190.00

Advt. Doll. Cream of Wheat Chef Doll. Printed in color on linen wearing his apron and chef's hat. Both sewn on, stuffed, 19". (Note: Mailed as single piece of cloth with doll and directions printed on cloth. Cut and stuff to make a home-made doll.) $125.00–165.00

Baby Doll: Mechanical celluloid. Baby doll with key wind-up mechanism which makes the baby crawl forward on hands and knees. Approximately 5½" long (slight depressed spot above right ear). $55.00–75.00

Doll: 16" rubber head and hand "Shindana" doll with knitted sweater and printed skirt, cloth body and feet (1969).
$55.00–85.00

Small Baby Doll: (1) Hair tufts and painted eyes and lips, wearing only diaper, 4". (2) Pincushion with cute doll's head wearing dunce cap, with feet and hands protruding from cushion. Cushion is torn and stuffing is coming out. (2 dolls)
$55.00–75.00 each

Folk Art: Mammy doll made of stuffed sock over glass bottle. Mammy wears long floral print gown, has overstuffed bosom, bandana and a pair of earrings. Meant to be filled with lead shot or sand to give sufficient weight for use as door stop.
$70.00–85.00

Occupied Japan celluloid kewpie-type girl in top hat, 7" including hat (2) Fisher boy doll, plastic with straw hat, bright print shirt, fish and net. 6½" including hat. (2 dolls)
$145.00–185.00 pair

Seven various sizes and types; rag doll, stuffed dolls, Black vote doll, Aunt Jemima, Puerto Rican stuffed and wire doll and two half-length "cover" dolls, ca. 1930/60. (7 dolls)
$55.00–85.00 each

Santa Claus doll dressed in full Christmas regalia, 15", Hong Kong Prod. Co. $55.00–85.00

Large stuffed doll with oil cloth head, dressed in long floral print gown, head dress, 3 buttons on stuffed socks for high-button shoes. The Soft Co. ca. 1930, 21". $185.00–250.00

Television personality dolls, Shindana Toys, ca. 1970. (1) 16" Redd Foxx; (2) 14" Dyn-O-Mite J.J. (Jimmy Walker); (3) 16" Rodney Allen Rippey. $40.00–55.00 each

Telephone Cover: Cloth body doll, oil-cloth head, half-length with full-length printed cloth dress. Ca. 1950. No markings.
$60.00–75.00

Composition/Stuffed: Four dolls. Three seated composition babies, each approximately 9" in varying states of surface peel. (4) stuffed doll, approximately 14" with large floppy hat and printed dress. (4 items) $70.00–115.00 each

Doll unmarked, all brown composition, jointed at hips/shoulders, molded/painted hair, painted eyes/mouth (closed), dressed in hand-made clothes, 9" (composition cracked/missing on both sides of head with left hand chipped), ca. 1900. $100.00–125.00 each

Black bisque-head lady character doll, Parisienne type. Negroid features, swivel neck, bisque shoulder plate. Fixed dark brown eyes, pierced ears, open mouth with teeth, quality brown mohair wig, kid body stained dark brown. Original white faille summer dress with a train. 15", unmarked, ca. 1870's. $2,700.00–3,750.00

Schoenau & Hoffmeister Black bisque doll. Brown sleep eyes, black mohair wig and jointed composition body, wearing original Hawaiian costume, 10", incised "1909."
$675.00–825.00

Small Black bisque-head doll. Fixed dark brown eyes, black hair wig and five-piece composition body, wearing a white lawn dress, 8", incised "P." $415.00–465.00

Black composition baby doll with blue sleep eyes, black cotton wig, pierced ears and bent-limb composition body. Wearing a red silk dress, 19½". $265.00–375.00

Pillow Rag Doll. Full-bodied, Black woman with arms outstretched, but truncated (no legs; made to sit on girl's pillow). 16" overall height to hemline of red/white polka-dotted dress with lace edged white apron, matching head scarf, button eyes and pasted-on nose and mouth. $150.00–220.00

Pipe-cleaner style dolls (2). Stitched eyes, nose and mouth, each 12". (2 items) $55.00–70.00 each

Rubber baby doll with moveable hands, feet and head, 17". Marked "Plated Moulds, Inc., 1961." Wearing white floral nightgown and panties. $70.00–100.00

Stuffed doll. Tall cloth homemade lady doll with oversized bosom, straw-filled body (tattered), straw hat, torn clothing, painted face, 24". $90.00–135.00

Wire frame doll, 11", built around a plastic face. Circular scrap cloth discs are pierced by wire to form the fancily dressed body, arms and legs. With hand-crocheted hat. $70.00–100.00

Wooden walking doll. Painted face and long dowels for legs with large shoes on (empty) cardboard cone-shaped string spool body. Armless with cloth dress. Made so it can walk by itself down a slight incline, 4¼". $75.00–105.00

Black baby with painted eyes, moveable hands and feet. Three tufts of hair (reglued rear end). Incised "Japan," 4½". Together with painted Black mammy figure. Heavy composition with appearance of carved wood. Head reglued. 6". (2 items) Japan - $70.00; Mammy - $115.00

Small celluloid gold-haired Black doll, 6½", marked on back "GR Made in Occupied Japan." $70.00–100.00

Antique boy doll with moveable joints and head, glass eyes, painted mouth and shoes. Cloth hair with hat missing (doll originally wore hat). Composition, 7¼", ca. 1870.
$450.00–675.00

Bisque doll, small 4" bisque doll, jointed at shoulders and top of legs, 3 tufts of hair on head. Incised "Japan," ca. 1930.
$70.00–90.00

Tiny bisque baby with moveable hands and feet. Three tufts of hair. Incised "Japan," 4". $60.00–75.00

Compo. Black boy baby doll with painted face, bent knees, moveable hands and feet, 8". Thumbs nicked.
$115.00–135.00

Clothes pin doll, 11". Young woman of clothes pin construction. Arms and legs moveable at joints; wearing pink floral dress, apron and bandana head dress. $60.00–75.00

Doll, Madame Alexander, 14" Black girl. Marked "Alexander C. 1965." Synthetic dark brown hair, cloth body, hard vinyl arms and legs (bent at knees), soft vinyl face with closed mouth, awake and sleep eyes; cries, w/pussy cat, blue gingham dress and matching bloomers, and only one knit bootie.
$565.00–650.00

Three Carmen Miranda-style dolls, each balancing a basket of fruit on her head, wearing a colorful dress. Two are stuffed rag; one is molded plastic. 7" to 10", ca. 1950–1970. (3 dolls)
$55.00–70.00 each

Three different dolls of varying composition – rubber, basket rag, varnished cloth. 6" – 10", ca. 1950–1970. $70.00–90.00

(1) Shimmy Bank/Doll. Neck on spring so it shakes its head with movement (of car?) or insertion of coin in back. Seated diapered baby holding fruit, wearing earrings and scarf. 7". (2) Rag doll (needs resewing at toe, heels and neck), 12". Dressed in red striped dress. (2 dolls) $35.00–50.00 each

German Black bisque-head infant doll, Armand Marseille, with brown glass sleep eyes and open mouth-inset lower teeth, cloth body with composition hands, 15".
$900.00–1,050.00

German Black infant doll, Armand Marseille, brown glass eyes, closed mouth, five-piece composition baby body, 16", bisque head. $975.00–1,125.00

German Black bisque-head doll, incised "Heinrich Handwerck/Simon & Halbig/Germany." Brown glass eyes, pierced ears, open mouth, inset teeth, ball-jointed composition body. $1,050.00–1,200.00

German Black bisque-head doll, Societe Francaise de Fabrication de Bebes et Jouets. Brown glass sleep eyes, black features, open mouth, ball-jointed, black painted composition toddler body, 16". $4,500.00–6,000.00

Schoehut Black boy doll with black molded hair, brown intaglio eyes. Wearing original blue cotton knickers and white shirt, shoes and stockings, 16", chipped paint on the hands, incised mark on the back. $2,700.00–3,300.00

Black composition character baby with painted features, cloth body and a checked flannel playsuit, 11½", ca. 1920's.
$145.00–200.00

Black bisque head character doll with fixed brown eyes and smiling open-closed mouth showing two rows of painted

teeth. Grey wig stylized in a top knot, cloth body with composition arms and legs. Original printed red dress/apron-white. 13". Crazing to arms and legs. Incised "N.I."
$1,050.00–1,200.00

Joel Ellis Doll: Black female, "Dinah." Jointed maplewood with painted metal hands and feet, wearing an original blue-striped cotton dress and white apron, 12½". Paint on the head is peeling (fair condition). $650.00–825.00

Rubber dolls, "Amos-Andra." 8" tall, in marked box with ad of Amos n' Andy Radio Show, w/accessories, Big Sun Rubber Co., ca. 1930. $125.00–165.00

Doll, unmarked, 11". All brown composition, jointed at hips/shoulders, molded/painted hair with one yarn pigtail (other missing), painted eyes/closed mouth. Paint cracked with some missing in hair. $125.00–150.00

Plastic, oil cloth, stuffed doll, ca. 1950. 11" tall with brown face/wool hair and red/yellow clothing. $100.00–115.00

Brown felt stuffed doll with beaded trim/jewelry, wearing black felt skirt with beaded trim, ca. 1950. $90.00–125.00

Entertainment

Booklet: "Porgy and Bess," produced by Samuel Goldwyn Motion Pictures, 1959 (photograph of Pearl Bailey inside).
$75.00–95.00

Sheet Music: "Who's That Knocking at the Door" composed and sung by Wm. Whitlock. Cover depicts two minstrels on stage - one playing banjo while other is doing the jig. "As Sung with Great Applause by William Whitlock at the Principal Theatres in the United States," 1846. $45.00–55.00

Sheet Music: Cole & Johnson's "The Shoo-Fly Regiment," "Rapasz Band March," "I'm Goin' Away" by Mack and Orth, A Great Coon Song; "Plantation Airs," "At A Darktown Cake Walk" by Charles Hale; "Old Black Joe" and "Play That Barber Shop Chord" (Bert Williams on cover) (7 items) $45.00–55.00 each

Sheet Music: "Ten Little Niggers" written by Frank Green with music by Mark Mason (b/w lithograph of G.W. Moore in circle w/vignettes surrounding circle), sung by G.W. Moore of the original Christy Minstrels, St. James Hall, Piccadilly.
$45.00–55.00

Theatre Flyers: 3" x 7¾", blue/black on white. "Are Coming. Pettengill's Minstrels and Splended Brass Band, 23 Star Performers! Newly Organized and Equipped will shortly visit the Principal Cities of the United States and Canada, headed by the Great Ethopian Comedian, the ONLY NICODEMUS JOHNSON in the WORLD, Charles Pettengill ... " Ca. 1890.
$45.00–50.00

Sheet Music/Flyer: Color lithograph of beautiful well-dressed woman. "She's the Real Thing My Baby," words and music by Theo. A. Northrop. Musical supplement to the *Cleveland Plain Dealer,* Sunday, January 20, 1901. $40.00–50.00

Theatrical Broadside, 6" x 20", advertising "Uncle Tom's Cabin" along with other plays/performances, printed in b/w by Cortland County Democrat Amusement Printing Establishment, Cortland, NY, ca. 1890, framed. $65.00–75.00

Movie Advertising Brochures: Norman Film Manufacturing Co. advertising brochures depicting all-colored cast movies of the 1920's and early 1930's. (5 items) $70.00–75.00 each

Movie Poster: (1 sheet) George Randol Production Presents "Midnight Shadow" with Frances Redd (The Cinderella Girl), Buck Woods and Richard Bates (Coal Dust and Ashes), red, blue and black on white. $95.00–110.00

Movie Poster: (1 sheet) Toddy Pictures presents "Harlem on the Prairie" with Mantan Moreland. Red, white and blue.
$225.00–250.00

Poster: Louis "Satchmo" Armstrong, "L'Ambassadeur Du Jazz Bruxelles," ca. 1958. Red and black on white, 14" x 21".
$110.00–125.00

Movie Poster: (1 sheet) Goldmax Productions presents Mantan Moreland in "She's Too Mean For Me." Red, white and black (damaged from folding). $95.00–115.00

Sheet Music: "Coon-Coon-Coon" by Gene Jefferson, music by Leo Friedman, introduced and sung by Lew Dockstader. Vig. photos of Dean and Johnson. Red, green, white and black cover. $45.00–50.00

Sheet Music: "Hap Hazard" by Winthrop Wiley. Yellow and black cover, ca. 1901. $45.00–50.00

Phonograph Records: Comedy. "Two Black Crows," Moran and Mack, 4 records, 8 sides, old 78s, Columbia Records, 1913. Part 1–4, records with original sleeves. $75.00–80.00 each

Phonograph Records: "Two Black Crows," Moran and Mack, 3 records, 6 sides, old 78's, Columbia Records, 1913. Part 1 through 6. Records with original sleeves. $45.00–65.00 each

Phonograph Records: Record Guild. Small 33 rpm record #2001P, produced by Record Guild of America, Inc., N.Y. Two colorful labels, 2 songs with vocal and full orchestra. (1) "Carry Me Back to Old Virginny" with label depicting elderly white-haired man with cane and wrapped in purple shawl with woman and by tree on hill overlooking cotton field. (2) "Blue Tail Fly" with boy in overalls looking in awe at red-coated plantation owner on prancing horse. $50.00–60.00 each

Phonograph Records: 1950 LPs. (1) Ethel Waters, "Shades of Blue" with dust jacket and J.C. Heard and his Orchestra.

Remington Records including "Am I Blue," "Taking a Chance on Love," "Cabin in the Sky," "Dinah," etc. (2) Josephine Baker, Avec Orchestra, Columbia Records with dust jacket including "Haiti," "C'Est Lui," "Sans Amour," etc. (3) Pearl Bailey, "Pearl's Pearls," Columbia Records with dust jacket, Mitchell Ayres Orchestra. (4) "Ella, Lena and Billie," Columbia with dust jacket including "Prisoner of Love," "All My Life," "Nice Work If You Can Get It," "Out of Nowhere," "My Melancholy Baby," "I'll Never Be the Same." (5) "Erroll Garner - Garnerland," Columbia with dust jacket including "Sophisticated Lady," "How High the Moon," "Am I Blue," etc. (6) "Joyce Bryant - Running Wild", Epic Records including "You Made Me Love You," "After You've Gone," "Lonely Girl," "Love Was Made for Me," etc. (7) Music of Africa series with dust jackets. #3 "Drums of East Africa." (7 records) $70.00–80.00 each

"American Folk Songs as sung by William's Jubilee Sungers," front/back covers are illustrated with b/w halftones, ca. 1900.
$45.00–60.00

Movie: "Roar of the Crowd," b/w advertisement for the movie showing the "Brown Bomber" in a fighting pose.
$45.00–60.00

Movie Program: "The Duncan Sisters in 'Topsy and Eva' with Noble Johnson as Uncle Tom," distributed by United Artists Pictures, 1927 (illustrated use of Black faces) $65.00–70.00

Sheet Music: (Bert Williams/William Walker - The Two Real Coons) (1) "I Don't Like No Cheap Man," Wms./Walker, with cover photo of McIntyre and Heath in blackface. (2) "Just An Old Friend of the Family," W/W's latest song hit, McPherson and Smith with cover photo of W/W. (3) "If You Love Your Baby Make Goo Goo Eyes," W/W with cover illustration of couple making goo-goo eyes. (4) "I May Be Crazy But I Ain't No Fool" by Alex Rogers with cover photo of Bert Williams. (5) "He's Up Against The Real Thing Now," Farber/Wms. with cover photos of W/W. (5 pieces) $65.00–75.00 each

Sheet Music: (1) "Blue Boogie" by John W. Schaum, 1946. Cover has 3 Sambo-style caricature heads with roly-poly eyes. (2) "Short'Nin Bread" by Jacques Wolfe, choral arrangements, Harold Flammer, Inc. 1933, 10 pages. (2 pieces)
$55.00–65.00 each

Sheet Music: "Coons in the Canebrake," M.S. Clayson, 1900 and 2 different versions of "Alagaza-Zam! Zam!" Abe Holzmann with cover illustrations of marching Black troops, and "Alagazam to the Music of the Band" by Sterling and Tilzer with color cartoon of marching band and drum leader. (3 pieces) $55.00–65.00 each

Sheet Music: "The Darkie's Dream" by Lansing and Giles, 1891, with b/w cover of old man seated at foot of tree dreaming of family and friends, with background of people picking cotton in field. $55.00–65.00

Sheet Music: 1920s. (1) "Ain't Misbehavin'," "Connie's Hot Chocolate," 1929 with color cover by Leff of saxophonist and

chorus line. (2) "I've got the Ol' Virginny Picanniny Blues," Joe McKierman, 1924 with color cover of Mammy seated outside farmhouse knitting with riverboat passing by. (3) "I Never Had a Mammy" by the Duncan Sisters, 1923 with color cover of Topsy & Eva (with Topsy in blackface).
$60.00–65.00 each

Sheet Music: Virginia. "Carry Me Back to Old Virginny," Jas. A. Bland, with half-cover color illustrations of family outside the house, under a thatched roof, with many playing banjo. Child and mother playing, young couple in conversation and with several onlookers at second-floor window. $55.00–65.00

Sheet Music: "Hap Hazard" by Winthrop Wiley with colored cartoon (by Starmer) of heavy man with derby and cane leaning against lamp post, 1901. Yellow and black cover, F.B. Mills, N.Y. $55.00–65.00

Sheet Music: (1) "I Only Thought I'd Call Around," by W.J. Moloney with cartoon cover man in doorway with woman in rocker. (2) "If the Man in the Moon Were a Coon" by Fred Fisher with cartoon cover of old man stealing a chicken. (3) "I'd Rather be Outside A Lookin' In" by Hamill/Snyder with cartoon cover of picture of man with high wing collar and bow tie. (3 items) $45.00–55.00 each

Sheet Music: (1) James A. Bland's great Ethiopian songs, "In the Evening by the Moonlight" published 1880. B/W cartoon cover w/church scene of shouting worshippers, winged angels. Bland listed as best Ethiopian songwriter in the world, author of "Oh, Dem Golden Slippers." (2) "Pray for the Lights to Go Out," Tunnah & Skidmore, with Guy E. Turpin, cartoon of preacher and his flock, 1916. (2 items) $55.00–60.00 each

Sheet Music: (1) "Jolly Me Along" by McDonald/Gumble, cover depicting two lovers kissing under the moon. (2) "Alagazam to the Music of the Band" by Sterling/Von Tilzer with cartoon cover depicting drum major leading a marching band. (2 pieces) $55.00–65.00 each

Sheet Music: (1) "Just Come Up and Take Your Presents Back." Von Tilzer/Sterling with sepia cover cartoon of woman at top of house steps shaking her fist at man knocked to bottom step. (2) "Home Sickness Blues," Cliff Hess with carciature cover picture scratching his head and dreaming of the past. (2 items) $50.00–60.00 each

Sheet Music: (1) "Knockin" by Eagle Mathews. Covers depicting red-coated top-hatted dandy. (2) "Coon in the Canebrake," M.S. Clayson. Cover depicting farm owner and dogs chasing people through cane. (3) "Alagazam" by Abe Holtzman. Cover illustration of marching troops. $45.00–55.00 each

Sheet Music: (1) "Memories of the Old South," Rudolph Thaler, 1908. Cover depicting elderly man dreaming of old times with wife in cotton field. (2) "When the Major Plays Those Miner Melodies," Wm. A. Wilander and H. DeCosta (ca. 1920). Colorful cover cartoon of miners gathered around saloon pianist. (3) "Show Me the Way to Go Home Babe,"

Morrow and Hebert, 1901, with colorful cover of soldier winking with his girl. $45.00–55.00 each

Sheet Music: Six items of sheet music. 1930's. Including Amos n' Andy cover of "3 Little Words" from "Check and Double Check," "Laud You Made the Night Too Long," "River Stay Away From My Door," "Song of the Bayou," "Underneath the Harlem Moon," and Duke Ellington's "Sophisticated Lady." (6 items) $55.00–65.00 each

Sheet Music: B/W on black. Amos & Andy, "Three Little Words" from "Check and Double Check"; Duncan Sisters, "I Never Had a Mammy" from "Topsy & Eva" (torn corner); Al Jolson, "Old Fashion Girl" from "Bombo" plus "Were You There" from "Negro Spirituals" arranged by H.T. Burleigh. (4 items) $55.00–65.00 each

Sheet Music: Presidential Election. "When a Coon Sits in the Presidential Chair" by Geo. R. Wilson, published by Chas. K. Harris, 1896, with cover halftone photo of the famous Wilson Family (on stage). $65.00–70.00

Song Book: Spirituals. Johnson, James Weldon, editor. *The Book of American Negro Spirituals*, Viking Press, N.Y., 1925, 183 pages (words and music). $55.00–65.00

Sheet Music: Turn-of-Century. "Coon-Coon-Coon." Jefferson/Friedman, 1901. Color cover of 3 men in red top hats and bowties with wide eyes forming the "OO" in each word of the title. $45.00–55.00

Lobby Cards: Movies/Our Gang. 5 theater lobby photos of "Our Gang." "Little Rascals" in Hal Roach's comedy "The Mysterious Mystery." Various sizes from 8¼" x 11¼" to 9¼" x 13". Soiled, worn, abused. Has a hole from being tacked up/torn down from lobby exhibits. (5 pieces, good condition) $65.00–75.00 each

Program: "de Paur's Infantry Chorus" Army Infantry Chorus' first civilian tour of America/Canada, presented by Columbia Concerts, Inc. 1945. $75.00–85.00

Plays: "The Coontown Wedding," "Plantation School Days" published by Walter H. Baker Co., Boston, Mass., 1930. $85.00–95.00

Button: "Joe Louis - World's Champion" on outer border of photo view of Louis in boxing pose. B/W with red, white and blue ribbon attached, 1¾" dia., ca. 1940. $55.00–65.00

Penny Sheet: Song "The Contraband's Adventure" published by Chas. Magnus, 12 Frankfort St., N.Y. $65.00–75.00

Sheet Music: "Everybody Loves the Man with the Jingle," music by Chas. E. Mullen (man smoking large cigar, flashing fist full of money), repaired at bind. $45.00–55.00

Plays: Denison's Blackface Plays "On Yo' Way Niggah!" "A Henpecked Coon," "Mush and Poke, Ash Haulers," "No Sense,

No How," "Coon Creek Courtship," "My Old Man's Sick," "Black Clouds" and "A Much Married Coon," 1929 T.S. Denison & Co., published, Chicago. (8 items) $70.00–80.00 each

Broadside: J. Morris & Co., N.Y. "Burning of the Lexington" …"Fairy Grotto…Otto Motty!" Also 2 Negro singers who will sing the Negro Extravaganza of "Jim a Long Josey!"… At close…performance, the Two Living Curious Brothers, From South Sea Islands…Hands and Feet Resemble…Spread Claws of an Eagle…" Ca. 1875. $160.00–170.00

Sheet Music: Famous names. (1) "Abraham Jefferson Washington Lee - You Ain't Goin' to Pic No Fuss Out of Me." "Terrific Coon Song Hit," Sterling/Von Tilzer, 1906 with color cover cartoon. (2) "The Booker T's are on Parade Today," Moran/Helf, 1908. (2 items) $50.00–60.00 each

Sheet Music: Mid-19th century. "Plantation Melodies","The Gum Tree Canoe" by S.S. Steele. B/W lithograph cover showing 2 lads seated on bench - 1 playing fife with banjo and tamborine at his feet, the other with music book *Plantation Melodies* open on his lap. Published by Geo. A. Reed, 1847, rare. $75.00–85.00

Sheet Music: Mid-19th century. "Poor Old Slave" by G.W. Griffin. Small sketch of the old man seated on stool, wearily resting his head and hand on his cane handle. Published G.P. Reed & Co., Boston, 1851. $65.00–75.00

Sheet Music: Misc. (1) "One Meat Ball" by Zaret/Singer, Leeds Music Corp., N.Y. (1944). Cover photos of Josh White and Jimmy Savo. (2) "The Dark Town Strutters Ball," Shelton Brooks, Feist Publisher, N.Y., 1934. (3) "Carry Me Back to Old Virginny," James A. Bland, Ditson Co., Boston, 1906. Half-cover color illustrations of family in courtyard, man with banjo. (4) "Every Race Has A Flag but the Coon," Heelan/Helf, Stern & Co., N.Y., 1900, as is condition. $45.00–55.00 each

Sheet Music: 19th Century. "Ash-Cake Shuffle" by D.A. Epler, Bergé Music Co., 1899, with color lithograph cover by J.E. Rosenthal of 8 young men and girls dancing with joy as Mammy removes the flat ash cake from the fireplace. (2) "Topsy Neber Was Born," Topsy's song dedicated to Mrs. Harriet Beecher Stowe. By Cook/Stanley, published by The Amphions, 1854. (2 pieces) $65.00–75.00 each

Sheet Music: "A Pickaninny Named Honey," "Everybody Calls Me Honey" by Lyons/Straight. Forster Music, published Chicago, 1919. With fine lithograph color cover of an appealing little boy holding a cute puppy standing before gate of large house. $65.00–75.00

Sheet Music: Tennessee. "In Dear Old Tennessee" by Fields/Newman with pictorial tinted cover of "a Tennessee Topsy." $50.00–60.00

Sheet Music: (1) Turn of Century. "I'd Leave Ma Happy Home For You," Heelen & Von Tilzer, 1899, with cover cartoon bust figure of woman with large feathered and ribboned hat singing the great "Oo, Oo, Oo" song. (2) The answer to the first, "I Wouldn't Leave My Home It I Were You." Sterling & Von Tilzer, 1899 with color cartoon cover illustrations of woman in long striped skirt, ruffled collar and very large feathered hat. (2 items) $50.00–60.00 each

Sheet Music: (1) O. Maude Huth's "Hush! My Little Coon," music and words by J.W. Wheeler. Back cover with "Hush! Pickaninnies" (1896). (2) May Irwin's great coon triumph "When You Ain't Got Money, Well You Needn't Come Around" (1898). (3) "Mandy Loves Me." Torn and fragile. (3 items)
$45.00–55.00 each

Sheet Music: "My Dusky Rose," Thomas S. Allen. Cover print of pair of young lovers with cotton field background, small border photo of Alf and Mabe Wilson, performers.
$75.00–80.00

Sheet Music: (1) "Old Black Joe" by Stephen Foster. Portrait cover of O.B.J. (2) "Sweet Memories of Dixie" - Laurence C. Jones. Cover illustrated sketch of 2 in rowboat and inset photo of L.C. Jones. (2 pieces) $40.00–45.00 each

Phonograph Records: (Amos n' Andy) Charles J. Cornell and Freeman F. Gosden pre-Amos n' Andy recordings (on Victor labels). "Oh, Look at That Baby"/"What'll You Do." (as Sam n' Henry) "Let's Talk About My Sweetie"/"All I Want to Do." (as Sam n' Henry) Sam's Speech at the Colored Lodge/Sam n' Henry at the Fortune Tellers." All 78's (ca. 1910). (3 records) $75.00–85.00 each

Phonograph Records: Southernaires. Album, "Decca presents The Southernaires in a Recital of Spirituals" including "Swing Low, Swing Chariot," "Go Down Moses," "Roll Jordan Roll," etc. Album #83 (5 records) in original jacket. 78 rpm. (5 records in 1 album) $85.00–95.00

Phonograph Records: Bert Williams (Black performer, often called America's foremost comedian, known for his black face act, ca. 1910) singing "Nobody" coon song on old 78 Columbia Phonograph Co. recording, song introduced by Bert Williams in follies of 1910. $75.00–95.00

Phonograph Record/Record Jacket: (1) Record: "Little Black Sambo," Caravan Records, Milton Cross and supporting cast. (2) Album cover "Little Black Sambo's Jungle Band." Victor, Paul Wing with orchestra illustrated color cover (front and back) of Sambo leading and all animals playing instruments. (2 items)   Record - $60.00–75.00; Cover - $50.00–55.00

Sheet Music: (1) "Alagazam" cake walk with full cover dipicting three rows of marching Black infantrymen. By Abe Holzmann, publisher. Feb. Feist, 1902. (2) "Rockin' Chair" by Hoagy Carmichael, Southern Music Publisher (1930) with cover depicting elderly man in rocking chair dreaming of a chariot ride. (2 items) $65.00–75.00 each

Sheet Music: Turn of Century. (1) "A Warm-up in Dixie" (Cakewalk March and 2-step), E.T. Paull, 1899 with fine color lithograph cover of 12 men and woman dancing uproariously in the full moonlight in a woods-clearing around a bonfire. (2) "Mammy Jinny's Jubilee - Shake Yo' Feet" by Gilbert/Muir, 1903, colorful cover depicting Mammy coming out of her cabin door to accept presents and congratulations on her 82nd birthday. (2 items) $40.00–45.00 each

Sheet Music: "Mandy Lou" by Thomas S. Allen with color lithograph cover of two young lovers in the river. Published by Daly Music Publisher, Boston, 1911. $40.00–45.00

Sheet Music: Turn of Century. (1) "Is Yo' Yo Is" by Marjorie B. Cooke and Carrie Jacobs-Bond, 1905. Cover photo print of tiny girl in long dress with bonnet in hand. (2) "I've Got a White Man Working For Me." Coon song by Andrew Sterling with cover photo print of Lizzie McKeever. (2 items)
$40.00–45.00 each

Sheet Music: "Who's That Knocking at the Door" by Wm. Whitlock. Sepia and b/w cover depicts two minstrels on stage, one playing banjo while other dances jig. C.G. Christman, printer, 1846, some staining. $55.00–60.00

Sheet Music: "De Bugs Am In De Co'n" - or "The Darkey's Lament," words and music by L.E. West, published by L.E. West, Rock Island, 1897. Photo cover of bent, old, bearded Black man with cane. $45.00–55.00

Sheet Music: "Dere Ain't Gwine To Be No Rine" by Lyles and Jackson (1905) with color lithograph cartoon cover of youth with sack of watermelons escaping from angry farmer climbing the fence of melon patch in pursuit. $50.00–55.00

Sheet Music: "I'd Rather Be Outside A-Lookin' In Then On the Inside A-Lookin' Out," Hamell & Snyder, with color cartoon of a "dandy." "Jolly Me Along," McDonald & Gumble, with cover of 2 silhouetted lovers in moonlight about to kiss. "I Only Thought I'd Call Around to See How You're Gettin' Along," W.J. Moloney, with cartoon cover. (3 pieces)
$45.00–50.00 each

Sheet Music: "If I Only Had a Dollah of My Own," Bogert and O'Brien (1900). Color lithograph cover with b/w halftone photo of smiling shoe shine boy in tattered clothing. Slight tears. $45.00–50.00

Sheet Music: "I'm Saving Up the Means to Get to New Orleans," Johnson and deCosta, with color cover of cotton picking and loading. "Ida Dunn (I'd A Done Most Any One for Ida Dunn)," J.E. Dempsey with cover photo of Press Eldridge in black face. "I Know Dat I'll be Happy till I Die," by Rogers and Feist, with cover cartoon of young man in derby hat. "In Dear Old Tennessee" by Fields and Newman, with cartoon cover of "A Tennessee Topsy." (4 pieces) $55.00–60.00

Sheet Music: (1) "I've Said My Last Farewell Toot-Toot Goodbye" by Rose and Fischer. Cover cartoon of man on freight train waving to woman. Corner photo of Emile Subers in blackface. (2) "Just Because She Made Dem Goo-Goo Eyes" by Queen and Cannon (1900). Cover cartoon of minstrels on stage and oval inset of top-hatted man. (3) "I Don't Know Where I'm Going But I'm On My Way," coon song oddity, Joe Bren (1905). Bright color cartoon. (3 pieces) $40.00–45.00 each

Sheet Music: Baltimore. "Back, Back, Back to Baltimore" by Williams and Van Astyne. Colorful caricature cartoon cover with top-hatted hobo walking in the cold and snow with his bundle over his shoulder. $85.00–95.00

Sheet Music: Early turn of century. (1) "I Ain't Got No Use For Sleep" by Ralph Bicknell. Color lithograph cover of "Dandy" in top hat, 1903. (2) "I Am De Leaden' Lady ob de Town," Theodore Lane Music Supplement of Hearst's Chicago Amer., 1902 with cover illustrations of lady in long orange gown and large hat with line of dandies in back awaiting her beck and call. (2 items) $45.00–50.00 each

Sheet Music: "Sam, The Old Accordion Man" by Walter Donaldson, Leo Feist Publisher, 1927, with color cover print of an old man happily singing and accompanying himself on an accordion, while three boys in the background dance to the music in front of a riverboat. $45.00–50.00

Sheet Music: (1) "Show Me the Way to Go Home Baby – Capers of A Captivatin' Coon" by Morrow/Herbert, Witmark & Sons. N.Y., 1901 with color caricature of winking soldier walking his girl with parasol. (2) "The Busted Blues" by C. Arthur Fifer, Fifer Publisher, 1919. With cover caricature of farm boy with wide brim hat, suspenders, knee patches and empty pockets turned inside-out. (2 items) $50.00–60.00 each

Sheet Music: "Smoky Mokes - Cake walk & Two Step. Publisher also with Humorous Darky Text." A. Holzmann, composer, Leo Feist, N.Y., 1899 with cover photo print of 4 young lads. (2) "Honey Boy" by Albert Wood, Evans Music Co., Boston, 1909, with cover of small child in center of large sunflower. (2 items) $45.00–50.00 each

Sheet Music: "They Made It Twice As Nice As Paradise and They Called it Dixieland" - Egan/Whiting with color cover depicting "Mammy" seated in bentwood chair telling a story to a White child on her ample lap. $45.00–50.00

Sheet Music: (1) "When Old Bill Bailey Plays the Ukulele" by McCarron/Vincent, Broadway Music Corp., N.Y., 1915 with color cover depicting elderly man seated on log playing ukulele in moonlight (covers only). (2) "Memories of the South" by Rudolf Thaler, Eclipse Publisher, Philadelphia, 1908. Cover of elderly man seated in chair daydreaming of wife in cotton fields. (2 items) $45.00–50.00 each

Sheet Music: "When the Major Plays Those Miner Melodies" by Wm. A. Wilander and Harry deCosta. Full color cover cartoon shows large group of rough miners enjoying the playing of the Black saloon pianist in foreground (ca. 1920?) Great wall display. $50.00–60.00

Sheet Music: "When You Sang Hush-A-Bye Baby To Me,"

words by Jesse G.M. Glick. Music by Logan and Olman. Forster Music Publisher, Chicago, with large full-page color illustration of Mammy in large wicker armchair with white baby in her arms, by Starmer, ca. 1925. $50.00–55.00

Sheet Music: Early 20th century. (1) "If the Man in the Moon Were a Coon." Fred Fisher, 1905, with sketch cartoon of top-hatted old man at chicken coop with chicken peering out of his rear pocket. (2) "Knockin' " - Eagle/Mathews, 1905, with cover illustration of top-hatted tuxedoed "Dandy" with long coat, spats and cane. $45.00–50.00 each

Sheet Music: "The Darktown Colored Band" by Harry S. Miller. Supplement to the *Examiner*, Feb. 23, 1896. Color lithograph cover by Forbes Co. of drawing by Weschler of young woman in long red skirt and yellow blouse, wearing top hat, playing a banjo with cupid band leader in top right corner. $70.00–75.00

Sheet Music: Turn of century. (1) "Hello Ma Baby" (Howard & Emerson) with cover cartoon of man phoning woman in feathered hat, 1899. (2) "I Ain't A-Goin' To Weep No More," G.T. Smith/Von Tilzer, 1900, with cartoon illustration cover of young man weeping copious tears. (3) "Josephine, My Jo" (McPherson & Brymn) with color bust figure on cover of young woman in ruffled dress top and large hat. (3 items) $55.00–60.00 each

Sheet Music: "Pray for the Lights to Go Out" (Negro Shouting Song). Color print with cartoon of preacher and his congregation by Gay E. Turpin. Small photo lower left of Al G. Field in blackface. Words and music by Tunnah & Skidmore. Published Skidmore, Kansas City, Mo., n.d. $55.00–60.00

Figural Images

Cast Iron Doorstop: Black female, matronly, 8¾", molded dress, paint missing, heavy. $125.00–145.00

Cast Iron Doorstop: Black female, matronly, 8¾", molded dress, heavy, excellent condition. $160.00–185.00

Ceramic, Black male, his body forms the lamp, light comes out of top of head, 24"–36". $350.00–375.00

Chalk statue: Black boy, eating watermelon, 14"-16". $210.00–225.00

Plaster sculpture of a young Black woman. "New York - Young Negress," by Jo Jenks. 16" bust, solid wood base w/brass title plate, ca. 1930. $225.00–325.00

Bisque Figurine: "Greetings from Dixieland," a souvenir cotton novelty. Small child eating watermelon, sitting on top of a bale of cotton, with cotton boll, original box, ca. 1930. $60.00–75.00

Pipe Rack: Iron, polychrome metal wall pipe rack with head of a young Black male wearing a hat affixed at the top center of the rack. $170.00–210.00

Iron Figurines: Old man playing banjo, woman clapping her hands, young girl sitting on a rock and a boy dancing the jig. All 2"–3" H., ca. 1920. (4 pieces) $110.00–125.00 each

Figurine: Chalk figure of an elderly man (voodoo doctor) wearing straw hat, sitting on a throne-type chair, bare feet, w/ pot holding a skull at his feet. 15½" H., painted brown, yellow and blue, ca. 1920. $300.00–375.00

Wall Brackets: Pot holders, chalk figures of girls eating watermelon. Red, green, yellow, brown and black. $115.00–125.00

Bisque Figurine: Black male carrying a basket and rooster under his right arm, w/tree stump in back, painted yellow, blue, brown, red and purple (pastel). 9" H. $215.00–300.00

Bisque Figurine: Black boy sitting beside a watermelon. 4¼" H., painted brown, red, yellow and green (pastel). Watermelon has been repaired. $115.00–125.00

Lawn Figure: Chalk, boy sitting with his hands holding his knees, with hole for a fishing pole. 15" H. $115.00–160.00

Mug: Clear pressed glass stein with pewter top "Frieherrly Tucker Sche Brauerei - Nurnberg" and an incised head of a negro on the top - attached to the glass handle. $145.00–195.00

Bisque Figurine: Black male in an Italian costume, playing a mandolin, 8" H. Painted in pastel light blue, brown, red, black and different shades of yellow. $250.00–325.00

Bisque Figurine: 5" young child on a pot, eating watermelon, painted brown, black and red. Germany. $140.00–165.00

Bisque Figurine: 6½" H. figure of young man wearing large showboat-type top hat, sitting in a chair with his legs straddling the chair's back, smoking cigar (which has fallen inside the figure). Pink, yellow, white and green. $225.00–300.00

Bisque Figurine: Outhouse, 3" baby peeking around the corner of the outhouse at another baby who is sitting on a seat. Caption "One Moment Please." Japan. $80.00–110.00

Sculpture: 8" H. bust of a black male entitled "Djura" by Thomas Paul Strader, 1948, Annapolis, Maryland. Plaster with greenish brown tones. $175.00–250.00

Figurine: Fine Venetian hand-blown glass figurine of man with West Indian or African modern dress. Standing figure with arms akimbo and legs apart, with high pompadour hair style, with striped high-necked T-shirt with rolled sleeves, full length trousers of clear glass with gold flecks. On 4¼" clear glass base. Overall height - 11". $500.00–600.00

Figurine Vase: Fine hand-blown Venetian glass. Blackamoor in medieval Venetian costume with clear glass jacket and pantaloons trimmed with milk glass color. Wide frilly glass cuffs on sleeves and at knees. Black glass head, hands and feet. Holding in hands (and to base) a large clear glass spiral cornucopia (bud) vase. On round 4" dia. clear glass base. 10" H. $500.00–600.00

Figures: Pair of china bathers. Happy native kids out for a good time on the beach(?) One in red trunks lying on his back with hands under head and left leg crossed on knee of other leg, 4¾" L. x 2½" H. Second in blue trunks on knees and elbows, 3¾" L. x 2½" H. Both with big, big smiles, wearing earrings. Made in Japan. (2 items) $45.00–60.00 each

Figure: Amusing china figure of a squat, large bossomed "Mammy" with floor length tan dress, broad brimmed hat and hands folded over tummy. Apparently handmade by molding clay over a telephone pole insulator and then reglazing. Marked "Stan. B." on base. 4½" H., 3" dia. $75.00–80.00

Decoration: Vargas woman holding sleeping child on left shoulder and carrying a basket of vegetables. Dressed in red & white dotted skirt and floral print blouse. $300.00–400.00

Decoration: Delicate old Vargas wax figure on wire skeleton. Woman in floral print skirt/blouse, wearing a turban head wrap. One of rare Vargas family figures of New Orleans vendors (marked on bottom of wood base). Sold 1890–1930's. (Arms and feet wax need replacing.) Ca. 1900. $225.00–300.00

Sculpture: "Teaching" by John Rogers. Group statuary, signed, part. 1866, plaster, original tan paint, 20" H. Depicting Uncle Ned with high boot he's been working on in hand while he instructs two children, girl standing with book in hand to his right and a younger boy at his feet. Note: "Some of the Southern States had statutes against teaching the slaves to read. When the war ended in the emancipation of the slaves, schools for their education were established all over the South and the adults who first learned…became voluntary teachers…as in the case of Uncle Ned." "This sculpture was hailed as a powerful commentary on the freed Negro's determination to educate himself and improve his lot by his own efforts." This highly collectible group is sought after by the Americana collector, second only the famous Rogers's "Slave Auction" group. $1,000.00–1,200.00

Hanger: Colorful plaster wall figure of walking child dressed in white jacket and yellow pants carrying an open red umbrella over right shoulder as protection from the rain with brass cup hook suspended from base to hold child's umbrella(?) or whatever suits the owner. 7½" H. x 6" W x 1" dia. $50.00–60.00

Hitching Post: Concrete jockey, painted red and white, wearing red cap, with right hand extended, on ovoid base. 25¼" H. $300.00–325.00

Ornaments: Beach boys. Pair brown glazed china full figures

of two young boys standing. Figure with left hand on left rear cheek, right hand on right thigh, wearing red swim trunks, green bathing shoes and towel draped over shoulders. Second figure seated with left knee up and holding the knee, wearing red swim trunks, blue bathing shoes and towel draped over shoulders. (2 pieces). $75.00–95.00 each

Ornament: Fisher boy, ceramic figure, painted white and blue and wearing yellow cap, seated with arms wrapped about his knees (but no fishing pole), smoking a cigarette. Paint peeled and/or peeling off. 8½" H. x 4¼" W. x 6¼" D.
$75.00–85.00

Ornament: Fisher Boy. Ceramic figurine of boy seated with arms wrapped about knees, hands holding a fishing pole, and smoking a cigarette. 8½" H. x 5" W. x 4" D. $80.00–100.00

Ornament: Fisher boy, cement figure painted yellow and red. Seated with arms wrapped about his knees, hands holding a fishing pole, wearing a red cap. 8¼" H. x 4" W x 6" D
$50.00–60.00

Fruit Bowl Centerpiece: Nubian. 2-pc. green majolica-type semi-vitreous china figural fruit bowl centerpiece, 13¼" H. Green leafage 10" dia. base on which 3 Nubian semi-nude girls in turbans (10" H) support a vase-form center column on their upraised hands. This column, in turn, holds a green leafage bowl, 12" dia. The Nubian girls are wearing gold necklaces and white, green, blue and gold vertically striped skirts. (Base, 12" H, can be used without top as a flower vase).
$225.00–325.00

Decoration: Vargas Figure. Delicate, old Vargas-style wax figure (on wire skeleton) of man with seaweed or faggots in bundle on his back and with a small alligator on a rope leash. Red checkered shirt. $300.00–400.00

Decoration: Vargas Figure, man with oar, striped shirt.
$300.00–400.00

Postcards: Fifteen cards including six colorful comic cards, 4 cards on cotton industry, turpentine industry, etc. (15 cards)
$15.00–22.00 each

Postcards: Five colorful postcards (1) "Dis Am Heben" - laughing boy with huge watermelon. (2) Black cherubs - 2 boys with palmetto hand-fans behind them so they appear to be winged cherubs. (3) Waiting for the parade in Dixie Land - 7 children on fence. (4) I've Hoed in Fields of Cotton - girl with hoe over shoulder. (5) Wash Day in Dixie - 2 women at large wooden washtub. 3 used (dated 1909-1917) and 2 unused. (5 cards) $15.00–22.00 each

Postcards: 4 old leather postcards and 2 souvenir folders - "Way Down South in Dixie" and "Down in Sunny Dixie." Both with many photos. (6 items) $20.00–30.00 each

Postcards: Nineteen, used/unused, 1900–1910, mostly comic and group of illustrated Post Card Co. (19 items)
$15.00–22.00 each

Postcards: 16 used/unused postcards, 1906-26, aspects of life in the South, Panama natives, watermelon feasting, kids, etc. and historical depictions - Crispus Attucks at the Boston Massacre, Lincoln and the Contrabands. (16 cards)
$15.00–22.00 each

Postcards: "Souvenir Folder of Dixie Land" with Old Black Joe on cover and containing "Watermelon Feast, Picking Cotton, Three of a Kind, Lollipops & Chocolate Drops," etc. Plus Dorton's Cotton Plantation, Turpentine Industry, Skin Game, Mischief Brewing (ca. 1910–1930). Plus 3 different cards of Little Sambo (from Sambo's Restaurants). (11 cards)
$15.00–22.00 each

Postcards: Two postcards framed together as a unit. "In the Cotton Field" – woman with towel wrapped about her head; man in cotton field w/large basket of cotton on his shoulders. Together with a J&P Coats Spool Cotton advt. with background of cotton field. Plus framed postcard of a semi-draped Algerian young woman. (2 frames) $15.00–22.00 each

Ornaments: Miniature Bisque Figures. Pair of babies, wearing white shorts, seated on ground with legs extended, each eating a large slice of watermelon. 2" H x 1½" W x 1½" D (2 figures) $75.00–80.00 each

Ornaments: Nodding Head. Plastic wide-eyed Betty Boop type or kewpie-style seated blue diapered 2-part baby holding a slice of watermelon, wearing a pair of brass ring earrings. Head set on spring so that it nods when moved or touched. 3¾" H x 2¼" W x 1¾" D. $50.00–60.00

Ornament: Outhouse. Bisque ornament of diapered child at open door of orange painted outhouse with child seated within. Printed marking "One Moment Please." Impressed "Japan." 2½" H x 1¼" W x 1½" D $40.00–45.00

Ornament: Misc. (1) Seated bisque Fisher Boy ornament (to set on edge of fishbowl), 4" H. (2) Bisque outhouse ornament (boy to left, child seated within), 2¼". (3) Terra-cotta like figure "Famous Louisiana Mammy" (holding tray with coffee pot & c/s), 5¼" H. (4) Boy's head pepper shakers (wearing beret), 3" H. (4 items) $50.00–60.00 each

Ornament: Rachel. Small bisque 2-part figure of "Mammy"-type with crossed eyes, wearing apron and hat, incised marking on back, "Rachel." Head attached by string making this a nodder. Charming item. 3½" H x 1½" W $80.00–90.00

Wall Hanging: Musician. Burlap sacking with cut-out cloth hand-appliqued scene of an island man in bright floral print shirt, pants and hat seated playing a guitar in front of a palm tree. 20" x 28". $75.00–90.00

Wall Ornament: Painted ceramic smiling woman's head, facing three-quarter right, wearing large single earring in right ear, wearing a neckscarf tied in a bow under the chin and a blue beanie with tassels. (Tip of bow tie missing). 6" H x 4" W x 2½" D. $75.00–95.00

Wine Bottle Decoration. Glass wine bottle (4/5 qt.) very cleverly and artistically overlaid and sculpted with a large face of man with wide toothy smile. (Minor peeling of paint on neck of bottle above decorated face.) $85.00–95.00

Postcards: Eleven different colored photo postcards, used and unused, ca. 1905–1910, published by Leighton, including watermelon scenes, cotton field scenes, alligator bait, Coon Town, etc. Fine lot. (11 cards) $15.00–22.00 each

Postcards: Work and Play. Fourteen cards including 8 dated 1906 - ?. Picking Cotton, Old Black Joe, Kids and A Mule, At the Beach, Fla. Barber Shop, Pulling Turpentine, Alligator Bait, Jackass, Rope-Quattie A Yard, together with photo reproduction cards: Duke Ellington (1934); Planting Sweet Potatoes (1862); Bessie Smith (1925); Eubie Blake and Noble Sissle (1922); Van Der Zee - Children at Dance Class (1928); Olive Band (1922). (14 cards) $15.00–25.00 each

Postcards: Cabin/Log Cabin. Seven different colored postcards, used/unused illustrating life in and around "My Old Cabin Home" and "De Cabin Home in Dixeland." Ca. 1905–1925. (7 cards) $15.00–22.00 each

Postcards: Puzzle. "Pick the Pickaninnies," mailable postcard with various flaps, numerous slots and 17 black and white children's heads pictured, Aunt Jemima-type pictured on front states, "Show Me All dem Eleben Pickaninnies at one time. I don't want to see no white trash." Ullman Mfg. Co., N.Y., 1907. $65.00–85.00

Postcards: Women. Seven postcards (1906-1911) of washer woman, snuff, banjo player & wife, log cabin with mother and 7 children, log cabin and mother with three kids. Mammy on steps, Mammy with mistress. 6 used, 1 unused. (7 cards) $15.00–22.00 each

Souvenirs: Ashtray. Metal figure of howling boy seated on chamber pot. Marked "Souvenir of Florida." Mouth wide open as ash receiver (Nat'l Prod., Inc., Chicago). 6" H. x 3" W. x 3½" D. $65.00–70.00

Souvenir Ashtray: Nodding Figure. Japanese china ashtray in form of a canoe with native paddling. Lower half of the body of a grass skirted native sets astride the canoe as an integral part, with the upper body and head of the native as a separate pestle-form that fits into the opening of the lower body and moves (bows or nods) as one puts out his cigarette…or one may use the pestle-form to tamp out the sparks. 5½" L x 3" W x 4½" H Marked "Florida." $45.00–55.00

Antique Andirons: Unusually fine pair of figural andirons of Black man, facing full front, in standing position, feet apart in a wide stance, hands on knees. Ca. 1800 or earlier. 19¾" H. x 13" W at feet, 9" W at shoulders. Made with exceedingly heavy shanks (or fire dogs), hand-wrought by a blacksmith. Very rare. $500.00–625.00

Bank: "Lucky Joe" Glass Bank. Glass container for Nash's Prepared Mustard (8½" size). Manufactured by Nash Under-wood, Inc., Chicago. Figural head molded in glass and a pair of large red lips (painted on paper) glued into place. Made with tin (sheet metal) screw-type lid with a center coin slot (ca. 1940–50). $30.00–65.00

Lawn Sprinkler: Sambo. Flat metal figural lawn sprinkler with round iron base and hose connection. Colorfully painted on both sides, front and rear views of young man in blue overalls with yellow hat and horizontal striped yellow shirt. Labeled "Sprinklin' Sambo." Dapco Products, Defiance, Ohio. 30" H x 8" W. $110.00–125.00

Doorstop: Antique iron figural doorstop of Aunt Jemima wearing long apron and head turban with hands on hips. 13" H, ca. 1890. Still retains a little of the original red, black and white paint. Rear base of figure has two projecting points to wedge and hold door open. (Weight 6½" lbs.) $225.00–250.00

Tobacco Humidor: Figural stoneware humidor in shape of stitched canvas sack (ceramic rope tied around center with "Good Luck" tag). Lid has a figure of a young man rising from the sack, wearing a tasseled fez and smoking a stub of a cigar. 8½" H., ovoid base shape, 5¼" x 4", with lid 4½" dia. $275.00–325.00

Decoration: Vargas Figure. Old man with faggots on his back and an alligator on leash. $300.00–450.00

Humidor: Figural porcelain tobacco humidor of young man, smoking pipe, balding (retreating hairline), wide shirt collar, at base 4½" H., 3¼" dia. at top. $200.00–225.00

Hitching Post: Concrete jockey, painted blue, green, red and white, wearing green and white cap, with right hand extended holding a ring (with lantern part). Lantern had been electrified. Paint scabrous and in need of repair. 25" H. $100.00–145.00

Victorian Chalk Bust: 15" H., ca. 1870. $425.00–500.00

Iron Figure: 3½" H., man, painted. $90.00–125.00

Iron Figure: 3¼" H., woman clapping hands. $90.00–125.00

Ceramic Head: Old man with beard, semi-bald head, made from cinders or black clay (gray tone). $110.00–$125.00

Mask: 8" iron face mask made from mold (same as death mask) with face features from top lip to hairline above forehead, has 4 holes which were probably used to tie around head, with rawhide when placed on head, it tends to make the head bow. (Obedience Mask?) Ca. 1840, very unusual and rare item. $650.00–800.00

Papier Maché: "The Ghost Story." 11" x 14", bas-relief, watercolor with painted frame, ca. 1900, very scarce. $1,000.00–1,200.00

Chalk Figure: Young man shooting dice with pair of large dice in front of him, as he kneels to throw dice, with glass ashtray,

Alexander Corp. Advertising Displays, Phila., Pa. 7" tall with 5" x 6" base, logo in chalk and also paper label, ca. 1940. $300.00–325.00

Bisque Figure: Two boys conversing, 8½" H., base has been repaired. $85.00–110.00

Staffordshire Whistle: Young man shining boots, 3¾" H., rare. $300.00–350.00

Andirons: Wrought Iron. Antique hand wrought, ca. 1810. Fire dogs with slave's head in top. Horseshoe or inverted U-foot, center circle with slave's head topped by open circle or ring (ring missing from one andiron). Early Americana, imperfect, illustrated in book *Antique Iron* by H.P. & N. Schiffer, Schiffer Publ. Exton (1979) p. 139, illus. C. 14½" H. Extremely heavy shanks. Very rare. $625.00–700.00

Mug: Ceramic toby mug of Black man with green eyes and green color. Minor edge chip. 5" H. $70.00–90.00

Folk Art

Needlepoint: 21" x 26", framed in contemporary frame. "Little Eva and Uncle Tom," ca. 1880, blue, red, pink, brown, gold and white, excellent condition. $375.00–425.00

Needlepoint: 5⅝" dia. cross-stitch of a small girl washing clothes in a tub with a doll sitting in front of the tub and clothes hanging on the line above her head, framed, ca. 1935. $95.00–150.00

Folk Art: Carved wood nutcracker in the shape of a man's head; eye, mouth and earrings are painted, ca. 1900. $300.00–350.00

Tablecloth: 51" square tablecloth (men playing banjos and eating watermelon), green, blue and red on a white background. $225.00–300.00

Tramp Art Box: Box hand carved with mirror lining and a photo of a Black male on the lid. Fair condition. $95.00–135.00

Carving: Wood carving, 29" H, of a man with exaggerated long legs, dressed in overalls, barefooted, holding a sack slung over his left shoulder in his left hand. Stands erect on 2½" H ovoid base. 31½" H. overall - has a drilled hole ¼" front and back. $175.00–250.00

Folk Art: Hand-carved miniature figures of man on mule with Mammy, "Dynamo & Chalcedony"; made of pine, copper wire and paper (in wooded box). Fine example of contemporary native art. 6½" x 3½" x 4½". $125.00–150.00

Folk Art: Wooden art deco cut-out figural ashtray stand (only) with swallow-tail coat, striped vest, trousers with orange stripe, white spats. 33¾" H. $225.00–300.00

Folk Art: Wooden cut-out figural stand with swallow-tail coat, red knee breeches, white shirt and stockings. Hands missing, rear portion of lower circular base missing. Ca. 1930. (Needs regluing at feet and tummy.) $90.00–110.00

Folk Art: Male/Female Dolls. 18" stuffed cloth doll of woman dressed red underskirt, red/white designed middle-skirt, dark blue-on-blue dress, brown/white w/red trim apron and brown plaid, trimmed in red, kitchen-type head cover. Eyes and eyebrows are stitched with pair of black cylinder beads for each eye. Nose and mouth and applied cloth. Legs are made of red wool with brown and white striped cloth for socks. Red kid leather shoes w/three white buttons. (Doll shows wear on face, shoulders and fingers – showing it was used as a child's play companion, and not just for display. Otherwise in excellent condition.) 19" stuffed cloth doll of man in blue cloth suit, trimmed in red w/red shirt and white silk bowtie, one brass button on coat and one metal button on shirt. Cap is blue trimmed in red and shoes are black kid leather. Eyes and eyebrows are stitched with three black cylinder beads for each eye. Nose and mouth are applied cloth. Brown/white striped cloth for socks. (This doll, although a match to the above doll, shows far less wear.) Ca. 1850. $300.00–350.00 each

Tie Rack: Burn-wood art. Two boys looking over fence with ties in their hands. "I rather guess we use some sense," on back board. "We hang our neckties on dis fence!" on front bar. Flemish Art Co., N.Y. #1083. $115.00–175.00

Primitive Watercolor: Cut out and applied to board. 3½" x 4½", framed (original) ca. 1840–60, extremely rare piece of early American Folk Art. $800.00–900.00

6" press wood figure of woman wearing apron with hands on hip. Ca. 1935. $95.00–125.00

Needlecraft: Five 11½" x 20" linen dish cloths with very colorful designs, depicting various Black images. Ca. 1925. $250.00–300.00

Card Stand: Butler. Wood cut-out primitive cartoon figure of butler with white painted shirt, big red lips, attached arms holding round wood card tray (or for glass ashtray). $200.00–250.00

Dish Cloth: Bright poplin cloth with print of two girls and a boy in garden with sunflowers picking tomatoes and watermelon in green border. (Faded) 15" x 25". $75.00–95.00

Literary Collectibles

Saturday Evening Post, Nov. 4, 1913. Caption: "According to the Sucker" by Harris Dickson. Illustration by Henry Raleigh of a Black man named Virgil Custard (inside article 2½" pages). 14" x 11". $90.00–110.00

Book: *Little Black Sambo* by Helen Bannerman, A Mary Perks

Book, The American Crayon Co., Sandusky, Ohio, Harter Publishing Co., 1931, John Sherman Bugg, 1943. 14 pages w/ color and b/w illustrations by Feru Bisil Peat, w/jacket.
$150.00–215.00

The Ten Little Niggers published by W.F. McLaughlin & Co., Chicago, Ill. 16 pages of verse, sepia tone, color lithos, Koerner & Hayes, Buffalo, NY. Ca. 1890. $350.00–475.00

Book: *The World of James VanDerzee; A Visual Record of Black Americans*, compiled and with introduction by Reginald McGhee, Grove Press, Inc., NY, NY, 1969. $150.00–185.00

Booklet: "Ten Little Niggers," accordion fold-out. 10 lithographed pages in solid colors of green, red, blue, brown and black, ca. 1900. $225.00–250.00

Book: *Old Voices* by Howard Weeden, Doubleday, Page & Company, 1904. $60.00–70.00

Book: *International Library of Negro Life and History*, two volumes. $110.00–125.00

Newspapers: 1840–1940. Miscellaneous articles on Blacks, per page. $45.00–55.00 each

Magazine: *The Southern Workman*, Vol. XXXI. No. 5, May 1902, published by the Hampton Press, Hampton, Va., with articles "Booker Washington's School Days at Hampton" by Nathalie Lord and "The Penn School on St. Helena Island," illustrated w/halftones. $185.00–215.00

Book: *Uncle John's Drolleries - Simple Addition by a Little Nigger*, McLaughlin Brothers, New York, spine repaired with mouse damage at the upper corner, color lithographs, ca. 1880. $185.00–225.00

Black Mother Goose Book arranged by Elizabeth Murphy Oliver and illustrated by Aaron Sopher, 1st limited edition (1969), color, Maryland Publishing Co., Inc. (autographed by both the arranger and the illustrator). $95.00–135.00

Books: *Native Son*, 1st edition, 1940, w/jacket and *Black Boy*, 1945. (2 items) $95.00–110.00

Books: *Who's Who in Colored America* (A Biographical Dictionary of Notable Living Persons of African Descent in America) edited by Joseph J. Boris, 1928-1929, 2nd edition, Who's Who in Colored America Corp., N.Y., N.Y., illustrated with halftones. 470 pages. $175.00–215.00

Books: Joel Chandler Harris, *Uncle Remus - His Songs and His Sayings* and *The Tar Baby and Other Rhymes of Uncle Remus*, illustrated by A.B. Frost and E.W. Kimble (2 items)
$150.00–175.00

Books: *The Complete Poems of Paul Laurence Dunbar; The Negro in Our History*, and *Kelley Miller's History of the World War for Human Rights*. (3 items) $125.00–175.00

Books: *Uncle Tom's Cabin* by Harriet Beecher Stowe, rewritten for young readers by Mary E. Blain, illustrated by Hugo Von Hofsten, Barse & Hopkins, published N.Y., together with *Eneas Africanus* by Harry Stillwell Edwards, illustrated by Ernest Townsend, Grosset & Dunlap, N.Y., w/jacket. (2 items) $75.00–115.00

Pamphlet: Slavery. "An Exposition of the African Slave Trade, from ca. 1840 to 1850, Inclusive." Philadelphia: J. Rakestraw, 1951, 8 vol. printed wraps, 160 pages, Sabin 23452.
$150.00–185.00

Pamphlet: Massacre. "The Massacre of Six Colored Citizens At Hamburgh, S.C. on July 4, 1876." 44th Congress, 2nd Session, House Report, 8 vol. 14 pages, integral title, untrimmed. Edges chipped, first leaf detached, light foxing. Includes quotes by Black congressmen regarding vigilante actions by Georgians against S.C. Blacks. $145.00–185.00

Pamphlet: Slavery. "An Address to the Anti-Slavery Christians of the United States." N.Y.: John A. Gray, 1852, 8 vol., blue printed wraps, 16 pages. Very light aging at edges, else very nice, interior library handstamp. Address on behalf of American and Foreign Anti-Slavery Society. $95.00–115.00

Pamphlet: Slavery. "A Northern Presbyter's Second Letter to Ministers of the Gospel of All Denominations on Slavery," by Nathan Lord. Boston: Little, Brown, 1855. 8 vol., removed 99 pages, integral title, saddle-stitched. Some rubbing and light soiling to outside leaves, last leaf chipped. Good condition. Sabin 42044. $95.00–115.00

Pamphlet: Slavery. "Anti-Slavery Catechism," by Mrs. (Lydia Maria) Child. Newburyport: Charles Whipple, 1839. 2 edition. "Does the Bible Sanction American Slavery?" by Godwin Smith. Cambridge: Sever and Francis, 1863. 12 mos. original blue printed wraps on first, second removed, 26 and 107 pages. Both nice with light wear. Sabin 12710, 82676. $95.00–115.00

Pamphlet: Slavery. "Slavery and the Remedy; or Principles and Suggestions for a Remedial Code," by Samuel Nott. Boston: Crocker and Brewer, 1856. 8 vol. printed wraps, 118 pages, saddle-stitched. Light chips to wraps, contents very good. Sabin 56060. $95.00–115.00

Pamphlet: Freedmen. "A Report on the Condition of the Freedom of the Mississippi...," by James E. Yeatman. St. Louis: Western Sanitary Commission, 1864. 8 vol., printed wraps. Good condition. $95.00–115.00

Pamphlet: Slavery: "Anti-Slavery Tracts No. 14 – A Fresh Catalogue of Southern Outrages upon Northern Citizens." N.Y.: American Anti-Slavery Society, 1860. 12 mo., 72 pages, integral title, saddle-stitched. Dampstains to most of text, otherwise in good condition (once a library book).
$95.00–115.00

Pamphlet: Slavery: "Anti-Slavery Tracts No. 4 – The New Race of Terror in the Slaveholding States, for 1859-60." N.Y.: Anti-

Slavery Society, 1860. 12 mo., 144 pages, integral title, saddle-stitched. Light damping throughout, title leaf partly separated.
$95.00–115.00

Pamphlet: Abductions. "Address…at Faneuil Hall, September 24, 1856…(on) Kidnapping from Our Soil (of Free Blacks)…" Boston: White & Potter, 1846, 8 vol., 42 pages, integral title, removed. First leaf dusted.
$95.00–115.00

Book: Keltzing, H.F. and Crogman, W.H. *Progress of A Race, Or, The Remarkable Advancement of the Afro-American Negro.* Atlanta: J.L. Nichols, 1899. Salesman's dummy, containing numerous examples of illustrations, and concept of text. 12 mo., blue cloth and red calf, with covers well worn. Includes halftone portraits of B.T. Washington, F. Douglas, H.B. Stowe, C. Sumner, W.H. Carney and many others.
$95.00–135.00

Pamphlets: Slavery. Bound volume of 7 pamphlets and 13 issues of the "Anti-Slavery Record" (#5–22, not inclusive), 1816 - 1857. 12 mo., calf and marbled boards, edges worn, wood engraved illustration in most issues of "Record."
$225.00–300.00

Pamphlet: Slavery. Henry, C.S., "Patriotism and the Slaveholders' Rebellion," N.Y.: Appleton, 1861. Slim 8 vol., 34 pages, integral title, saddle-stitched. Some aging, small library stamp.
$65.00–110.00

Pamphlet: Slavery. Five "Anti-Slavery Tracts," Nos. 1, 7, 10, 11, 15, all issued by the American Anti-Slavery Society, ca. 1859-1860. 12 mos., 7-20 pages each. Very light wear. Good condition.
$75.00–110.00

Autograph: Booker T. Washington. Typewritten letter on "Booker T. Washington, Tuskegee Institute, Alabama" stationary to parent of one of his students at Institute during his term as principal, dated October 10, 1911. $185.00–225.00

Book: Publisher's salesman sample, *The Story of My Life and Work* by Booker T. Washington, W.H. Ferguson Co., Cincinnati, Ohio, 1900, illustrated with b/w halftone. $95.00–115.00
Book: *Organized Labor and the Negro* by Herbert R. Northup, Harper and Bros., Publisher, N.Y., and London, 1944.
$75.00–85.00

Book: Children's Book. *Unkle Rastus' Christmas Tree* designed and written by S. Herbert Voorhees, illustrated by Mildred C. Hayes, 1921. Drawings, colored with crayons, (not original).
$95.00–155.00

Books: *The Black Family in Slavery and Freedom 1750–1925* by Herbert G. Gutman; *Documents of Upheaval* (selections from William Loyd Garrison's *The Liberator 1931-1865*); *Time on the Cross* by Robert William Fogel and Stanley L. Engerman and *The Slave Catchers* by Stanley W. Campbell. (5 items)
$175.00–225.00

Books: Booker T. Washington, *Character Building; Working With the Hands; My Larger Education* (all by Washington);

and *Selected Speeches of Booker T. Washington edited by E. Davidson Washington,* 1932, 1st edition. (4 items)
$115.00–200.00

Books: *Goodbye to Uncle Tom* by J.C. Furnas; *American Slavery and Colour* by William Chambers; *John Brown's Body* by Stephen Vincent Benet; *Emotion at High Tide* (Abolition as a Controversial Factor, 1830–1845) by Henry H. Simms; and *The Adventure of an African Slaver*, a true account of the life of Captain Theodore Canot. (5 items) $185.00–245.00

Pamphlet: "Four Negro Poets, The Pamphlet Poets" published by Simon & Schuster, Inc., 1927 (Works of Claude McKay, Jean Toomer, Countee Cullen and Langston Hughes.)
$115.00–195.00

Children's Books: *The Story of Little Black Sambo*, Wee Books for Wee Folks, w/jacket and *The Story Book of Cotton* by Maud and Miska Petersham. (2 items) $95.00–145.00

Book: Hinton, Richard J., *John Brown and His Men with some Account of the Roads They Traveled to Reach Harper's Ferry*, N.Y., revised (1894), w/numerous illustrations. 752 pages.
$110.00–165.00

Books: Antebellum. Seven titled original editions or photographic reprints. All volumes deal with slavery in antebellum South. All in publisher's cloth, 2 with dust wrapper, in very good condition, several very fine. Includes essays and biography of Robert Toombs by Ulrich B. Phillips, biography of James G. Birney, and 2-volume set on plantation documents, edited by Phillips. (8 volumes) $95.00–115.00

Books: Anti-Slavery. Group of thirteen volumes: biographies, historical analyses, and reprints of contemporary anti-slavery accounts. All in original publisher's cloth, few with dust wrappers, in very good condition overall, many very fine. Includes reprints of works on fugitive slaves: McDougall - *Fugitive Slave*), Siebert - *The Underground Railroad from Slavery to Freedom*, the abolitionist movement, and the colonization efforts prior to the Civil War, *Report of Mr. Kennedy of Md.* plus biographies of the Beecher family, William Jay and others.
$125.00–175.00

Books: Authors. Group of ten volumes, most initial editions, original clothes, all but one in dust wrappers, either by or about 20th century Black American authors. Very good condition, few with moderate wear at edges. Includes volumes by Richard Wright, Early Conrad, Cynthia J. Prime, Howard W. Odum, plus volumes about Negro playwright, William Stanley Braithwaite, Black French writers, others. $165.00–215.00

Books: Autobiographies, etc. 11 books including Gregory's *Nigger*, Quarles, *The Negro in the Making America; Soul Food - Illus. New Testament*; Griffin's *Black Like Me*; Allen, *Great Black Americans*; Lester, *To Be a Slave, Judge Horton & The Scottsboro Boys, Autobiography of Malcolm X, Black Rage*; Grier/Cobb, Wright's *Uncle Tom's Children* and *Angela* by "The Professor." All paperbacks. Various editions and condition. (11 books) $45.00–55.00 each

Books: Biographies. Gathering of 9 titles, all biographies or autobiographies of prominent Black Americans, or those involved in the abolitionist or anti-slavery movements. Original cloths, 6 w/dust wrappers, in very nice condition overall, few moderately worn. Includes volumes on Ethel Waters, Owen Lovejoy, Eldridge Cleaver, Pierre Toussaint, Robert S. Abbott, Edward Seaward, Albion W. Tourgee, Father Divine, and E. Frederic Morrow. $115.00–145.00

Book: Black Migration. Bontemps, Arna and Conroy, Jack. *They Seek A City.* Doubleday, Doran, Garden City, 1945. 8 vol., 266 pages. First edition. An account of Black migration within the U.S. with special attention on Chicago and the Midwest. $55.00–65.00

Pamphlet: Emancipation. "Free Negroism" (N.Y., 1862). 8 vol., 32 pages, saddle-stitched. Some wear, small library stamp, fair condition. $75.00–95.00

Pamphlet: Slavery. Tucker, St. George. "A Dissertation on Slavery: With a Proposal for the Gradual Abolition of It, in the State of Virginia." N.Y., 1861. Reprint of 1796 original edition. Tall slim 8 vol., 104 pages, printed front wrap, which is detached and chipped. $75.00–115.00

Pamplets: Slavery. Beecher, Charles. "The Duty of Disobedience to Wicked Laws: A Sermon on the Fugitive Slave Law," N.Y., 1851. "The Equality of All Men Before the Law…" Speeches by William D. Kelley, Wendell Phillips, Frederick Douglass. Boston, 1865. 8 vols., 22 and 43 pages, first removed, w/ penciled presentation by author. Some wear, good condition. $75.00–115.00

Book: Talley, Thomas W., *Negro Folk Rhymes: Wise and Otherwise; With a Study.* N.Y.: Macmillan, 1922. First edition. Thick 12 mo., green cloth XII and 347 pages, very good condition. $95.00–125.00

Flyer: (Fold, 4 pages) "The Negro in the Cars – White Workingmen Disfranchised." (Four-page political give-away, in the State of Pennsylvania, citing a new law giving the Negro the right to board any car on the railroads of Pennsylvania. This flyer was distributed against the Negro of Pennsylvania and Ohio), ca. 1867. $85.00–125.00

Book: *Ten Little Niggers.* Bo Peep Series, McLaughlin & Bros., N.Y. 1896, cover has been repaired with tape and bound with black cotton. $225.00–350.00

Book: *Black Boy* by Richard Wright (A Record of Childhood and Youth), Harper & Bros. Publ., N.Y. and London, 1945, 1st edition, w/jacket. $65.00–95.00

Book: *White Supremacy and Negro Subordination: or Negroes a Subordinate Race and (So-called) Slavery Its Normal Condition* (with an appendix showing the past and present condition of the countries south of us) by J.H. Van Evrie, M.D.; Van Evrie, Horton & Co., N.Y., 1868, 2nd edition, 405 pp., illustrated, loose spine. $110.00–165.00

Almanac: Slavery. "The American Anti-Slavery Almanac for 1836." Vol. I, No. 1, Webster & Southard, boston, 46 pages, w/ badly chipped spine, text intact. $95.00–125.00

Letter: Slavery. Letter from Fayettesville, NC, written March 22, 1859, w/reference to the mortgage of a Negro boy - "I shall leave with Roy & Pearce, Mr. Blount's note for $350 - the mortgage upon a Negro boy and a policy of insurance on the boy's life for $350 & Curtis' note for $200 for your complete security…signed…" 4 pp., script, folded, good condition. $135.00–185.00

Autograph: Paul Lawrence Dunbar. Typewritten letter, written to Edwin H. Hackley, Esq. of Philadelphia, Pa., dated October 31, 1904, signed "Paul Lawrence Dunbar." $250.00–325.00

Book: Minstrels. Two Minstrel books: (1) Newton, Harry L., *Laughland - A Merry Minstrel Book*, T.S. Dennison & Co., Chicago, (1909). Small 8 vol., 107 pages + advt. Paper cover with caroon of 2 minstrels with tiny dog. (2) Wheeler, H.H., *Up to Date Minstrel Jokes*, Walter H. Baker Co., Boston, (1910), 71 pages. Paper wraps. Plus "Female Minstrel Jokes." 31 pages + "Mistaken Identity," an Ethiopian Farce in One Scene, by Geo. H. Coes; "Badly Sold," a Negro Act in 2 Scenes, by Geo. H. Coes, Music and Elocution. Negro Sketch in one act - Geo. H. Coes, "Black Blunders" Ethiopian Farce in 2 scenes, by Geo. H. Coes. (2 items) $75.00–95.00 each

Book: Frank, Gerold. *An American Death/The True Story of the Assassination of Dr. Martin Luther King Jr. & The Greatest Manhunt of Our Time,* Doubleday, 1972. 8 vol., 467 pages w/ dust jacket with 31 illustrations. $65.00–75.00

Book: National Book Award Winner. Jordan, Winthrop D., *White Over Black, American Attitudes Toward the Negro, 1550–1812.* Univ. of North Carolina Press, (1968). 8 vol., XX 651 pages. Published for the Institute of Early American History & Culture. Bancroft Prize Winner. $45.00–55.00

Book: Negro Race. Williams, George Washington, *History of the Negro Race in America*, Bergman Publ., N.Y. (1968). 2 vol. XIX, 481 pages: XIII 611 pages. Reprint, 1st publ. 1883. *Negro Race in America from 1619 to 1880/Negroes As Slaves, As Soldiers and As Citizen*s written by the first colored member of the Ohio legislature. (2 volumes) $75.00–95.00

Books: Non-fiction. 11 books including E.L. Lee, *C.H. Mason - Man Greatly Used of God*; Cleveland, *Without A Song, Soul Word, Soul to Soul, Black World*; Peck's *The Life and Words of Martin Luther King, Jr.*; Davidson, *Frederick Douglass Fights for Freedom*; Allen, *Great Black Americans*; Cohen "Cool Cos" Griffin, *Black Like Me*; and Davy's *Mr. Creator's Borrowed Brown Hands.* All but first are paperbacks. Various editions. (11 books) $35.00–45.00 each

Books: Novels. 6 books including Thom Demijohn's *Black Alice*, Doubleday, Garden City, (1968); James E. Nash, *Poor*

Teddy Black, Harper, N.Y., (1970); Blough's *The Brass Ring*; Alex Haley, *Roots*; Williams, *The Man Who Cried I Am*; and Cato, *Chindera*. Latter four are paperbacks. Various editions. (6 books) $35.00–45.00 each

Book: Novels. Three old timers. Fast, Howard, *Freedom Road*, Duell, Sloan & Pearce, N.Y., (1944). 8 vol., 263 pages. Innter front spine loose. Stowe, Harriet Beecher, *Uncle Tom's Cabin*, Grosset and Dunlap, N.Y., n.d., 8 vol., 442 pages. Dixon, Thomas, Jr., *The Clansman, An Historical Romance of the Ku Klux Klan*, A. Wassels Co., N.Y., 1907, 8 vol., 374 pages. Cover detached. Frontispiece torn. (3 books) $75.00–95.00 each

Book: Caribbean. Four titles, each dealing with Blacks in the Caribbean, primarily Martinique and Jamaica. Original publisher's cloths, one in dust wrapper, very nice overall. Includes Gladstone and Gripper, *Correspondence on the Present State of Slavery in the British West Indies...* (1972 photo reprint); Sells, *Remarks on the Condition of the Slaves on the Island of Jamaica* (1972 photo reprint); Phillippo, *Jamaica: Its Past Present State* (1971 photo reprint); Skater, *The Caribbean Family: Legitimacy in Martinique* (1977). $65.00–75.00

Book: Children's. Montgomery, Frances Trego. *Billy Whiskers in the South*, Saalfield Publ., Akron, 1917. 148 pages with 16 color illustrations by Will Fitzgerald. Large 8 vol. colorful cover caroon of the goat (Billy Whiskers) butting a man with the stolen watermelon. $75.00–95.00

Book: Swearingen, Estelle Margaret, *Pickaninny*, Duffield & Co., N.Y., 1925. Small 8 vol., 132 pages, introduction by Ruth Comfort Mitchell, illustrated by E.W. Kimble. $55.00–65.00

Books: Children/Youth. Seven books including *Little Black Sambo, Fat Albert, Five Little Gifts, Jungle Heroes, Our Little Ethiopian Cousin, Afoot and Afloat in Burma* and *The Jackie Robinson Story*. Various editions. $125.00–155.00

Books: Civil Rights. Group of 8 books, original cloths, all but one in dust wrappers, all related to the Civil Rights effort in the U.S. South during the 1960's. All very nice, few with light wear at edges. Includes: Huie, *Three Lives for Mississippi*, 1965; King, Martin L., Jr., *Strength to Love*, 1963; Von Hoffman, *Mississippi Notebook*, 1964; Meredith, James, *Three Years in Mississippi*, 1966. $125.00–145.00

Books: Civil Rights. Group of 10 volumes, each on the Civil Rights Movement in the United States in the 1960's and 1970's. All in cloth save one in wraps. All but one with original dust wrappers. Very good condition overall, some dust wrappers moderately worn. Includes volumes on Watts, J.F. Kennedy, the Black Panthers and the Black Power Movement. $125.00–175.00

Books: Civil Rights. 4 titles, original editions and photographic reprints, all dealing with slavery and the Civil War. Original cloths, two with dust wrappers in very good condition overall. Includes Wagandt, *The Might Revolution; Negro Emancipation in Maryland. 1862-1864*, 1964; Schluter, *Lincoln, Labor and Slavery*, 1965; Kirke, *Down in Tennessee, and Back by Way of Richmond*, 1971; Logan, *The Great Conspiracy: Its Origin and History*, 1971. $95.00–110.00

Books: Howard, Oliver Otis, *Autobiography of Oliver Otis Howard, Major General U.S. Army*. Books for Libraries Press, Freeport, N.Y., 1971. 2 volumes: xi 602 pages, ix 610 pages; *The Black Heritage Library Collection*. First publ. 1907, reprinted 1971. Mint condition. (Note: Howard, Commissioner Freedmen's Bureau and founder Howard University.) $65.00–75.00

Book: Friends and Slavery. *The Discipline of the Society of Friends, of Indiana Yearly Meeting*, with Richmond, E. Morgan & Sons, 1864. Small 8 vol., 146 pages with section of Friends belief of the repugnancy of slavery to the Christian religion (from the center of the midwest underground railroad during the Civil War). $65.00–85.00

Book: Haiti. Vandercook, John W., *Black Majesty*, Literary Guild of America, N.Y., 1928, 8 vol., 207 pages plus advertisement with dust jacket. Illustrated by Mahlon Blaine. This is a fascinating story of Haitian native fight for independence led by Christophe. $45.00–65.00

Book: Harlem Pictorial. Schoener, Allon (editor), *Harlem on my Mind/Cultural Capital of Black America 1900/1968*, Random House, NY, 1968. First printing, 255 pages with dust jacket. Introduction by Thomas Hoving. (Numerous newspaper articles and hundreds of photos.) $55.00–65.00

Books: Jokes. The Star Stories, *Funny Jokes and Funny Stories*, Western Printing and Litho. Co., Racine, n.d. (ca. 1920), 12 mo., 64 pages. Paper wraps, color cover w/Ray Gleason illustration of laughing heavy-set minstrel w/polka dot bowtie. *New Coon Jokes*, Arthur Westbrook Co., Cleveland, small 8 vol., 64 pages(?), rear cover missing, front cover loose and torn. Color cover of top-hatted man seated on watermelon w/small slice in hand, razor stuck in watermelon. (2 books) $75.00–95.00 each

Book: KKK. Dixon, Thomas. *The Clansman. An Historical Romance of the Ku Klux Klan*, Grosset & Dunlap, NY (1905). 8 vol., 374 pages. Illustrated with photos from the movie "The Birth of a Nation" with dedication to "My Uncle Colonel Leroy McAfee, Grand Titan of the Invisible Empire Ku Klux Klan." $55.00–65.00

Books: Magazines. Four volumes, each an analytical guide and index to different early 20th century U.S. Black magazines. Each very fine, black cloth, contents excellent. Includes guides to *The Voice of the Negro, The Colored American Magazine* (2 volumes) and *Alexander's Magazine*. $65.00–75.00

Books: Minstrels. Lawrence, John E., *Minstrel First Parts* (series), T.S. Dennison and Co., Chicago, 1922-24, paper wraps, small 8 vol. *Dennison's Alabama Minstrel First Part*, 32 pages, 1922; *Dennison's Dixie Minstrel First Part*, 39 pages + ads, 1924. (2 items) $75.00–95.00 each

Books: Minstrels. Lawrence, John E. *Minstrel First Parts* (series), T.S. Dennison and Co., Chicago. paper wraps (1928-29). *Dennison's Old Virginia Minstrel First Part*, (1920), small 8 vol. 36 pages; *Dennison's Louisiana Minstrel First Part* (1928), 38 pages. (2 items) $95.00–110.00

Newspaper: Abolitionist. *The National Era*, Wash. (1) August 10, 1854, with lengthy reports on 33rd Congress, 1st Session, Free democratic convention, Fugitive Slave Act – Unconstitutional. (2) March 3, 1853, several reviews of books on white slavery, etc. (2 items) $70.00–85.00 each

Newspaper: Atkinson's *Saturday Evening Post*. Phila. July 4, 1835. Report, "The White Slave," concerning impending trial in Baltimore of a young girl alleged by the claimant to be the daughter of his mulatto slave stolen from him but professed by a colored man to be his adopted daughter left with him years before by a white woman who said this was her mulatto daughter… Also the paper reports in "The Slave Trade" of a case pending in N.Y. following the arrest of 2 prominent citizens for bringing slaves from Africa. $70.00–85.00

Newspaper: Comics. *The Illustrated Record* (The Largest Newspaper in the World), N.Y.C., Sept. 7, 1895, with several illustrated jokes on the cartoon page, "The Joker."
               $65.00–75.00

Newspaper: Fugitive Slave Act/Kansas Territory, *The National Era*, Wash., D.C., July 20, 1854, with lead article on Movements in Kansas (Abolition of Slavery), Speech of Garret Smith on Mexican Treaty and Monroe Doctrine, 33rd Congress - 1st Session (Repeal of Fugitive Slave Law), etc.
               $55.00–65.00

Newspaper: *The National Era*. Wash., D.C., July 27, 1854. Most of back page given to publication of "The Nebraska Act/An Act to Organize the Territories of Nebraska and Kansas." (Note: This act was very important in the events leading to Civil War when signed by Pres. Pierce, May 20, 1854. It proclaimed that two new territories should be free of slaves as voted by its citizens, thus reversing the policy regarding extension of slavery established by Missouri Compromise of 1820 for Louisiana Territory.). Various folds cracked. $55.00–65.00

Pamphlet: Slavery. Non-Interference by Congress with slavery in the Territories. "Speech of Stephen A. Douglas of Illinois, in the Senate, May 15/16, 1860." 32 pages, 8 vol., Lem Towers, Printer (R), self wraps, covers fly-specked. $65.00–75.00

Pamphlet: Webb, General J. Watson, "Speech of _____ at the Great Mass Meeting/On the Battle Ground of/Tippecanoe/60,000 Freemen in Council." 8 vol., 20 pages, self wraps., n.p. (N.Y.?), n.d. (ca. 1855). Apparently reprint of lengthy article appearing Oct. 14th?, in *The Morning Courier and N.Y. Enquirer* (N.Y. City). J.W. Webb was proprietor and editor.
               $65.00–75.00

Pamphlet: Violation of Civil Rights. Message of the President of the U.S., Feb. 19, 1867 in compliance with a resolution of the Senate calling for information in relation to violations of the Civil Rights Act, stitched 8 vol., 43 pages, 39th Congress, 2nd session, Senate Exec. Doc. #29. $65.00–75.00

Advt. Booklet: Regal Shoe. 4-page advertising brochure "The Regal Shoe - For Men & Woman - $6.00 shoe for $3.50." Cover with sepia litho by W.F. Powers, N.Y. (1900) of 2 little kids and 2 babies by a fence. 10" x 6½". $55.00–65.00

Pamphlet: Little Henry & His Bearer, (As above) with last 2 pages torn but complete. $70.00–90.00

Books: Africa. Group of 11 titles, most first editions, all 8 vol. original cloths, all in dust wrappers, in good to better condition overall. Subjects cover various aspects of life and politics in South Africa, plus neighboring lands, including Rhodesia. Includes several biographies, travel accounts, struggles of Blacks within the South African system, etc. (11 books)
               $75.00–95.00 each

Books: Africa. Large gathering of 30 volumes, mostly 8 vol., most with dust wrappers, all volumes dealing with Africa, emergence of new nations, the sociological struggles against former colonization, tribal histories, and other subjects including some volumes on Nigeria and other specific nations. (30 volumes) $45.00–55.00 each

Books: Africa. 7 volumes and later editions, 8 vol., all but one with dust wrappers, in very good condition overall, all volumes dealing with Central Africa, primarily Uganda, Tanganyika (Tanzania) and Kenya. Includes Thomas, *Warrior Herdsmen*, 1965; Gaiti, *Africa is Adventure,* 1959; Leakey, *White African*, 1966; Huxley, *With Forks and Hope*, 1964; Cole, *The Prehistory of East Africa*, 1963; Rothchild, *Toward Unity In Africa*, 1960; Werner, *A First Swahili Book*, 1930. (7 books)
               $45.00–60.00 each

Pamphlet: "Little Henry & His Bearer." Amer. Tract Soc. (#107) printed by Flagg and Gould, Andover, n.d. (ca. 1825). Removed, 32-pages. Woodcut cover with Black man carrying white child. Clean. $90.00–125.00

Pamphlet: Slavery. (Wise, Henry Alexander) Substitute for the Report of the Committee on Federal Relations (at the Virginia Convention), March 9, 1861. 7 of 9 pp (n.p.) an appeal by Wise to Confederates of Va. still in Union to get a determination on points of difference and dissension of Federal Property and D.C., African slaves, fugitive slaves, etc. Stained, 7 of 9 pages, unbound. (Note: Henry A. Wise, Gov. of Va., refused to reprieve John Brown, first opposed secession, became Confederate general.) $75.00–85.00

Books: James Baldwin. *Nobody Knows My Name: More Notes of a Native Son, The First Next Time, No Name in the Street.* N.Y.: Dial, 1961, 1963, 1972. 3rd printing of first, others first editions. 8 vol., cloth, first two with dust wrappers, in good to very good condition overall. (3 volumes) $45.00–60.00 each

Books: Biographies. Group of 13 titles, all biographies or autobiographies of mostly 20th century Black Americans, with few on earlier well-known Blacks. 8 vol., all but one with dust wrappers, in very good condition overall, some dust wrappers lightly chipped, few volumes moderately worn, one with spine well worn. Includes volumes on Rev. William Holmes Borders, Benjamin E. Mays, LeEha Whitfield, Peter Still, Mary McLeod Bethune, Rev. James H. Robinson, Archibald Grimke, Christophe, Charles W. Chestnutt, Geo. S. Schuyler, and Bert Williams among others. (13 volumes) $55.00–65.00 each

Book: Illustrated. *The Old Folks at Home*, illustrated by G.W. Brenneman, publ. White & Allen, N.Y./London, 1888. Illustrated cover, softbound, ribbon bound, 8 vol. (with added words and music by Stephen Foster.) $95.00–160.00

Books: Africa. 5 titles, all relating to the Congo. Various 8 vol. all but one with dust wrappers, in good to better condition overall. Includes Merriam, *Congo: Background or conflict*, 1961; Bellotti, *Fabulous Congo*, ca. 1955; Carlson, *Monganga Paul – The Congo Ministry and Martyrdom of Paul Carson, M.D.*, 1966; Deans, *Muffled Drumbeats in the Congo*, 1961. Inscribed by author at front blank. Latouche, *Congo*, photographed by Andre Cauvin, 1945. (5 books) $75.00–85.00

Books: 12 books on American plantation and slave life, African slave trade, etc. including *Black Cargo, Eden, Mandingo, Heir to Falconhurst, The Street of the Sun, August Heat, Black Love, Chinaberry, Dark Don't Catch Me*. All paperbacks, various authors, editions and conditions. S.W.A.F. (12 books) $45.00–50.00 each

Book: Wright, Richard. *Native Son*, Harper & Bros., N.Y., 1940, 8 vol. XI 359 pages. $45.00–65.00

Book: Plays. Green, Paul, *Lonesome Road/Six Plays for the Negro Theatre*. With introduction by Barrett H. Clark. Robt. M. McBride, N.Y. 1926, first edition. Small 8 vol., XX 217 pages + advt. Floral cloth binding, paper labels. $95.00–145.00

Book: Race Relations: Interesting group of 20 volumes, all 8 vol. most in cloth, many with dust wrappers, in good to very good condition overall, all titles dealing with the political, sociological or physiological struggle by Blacks to achieve equality in the United States, 1940's-1970's. Includes several well-known titles, plus numerous less publicized or rather technical volumes. $95.00–135.00

Book: Reconstruction. 12 titles, all dealing with Blacks in the post-Civil War era, especially reconstruction in the U.S. South. Original cloths, most with dust wrappers, in very good condition overall. Includes photographic reprints of contemporary accounts, modern studies, narratives, recollections, etc. $95.00–135.00

Book: Roots/Africa. 14 volumes, original cloths, most with dust wrappers, in very good condition overall, subjects dealing with African native tribal literature, customs, and the struggle against slavery and colonialism. $95.00–135.00

Book: Spirituals. Johnson, James Weldon (editor). *The Book of American Nergo Spirituals*, Viking, N.Y., 1925, 187 pages (with musical arrangements). $75.00–95.00

Book: Uncle Remus. Harris, Joel Chandler. *Told by Uncle Remus - New Stories of the Old Plantation*. McClure, Phillips & Co., N.Y., 1905 w/18 full page illustrations by A.B. Frost, J.M. Conde and Franke Verbeck. 8 vol, 295 pages, marred cover. $125.00–145.00

Book: WWI/Two Black Crows. Mack, Charles E. (of Moran and Mack). *Two Black Crows in the A.E.F.*, Bobbs-Merrill, Indianapolis, 1928. 8 vol, 340 pages. Soiled cover (Moran and Mack, 2 black-faced comedians of early radio and phonograph records, known as the "Two Black Crows," predecessors of Amos n' Andy). $75.00–95.00

Newspaper: Abolitionist. *The National Era*, Wash., D.C., June 15, 1854, with lengthy front page letter to "The Friends of American Liberty/The Legal Tenure of Slavery/The Colonial Legislatures Had No Authority to Legalize Slavery," signed (in print) William Goodell. $65.00–75.00

Newspaper: Abolitionist. *The National Era*, Wash. (1) July 13, 1854. Lengthy reports on Political Movements & The South, The Movement and its Supporters (Nationally), The Administration and Its Supporters (N.Y.), Slavery in Russia. (2) June 29, 1854, with reports on the Nebraska Bill - Will Slavery, if Permitted, Go Into Nebraska, Settlement of Kansas, 33rd Congress-1st Session; and a lengthy account of Col. Fremont's Exploration of the Central Railroad Route to the Pacific. $65.00–75.00 each

Books: Biographies. 7 titles, various 8 vol., original cloths, some with dust wrappers, in good to better condition overall, all titles being biographies of quite prominent Black Americans, primarily late 19th century. Includes 2 different biographies of George Washington Carver by Rackham Holt or Lawrence Elliott (2 copies of each title); biographies of Booker T. Washington by Basil Matthews, Portia Washington Pittman, by Ruth Ann Stewart, W.E.B. DuBois by E.G. Sterne, and Frederick Douglass by Shirley Graham, plus a fair copy of *My Larger Education* by B.T. Washington, 1911. (9 volumes) $75.00–95.00 each

Books: Sports. 6 titles, first and later editions, 8 vol., original clothes, all with dust jackets, in very good condition overall, some moderately worn or with few internal markings, lot also includes one duplicate. Includes biographies or autobiographies of Muhammad Ali, Jesse Owens, Jackie Robinson, Althea Gibson, plus one volume by Bernie Casey, and a study of the Black athlete by Jack Olson. (7 volumes) $45.00–50.00 each

Books: Children's. *Topsy*, die-cut book cover of small girl holding a slice of watermelon and marked "Topsy" across her surplice apron. No author, n.d. McLoughlin Bros., N.Y., (ca. 1890). 10 pages, 8¾". $75.00–95.00

Books: Fiction. Group of 10 volumes, all novels by Black writers, all 8 vol., in dust wrappers, in good to very good condition, few with minor markings. Includes: Venter, *Dark Pilgrim*, Philadelphia, 1959; Lamming, *In The Castle of My Skin*, N.Y., 1954; Portune, *Show Me the Way*, Garden City, 1960; Nern, *Black as Night*, Boston, 1958; Wahl, *The Invisible Glass*, N.Y., 1950; Carroll, *White Hills*, N.Y., 1964; Smith, *A Walk in the City*, N.Y., 1971; DeJongh and Cleveland, *City Cool: A Ritual of Belonging*, N.Y. First editions. (10 volumes) $60.00–75.00 each

Books: Biographies. 10 titles all biographies or personal writings of notable mid-20th century Black Americans, primarily those connected with Civil Rights and Black Power movements. 8 vol., original cloths, most with dust wrappers, in good to very good condition overall. Lot includes two duplicates. Includes: Brown, *Manchild in the Promised Land*; Cleveland, *Soul on Ice*; Cleaver, *Post-Prison Writings and Speeches*; 2 copies; McKissick, *3/5 of a Man*; Chisholm, *The Good Fight*; Wright, *Black Boy*; Evers, Medgar, Mrs. *For Us, the Living*, 2 copies; Mitchell, H.L., *Mean Things Happening in This Land*; Bailey, Pearl, *The Raw Pearl*; Sopher, *Up From the Walking Dead; the Charles McGregor Story*. (12 volumes) $40.00–55.00 each

Books: Music. 8 titles with original cloth or publisher's binding. All but one with dust wrappers, in very good condition overall, one ex-library. Includes: Hughes, Langston, *Famous Negro Music Makers*, (ex-library); Bontemps, *Chariot in the Sky: A Story of the Jubilee Singers*, 1951; Ramsey, Jr., *Been Here and Gone*, 1969; King, editor; *Beneath the Underdog: His world as composed by Mingus*, 1971; Stevenson, *Singing to the World: Marian Anderson*, 1963; Heilbut, *The Gospel Sound*, 1971; Knight, *Jimi: an Intimate Biography of Jimi Hendrix*, 1974; Haralambos, *Right On: From Blues to Soul in Black America*, 1975. $50.00–60.00 each

Book: *The Slave Catchers (Enforcement of the Fugitive Slave Law, 1850–1860)* Stanley W. Campbell, The University of North Carolina Press, Chapel Hill, LC 79-109463 w/jacket, 1970. $55.00–75.00

Book: *Emotion at High Tide (Abolition as a Controversial Factor, 1830–1845)* by Henry H. Simms, Wm. Byrd Ress, Inc. Richmond, Va. bd/dist. by Moore & Co, Inc., Baltimore, Md., 1960. $75.00–95.00

Payroll Voucher: (Civil War - Colored Servant Volunteer) "Voucher #359 - Paid on the 10th of Sept. 1864, G.C. Wethbuer, Capt. C.S.V. (U.S. crossed out) from the 1st of August 1864 to the 31st of August 1864, Pay...Subsistence...Forage... clothing...$126.00 (Officer being paid for himself and Colored servant during the war.) $75.00–100.00

Same as above: "Paid the 10th Sept., 1864 - John Dillenback, 2 Lieut. Co. "B" 20 N.Y. Cav. from the 30 of April 1864 to the 31 of August 1864 Pay ...Subsistence...Forage...Clothing... $445.59, Voucher #358. $75.00–100.00

Broadside: Propaganda, 8" x 11" (Martin Luther King sitting w/group attending, supposed Community Training School. Record of supposed participation w/Communist Organizations is printed front/back of sheet.) Probably distributed by Racist group sometime in the late 1960's. $75.00–90.00

Book: *I Have A Dream (The Story of Martin Luther King in Text and Pictures)* by the editors of Time-Life Books, 1968. $50.00–60.00

Book: Our Gang. Packer, Eleanor Lewis, *A Day with Our Gang*, Whitman Publ. Racine, 1929, 8 vol., 20–page, numerous pictures by Stax. (rough cover at binding) $75.00–95.00

Newspaper: *The National Era*, Wash., D.C., July 13, 1854. Lead article: "Movements in Nebraska and Kansas." Others include "Fugitive Slave Law," "The Legal Tenure of Slavery," etc. Partially soiled, apart at some folds. $65.00–75.00

Pamphlet: "The Praying Negro - An Authentic Narrative." Amer. Tract Society (#92), 4th edition of 6,000, 4 pages (R) n.p., n.d. (ca. 1820) with a nice woodcut illustrating the title. $75.00–100.00

Pamphlet: Civil War. Smith, Goldwin. "The Civil War in America – An Address Read at the Last Meeting of the Manchester Union & Emancipation Society." Simpkin, Marshall, Manchester 1866, small 8 vol., 96 pages. Fine copy. British view of slavery in U.S. Sabin, 82675. $100.00–145.00

Books: 6 near mint copies, 1960's – 1970's, all w/dust jackets, 4 to 8 vol., including Campbell's *Maryland in Africa/The Md. State Colonization Society, 1831-1857*; Gara, *The Liberty Line/The Legend of the Underground Railroad*; Ranson/Sutch, *One Kind of Freedom/The Economic Consequences of Emancipation*; Fishcher's *The Segregation Struggle in Louisiana 1862-77*; Dillion's *Elijah P. Lovejoy, Abolitionist edito*r and Dummond's *Anti-Slavery/The Crusade for Freedom in America*. $40.00–50.00 each

Scrapbook/Album: Wooden covered "Travel" scrapbook with Mammy and Child, jigsaw cut-out and handpainted figure applied to cover. 13" x 17½". $125.00–160.00

Sign: RR Segregation. Savannah & Atlanta Railway cardboard sign "Colored men" dated January 4, 1927. M&B Signs. $95.00–110.00

Stock Certificates: Tobacco. 7 stock certificates issued (ca. 1913-1924) by the Tobacco Products Corp. (Va.) both Preferred and Common, 4 different colors up to 100 shares, each with lithographed headpiece of man, woman and child working in large tobacco field. (7 certificates) $55.00–75.00 each

Stock Certificates: Tobacco. 6 stock certificates (ca. 1912-1924) issued by Tobacco Products Corp. (Va.) Common Class A, and Preferred, 2 each, 5 shares, 10 shares, and 100 shares, 3 different colors, each with lithographed headpiece of man, woman and child working in large tobacco field. (6 certificates) $55.00–75.00 each

Books: *Black Abolitionists* by Benjamin Quarles, Oxford University Press, N.Y., 1969, LC 69-17766 w/jacket.
$40.00–45.00

Book: *The American Race Problem* by Edward Bryon Reuter, rev. and w/intro. by Jitsuichi Masuoka, Thomas Y. Crowell Co., N.Y., 1970, LC 70–109904 w/jacket. $30.00–35.00

Books: Negro Heritage. 10 volumes Negro Heritage Library, including Dannett, *Profiles of Negro Womanhood*, 2 vol.; Cain, *The Winning Road to Freedom*; Evan, *Emerging African Nations*, 2 vol.; Cain, *Negro Heritage Readers for Young People*, *Negros in Public Affairs and Government;* Davis, *The American Negro Reference Book,* 2 vol., Martin Luther King Treasury. Matched bindings, Educational Heritage, Inc., Yonkers, 1964-1966. (Each volume 350/450 pages.) $45.00–65.00 each

Money

Coin: Slave Token. "Aylesbury Token 1796" with stand of flags and liberty cap. Reverse: Head of King James (worn), rim marked "To The Friends for Abolition of Slaves." Copper, 1⅛" dia. (C & H #7). Rare. $180.00–225.00

Coin: Trade Token: "Mrs. Newsham The White Negress" with relief full figure of woman. Reverse imprinted "To Be Had at the Curiosity House/City Road/near Finsbury Square/London/1795." Large cent size. Copper. $180.00–225.00

Coin: Advt. Lucky Token. "It's Lucky to Drink Green River Whiskey." Reverse: Top-hatted groom holding horse. "G.R.W. The Whiskey Without Regrets." 1¼" dia. brass.
$35.00–45.00

Coin: Civil War Penny Token: Obverse: "Liberty & No Slaves" with relief head Miss Liberty, 1863. Reverse: Relief of shield, stand of flags and liberty. $180.00–225.00

Coins: Republic of Haiti: Five brass coins. Obverse (heads) with man's head facing left. Marked "A. Petion-President- An 14" (ca. 1817-1818). Reverse: (tails) Marked "Republic D' Hayti 25 C." with stand of cannons, crossed flags and palm tree. (Note: Jan. 1, 1804, Haiti declared its independence from France under leadership of Jean Jacques Dessalines. Later, after A. Petion served, Henri Christophe declared himself as King Henry I.) (5 coins) $45.00–55.00 each

Coin: Slave Token. "Am I Not a Woman & A Sister - 1838." Depicts kneeling woman in chains. Reverse: "United States of America - Liberty." Large cent size. Copper. $180.00–225.00.

Novelties/Souvenirs

Memo Board: Slate material, Black female on top, matronly, excellent condition. $65.00–85.00

Pincushion: Black female, matronly, standard condition, cloth head. $50.00–75.00

China, Small Figurine: Black boy drummer, 4½".
$45.00–55.00

Cookie Jar: 12½" (Mammy) gray/brown, no markings, ca. 1935. $175.00–250.00

Ashtray: Baby with mouth open wide sitting on a chamber pot, 6½" white metal, ca. 1940. $75.00–110.00

McCoy Cookie Jar: 12" Mammy standing with her hands in front, "Cookies" in raised letters on the bottom-front, white w/hand painted face and hands, detailed color, ca. 1945.
$155.00–225.00

Thermometer: Pressed wood, baby peeking from behind the thermometer, Multi Products, 1949, 5½" H. $55.00–65.00

Paperweight: Iron, 4½" H, "Mammy" dressed in blue, red and yellow. $95.00–110.00

Staffordshire Whistle: Man in white suit and red bowtie shining boots, 3⅞" H., ca. 1880. $185.00–250.00

Bell: Modern brass figural bell of Black angel, 4" H, ca. 1950.
$65.00–75.00

Match Safe: Bisque, 4¼", Black male dancer, ca. 1890.
$95.00–140.00

Syrup and Pepper Shaker: F & F Mold & Dye Works, red plastic, ca. 1950. (2 items)   Syrup - $55.00–75.00
Pepper - $45.00–55.00

Metal bell: Yarn doll attached; broken sugar-doll (leg and arms are missing) and a bisque figurine of "dapper dandy" in pink top hat, sporting cane (head has been repaired). (3 items) $45.00–55.00 each

Nodder: 7½" H w/feet missing (?) woman wearing a yellow hat with flowers in her hair, a red and green shawl with floral decoration and a red and yellow dress, oversized head, composition, ca. 1895, needs repair. $75.00–95.00

Puppet: 13" H pressed wood head with cardboard body and red, white and blue dress, ca. 1950. $75.00–85.00

Note Pad Holder: 11¾" wood - green, brown and red, ca. 1940. "Mammy" memo. $55.00–65.00

Note Pad Holder: 10½" pressed wood, ca. 1940. Yellow, brown, red and blue "Mammy" memo that holds pencil.
$55.00–65.00

Puppet: "Jumbo The Jiver," Talent Product, Inc., N.Y.C., 1948, original box. $210.00–250.00

Record: "Little Black Sambo" narrated by Don Lyon, part 1 and 4 (of four parts). $95.00–110.00

Art Deco: Cigarette dispenser of woman's head/face on a

cigarette container with pull lever which dispenses cigarette through her mouth, wood tinted, ca. 1920. $185.00–250.00

Ashtray: Iron. "The Man in the Moon is a Coon" is the theme of this tray which has the relief of a Negro's face in the bowl. 4¼" dia., rare, ca. 1915. $185.00–250.00

Nodders: Pair of 7" H bisque nodders. Male with a knife and a slice of watermelon in his hands. Female is eating a slice of watermelon. Painted in pastel colors, Germany, bisque, ca. 1900. $600.00–750.00 pair

Nodder: 3" H metal figure of a man smoking a pipe, seated on the back of a seashell - painted red, green and brown.
$115.00–135.00

Boot Scraper: An iron boot cleaner with a pair of brushes and a tray (Black male sitting on top of a loop). $475.00–575.00

Plate: 9½" dia. handpainted dinner plate (woman in a blue dress, wearing a bonnet, carrying eggs under her arms, walking toward an elderly gentleman sitting on a crate in the barnyard, chickens in the background and a cantelope in the foreground). Brilliant colors, Saxe Blank, with raised flowers on the edge. $300.00–325.00

Egg and Outhouse: (1) China egg with child's head emerging from egg shell. Reverse has bare rear beginning to emerge. (2) Bisque Outhouse Child in diaper at open door of outhouse with seated child within. Base marked "One Moment Please." (2 items) $95.00–125.00 pair

Ashtray: Nodding Head. Bronze finish metal ashtray with painted metal standing figure of barefooted cigar smoking. Young man wearing yellow hat, turquoise blue shirt and red pants. Head is spring-fitted to nod with motion or vibration. 5" H x 4¼" W x 3½" D. $75.00–95.00

Ashtray Stand: Butler. Wooden cut-out figure of butler wearing black swallow-tail coat, white shirt, red vest, yellow-striped blue trousers and white spats. Octagonal piece of wood on hands to hold glass ashtray (missing). Double square base set at diamond point. 35½" H. $185.00–250.00

Broom Holder: Antique iron figural broom holder and wall decorations. Made to screw to wall or inside cupboard door. Holder in form of young boy with hands clasped before him to grasp and hold broom handle. Spring hidden behind boy's shoulders gives moveable arms leverage to hold brooms weight. 5" L x 2" W x 1½" D. $185.00–225.00

Chains and Miniatures: (1) Metal pedestal topped by winged child with chain atop head to serve as watch chain and fob. (2) Plastic cube containing skill game with head and opposite side with pair dice, serving as ornament on key chain. (3) Miniature terra-cotta choir boy with broom, 1⅞" H. (4) Miniature chalk figure of seated child, 1¼" H painted. (4 items)
$55.00–75.00 each

China: McCoy. Large semi-vitreous china Aunt Jemima figural "Cookie Jar." Cover: Aunt Jemima's head to waist, wearing bandana head scarf; Base: With floor length dress, has molded raised letters "Cookies" at front hem and underside of base has impressed word "McCoy." 11" H. $155.00–225.00

Rag Doll Door Stop Bottle: 16" H, "Mammy"-type wearing a red bandana. Beaded eyes, stitched mouth and nose (formed), original clothes. Bottle filled with coarse sand, ca. 1890–1900.
$95.00–150.00

Master Salt: 9" H, heart-shaped face Mammy, red, brown, white and blue, with spoon in her hand. $45.00–65.00

Brushes: Pair of brushes, "Pickaninny" and "Mammy" in original container. Mint condition. Made by Woonsocket Brush Co., R.I. $185.00–250.00 pair

Salt/Pepper Shakers: Ceramic, heads of cook/chef, 3½". "Souvenir of Tolchester Beach, Md." Brown, red/white, ca. 1940. $65.00–75.00 pair

Salt/Pepper Shakers: Ceramic, two children sitting in basket. Red, yellow, green, white, brown/white. Japan, ca. 1940.
$45.00–95.00 pair

Salt/Pepper Shakers: Metal, 2¼", cook/chef. Red, white, blue/brown, ca. 1950. $75.00–95.00 pair

Flower Holder: Ceramic, small girl standing beside ear of corn. Yellow, green, red/brown. 5" x 4¾". Ca. 1950. $45.00–55.00

Chalk Figurine: 14" young couple out for a stroll. Woman sporting umbrella/straw hat; man smoking cigarette and wearing flower in lapel. Blue highlights, red flowers, gold trim (ties, shoes, bows). Ca. 1910. $375.00–425.00

Outhouse Ashtray: China, person in an outhouse with another person looking around the corner, orange, brown/black, 2½" marked "Japan" incised and stamped. Ca. 1935.
$35.00–45.00

Figural Ashtray: Cast iron, 2½" iron figure of an old man sitting on a box playing banjo. Ca. 1920–30. $125.00–145.00

Golfing Bottle Opener: Iron, golf caddy w/19th hole marker in the front and hands on the bottle in the bag on his back, plated clubs, white bag, orange shirt, green trousers, brown shoes on green base, 6" H., ca. 1910. $225.00–300.00

Bisque Figure: 3" x 3½" baby sitting on bale of cotton eating watermelon, "Cotton from the Ol' South" on both sides of the bale with an opening in the top. Ca. 1940. $95.00–125.00

Bisque Figure: 3" x 3½" baby boy and girl sitting on a chamber pot. German, ca. 1900. $75.00–95.00

China Plaque: Young Black boy shooting craps with dice attached to a base. 3¼" x 3⅜". Brown, blue, yellow, white/black. Ca. 1940. $45.00–55.00

Wall Match Holder: Chalk, young boy eating watermelon, painted in brilliant colors, ca. 1940. $75.00–95.00

Recipe File Box: Plastic box w/head of Black woman in relief on front of box, ca. 1950. $65.00–75.00

Straw Wisk Broom: Black female, matronly, red checkered head rag, red checkered apron. $55.00–65.00

Wood Stick Pin: Golliwog, 1". $45.00–75.00

Ceramic Plate: Blacks picking cotton, 12", no paint missing. $75.00–95.00

Wood Tie Rack: Black man with small box hat, red uniform (porter) on top. $125.00–150.00

Wood Pipe Holder: Black man with small box hat, red uniform (porter) as holder, mouth holds cigarettes. $155.00–175.00

Metal Cigarette Lighter: Black boy with a place in the rear for cigarette, electric operation. $155.00–225.00

China Bell: Black female, china bell clapper, painted, original 5–8". $55.00–75.00

Pepper Shaker: Wooden "Pappy" head with chef's cap. Black, red/white, 5", ca. 1945. $55.00–65.00 pair

Bell: 4" Black head w/scarf , red and white dress. Souvenir from "The Natural Bridge." $45.00–55.00

Fishbowl Figure: 12½" metal boy with blue pants/red shirt in fishing pose. $95.00–125.00

Wall Plaque: Chalk, 5½" (head of man) - red, yellow, blue/brown. Ca. 1950. $35.00–45.00
Wall Plaque: Chalk, 5¾" head of man wearing straw hat. Red, yellow, blue/brown. Ca. 1950. $45.00–65.00

Bell: Ceramic, 5" woman in apron mixing something in bowl. Red, green, yellow, white, brown/black. Ca. 1950. $45.00–55.00

Bisque Figurine: 3½", two kids sitting on a fence with pot between them "Two souls with but a single thought." Orange, red, black/brown. Made in Germany. Ca. 1930. $125.00–175.00

China Ornaments: Natives. (1) Pair china salt and peppers. Woman's bust figure (salt) with top-knot hairdo set with bone ornament. Man bust figure (pepper) with ring thru nose and wearing tiger-teeth necklace, 3" H; (2) Pair tiny china native babies in grass skirts. One has green skirt w/one hand to jaw, other to hip. The other has blue skirt, hands on hips, 2" H; (3) Child w/yellow-dotted green wrap-around skirt and playing a large bongo drum (2½" H). (5 pieces) $75.00–95.00 each

Clock: Dixie Boy Blinking Eye. Small wall clock in the shape of man's head with green hat and red necktie. The eyes move sideways and red necktie (pendulum) swings as clock runs. Key wound (w/key). Mfg. by Lux Clock Co., Waterbury, Conn. (Ca. 1925?) 9½" H x 4" W x 1" D. $200.00–250.00

Letter Opener/Pencil: Ivorine celluloid alligator, 8" long. Head of boy on top of pencil protruding from alligator's mouth. Tail sharpened to serve as letter opener. $45.00–55.00

Coat Rack: Sunny Jim figural. Bronzed iron hanging wall rack with high relief head of smiling boy wearing floppy hat. (May be used either as hat/coat rack or tie/belt bar.) Ca. 1900. Approximately 13" L x 7" H. $225.00–300.00

Measuring Stick: Slaves. Most unusual handmade wooden stick or gauge with an attached wooden slide. Together resembling the height gauge found on a doctor's office scale. Fits into a wooden board or platform. Found on the eastern shore of Maryland and purported to have been used to note the height of slaves for the owner's records or for the auction market. Pole height approximately 7', platform 7" x 15" (ca. 1840.) $475.00–600.00

Minstrel/Medicine Show Sign: Unusual and attactive large two-sided cut-out figure of minstrel man dancing and strumming banjo. Colorfully painted, broad smiling, red-lipped man in green jacket, peppermint striped pants and shirt, green socks with red dots. 55" to top of head, 60½" to neck of banjo, 36" W x ¾". Outdoor sign used to attract customers to the minstrel show at a carnival (ca. 1900–1910) or a contemporary sign hung as a visual attraction at a western medicine show. (Found hidden in a barn in western South Dakota) Very rare. $3,500.00–$4,500.00

Perfume Bottle: Golliwog. Art Deco frosted glass bottle, ovoid shape with white/black dotted collar and fitted with stopper which has a black glass golliwog head. Fitted piece of fur representing hair. Appearance of a large kettle with a native inside. 3¼" H x 2⅛" W x 1¾" D. $65.00–75.00

Pillow Doll and Cushion. (1) Pillow doll of woman wearing bandana, adorned by real glass beaded earrings and necklace, made by sewing fabric flat to pillow and attaching stuffed arms and legs. Approximately 14" x 11" plus extending arms and legs (overall 16½" x 18"). (2) Cloth pillow, straw filled, with printed front panel of dockside scene of laborer moving bale of cotton and words and musical notes overhead. "Old Man River" paddle wheel steamboat in background. 10" x 9". (2 pieces) Doll - $45.00–55.00; Pillow - $65.00–75.00

Planters/Match Holders. Pair figural hand-painted Tawny Tots. Each a different small child on rectangular base standing alongside round tub. Made to hold small plants, candles or matches? 4¾" H x 4" W x 2" D. $35.00–45.00 each

Planter/Match Holders. Two figures, as above, each different child in different color clothing. (1 child with four puppies) (2 pieces) $35.00–45.00 each

Plate: China. Semi-vitreous china plate with imprint of two cards. Pair of aces (ace of hearts and ace of spades), woman representing theater (hearts) and native with spear, feathered headdress and club (ace of spades). "Roi du Congo." Plate "Terre de Fir mfg. by Chow Le Roi." 8" dia.

$85.00–125.00

Plate: Liverpool. Early cup plate with b/w transfer print of dancing man and fiddler on barrel with 5–line verse below "_____ Me wi' dance de sha sha - Me wi' dance de cotch reel ——— etc., etc." 5½" dia. Age cracked. Ca. 1840.

$125.00–175.00

Salt/Peppers: Aunt Jemima/Uncle Mose. 3½" H., F & F Mold & Die Works, Dayton, Ohio. Jemima with red dress and head kerchief with white apron, neckerchief. Holding white plate. Mose with yellow trousers, red coat and holding top hat. (2 pieces)

$65.00–95.00 pair

Salt/Peppers: Child in red diapers seated on green cucumber. Ceramic (Japan) 2¼" x 3¼" (scarcer than a similar set of children on ear of corn). (2 pieces) $45.00–55.00 pair

Salt/Peppers: Semi-vitreous figural clown or magician shaker in clown make-up, ill fitting clothes, and top hat. 3½" H. Magic box shaker with side handles marked "Magic" impressed in mold. 3" x 2¾" x 1⅜" H. (2 pieces) $45.00–55.00

Salt/Peppers: Aunt Jemima and Uncle Mose Salt and Pepper, manufactured by F. & F. Co., each 5½" H. Red plastic base color, painted white, yellow and blue, paint beginning to wear. Together with a bisque outhouse ornament of small boy standing outside awaiting his turn, with tiny face peering out from hole in door. 2½" x 1½" x ⅞" D. (3 pieces)

Salt/Pepper–$45.00–55.00
Outhouse–$45.00–65.00

Salt/Peppers: African. Pair black high-glazed porcelain Shakers of natives' heads with gold neck bands and one with gold top-knot. 4" H (one has small dime-size chip re-glued at base line). (2 items) $45.00–55.00

Salt/Pepper: China. Pair small "Mammy" figural salt and pepper set wearing white apron and red head kerchief and with arms akimbo. 2¼" H x 2" W x 1½" D. (1 figure repaired) (2 figures) $25.00–30.00 each

Salt/Pepper. Two "Mammy" figures of similar busty cooks, white dress with yellow aprons, one souvenir marked "Toronto, Canada", both with long black hair and arms on hips, one 2⅛" H, other 2¼" H. Plus a chef figure wearing white chef's hat and wrap-around jacket and blue pants. 3" H. (3 items)

Salt/Pepper – $45.00–55.00
Figure – $25.00–35.00
Chef – $25.00–35.00

Salt/Peppers: Salty and Peppy. Pair semi-vitreous china shakers. He is a figural head with big grin, wearing white collar and tall chef hat. Marked "Salty", signed by the ceramist "Jean."

(3½"H x 2½"W x 2"D) She is a "mammy" figural head with broad smile, open mouth, tongue out, wearing white collar, red tie and red polka dot on white head kerchief marked "Peppy." 2 small chips on back of head. (3" x 2¾" x 2"D.) Handmade. (2 pieces) $50.00–70.00 pair

Smoking Tray: Sunny Jim figural. Bronzed iron double-lobed tray centered around high relief head of smiling boy with floppy hat. Fitted into circle in left lobe is bronzed iron cup with ear of corn design to hold cigars (2½" dia. x 3⅜" H). Fitted into circle in right lobe, cup with same corn pattern for cigarettes (1⅞" dia. x 2¼" H). Copper matchbox holder screwed to top center. Tray itself measures 8" x 9⅜". Ca. 1900. $275.00–400.00

Spice Rack/Spice Shakers. Set of 4 painted china figural "Chef" shakers marked "All Spice", "Clove", "Pepper", "Salt". Each 3" H x 1½" W; fitted into a wooden rack, 6" L x 2" D x 3⅜" H.

$100.00–150.00 set

Spice Set and Syrup: Six-piece Aunt Jemima Spice Set manufactured by F & F Mold & Die Works, Dayton, Ohio. Each marked on base "Aunt Jemima." Each plastic figure painted black and white wearing white apron, red head scarf and holding a plate. Separates at waist into 2 pieces. Aprons marked "Nutmeg" "Allspice" "Ginger" "Paprika" "Cloves," and "Cinamon." Several overpainted on aprons and names rewritten. 4" H plus matching 5½" Aunt Jemima syrup pitcher, red overpainted with lid and handle polish motted as though affected by salt, air or hot water. (7 pieces)

Spice set , repainted - $125.00–145.00.
Syrup, repainted - $35.00–45.00

Stationery Portfolio: Canvas folder for stationery with hand-painted figure of straw-hatted "Dandy" in peppermint striped knickers, long black stocking, red-dotted white shirt, blue flowing tie, long red waist sash. Holding Valentine in right hand; floral bouquet in left (ca. 1910) 9½" x 7". $75.00–95.00

Diaper Dan: Full-standing figure of baby in diapers peeking from behind the thermometer. Marked "Multi-Products, Inc. 1949" pressed fibre, 5½"H. $45.00–50.00

Umbrella Stand: Oak umbrella and cane stand with slated staves on three sides, cleverly and humorously carved on the front side with a man stealing a chicken from the coop yard. Man's lapel has a button "Vote for Lincoln." Rectangularly shaped, 10½"W x 11"D x 25½"H. (ca. 1925) $325.00–375.00

Ashtrays: China. (1) Man's head (porcelain) with wide open mouth; long lower lip to hold cigarette. 3½"L x 2¾"W x 1¼"H. (2) Large figural toilet ashtray. Large boy pulling a small boy pushing a porcelain toilet commode on wheels with wooden cover. 4½"L x 2½"H x 2"W. (2 pcs).   Head - $35.00–45.00
Toilet - $45.00–55.00

Ashtrays: Commodes. (1) Figural china ashtray. One child pulling; one pushing a wheel commode. 5" L x 2½" H. (2) Figural ashtray of two children at water's edge pulling a high fish. Large commode behind them. 4¼" L x 3½" H. (3)

Miniature child either pushing or trying to climb up to the commode. 2" L x 1¼" H. (4) Outhouse bisque ornament child on commode inside; one outside marked "Next." (4 items)
$45.00–65.00 each

Salt/Pepper Shakers: 5" H Aunt Jemima/Uncle Mose by F & F. Red plastic w/white, black and yellow paint.
Repainted - $65.00–75.00

Ashtrays: Three china "Mammy" figural items wearing red dress, red head kerchief and white apron with mixing bowl and spoon in hand. Salt and pepper with "New Orleans" printed on aprons. Back opens on third matching figure to hold toothpicks. Each 3" H. (3 items) $65.00–75.00 each

Ashtrays: Three different size "cotton bale" boxes. Cotton and burlap covered. (1) Decorated with "Jemima" type, marked on apron "Souvenir New Orleans, La." 3 dimensional, 5" x 5½" x 5"; (2 & 3) Aunt Sally's Creole Pralines with flat paste-up figures of Aunt Sally. 5" x 5" x 6" and 6½" x 3" x 3". $55.00–65.00 each

Pincushion: Small figure (bisque or plaster) of child seated on hassock beneath a tree eating a slice of watermelon. Small block of wood supporting the hassock has a paper band around it, printed "Educational Souvenir/Hattiesburg, Miss./Jos. Hollander Nov. Co., Baton Rouge, La. Pat. Feb 7-39". Hassock serves as a pincushion. Figure sits beneath the tree which is natural cotton blossom. Figure approximately 1⅜" H, overall 4". $55.00–65.00

Salt/Pepper. China chef shaker ("P") in white coat, apron and hat with gold ladle, marked "Split Rock." 4½"H. China "Mammy" shaker ("S") with white dress, apron and head kerchief with gold rolling pin in hand. Marked "Hand Painted," 4" H. (2 items) $55.00–65.00 pair

Pot Holder Hanger: Painted chalk twin figure wall ornament of boy and girl side by side, holding and eating a large slice of watermelon. Two hooks project from base of ornament serving as hangers for cloth pot holders. 5¼"W x 5½"H x 1½"D.
$65.00–75.00

Cotton Bale Ornament: Souvenir cotton bale with miniature bisque figure of child on top seated in cotton eating a slice of watermelon. Marked "I Am From Dixie/Miniature Cotton Bale/Souvenir New Orleans, La." 2½" x 2" x 2¾".
$45.00–65.00

Bells: Jemimas. (1) Aunt Jemima bell with wool head and arms on wooden bell handle dressed in bandana, white-dotted red dress with white apron. Marked on lower hem "New Orleans, La." 6"H; (2) Painted "Jemima" face on handle of bell with gingham gown, apron marked "Mammy's/Ring Bell for Service" 4" H; (3) Plus small semi-vitreous bell. 3" H. (3 bells)
$45.00–65.00

Bell: New Orleans. Figural call bell with maid dressed in floral print dress with apron marked at lower hem "New Orleans, La." Plus Japanese bisque ornament of child with goose pecking at him. Marked: "The Early Bird Catches the Worm" (2 pieces) $45.00–65.00 each

Decorative Kitchen Aids: Pair of wood-turned figural salt and pepper shakers, 2½" H; (2) Turned wood "Chef" shaker, 2½" H; (3) Turned wood decoration "Borneo" with woman's head, 4½" H; (4) Natives with wood-turned heads on natural seed pod bodies in wooden canoe, 4½" L x 4½" H; (5) Two native wood-turned heads on natural seashell bodies. (6) Turned wood decorative native girl, marked "African Men," 4" H. (6 items)
$35.00–45.00 each

Decorative Kitchen Aids: Brass pipe figure of porter with red hat (on brass base) carrying a pair of clown-head teapot-shaped, brass-handled salt and pepper shakers. Figure 9½"H approximately 7½"W x 3"D.   Teapot - $65.00–85.00
Salt/Pepper - $55.00–60.00

Decorative Kitchen Aids: (1) 10" plaster figure of native with jardiniere at his left (for planter or candle holder). (2) Chalk figure pop-eyed moron holding basket before him. (3) 7" leaf-form ashtray with nude native girl (edge chipped). (4) Decorative angel with bouquet. (5) 6" native girl dancer. (6) "Chef" china decoration. (7) 4½" pair tall hatted "chef" shakers. (7 pieces) $25.00–35.00 each

Figure and Doll. (1) Nodding-head plaster baby with apple and banana (head on spring). (2) Stuffed dog, figural shaped, printed figure on cloth - boy in overalls, holding an apple. (2 pieces) $25.00–35.00 each

Homemaker's Aids: (1) Jemima, Misc. Figural "Jemima" maid call bell, stuffed head and with duster in hand, 6"H. (2) Figural "Jemima" pincushion, 4½" H (in original box). (3) "Jemima" grocery list. Flat cut-out figure with turned down arms holding adding machine paper roll 2½" W to list needs, phone numbers, etc., 9¾" L x 4¼" W x 3" D. (3 items)
$35.00–45.00 each

Jewelry and Miniature Decorations: Pair sterling "Sunny Jim" cuff links, miniature dolls and pendant, pair sterling earrings with obsidian heads, enameled spring pin, porcelain pin, drummer boy, ceramic pin of native with headdress.
$100.00–125.00 each

Kitchen Aids: (1) Fine crocheted pair pot holders which button to collar of a crochet bonnet around smiling baby's face, plastic 15"x 16"W; (2) clothes pin bag with "Jemima" flat cut-out wood head with pasted features with wooden bowtie marked "Riverside, Calif." to which is thumb-tacked a red and white dot (blouse) bag. 11" x 7"; (3) "Jemima" wood cut-out note pad holder for kitchen use, ca.1930 (apparently mate to #2) having bowtie ribbon on headdress and same paste up features. (3 items) $35.00–45.00 each

Kitchen Aids: (1) Set of 5 china shakers with bas relief figures of chef or cook on each shaker. Each has different color cap-neck, 3" H (one has age crack). (2) Frosted glass syrup pitcher with painted decorations circling the center of Sambo

and Tiger. 5½"H. (6 pieces) $35.00–45.00 each set
$55.00–75.00 syrup

Grocery List Board: Rectangular plywood board with painted "Jemima" type with finger to chin "Recon Ah Needs?" with a list of 22 essentials for kitchen from apples, bananas and bread to soap, sugar and tea, with peg holes (no pegs), red and black on pine. 8¼" x 6". $65.00–85.00

Kitchen/Beauty Aids: (1) Crocheted "Mammy" hot-pot holder (red, white and black); (2) cut-out material and appliqued hair spray can cover; (3) "Avon Small World" cologne 2 ox. glass bottle with figural head stopper (in original box); (4) b/w napkin clip salt and pepper; (5) decorative plastic lipstick case. (5 items) $35.00–45.00 each

Kitchen Aids: (1) Miscellaneous decorative hot-pot holder; (2) miniature iron frying pan with base relief "Aunt Jemima" head (approximately 3" dia. x 4¾" L at handle); (3) china figure "Jemima" salt, 4" H; (4) wood jig-saw cut-out salt with painted figure "Lisa," 2½" H; (5) pair seated children S&P, 3¾" H; (6) miniature bisque figure of seated baby eating slice of watermelon. (7 items) $35.00–45.00 each

Pillow: Large soft pillow with transfer b/w print of Nanny with her little charge seated in her lap with side-by-side poems to be read to the child, "Play You's Er Squirrel, Chile," 17" x 20". $100.00–125.00

Salt/Pepper: (1) Pair china chef and cook (each with ladle), 3⅛" (chef reglued); (2) Aunt Jemima and Uncle Mose plastic S&P. F & F Mold & Die Works, Dayton, 3½". (3) Luzianne Coffee Maid (plastic) woman with coffeepot and C&S, 5½". (5 pieces) $35.00–45.00 each

Salt/Pepper, Etc: (1) Unusual seated china figure of man with banjo across his knees (2 separate pieces) salt and pepper, 4" H x 2½" D x 2¼" W. Banjo, 3¾" L; (2) China chef & cook pair, each with ladles, 3¾" H; (3) 2 china salts - chef's with ladles, 3¼" H; (4) oversize Toby-like coffee mug with woman's face, 4¾" H. (7 pcs.) S & P – $35.00–45.00 each; Mug – $45.00–65.00

Decorations: Miscellaneous. (1) white and gilded plaster lamp, man dressed as gaucho, 22" H (plus lamp harp). (2) Pair white semi-vitreous china figural vases, gold caddies, 8" H (1 golf bag). (3) Large "Aunt Jemima" McCoy cookie jar, 12" H. (4 items) Lamp - $110.00–135.00 ;
Vase - $85.00–110.00;
Cookie Jar - $115.00–250.00

Fish Bowl Figure: Seated boy in red shirt/blue pants with right arm up as if holding fishing pole. Hand has opening to hold pole, cast metal, 12" tall, ca. 1925. $210.00–250.00

Shackles: Pair early iron handcuffs with 3 double links separating each cuff and brass ring holding 2 keys. (Black Collectible with documentation) $200.00–225.00

String Holder: Homemade, cut-out, flat wooden doll with pasted loose-leaf paper reinforcement circle eyes, red painted nose. Hole for mouth through which string is pulled. Cloth jumper suit with attached flat cut-out wooden feet with brass cupholder, made to serve as a combination string server and pot holder. $85.00–110.00

Salt/Pepper Shakers: Aunt Jemima/Uncle Mose, 3½". $35.00–45.00

Vase: "Mammy" figural vase with basket (to hold flowers and water) on back, 5¾" H. $40.00–50.00

Wall Decoration: Miniature 3-dimensional head of young boy wearing bowtie and fancy fez-type cap with side pom-pom, painted brown, black, red and yellow pottery. Ca. 1890. $110.00–125.00

Souvenir Cotton Bale Ornament: Bisque baby wearing red cloth hat sitting on bale of cotton eating watermelon. Bale marked "I'm From Dixie - Memphis, Tenn." Ca. 1900, 2" x 2½" x 3". $65.00–75.00

Souvenir Cotton Bale Ornament: Bisque baby (as above) but marked "I'm From Dixie - Savannah, Ga." $65.00–75.00

Souvenir Outhouse: Bisque ornament of diapered child looking in outhouse door at child seated therein. Marked "Next" and "Galveston, Tex." 2½" H., Japan. $40.00–50.00

Souvenir Outhouse: Bisque ornament of diapered child looking in outhouse at child seated therein. Marked "Please" and "Long Beach, California. 1934." 2½" H., Japan. $40.00–50.00

Souvenir Sachet: Small envelope, ribbon tied, illustrated w/ charming watercolor (lower right) of two small girls dressed in yellow/purple dresses. Upper left corner of gate post entranceway illustrated, marked "St. Augustine, Fla. w/Loving Easter Wishes." 2¾" x 3½". Ca. 1900. $210.00–250.00

Souvenir Spoon: Hanging of John Brown. Sterling silver souvenir teaspoon, "Execution of John Brown, Dec. 21, 1895/ Charleston, W.,Va." with engraved scene of the hanging in bowl. $200.00–225.00 mint

Souvenir Spoon: Sterling demitasse spoon, souvenir of "Daytona, Fla." in bowl; "Sunny South" with head of boy at tip of handle. 4¼" long. (Relief-image) $155.00–195.00

Souvenir Thermometer: "Mammy" wood cut-out figure on round wooden board with thermometer to her right. 5" dia. souvenir, marked "San Lorenzo, Calif." $45.00–55.00

Candy Dish: Swami. Figural white china serving dish of seated swami or fortune teller in gold/red edged robe and turban, with bowl in hands. 7½" H x 7" x 7". $50.00–65.00

Pillow Rag Doll: Young woman doll, manufactured head, apparently cut off and attached to handmade stuffed rag or

sock body, truncated and attached to round flat cardboard disc (no legs, made to sit on pillow), wearing very colorful patchwork quilt style wide skirted dress and bandana. 16" H.
$100.00–150.00

Dolls: Pincushion. Two pincushion "Jemima" type figural dolls. (1) 4" H with red and white polka dot dress and bandana, pipe cleaner arms, flat bottom, and tape measure in hem (Japan); (2) 5½" H homemade, painted face with red printed dress, apron, bandana and brass earrings. (2 dolls)
$45.00–70.00 each

Souvenir Doll: "Dinah," cotton novelty doll made by Hollander Novelty Co., Baton Rouge, La. Wooden dowel body, wire arms and cotton bloom atop head. Red/white polka dot dress and white apron. Ca. 1940. With original carton. 7½" H.
$85.00–110.00

Wall Decorations: Pair of cast iron wall plaques in shape of frying pans. Bas relief busts of elderly whiskered man in one; woman with headkerchief in other. Painted, marked "John Wright." 4½" x 3½". (2 items) $65.00–75.00 each
$135.00–165.00 pair

Wall Decoration: Little Black Sambo carrying an umbrella with tiger behind him. Colorfully painted semi-vitreous china, with slight paint chips on cheek and umbrella. 5¾" x 6¼".
$45.00–65.00

Wood Carving: Sculptured head of Black male wall decoration, heavy ebony or rosewood. 7" x 9" x approximately ¾" thick. $85.00–110.00

Measuring Cups: Set of 4 different size handled mugs or cups, each painted with large white lips, red nose, blue/white eyes, yellow cap with gold hair. Marked ⅛, ¼, ½ and 1 cup.
$180.00–225.00

Masks: Cardboard Halloween mask with big red lips, broad nose and large white eyes, USA. $45.00–65.00

Match Holder: Bellhop bust figure with big wide grin. Metal, red and black w/polka dot bowtie. Wood matches fit into hollow pill box hat and user may strike match on teeth. 3½" H. (Coon Chicken Inn symbol unmarked.) $110.00–125.00

Letter Opener: Black Boy. Brown patinated bronze oversized letter/newspaper opener with figural handle in form of broad smiling youth wearing large floppy yellow hat and green jacket. Ca. 1890. 13½" L. $45.00–65.00

Letter Opener/Pencil: Ivorine celluloid alligator, 6½" L. Head of boy on top of pencil protruding from alligator's mouth; tail sharpened to serve as letter opener. $25.00–35.00 each

Pictorial Images

Painting: 28" x 34" (nude study - woman), no signature, ca. 1940's. $550.00–650.00

Oil Painting: "Black Madonna and Child," oil painting with gold/silver trim, inscription in Polish across bottom, framed, ca. 1900. $450.00–575.00

American Folk Art: Primitive watercolor on board, 3½" x 4½", framed. Woman with small tree limb in an upright striking position (limb cut-out and applied to board). Yellow, light/dark blue, brown/black. Ca. 1840–1860. $450.00–575.00

Watercolors: Two 3" x 3½" pictures of an elderly couple by Elise C. Burns (both are signed) in one frame, ca. 1900.
$600.00–700.00 pair

Pencil Drawing: Black woman, 16" x 20", b/w, inscribed "To Brenda from Johnny," attributed to J. Frailey, ca. 1960.
$325.00–400.00

Painting: Two women leaning on a wall, both with their eyes closed, 25½" x 34", ca. 1930. $300.00–400.00

Watercolor: Beautiful 7½" x 9½" portrait of an elderly gentleman w/white-gray beard in an overcoat and hat, by MBI, M.B. Irwin, ca. 1890, framed. $300.00–400.00

Pen and Ink Drawing: Original drawing by Kemble. "29" (elderly gentleman with teeth missing wearing engineer-type cap and sporting a beard), b/w, 4½" x 6½", framed.
$450.00–500.00

Watercolor: Young couple kissing on a rail of a fence by "Tito," 10" diameter (round), ca. 1935, framed. $450.00–500.00

Painting: A very fine painting of a boy in a straw hat holding a kitten under his right arm with his finger in his nose, snubbing, with the caption "Taint Your Cat," unsigned, 13" x 17," framed, ca. 1890. $2,000.00–2,200.00

Painting: Elderly gentleman is standing in a doorway, shadows of other people are in the background; the gentleman is looking at the stars with the caption, "I wonder ef dat could be de same old star!" Initialed "HMD," ca. 1890, 13" x 18".
$675.00–775.00

Charcoal: 16" x 21", b/w charcoal of a young woman holding a cat in her arms, framed, ca. 1900. $225.00–250.00

Print: "Aunt Chloe's Horticultural Pets." B/W print on drawing by S.G. McCutcheon. "Aunt Chloe" in shawl and headscarf tending plants in wooden soap box on kitchen table. Second boxed plant on chair. Her husband lighting his pipe by fireplace/ stove in background. (R) *Harper's Weekly*.
$65.00–75.00

Watercolor: Blacks in tobacco field, artist unknown, 12" x 17".
$550.00–675.00

Watercolor: Street scene, 11" x 17", Black couple walking on sidewalk looking at vendors' (oyster/fish) carts. By Dox Thrash, signed, ca. 1935, framed. $350.00–450.00

Black males, five farm workers, photograph. (Watch for reproductions). $125.00–150.00

Black male, charcoal photograph with convexed glass, unknown, excellent condition. $200.00–300.00

Black males playing dice, gambling, "Skin Game," black/white, dated 1898, 22" x 18", original. (Watch for reproductions.) $275.00–375.00

Black family standing in front of cabin, original. $250.00–350.00

Black kids eating watermelon, stereoview card, colortone. $45.00–55.00

Black male and female, leaning on pile of towels, 5" x 4½", unsigned. $30.00–40.00

Black female, leaning on pile of towels, 5" x 4½", unknown. $30.00–40.00

Black female, standing, black dress and hat, oval-shaped backing, unknown. 9½" x 5½". $40.00–65.00

Black male, seated, cane in hand, watch chain on vest pocket, unknown, 7½" x 4½". $40.00–65.00

Photo Poster: Dick Gregory for President, 22" x 29", blue and white, 1968. $250.00–275.00

Photo Poster: Huey Newton, Black Panther Party, 23" x 30", black and white. $175.00–225.00

Stereo Views: Underwood & Underwood, black/white views, "5678 Cotton is King" plantation scene with pickers at work, Georgia. $35.00–45.00

Tin Type: 6th plate, tinted (elderly woman in very pretty dress, holding a cat in her lap). $200.00–275.00

Glass positive of an elderly gentleman sporting beard/mustache, 6½" x 8½", identified on back, Henry Hunger. Ca. 1895. $200.00–275.00

Photograph: 7½" x 9½", elderly migrant worker or share cropper sitting in doorway of wood frame house. Ca. 1905. $75.00–85.00

Circus Photograph: 3¾" x 5¼", b/w early circus performers, a couple in their stage dress, identified as "Al E. and Mamie Holmes," "Zur Familie Longeld Mois. Grusse 19 14/VII," unframed. $200.00–225.00

Watercolor: Two young children holding hands "Little People" by E.J. Kane, 1959. 10" x 14". $375.00–425.00

Painting: Portrait of a woman in a yellow blouse/top, signed Maria Jackson, ca. 1970. 25" x 30". $145.00–200.00

Painting: Contemporary painting of an elderly man in a straw hat. 36" x 48". $100.00–175.00

Charcoal: Sketch of "Coal Miner" by Seth Wood. Right profile in miner's cap with crossed miner's picks under his neck. Faded pencil caption, "Yassah Mistah! Ah Wants a Job but I cain't git it." 6¾" x 9" - 9" x 12" including the margin, framed. $175.00–200.00

Painting: Group of 8 persons ice skating on a lake. The head of another protrudes through an opening in the ice where he had fallen and is seemingly being ignored by the group. Ca. 1900, signed A.B. FROST. 15½" x 27". $1,100.00–1,500.00

Williams and Walker: Pair of very colorful lithographs depicting Bert Williams and his partner with wives, titled "The Cake Walk." 16" x 17", oak frames, water stained, ca. 1910. (2 items) $375.00–450.00 ea

Brass Wall Plaque: 4 x 4½", head of young boy wearing old hat. Caption "Bred in Old Ky. - Peerless and Me" at bottom of plaque. $200.00–300.00

Painting: Oil painting of an elderly gentleman smoking a pipe on an 11¼" diameter walnut plaque, signed Ulrick A. Ambroise, ca. 1930. $225.00–275.00

Painting: Oil painting of a young girl's head looking toward the right, wearing a blue and white dress, hair braided, 10" x 13", framed, unsigned, ca. 1900. $425.00–575.00

Painting: Oil painting of a woman smoking a cigarette with a mug sitting on a table in front of her. Black, white and greys, 23" x 32", signed C. Diggs, ca. 1950. $350.00–450.00

Wall Plaque: 6" x 8¾" (chalk) Little Black Sambo with an umbrella, base has been repaired, painted blue, yellow and two shades of brown, with red lips, ca. 1935. $125.00–145.00

Calendar: Paul Laurence Dunbar. 1913, illustrated with b/w halftones, accompanied with verse by Dunbar. $200.00–250.00

Drawing: Charcoal and chalk portrait of a dignified woman, bust length, profile of the left side of the lady wearing an upswept pompadour hairdo, high-necked lacy gown with pince-nez glasses, earrings, pendant brooch and pinned lady's openface lapel watch. Signed Egan, ca. 1900. 16¾" x 14". $350.00–450.00

Drawing: Crayon and wash. Hand-tinted crayon drawing of a woman with three children conversing with a woman holding a jug. Signed Marry Godard; title on the back - "Saturday Errands." Ca. 1950, 11" x 14". $300.00–400.00

Painting: "The Gossips," oil painting of two older women both wearing shoe-top length dresses - one lady is wearing an off-white head scarf; the other is in blue wearing a man's style hat. One character is outside of a fence-gate, and the other is in the yard - talking to each other. Background center: two-story cottage with farm area at the left background. Signed H. Brenner. 18" x 24" $300.00–400.00

Painting: Oil painting. Study on canvas of a male model, full figure, profile, facing right, bare chested, wearing trousers to midcalf and bedroom slippers. Signed T. Johnson. 20" x 16".
$300.00–400.00

Painting: Oil painting of full standing female nude artist's model, facing 2/3 front with right hand raised holding a draped pole. Unsigned, reverse side of canvas and stretcher "Ingersoll," 30" x 24". $300.00–375.00

Painting: Large oil painting on canvas of nude woman wearing only a turquoise ring and red barrettes in her hair, seated sideways in a French Provincial-style upholstered back and seat chair facing the observer. Unsigned, back of canvas "Galwey." 36" x 30". Some damage (small holes in one area.)
$375.00–500.00

Painting: Oil portrait. Bust portrait of young woman with earrings, wearing light green blouse. Oil on pressed board, signed "1.1 Jessie Lee." Reverse marked in ink "Jessie Lee Stewart Dasile May/June 1950." 16" x 12". $200.00–250.00

Painting: Charming oil painting on pressed board of young girl wearing blue/white checkered dress and red bandana over her bow-tied plaited hair. Holding large slice of watermelon in both hands with eyes rolling upward in ecstasy; the juice dripping from her lips. (She seems to say "My that's good.") Signed l.f. "C.W. Schuman '43." 16" x 12". $350.00–450.00

Watercolor: Caribbean. Watercolor of dock scene, West Indies, with foreground figure of woman in green blouse and red skirt wearing red bandana, carrying a basket on one arm and pineapple in hand while two small groups (2 men left and 2 women right) stand near docked group of fishing sailboats. Signed "1.1., A. Moroso." 13" x 10". $200.00–275.00

Watercolor: Watercolor and pencil outlined drawing of a young woman with hands clasped behind her head, apparently reclining nude, on a chaise wearing only a diaphanous negligeé and slippers, signed "John Carroll (or John Cassoll)", l.r., approximately 14" x 12", n.d., n.p.
$300.00–400.00

Watercolor: Wash Day. Painting of woman pushing a home-made wheelbarrow filled with dirty clothes (?) past a background of high fence with clothesline seen beyond. Signed, l.r., "Stickney/Augusta, Ga., July '51." $85.00–110.00

Photograph: Small Black boys, photograph print, eating corn. (Watch for reproductions.) $85.00–110.00

Three 5" x 7" b/w views depicting six kids standing in front of a large door. One photo is a blow-up of a kid in the group of three, ca. 1930. $60.00–75.00

Three small boys, shabbily dressed, with large wedges of watermelon, posing on a paved surface. Ca. 1935.
$65.00–75.00

Harry Belafonte promotional photo, tinted, 16½" x 10¾", ca. 1950. $110.00–125.00

Black and white, 8" x 10" of a man and woman dressed up for the stage, posing in a dancing position, performing during an act with two small insert photos of the same individuals in street clothes. Ca. 1920, framed. $125.00–150.00

Photograph: Promotion photograph of Mery Lou Williams, jazz pianist and composer, tinted. 12" x 24½".
$145.00–165.00

Photograph: Ambrotype. 6th place, 3" x 3½" (man wearing masonic apron and ribbon). Portrait of a Black individual belonging to a closed order fraternity. Ca. 1875.
$400.00–500.00

Photographs: Three photos of adults (two women each carrying a purse and an elderly gentleman wearing a beard.)
$45.00–70.00 each

Photograph: Middle-age woman (studio) and postcard (linen comic) "Honey You Sure Made a Big Hit with Me! Let's Play Around" (small boy with a bat on his shoulder speaking with pretty bashful girl looking over a fence.) (2 items)
$40.00–60.00 each

Photograph: Promotional picture of Dizzy Gillespie, signed in print, 14" x 25", framed and tinted, ca. 1950.
$125.00–150.00

Photograph: Two b/w photos of Negroes working in cotton gins, 7" x 9" (both), mounted on boards, The Philadelphia Museum. $60.00–70.00

Photograph: 6½" x 8½", tin type (young woman wearing a straw hat in a studio pose), tinted, ca. 1890. $130.00–150.00

Martin Luther King: 8" x 10" press photo of Martin Luther King giving his wife a tremendous affectionate hug, b/w, framed. $110.00–165.00

Photograph: 4½" x 6¼" sepia tone photo of elderly couple posing, seated on a chair in front of a cabin, mounted on a board and framed. $75.00–85.00

Postcards: (26) color views depicting Blacks working and in comical situations, mostly unused. $15.00–20.00 each

Postcards: (12) very colorful greetings, mostly unused.
$15.00–20.00 each

Postcards: (11) very colorful Raphael Tuck & Sons "Dilette" comical postcards "Happy Little Coons" Series II and IV, unused. $20.00–30.00 each

Fortune Teller Print: 12" x 17" old woman telling a young woman's fortune, color, ca. 1900. $145.00–175.00

Cruickshank Print: (reproduction) 13" x 16", "Blind Man's Bluff" by Robert Cruickshank, ca. 1935. $95.00–125.00

Poster: 22½" x 28". "World's Champions and Past Greats of the Prize Ring," b/w halftones of such boxing greats (Joe Louis, Sugar Ray Robinson, Joe Gans, Ike Williams and others.) Distributed by Champs of Sports, 59 South Pearl St., Albany, N.Y., ca. 1947. Orange/black on white. $145.00–175.00

World War I Print: "Colored Man is No Slacker," printed "1918 E.G. Renesch, Chicago," 16" x 20", (soldier saying goodbye to his sweetheart, with troops marching in the background), framed. $195.00–275.00

Print: "Far From the Madding Crowd - Little Study in Black and White," Small baby in a bed, surrounded by white pillows and sheets with small tears. 9" x 12", ca. 1910, original. $85.00–125.00

Printer's Block: 1½" x 2½" cut linoleum printer's block, mounted on wood (Black male, minstrel-type face, dressed in jitter-bug fashion clothes), ca. 1930's. $115.00–145.00

Map: "Eagle's Eye View of Weber City (INC.), Andrew H. Brown, Map Maker, (Amos n' Andy souvenir map), framed. $95.00–125.00

Cartes De Visite: Men. Two early cartes de visite of seated men, each with military-style (Civil War) hat or uniform jacket, one with elaborate watch chain, both from the studio of "C.A. Garrett's - Salem, N.Y., photographer." (Two cards) $75.00–95.00

Motion Picture: 8mm. Castle Film fun cartoon "Little Black Sambo," #757 b/w film (ca. 1940–1950) on 5" reel. $125.00–200.00

Motion Picture: 16mm. Life of Martin Luther King, Jr. "I Have A Dream." BFA Educational Media, Santa Monica, CA, produced by CBS News, b/w film, 35 minutes length on 12" dia. reel. Chronology of the U.S. Civil Rights Movement of the 1950/60 period from boycott to sit-ins, freedom riders, mass demonstrations and development of "Black Power." (Made for social studies on junior/senior high school, college and adult level.) Gripping, historic film! $195.00–275.00

Photograph: Photograph of Old Baltimore church identified by handwritten title in lower margin "Calvary Baptist Church, Park Ave. & Biddle Str., Baltimore, Md. Erected 1884. Under supervision of Rev. P.H. A. Braxton, Pastor." 10¼" x 13½" plus title and margin (15 x 18½" overall). J. Molgland, photographer. Photo shows large grey stone church with bearded pastor standing in doorway talking to a woman parishioner. (Note: The southeast corner of the Balto. Life Insurance Co. parking lot now stands where this church originally stood.) $125.00–175.00

Publicity Poster: Lithograph of 4 young Blacks sitting on carton w/banjo. Lithograph for sheet music booklet. $75.00–95.00

Frederick Douglass: Framed halftone, engraving by E.A. Wright, Phila., "With sentiments of highest regard, very truly yours, Frederick Douglass." 8" x 10" $95.00–165.00

Old man with jug walking in the snow by E.W. Kemble and "The Effects of the Proclamation - Freed Negroes Coming Into Our Lines at Newbern, North Carolina" from *Harper's Weekly*, Feb. 21, 1863, b/w photo of Mrs. Henry Ward Beecher. (3 items) $75.00–95.00

Civil War Print: 18" x 21½", Kurz & Allison, "Storming Fort Wagner." Negro troops charging fort. Color, framed. $125.00–175.00

Spanish American War Print: 12½" x 18¾", b/w, (Negro Rough Riders charging into battle) by Fletcher C. Ransom, 1898, framed. $200.00–225.00

Document Box: Lincoln Freeing Slaves. Black painted wooden box with fine print glued and lacquered to top cover of symbolic scene of Lincoln freeing slaves. Depicts bowing slave with shackles broken, kissing left hand of President Lincoln, who stands with one foot on broken chain and his right hand aloft proclaiming emancipation. Cracked lower left into print with brittle, fragile and chipped edges all around. $200.00–250.00

Greeting Cards: Seven different greeting cards (ca. 1940–72) including Raggedy Ann, Beloved Belinda and the Chocolate Day (storybook Hallmark Greeting), Alan Sues Inflate-Me Greeting Balloon (Girl-Put a Little Color in Your Life), "For Yo' Birthday," "Ah Sho' Is Sorry About Yo' Accident," "Please Get Well Honey Dew" (depicting a child eating a melon), "Dist Ain't No Puny lil Birfday Wish," and "Ah'm Sending You a Barrell O' Love." (7 cards) $13.00–15.00 each

Photos: CDV/Tintype. (1) Fine early CDV of small child and maid. Girl approximately 6 months to 3 years holding a bisque doll standing on a chair and being held and cared for by teenage maid wearing striped uniform gown and apron. Photo by Evans and Prince, York, Pa. (2) Early tintype half-length portrait of handsome young man wearing fox hunt outfit or brass buttoned livery. (2 photos) $125.00–150.00 each

Photos: Children. 1880/1920 various sizes, snapshots and studio - infants, little girl with high-button shoes (Lexington, Ky.), boy with derby hat, communion for ad, young girl with long curls reading a photo book, children in cornfield, etc. (9 photos) $25.00–35.00 each

Photograph: Nine children on single photographic copy print, all nude little boys and girls crying or gazing solemnly or curiously into camera. Marked "Alligator Bait." Copyright by McCrary & Branson, 1897, Knoxville, Tenn. 6½" x 20". $25.00–35.00

Photograph: 8½" x 7¼" (plus margin). Boy eating watermelon of very happy, toothy, grinning, barefoot boy in overalls and straw hat seated on a crate with large slice of watermelon in hand, an uneaten portion of melon on plate at his side and lot of rind at his feet. Ca. 1920, copy photo with some retouching in negative. Unsigned, undated. $95.00–115.00 for reprints

Photograph: Boys. Two group photos. (1) 3 young boys seated on a curbstone, the lad in center with elbows on knees and fist holding chin with kids on left and right eaching holding a small tree branch. (2) two children (brother and sister?) seen through the barrel of a large playground sewer pipe. Each photo 7¼" x 9¼", unmarked, undated. (2 photos) $25.00–35.00 each

Photographs: Watermelon. Double photographic copy print of 10 children, seated on or hanging over a fence watching man with whole watermelon at his feet and tiny child at his side marked "Gimme De Rine." Second photo (side-by-side) the disappointed kids are aghast as man devours watermelon without offering them any and tiny child howls in protest. Copyright 1898, McCrary & Branson, Knoxville, Tennessee. 7" x 19½" plus margins. (2 items) $25.00–35.00 each

Photographs: Women. Two framed women's photos, (1) oval full length photo, ca. 1910, buxom woman with full length gown, ribbon bow-tie, standing by a rustic stand. (2) Hand-tinted portrait, ca. 1930, right profile of woman with bobbed hair wearing pearl necklace. (2 items) $45.00–65.00 each

Stereographs: Breast Feeding. "Free Lunch." (1) Geo. Barber, Niagra Falls, 1889. (2) Keystone View Co., B.L. Singley, Meadville, 1897. (2 cards) $25.00–35.00 each

Stereographs: Occupations. Lots of photos, snapshots and studio, various sizes, 1890–1940's including 2 railroad porters (?) in uniform, cotton warehouse, laborers, barber (in front of his shop), cotton field outside old log cabin, dum trunkman (1920's), horse and wagon by stable with man and son, soldiers. (9 photos) $25.00–35.00 each

Stereographs: Chickens and Possums. Four (4) different Keystone View Co. cards: "I's Bound to Hab a Christmas Dinna" (1898); "De pic ob de hull roost" (1899); "Possum fo' Dinna, Suah" (1899), Universal Photo Art Co.; C.H. Graves "Deed Judge, I ain't stole no chicken," (n.d.); Underwood & Underwood "The End of Mistah Possum - O a jolly out-of-door feast preparing for darkies & dogs," (1904). (6 cards) $35.00–45.00 each

Stereographs: Children. 10 early stereo cards, including "Doing Business on a Small Scale," (child seated on potty on a scale); W.M. Chase "Mother Nit-Picking Thru Child's Hair;" Underwood & Underwood, Strohmeyer & Wyman, "A Still Hunt (Parents Nit Picking); B.W. Kilburn, "Simplicity," 1887; Keystone View, B.L. Singley, "I isn't bin borned very long," 1897; "The Interrupted Game," 1896; Perfec, H.C. White, "Three of a Kind," 1901; Keystone View, "It's al 'us washin' day," 1898. (10 cards) $35.00–45.00 each

Photographs: 2 photographs of boys. (1) Stopping child, hidden within a large see-through umbrella, petting a small forlorn-looking puppy, 18" x 15". (2) 4 boys at a sand pile watching another boy doing a complete flip (snapped while the young acrobat is completely upside down and attention of the onlookers is on the photographer rather than the the the young acrobat's feat. Spot on far right (on boy's jacket), 19" x 13". (2 photos) $25.00–45.00 each

Photograph: Serviceman. Hand-tinted photo of young man in sailor's uniform (U.S. Navy) in original ovoid capital frame with patriotic emblems: stars in corners, eagle with shield and U.S.A. at top margin, side emblems of American flags, ca. 1917-1920. Photo 15" x 10", frame overall 19½" x 13".
$75.00–95.00

Stereographs: Comedy. 4 pairs of early comic stereo cards. (1) Trouble head/Trouble Behind. (2) "By Jinks! I coulda sworn I saw a little darkey in the melon patch/Dis Am de mos' narrerest escape dis chile eber had" (dated 1897). (3) "Ten Jamaica nigger boys Feasting on Pine/One Had Too Much, Ten There Were Nine." (4) "Look out dar, sumfin's gwine to drap/sumfin' did drap." (8 cards) $15.00–25.00 each

Stereographs: 12 stereo cards on cotton planting, growing and marketing, including five by B.W. Kilburn (1892): "Cotton Picking in full blast," "Morning Start in Cotton Field," "Pickers grouped in cotton field," "Our Little Cotton Coop," "The Lone Picker." Three Underwood & Underwood cards including "Away Down among de Cotton & de Coons, Louisiana," "Shipping cotton from Levee, Texas," "Picking Cotton, Georgia." Keystone: "Picking Cotton on a Mississippi Plantation." Universal, C.H. Graves: "Way Down South in fields of cotton" and two different views, Strohmeyer & Wyman: "Cotton is King," "Plantation Scene, Georgia." (12 cards) $15.00–25.00 each

Stereographs: 12 on cotton, planting, picking, etc. Nine Keystone View Co. cards 1898/99 (one duplicate) including "A Typical Texas Cotton Field at Planting Time"; "Picking Cotton on a Mississippi Plantation"; Plantation scene with pickers at work, Georgia; Hoeing Cotton, Dallas, Texas, "We's Done All dis s'mornin"; Levee, New Orleans, A family of cotton picker, Ga.; "If Dat Dog Wasn't watchin' I'd kiss you," plus unmarked card "Picking Cotton," S & W, U & U Plantation scene, Ga., M.H. Zahner, Cotton is King or Plantation Scene. (12 cards) $25.00–35.00 each

Stereo Cards: Eating. Kilburn Bros., 1879, "Distinguished Southerners, Grinding Cane"; Strohmeyer & Wyman, 1890, "Ten Minutes for Refreshment"; Strohmeyer & Wyman, 1892, "Golly Dis Am Paradise"; B.W. Kilburn (James M. Davis), 1897, "I feel obliged to removed this temptation from the eyes of a weaker brother"; S & W, 1897, "Reality"; Keystone View Co.; B.L. Singley, 1902, "Turkey Invades Africa"; H.C. White, 1901, Perfec 1903,"Get on quick Rastus, he done got it mos' eat up." (7 cards) $25.00–35.00

Stereographs: Comic and Lovers. 17 cards including "Warranted All Wool," "Mammy's Little Honey Boy," "Mammy's

Little Alabama Coon," "Expecting a Caller" (fishing), "The Lover's Duet," "Dreaming of Sambo," "Honey, Does Yo Lub Yo Man?", "Caught in the Act," "Yo shuah dem stockins won't black de legs?", etc. (17 cards) $15.00–25.00 each

Stereo Card: 15th Amendment. Early stereo card, J.N. Wilson, Savannah, Ga., dated 1871. "15th Amendment bring his crop to town." (Man on back of steer pulling a cart.)
$45.00–60.00

Stereo Cards: Five Southern homes depicted. Two Perfec. H.G. White & Co., 1903. (1) Typical Negro Cabin, Louisiana, (2) "Dars been free two times, two tree times & one lawk kno' how ma times." (large family). Two Littleon Views. (1) Uncle Tom's Cabin, (2) "A Picturesque Southern Home" plus Keystone View Co. "A Humble but Happy Home Down South in Dixie Land." (5 cards) $15.00–25.00 each

Stereographs: Misc. Twelve cards including "It's so easy to be lazy," (boy on horseback), Hauling Logs - at Daytona, Fla. (oxen team); children on goat cart, "Sponge Market at Key West," "In the Sugar Fields of Louisiana," "2 Pretty Girls in Sugar Cane Plantation, La."; "Uncle Tom and Little Eva," "The Pastoral Visit," etc. (12 cards) $15.00–25.00 each

Stereographs: Two early stereo cards of Washington, D.C. Scenes photographed and published by Kilburn Brother, Littleton, N.Y., 1889. #5056 "The Merry Market Maid, Wash."; #5065, "The Merry Bootblacks, Inauguration." (2 cards)
$25.00–35.00 each

Stereographs: 2 early stereo cards. (1) W.M. Chase, "Chimney Sweeps." (2) J.N. Wilson, 1874, Savannah, Ga. "Florida Cracker Going to Market." (2 cards) $35.00–50.00 pair

Posters: Black Culture. Three different posters for the same event taking place at Bowling Green State University during "A Week of Black Culture - Feb. 7-13, 1971." (1) Roberta Flack (black type on turquoise) 23" x 17½", (2) Photo prints of Roberta Flack, Mango Santamaria, Leon Thomas & the Presidents, 22" x 14". (3) Photo print of black and white eggs, one black egg already hatched, 23" x 17½". (3 posters)
$35.00–45.00 each

Posters: Bull Durham. Four colorful reprints of "Genuine Bull Burham Smoking Tobacco" including (1) "Without a Match." Two hunters in pasture; (2) "My! It Shure Am Sweet." Couple seated on pasture fence, backs to viewers and can be seen kissing through a hole in their tattered umbrella. (3) "My! it shure am sweet tastan." Front porch of general store with mammy in rocker. (20" x 24½" and 25½" x 18") (3 posters)
$75.00–95.00 each

Print: Large b/w multi-scene print titled "Onward" with numerous scenes and/or portraits: Abraham Lincoln (u.l.), Fred Douglass (u.r.) and Booker T. Washington (l.c.) with 4 paragraphs on Lincoln and Douglass (top border) and The Tuskegee Institute and Booker T. (lower margin) with left hand vignettes-house where Lincoln was born, Tuskegee

drawing room, Tuskegee lab and general view of Tuskegee (right), vignette of Douglass learning to read, Tuskegee machine shop and house were B.T.W. was born. Printed, W.L. Haskell, 1903, 20" x 16". Soiled. $125.00–145.00

Print: Civil War. "Avoiding the Draft," b/w print of sketch depicting line of Black men lining up before a table where agents of Northern States enroll and hire Negro substitutes at Norfolk with doctor in background giving a physical exam to one of the substitutes. (Note: This new type of human market allowed anyone who could afford it to buy a substitute for the Northern States draft.) (R) *Frank Leslie's Illustrated Newspaper*, Sept. 3, 1864. 8" x 10½". $75.00–95.00

Print: B/W print after artist's sketch titled "Colored Troops Under General Wild, Liberating slaves in North Carolina," depicting soldiers welcoming slaves and vice versa with long line of marching troops. (R) *Harper's Weekly*, Jan. 23, 1864.
$45.00–65.00

Print: B/W print after newspaper artist's sketch titled "Escaping Union Officers Succored by Slaves." (R) *Harper's Weekly*, Mar. 12, 1864. $45.00–60.00

Print: Kurz & Allison colored lithographic print "The Fort Pillow Massacre, "April 12, 1864, Union Troops (Maj. Booth, Com.)" Depicting Confederate troops, under Gen'l Forest, slaughtering civilian men, women and children as well as attacking Union positions. Copyright 1892, Kurz & Allison, Chicago. 14½" x 20¾" plus title and wide margins.
Reproduction – $75.00–100.00

Print: Civil War. "The Negro in the War - Sketches of the Various Employments of the Colored Men in the U.S. Armies." B/W print of sketches by C.E.F. Hillen. Center sketch of "Battle of Milliken's Bend" surrounded by ten border sketches: Bldg. Roads, Blacksmith's Shop, In the Trenches, Scouts, Teamsters, Washing in Camp, Driving Cattle, Unloading Gov't Stores (from steamer), Cooking in Camp & On Picket. (R) *Frank Leslie's Illus. Newspaper*, Jan. 16, 1864, 16" x 21".
$45.00–60.00

Print: Comic. Waterberry's Secret or How to. Five cards from set of six. Colored prints issued advertising "Pedro Cut Plug," "How to Milk in Fly Time," etc. 9" x 10½" each. (5 pieces)
Each - $55.00–65.00;
Set of 6 - $275.00–325.00

The following prints are all original Currier and Ives lithographs of the famous Darktown Series. Each approximately 11" x 14" plus margins.

Prints: Currier & Ives. "Darktown Bowling Club. Watching for a Strike and Bowled Out." (Latter with lower marginal right side tear just to the print.) Matched pair, 1888, framed together, single frame, glass both sides. (2 prints)
$500.00–600.00 pair

Print: Currier & Ives. "The Darktown Bowling Club. Bowled Out." 1888 as above. $250.00–300.00

Print: Currier & Ives. "Watching for a Strike." Tear center top just into print. $250.00–300.00

Print: Currier & Ives. "Darktown Law Party. - A Bully Time." 1888, bull upsetting picnic table. "Music in the Air," 1888, bull in distance sees picnic table covered with red umbrella. Matched pair, framed together, glass both sides in single frame. (2 prints) $500.00–600.00 pair

Print: Currier & Ives. "Darktown Race. Facing the Flag. Match between 'His Lowness' and 'The Stretcher' for de gate money." Two horses at judge's stand - "Coony Island Jockey Club." 1892. Soiled, tears at top and right margin. $250.00–300.00

Print: Currier & Ives. "Darktown Race - Won by a Neck." ("Golly dat gyraffy neck does de bizness.") 1889. $250.00–300.00

Print: Currier & Ives. "Darktown Tally-Ho" - "Straightened Out & Tangled Up." 1889, team of 4 jackasses pulling stage-coach and running away. Matched pair, framed together, glass both sides, single frame. $500.00–600.00 pair

Print: Currier & Ives. "Darktown Tournament - Close Quarter" and "First Tilt" (1890). White washers arguing and fighting. Matched pair, framed together, glass each side, single frame. Minor foxing. (Two prints) $500.00–600.00 pair

Print: Currier & Ives. "Darktown Tournament - Close Quarters." 1890. White washers battling it out with their brushes as the policeman rushes in to stop the fight and onlookers roar with laughter. (One of above pair) $250.00–300.00

Prints: Currier & Ives. "Obdurate Mule/Going Back on the Parson." Mule refuses to move on railroad track despite fire under him, train approaching. "Penitent Mule/The Parson of Deck." Matched pair, framed together. (2 prints) $500.00–600.00 pair

Prints: Currier & Ives. "White Dog's Got Him" and companion print "De Black Dog Wins." Dog Fight Arena. Matched pair, framed together. (2 prints) $500.00–600.00 pair

Print: Currier & Ives. "Wrecked by a Cow Catcher." Cow has butted engine and one coach off the track. $250.00–300.00

Print: Going for a shine. "He Kin Knock de stuffin outen a mule." Large oversize fighter in top hat with his retinue. 1888. 14½" x 10" plus wide margin. Mint condition. $250.00–300.00

End Darktown Series

Print: Duel. "The Savannah Duel," b/w print depicting rifle duel between two former slaves over a question of politics. (R) *Harper's Weekly*, June 27, 1868. 7" x 11" $45.00–60.00

Print: Print of Thomas Nast drawing titled "The Emancipation of the Negroes, January 1863 - The Past and the Future" with a large circular scene at center of family around a large wood-burning stove with vignettes surrounding, including (on left) scene of slaves being whipped, being sold at public auction; (on right) children waving goodbye to mother and crossing to public school and worker receiving pay at cashier's window. Removed from *Harper's Weekly*. 14½" x 20½". $45.00–70.00

Prints: E.W. Kemble. Two b/w prints of drawings by E. W. Kemble. (1) "Ignorance is Bliss," depicting white-bearded old man unaware of his leaking jug, 12½" x 9" plus margins. (2) double illustration for "Kite Time in Coonville." (R). (2 items) $45.00–65.00 each

Print: Flower Seller. Colored photo-print of drawing by Elizabeth O'Neill Verner of a tired old woman smoking a pipe, wearing shawl, bandana head scarf and long dress with full length apron, seated on a crate holding a bouquet of flowers with a large basket of flowers at her feet. Titled "Sit Down and Rest a Little While." (Water stained in lower margin not affecting print.) 6¾" x 5¾" plus title and margins. $95.00–115.00

Prints: Pair pencil-signed prints of Women Flower Sellers. (1) Woman seated with two large baskets of flowers and holding a small bouquet for inspection. (2) woman standing with large basket of flowers on her head. 8" x 6" (repros.) but with original pencil signature. $65.00–75.00 each
$140.00–175.00 pair

Print: Greenwood. Signed original lithographs signed in pencil l.r. "Marion Greenwood." Titled on reverse label "Mississippi Girl." Well-known model "Ruby" (from Miss.) posed. Depicts seated young woman, ¾ length, facing half right with left hand on top rail of chair, right hand in lap, wearing low-cut slip beneath her unbuttoned blouse. Limited edition published by Associated American Artists, ca. 1935–1940. $175.00–225.00

Prints: Greeting Cards. 2 Southern Tradition series greeting/birthday cards, printed in multi-color from original paintings by Jack Meyers (ca. 1975) of country General Stores. (1) 3 old men and women with infant in arms on porch, children in foreground. (2) Old man and boy w/dog on porch, woman feeding children in foreground. $16.00–20.00 each

Print: Jury Bound. B/W print of sketch by S.G. McCutcheon titled "Drawn on the Jury" depicting family surrounding father who perplexedly reads jury summons. (R) *Harper's Weekly*, Dec. 28, 1878. 15" x 10½". $45.00–60.00

Print: Old Times. B/W cover print of drawing by W.L. Sheppard, titled "Old Master & Old Man - a New Year's Talk Over Old Years Gone," depicting two elderly men, B/W, seated by fireplace reminiscing. (R) *Harper's Weekly*, Sat. Jan. 11, 1890. $45.00–60.00

Print: Marriage Certificate. Large document "Certificate of Marriage" printed in oval surrounding a horseshoe with b/w scene within of a priest marrying young couple. Printed form

"This certifies…" to be filled in. United border with white chain encircling oval. Marked L.L. "copyrighted 1910 P.P. & F. Co., Chi." 20" x 15¾". $40.00–60.00

Print: Philadelphia Centennial. B/W cover picture (R) *Frank Leslie's Illustrated Newpaper*, N.Y., Aug. 5, 1876, titled "The Centennial Exposition. Statue of the freed slave in Memorial Hall" depicting the statue of the slave holding the Emancipation Proclamation being viewed by numerous museum goers. $45.00–75.00

The following 18 color lithographs contain 11 from the charming "Pore Lil Mose" comic series by R.F. Outcault, noted cartoonist. Each is 10½" x 14" printed and published by N.Y. Herald Co. 1901/02, printed on white stock, with lengthy poem in center and colored cartoon vignettes and illustrations completely around each border adding a visual delight to each section of the humorous poems of this series. (Note: R.F. Outcault, listed in Blackbeard & Williams "The Smithsonian Collection of Newspaper Comics" as "father of the modern comic"; premier figure of juvenile genius and subversion in comic was…R.F. Outcault's Yellow Kid, immediately followed by Rudolph Dirk's…Katzenjammer Kids. Subsequent demon children of the early Sunday comics… Outcault's Buster Brown and his Hogan's Alley.") Each of first 10 lithographs has a tiny triangular piece missing from the upper right corner; others are in excellent condition.

Comic Lithograph: "Pet Chicken." $65.00–75.00

Comic Lithograph: "He Treats His Friends to Soda Water." $65.00–75.00

Comic Lithograph: "He Builds an Airship." $65.00–75.00

Comic Lithograph: "He Spends a Week on the Farm." $65.00–75.00

Comic Lithograph: "…at Coney Island." $65.00–75.00

Comic Lithograph: "Mouse Houn." $65.00–75.00

Comic Lithograph: "Send His Pa A Venture." $65.00–75.00

Comic Lithograph: "He buys His Mammy a Hat." $65.00–75.00

Comic Lithograph: "He Goes Bathing." $65.00–75.00

Comic Lithograph: "Happy Lil Sal as the Queen of the May." $65.00–75.00

Comic Lithograph: "He Visits Baxter Street." $65.00–75.00

Comic Lithograph: "He Takes a Ride on the Car." $65.00–75.00

Comic Lithograph: " …& His Hatchet." $65.00–75.00

Comic Lithograph: " …at Central Park." $65.00–75.00

Comic Lithograph: "He Takes a Sail." $65.00–75.00

Comic Lithograph: "He Calls on Edison." $65.00–75.00

Comic Lithograph: "He Visits the War Works." $65.00–75.00

Print: Post-Civil War School. B/W print of drawing by A.R. Waud titled "Zion School for Colored Children, Charleston, SC." (R) *Harper's Weekly*, Dec. 15, 1866, depicting teacher/ minister speaking to large student body of over a hundred children within large church room. $65.00–75.00

Print: B/W print of sketch by Edwin Forbes titled "Cotton team in North Carolina." (R) *Harper's Weekly*, May 12, 1866, depicting former slaves moving a large wagon load of cotton down the road. (Edge tears on right margin and lower margin into title and print.) $65.00–75.00

Print: Religious. Three B/W prints (1) "My Faith I place in Thee" depicting a woman clinging to a large granite cross with an angel hovering to her left. Publ. by E.G. Renesch, Chicago, 1919, marked l.r. Several 1½" to 2" tears and a crease from top center to lower third right, 20" x 15¼". (2) "The Little Shepherd" seated child with shepherd's crook and large sheep with flock in backround. Marked l.r. "1911, Otto Scheible, Chicago." 20" x 16". (3) "Heavenward" with large central long-haired angel surrounded by winged cherubs. Marked l.l. "P.P. & F. Co., 1911." (3 items)
$210.00–250.00 each

Print: Seesaw. Colored litho. print of painting by J. Wells Champney depicting b/w children at play, the boy and girl (at creek side) seesawing on a plank set on an overturned decaying rowboat marked "The Union." 7" x 10¼". $65.00–75.00

Print: Large colorful print of an original painting signed "S.G." (ca. 1875) with scene set at a clearing by a stand of large trees where, in foreground, two boys are playing seesaw on a heavy plank set across a large tree stump with a third boy holding a younger child seated back on the stump watching the exercise. Rare. 13" x 19" plus margins. $375.00–500.00

Print: South. "Levee Scene on the Mississippi." 1878, special reprint for Mississippi Lime Company, Alton, Illinois. W.J. Morgan & Co. Litho & Publ., Cleveland, O. (ca. 1935). 10¾" x 15¾". Depicting men dancing, playing banjo, gambling and lazing at the waterfront with six or so side-paddle wheelers at the dock (background). $75.00–95.00

Print: Story Telling/Circus Parade Viewers. Two B/W prints of drawing by R.N. Brooke. (1) "The Coon Hunt - Telling Stories Round the Camp Fire." (2) "Seeing the Circus Pass- A Virginia Sketch" depicting large group of b/w kids at a fence gate watching open-mouthed. (R) *Harper's Weekly*, Dec. 14, 1872. $65.00–75.00

Print: Spanish American War. Colorful lithograph "Charge of the 24th & 25th Colored Infantry & Rescue of Rough Riders at San Juan Hill, July 2, 1898." Print depicts U.S. troops (with Black flag bearer) reaching the stone wall barricade behind which the Spanish troops are still very active; two trooper have carried the U.S. Flag to the top of the blockhouse but are still engaged in fighting. Kurz & Allison, Chicago, ca. 1899. 20" x 27½", fine clean print. $250.00–325.00

Lanten Slides: Series of small size glass lantern slides (1¼" x 5") including (1) Jing-Jing hab some fun - 2 slides; (2) Good Evening, Good Night - 3 slides; (3) Zulus - 2 slides; (4) Mr. Long & Mr. Short - 2 slides; (5) Elephant Goes for a Walk - 2 slides. (11 slides) $45.00–65.00 each

Misc.: "Little Miss Muffett (#498) w/Spider, Dixie Boy Flaslight (Fire) Crackers (with boy eating watermelon), Maid Aid Brochure, Postcards (slave quarters, Jocular Jinks, etc.) (5 items) $25.00–30.00 each

Prints: "Ice Cream Racket. Freezing In" and "Thawing Out," 1889. ("Oh dat lubly cream! Seems as I could nebber get enuf" and "Guess yous done got enuf dis time". Matched pair, framed together, back to back, glass both sides, single frame. "Thawing Out" in upper left corner creased but not into print. "Freezing In" in upper right corner creased. (2 prints) $150.00–175.00 each

Prints: Inititation Cermonies of the Darktown Lodge. 1887. "The Grand Boss Charging the Candidate" and "The Candidate Charging the Boss." (The candidate being a boat mascot.) Matched pair, framed together, back to back, glass both sides, single frame. (2 prints) $100.00–150.00 each

Print: War in Virginia. B/W print of sketch by Edwin Forbes, "Contraband Coming into the Union Camp." (R) *Frank Leslie's Illustrated Newspaper,* Aug. 20, 1864, depicting a conestoga wagon-load (elderly, women and kids riding) drawn by horse, mule and oxen with men walking alongside. $65.00–75.00

Print: Watermelon Eater. Print of young girl eating a large slice of watermelon, 13" x 9½" plus title and margin. $55.00–65.00

Print: Watermelon Lover. Color print, hand touched half-tone, titled, "The Feast" of 3 young barefoot boys seated by heavy-vined fence. Center boy, looking seriously at onlooker, holding a huge half-watermelon, while the boys on either side, look laughingly at each other, each with a quarter melon. 13½" x 18¾". Repaired and hand colored to hide the defects. $145.00–175.00

Print: Watermelon. Colored print depicting group of kids (11 in all) peeking over fence at a small child in foreground eating a large slice of watermelon. Print signed "Teyton '05" in original dark oak frame marked "Watch on the Rine" to match title on print. 4½" x 10" plus margins. Torn at far right margin (not into print). $55.00–65.00

Print: Valentine. B/W print titled "Homage to St. Valentine" of drawing by Alfred Kappes, (R) *Harper's Weekly,* Feb. 12, 1887, depicting young man standing outside log cabin window where young woman admires the Valentine gifts left by her man. 16" x 11" overall. $55.00–65.00

Print: Victorian Die Cut. Beautiful colorful die-cut lithograph of man in swallow tail coat, top hat and red peppermint-striped trousers on the back of a large striding ostrich, ca. 1880. 10" x 8". $55.00–65.00

Print: Five colorful Victorian die-cuts: (1 & 2) Messengers (left, right profiles). (3) Old man looking aghast (bust). (4) Mammy with bowtie and knotted head kerchief (bust) (5) Little baby asleep in grass with large sleeping pig. (Each approximately 2¼" x 1¾".) (5 items) $110.00–155.00 each

Print: Two die-cut figures of boys, one sprawled out lying on stomach with one hand on chin apparently interested in story being told by second boy seated on his haunches, gesturing with right hand. 10" x 4¾". (2 pieces) $110.00–155.00 each

Postcards: Cartoon/Comic. 25 postcards, used and unused, 1905–1948, greetings. (25 cards) $11.00–15.00 each

Postcards: Children/Nudes. 15 postcards, used and unused, 1904-56 with children at work and play; native women, nudes and semi-nudes. (15 cards) $11.00–15.00 each

Postcards: 16 postcards, used and unused, all different, from cotton planting, picking, transporting to processing. Ca. 1905–20. (16 cards) $11.00–15.00 each

Postcards: Log Cabins, Industry. 23 postcards, used and unused, ca. 1910, including 6 cards of log cabins, many of various types of transportation, etc. (23 cards) $11.00–15.00 each

Postcards: Misc. 35 cards, used and unused, U.S. and Foreign, ca. 1910–1970. (35 cards) $9.00–15.00 each

Trunk: Humpback. Fine sheet metal rounded top trunk with wooden strip supports and brass corners (ca. 1880) decorated inside with colorful lithographed print of "dandy" dancing to the music of his piano-playing girl dressed in fine, big-bustled Victorian dress. 36" x 22" x 18". $400.00–500.00

Spiritual and Prints: (1) "Swing Low, Sweet Chariot," Negro spiritual printed on linen (word and music), 13" x 11". (2) Three B/W prints, framed together, "The Cabbage Patch," "Robinson - The Man's 'fraid of his own shadow," "Misto Bradish's Nigger." (2 items) $45.00–65.00 each

Print: Large b/w photo copy half-tone print of young boy putting on a man's hat with cigarette in band. Signed l.l. "Karl Marshall," 14" x 18". $45.00–60.00

Painting: Oil painting on board. Singing guitar man, signed l.r. "M. Billy." 20" x 16". $500.00–600.00

Print: WWI colored lithograph "Our Colored Heroes." Depicting American soldiers, Henry Johnson and Needham Roberts, while on sentry duty engaged in hand-to-hand combat with a large number of helmeted German soldiers in a raiding party in bright moolight, with an American group in distant background rushing up to get into the battle. On lower left is a shield-shaped imprint titled "Honored As Heroes" with General Pershing's communique citing Johnson and Roberts for their deeds of bravery for which they received the Croix de Guerre. Lithograph by E.G. Renesch, Chicago, 1918. Clean, fresh print, 16" x 20".
$250.00–350.00

Print: "Colored Man is No Slacker." Colored halftone print of a WWI soldier saying good-bye to his wife in a flowered bower while a long line of his fellow Black infantrymen march behind with an American flag waving. Marked l.l. "E.G. Renesch & Co., 1918." 19½" x 16". $75.00–95.00

Print: "True Blue." Color halftone print of a mother with three children standing before a cheerful fireplace (interior) with a photo centered above the mantelpiece of the absent father shown in an American Doughboy's uniform, surrounded by prints of Washington, Lincoln and Wilson. The little girl in center foreground holds a Black baby doll. Marked l.l. "E.G. Renesch, Chicago, 1919, publisher." 20" x 16", very minor edge tears. $150.00–175.00

Print: Emancipation Proclamation. Colorful composite print with large center oval, surrounding small oval portraits and four side vignettes. Large center oval (topped by large American eagle, shield and stand of flags) of Abraham Lincoln holding pages of the Declaration of Independence on which can be read "All men are created equal...". Center oval surrounded by vignettes of Miss Liberty with Black and White boys. Booker T. Washington with quote, WWI troops charging and contemporary urban scene and four oval portraits of Paul Dunbar, Frederick Douglass, Lt. Col. Otis B. Duncan and Lt. Col. Franklin Dennison. Lithography by Renesch, Chicago, 1919. 16" x 20".
$200.00–250.00

The following seven lots are colorful offset lithographs printed in *Judge* magazine, various issues, turn-of-century (1896-1902), all by cartoonist/humorist "Zim" and lithographed by Sackett & Wilhelms Litho Col. N.Y., each 13½" x 10¼" (R).

Print: Zim. "A Sagacious Animal." Mule outsmarts Grandpa.
$50.00–60.00

Print: Zim. "The Great Sprint at Blackville." The starter of the race used an antique pepperbox pistol to start the race.
$50.00–60.00

Print: Zim. "How the Blackville Handicap was Won." Rockets make the horse a winner. $50.00–60.00

Print: Zim. "The Great Fourth of July Handicap at the Blackville Track." A sure thing becomes a cropper when all 4 horses drop dead at the quarter-mark. $50.00–60.00

Print: Zim. "The Best Laid Plans Oft Fail to Hatch." Winning a turkey shoot against the odds. $50.00–60.00

Print: Zim. "Our Comic Artist's Nightmare." His favorite characters take Vengence. $50.00–60.00

Print: Zim. "How the Great Football Game Was Won. Blackville vs. Shantytown." Blackville had no chance until their manager painted the football to look like a watermelon. $50.00–60.00

Watercolor: Menu. Handpainted illustrated menu for Cotillion dated Dec. 31, 1938, with pelican chasing little boy holding balloon. (1939). 9" x 12". $125.00–150.00

Watercolor: Portrait. Man with white beard wearing straw hat and smoking a pipe. Signed l.r. "Koehle," 8" x 6".
$125.00–175.00

Watercolor: Watermelon. Watercolor of boy with outstretched legs seated by "No Trespassing" sign and wire fence of watermelon patch, eating a large piece of watermelon and keeping a watchful eye out for the farmer. n.p., n.d., marked by consignor as drawn by Ruby Anderson, 13 yrs. 13½" x 10", creased rough margins. $125.00–175.00

Print: Progress of Liberty. Large poster, publ. by Geo. M. Rewell & Co. Cleveland, 1886, titled "Progress of Liberty" with large center of statue of Lincoln emancipating the slaves (Freedom Memorial) surrounded by eleven ovals and rectangular scenes on each side w/Lincoln Univ., Harvard Univ., Berea College, Claflen Univ., Wilburforce U. and Atlanta U. on the right with White House, Senate, Hampton, Normal, Fisk Univ., Lincoln Inst., Leland Univ., Tougaloo Univ. and Bishop College with various other schools pictured and brief history of the Emancipation Proclamation and Canons of Race Progress. 33¾" x 24" plus margins. (Apart at one of the folds. Laid down on cardboard to serve as advt. poster recruiting sales people as well, marginal soiling and staining.) $175.00–200.00

Print: Spanish American War/Genealogical. Colorful lithograph titled "Afro-American Historical Family Record" with center area left blank for genealogical facts as: grandparents, parents, births, children, marriages. Surrounded on all four margins by scenes and portraits. At top are 24 cigarette-card size pictures of 24 U.S. presidents, Fred. Douglass, 13 portraits of leaders, educators, ministers, editors plus 4 rectangular scenes (on left) of last auction of slaves, picking cotton, hat of a slave, etc. and 4 scenes (right) Tuskeegee Institute, progressive farming, school house and home of freeman. Bottom margin with two Spanish American War battle scenes, Battle of Quaimas and Charge Up San Juan Hill. Publ. by Hist. Publ. Co., Augusta, Ga., 1899. Copyright J.M. Vickroy, Terre Haute. (soiled and stained in margins only.) $175.00–200.00

Print: WWI - Emancipation Proclamation. Composite print with large center oval of Lincoln honoring Lt. Otis B. Duncan and Lt. Col. Franklin A. Dennison. Lithograph by Renesch, Chicago, 1909. 16" x 20" (soiled).
$110.00–125.00

Original Block Print: Preacher. Original woodblock or linoleum print titled "Announcing Text" signed "E. Hargevaes," depicting tall preacher behind lectern with hand on Bible and right hand gesturing. 10" x 4½". $95.00–150.00

Pencil Sketches: 2 pencil portraits signed "Koehle." (1) Pipe-smoking man with old hat, 8" x 6"; (2) Profile (2/3 right) of man with long pipe and seaman's hat. Marked on back "Fisherman of Rio Grande do Sail," 6" x 8" (possibly pencil and ink). (2 drawings) $110.00–125.00 each

Pencil Sketches: Turkey Trot. Four panel pencil drawing of girl with turkey learning Turkey Trot (but the grizzly bear ?). Of original Kemble, drawn by Calist A. DeVaul, dated 1913. $95.00–110.00 each

Photo Album: Midwest. Old velvet-covered "Souvenir" album with ornate clasp, filled with family photos from wealthy family relatives and friends of Illinois area including approximately 76 large studio portraits and miscellaneous cartes de visite; mother with children, children with toys, man with gold-headed cane & hat, etc., ca. 1880–90's. Plus loose group studio pictures of horses w/carriage, girl in communion dress, woman in fur coat; Lincoln pencil sketch, several snapshots from 1920's with old automobiles.
$200.00–225.00

Stereopticon Views: At Work/Play. Comospolitan & Keystone views including seven at work - Southern Fla. Ltd. Train, Mining Phosphate (Tenn.), Turpentine Farm (Savannah), Picking Cotton (Miss.); Hoeing Rice (S.C.) Plus two watermelon comics. (9 views) $15.00–20.00 each

Print: B/W print of drawing by S.G. McCutcheon. (R) Harper's Weekly, April 12, 1870, titled "The Soup Kitchen Charity" depicting a man bringing hot soup, bread, etc. to family with woman sick in bed. $65.00–75.00

Prints: Two prints of sketches by Alfred Trauble. "Sunday on the Mosquito Coast - Moravian Missionary Preaching." Above second print, "The Impending Feast - A Scene on the Mosquito Coast." (R) from Harper's Weekly, May 9, 1874. Tear through upper print. $65.00–75.00

Print: Bicyclist. Reprint of Currier & Ives Darktown Series "Creating A Sensation." The bully boy on a bicycle (high front-wheeler), The plasterer and his wheelbarrow have been upset and run-away mule frightens a woman into a tree. 9" x 12½" plus title and margins. $70.00–85.00

Print: "One Look at Your Angelic Face and I am Yours Forever." 8" x 11" color lithograph, ca. 1870, framed.
$200.00–250.00

Print: Civil War. B/W print of an artist's drawing titled "Scene in the Military Market at Beaufort, SC" depicting large crowd with soldiers and sailors dickering with the civilians for vegetables, poultry and meat. 10" x 15" (R) Harper's Weekly, ca. 1862. $65.00–75.00

Stereoptic View: "Picking Cotton, Louisiana." Two adults in field with child in foreground. Underwood & Underwood, #1221. $20.00–25.00

Stereoptic View: "Golly! dis am cheper dan twofers." Young boy stealing puff from drunk's cigar. B.L. Singley, 1897, Keystone #6051. $16.00–20.00

Stereoptic View: "Free of Us is Cullu'd and Free Spotted." Young girl/boy with puppies. B.L. Singley, 1899, Keystone #9524. $16.00–20.00

Stereoptic View: "Cabin Home, Petersburg, Va." Three persons outside cabin with small kid sitting near corner of cabin. Kilburn Bros. #885. $16.00–20.00

Stereoptic View: "Happy Hours." Young girl picking boy's head. American Ill'd Tropical Series. 4" x 7". $16.00–20.00

Stereoptic View: "15th Amendment, or The Darkey's Millennium, 40 acres of Land and a Mule". Elderly man on back of mule, pulling cart with young boy walking in front. St. Augustine, Read Bloomfield's Historical Guide, 4" x 7". $16.00–20.00

Stereoptic View: Elderly man riding cart pulled by bull. Ca. 1875. 4" x 7", numbered 613, sepia. $16.00–20.00

Stereoptic View: "Swamp Cypress." Man leaning on tree in swamp. Signed "Upton #357, Ashmead Bros., #317 (Florida Views) 4" x 7" sepia. $20.00–25.00

Print: "Wash Day." Woman washing while young boy looks on. Photo by John H. Tarbell, 8" x 10" b/w halftone.
$65.00–75.00

Print: "Reminiscenes." Elderly man sitting in chair looking at pictures of Abraham Lincoln in book. Tarbell, 1898, 8" x 10" b/w halftone. $65.00–75.00

Print: "An Anxious Moment." Boy coming through hole in fence with two watermelons. Tarbell, 1897, 8" x 10" b/w halftone. $65.00–75.00

Print: Tiger stalking "Little Black Sambo" with umbrella. Color; 8½" x 11", framed. $75.00–95.00

Cut-Out: Three young girls dressed in their "Sunday best" out for a stroll with umbrella being carried by one in center. Mounted, (break) on one leg of trio, 6" x 8" color lithograph, ca. 1890. $75.00–95.00

Carte De Visite: Small boy with Civil War cap. Bowdoin,

Taylor & Co., 204 King, Alexander, Va., ca. 1875.
$75.00–95.00

Poster: Bull Durham. Three colorful advertising reprints.
$65.00–75.00 each

Print: Egyptian. Large colored engraving from painting by Ernest Mormand, 1895. Egyptian prince or pharoah consulting with advisor (chief harem girl) on purchase of several b/w slave girls. 15" x 25". $95.00–125.00

Prints: Fowl/Foul. Two colored comedy prints. (1) two children with boxing gloves in a ring with flag "Champion" hanging with rooster running near wording "Foul." Nat'l Art. Co., 1905. 8" x 10". (2) Frd. cute print of little girl hugging a little boy being frightened by a vicious barking dog annoyed by the dead chicken in the boy's hand. 10" x 8". (2 prints) $65.00–75.00 each

Prints: Misc. (1) Print of boy apparently preparing to urinate through hole in fence who has look of pain as a large goose on the other side of the fence pecks at him through hole. (2) Six-part printed cartoon from 1880's magazine (R) titled Solution of boys solving problem of stealing a watermelon from field guarded by large bull dog. (2 items)
$65.00–75.00

Print: Post Civil War. Large sepia and b/w print published by Geo. M. Rewell, Cleveland, titled "Colored Chieftains" with numerous oval portraits (both left and right) surrounding portraits of Lincoln, Fred. Douglass, various post-Civil War U.S. Congressmen. Below are portraits of Grant and various Abolitionists with write-ups of "Milestones of Progress" and "The Pioneers" and "Noble Words." Dated 1885, 30" x 24", laid down on cardboard for use as poster to create sales and recruit sales agents. Several tears in margins include piece 3" x 1" missing right center into print; large crease and tear lower margin center into print. $200.00–225.00

Stereoptic View: "Pickers Grouped in Cotton Field." Six persons in cotton field, James M. Davis, #6951, Kilburn, 1892. $20.00–25.00

Stereoptic View: "A Field of Snowy White - A Cotton Plantation near Dallas, Texas." Man carrying basket of cotton on shoulder. Berry, Kelly & Chadwick, 1907.
$20.00–25.00

Stereoptic View: "Ten minutes for Refreshments." Boy holding bottle while pig sucks on nipple. Strohmeyer and Wyman, 1892, Underwood and Underwood. $20.00–25.00

Photo: Cabinet. Young boy in cart being pulled by bull on main street, Jacksonville, Fla. - (signs can be be stores/shops) 4½" x 7½", mounted on board. $85.00–100.00

Stereoptic View: "Cotton Field." Heavy-set woman with basket of cotton on head/five other persons in field, picking cotton. "Characteristics Southern Scenes." Photo by J.A. Palmer, Aiken, S.C. #179. 4" x 7". $30.00–45.00

Tin-Types: Fifteen different small photos.
$110.00–150.00 each

Imperial Cartes: Nine different rare photos of young men/women taken by Davis Premium Gallery. Highest awards at the World's Cotton Exposition and State Fairs (a few are identified on reverse.) $65.00–75.00 each

Photo: "N.A.A.C.P. War Time Conference." July 12-14, 1944, 8 p.m. "To Point Social Legal Action for the Future of Baltimore Negroes." (Panoramic view of conference participants) Patton's Studio, Chicago, 8" x 36", framed.
$200.00–225.00

Broadside: (Minstrel) "Cool Burgress Minstrels and Rollin Howard's Opera Bouffe Company featuring Nicodemus Johnson played by Burgess, The Comical Darky. J. Gibson, City Hall, Providence, Friday Evening, April 16, 1869." 9½" x 28", framed. $250.00–300.00

Photo: Hazel Scott - Pop Singer of the Fifties. 11" x 24", tinted, print autographed, cropped, framed. $70.00–90.00

Photo: Al Hibler - Pop Singer of the Fitties, 14" x 25", tinted, print autographed, cropped, framed. $70.00–90.00

Print: "Currier & Ives" American Jockey Club Races; Jerome Park…Tom Bowling winning the Jerome Stakes for 3 year olds, value $5,000; Dash Two Miles; October 4th, 1873. (Unofficial Time 3:40). Merodac - Springbok - Fellowcraft - Count D'Orsay - Tom Bowling, keyed above title, J. Cameron on stone., 16, (6" x 26"). 4, (24" x 32" Horses under saddle, broadside to right Clubhouse in rear) 1873, slightly stained/faded w/hole size of pencil above the letter "M" in American, repaired tear - 4½" above clubhouse flag, unframed, very rare print. $1,000.00–1,200.00

Prints: "Trust." Young man flirting with young woman while stealing a pie from her vending stand. Francis Brundage, Rapheal Tuck & Sons Co. Ltd., 1903. 16" x 20" slightly stained framed. $250.00–350.00

Print: "No Trust." Female vendor looking at young man searching for funds to pay for merchandise, looking forlorned, because he is to receive no credit. Francis Brundage, R. Tuck and Sons, Co., Ltd., 1903. 16" x 20" color, sl. foxed at top (does not affect print), framed. $250.00–350.00

Print: "Peter Jackson: British Boxer." "Peter Jackson" signed in print - "A.D. Bastin" in pencil, London publ. Jan. 1894 by Cadbury Jones & Co., 60 Haymarket, S.W., N.Y., Fishel, Adler & Schwartz, copyright reg. prtd., in Vienna, w/seal ATT 150, 22" x 28", b/w eng., framed sl. foxed on border. $250.00–350.00

Engraving: Calendar. "New England Mutual Life Insurance

Co., Boston Mass., 1901 - The Boston Massacre" by Frank T. Merrill "First Blood of the Revolution, March 5, 1770." The Death of Crispus Attucks) American Bank Note Co., N.Y. & Boston, 13" x 15", b/w. $95.00–125.00

Prints: Four early 19th century lithographs of Native Africans, hand colored, 7" x 9½", J. Grasset Souvenir, inv. direx., J. Laroque, Sculp. $250.00–350.00 set

Postcards: 13 different portrait photo views of children/adults, us/uns, ca. 1915. $20.00–25.00 each

Print: "Native of Benguela"/"Native of Angola" (male and female) Dr. Pritchard's Natural History of Man tinted engraving, ca. 1840, 5½" x 9", framed. $100.00–150.00

Photos: 13 different sepia views depicting children/people at work in/around Jacksonville, Fla./Savannah, Ga. 4½" x 5" on Eastman Kodak Co. board. $20.00–25.00 each

Photo: "Honey does ye Lub Yo Man?" Preacher marrying couple while family looks on in humor and satisfaction. Knaffel & Bro., Knoxville, Tennessee, 1897. 10" x 12", framed. $110.00–135.00

Photos: Family Album with approximately 600 snapshots of outings, individuals, pets and family of a New London, Conn. family, ca. 1912-1925. $225.00–275.00

Magic Lantern Slides: Two boxers dressed in striped pants, dress coat and top hat. 3¼" x 4¼" color, framed/numbered "2" and "3". $45.00–65.00 each

Photo: Roy Hamilton - pop singer of the Fifties. 11" x 14", tinted, autographed in print, framed. $80.00–115.00

Photo: Dinah Washington - jazz and pop singer. 11" x 14" tinted, autographed in print, framed. $90.00–125.00

Poster: "The Saturday Evening Post" - Sept. 13, 1941. Man O' War, all-time champion, age 24, nuzzling William Harbut, his groom since 1930, at Faraway Farms, Kentucky, where the great horse still stands at stud. 22" x 28" unframed. $75.00–85.00

Print: "Prayer Meeting in a Contraband Camp. Washington 1862." Group of people shouting and dancing with woman being blessed by elderly male. Engraved by J.J. Cade, N.Y., A.D. Worthington & Co., Pub., Harford, Conn., 1887, 5½" x 7", tinted, unframed. $75.00–85.00

Print: "Life in Philadelphia." Fashionably dressed couple, ca. 1836, 6" x 7¼" tinted, trimmed, unframed. $75.00–85.00

Print: "Life in Philadelphia. A Black Ball." Five persons w/captions, on dance floor, praising each other, ca. 1836, 9¼" x 7½", tinted, trimmed, unframed. $75.00–85.00

Film: 16 mm. "From Slave Cabin to Hall of Fame." Life of Booker T. Washington. 2 reels, 800 ft. $150.00–225.00

Print: "Power of Fashion." (Small boy smoking cigar, seated on stoop with dog, color by LaFosse, 1853, 24" x 30" cropped, very nicely framed, matted. $350.00–425.00

Calendar: Four different blotters by J.P. Alley Adv., "Fairfield Farms Dairy," color. Southern Art Corp., 1920 calendar on three of four. (1922) $75.00–80.00

Print: "Southern Exposure." Small girl w/back in air, scrubbing marble steps with brush. B/W eng., signed in pencil "Tom Mabon" along with title and inscribed on reverse "November 22, 1934 - Presented to G. Norman Anderson by Tom Mabon." 7" x 8½", framed. $150.00–200.00

Imperial Carte: Mammy with baby on lap. Used as New Year's greeting in 1891, signed "James Maxwell Bennett, Jan. 1st, '91," photo by Jacob Stealey, Weston, W.Va. $150.00–200.00

Print: "dat Little Ole Log Cabin." Three children on steps of cabin. J.H. Tarbell, b/w halftone, 8" x 10". $55.00–65.00

Print: "After the Bath." Naked child with tears in eyes while three others are looking on. Bertrice To-nesen, b/w halftone, 8" x 10". $65.00–75.00

Print: "I'se a Little Alabama Coon." Small boy picking banjo sitting on box. Swarthout, b/w halftone, 8" x 10", 1897. $65.00–75.00

Print: "Reading the Crystal." Elderly woman telling young woman's fortune. Color reproduction from original painting, 8" x 10". $65.00–75.00

Photo: Black exercise boy with five horses outside stables. B/W, 8" x 10". $85.00–125.00

Print: "Pore Lil Mose - Sends his Pal A Valentine." Comic by R.F. Outcault, color, 11" x 14" framed, ca. 1910. (Mat portion of print slightly stained.) $65.00–75.00

Print: Two men, one in tattered clothes holding dice in one hand; money in the other, looking for explanation from smartly dressed other caught in act of cheating, with a look on his face, as to say "Who, Me?" 18" x 26" color litho. poster, blank, ca. 1910, framed. $165.00–200.00

Prints: 2 different Black posters by Harlan Tarbell of Black Face Minstrels, printed by T.S. Dennison & Co., Chicago, 11" x 17", color lithograph, ca. 1910. $110.00–150.00 each

Imperial Carte: A very nice photo of gentleman with large book in hand (possibly a pastor). Photo by Lauf, Philadelphia, Pa., ca. 1885. $55.00–75.00

Imperial Carte: Two photos of differently smartly dressed

boys, Kenyon & Son, New London, Conn., ca. 1885.
$55.00–75.00 each

Tin-Type: Mammy/child identified "Jenny Jolly/John Carhart," inscribed on face, a very nice photo. 3½" x 5".
$125.00–150.00

Tin-Type: Nurse with two children, identified "Carhart Van and Amanda." 2½" x 3½".
$75.00–100.00

Imperial Carte: Nurse/children identified - "Jane, Carhart, Van and Wallale," trimmed.
$60.00–75.00

Postcards: 20 different linen/WB views depicting work/comic views, us/uns.
$20.00–25.00 each

Postcards: Souvenir folder. 9 different b/w color views of Hampton Institute, Hampton, Va. (10) $15.00–20.00 each

Postcards: Two different photo views of boy climbing palm trees, us/uns.
$11.00–16.00 each

Postcards: An interesting lot of 12 different b/w/sepia photo views depicting Blacks, us/uns. $11.00–16.00 each

Print: "Opossum up a gum tree. His tail his body follow. Raccoon quickly him see...Looking out o' hollow." (Vignette of female with straw hat.) color lithograph R.R. Soanlan-Ward Morton, Pub. by J. Mitchell Library, 33 Old Bond Street, London, 8" x 11" framed.
$175.00–250.00

Photo: Sugar Ray Robinson (boxer). 16" x 24", tinted, autographed in print, framed.
$200.00–250.00

Photo: Ella Fitzgerald, jazz/pop singer. 14" x 25", tinted, autographed in print, framed.
$150.00–175.00

Carte De Visite: Full body shot of sailor. Ca. 1870, F.P. Kenyon & Son, Photographers, New London, Conn.
$150.00–175.00

Photo: Celluloid, 6" dia. Beautiful woman in evening dress, studio pose, tinted.
$120.00–145.00

Photo: Lionel Hampton, band leader. 14" x 23", tinted, autographed in print, unframed.
$120.00–145.00

Print: Joe Louis, boxer. 8" x 11" color photogravure.
$145.00–165.00

Cut-outs: Five different 11" tall cut-outs (cake walk) mounted on board, ca. 1895.
$200.00–275.00

Photo: "Alone." Small boy sitting at base of column of what looks to be front porch of Southern plantation estate. Taken by Frank Gould, Towson, Md., 11" x 14", title and name on mat in pencil, unframed.
$75.00–95.00

Photo: Ambrotype. Grey hair man w/Masonic apron around waist, standing beside table (studio pose) with a book or missal in left hand resting on table. 6th plate (case broken), ca. 1870. This item depicts the involvement of Blacks with the Masonic order at an early date in our history. Extremely rare.
$575.00–675.00

Civil War Memorial Discharge: (Easel-shaped monument in a memorial park background.) "To whom it may concern. Know ye that James H. Bryan, a private of Captain Hakey's Company K, 4th Regiment, U.S. Colored troops infantry volunteers, who was enrolled on the first day of September 1863 to serve three years during the war is hereby discharged from the service of the United States this 18th day of May 1865 at Fortress Monroe, VA...Said James H. Bryan was born in Frederick City and County...Maryland, is 26 years of age..." 22½" x 30", framed, slightly soiled, rare.
$500.00–600.00

Print: "Reproduced in facsimile from the original painting by Winslow Homer for Lawson Valentine Co. by Armstrong & Co. Litho., The Riverside Press, Cambridge, Mass." Three mule skinners lying outside tent with one peering out of tent, mules grazing to left with covered wagons, barrel in right foreground. This print was originally used as advertising sign, has been cropped. 17" x 27½", unframed.
$200.00–225.00

Print: Large number of political posters, local elections, mainly Philadelphia, for various offices of Mayor, City Council, Judge, City Commissioner, all as found, used and/or abused, after elections, approximately 8 including 13 duplicates. (Of national prominence, W. Wilson Goode, who became first Black mayor of Philadelphia.) (28 posters)
$45.00–65.00 each

Print: "The Feast." Three young boys with straw hats eating watermelon. Jos. Hoover & Sons, Phila., 1903, #627 color lithograph, 16" x 20", unframed.
$75.00–95.00

Charcoal Portrait: 14" x 18", b/w (well-dressed elderly gentleman with beard). Ca. 1895, framed.
$175.00–250.00

Tin-type: Baby seated in red chair, 8" x 10".
$125.00–175.00

Print: "How Union Soldiers Got Their Mail - Taken Before Petersburg, August, 1864." 10 soldiers sitting outside mail tent, including Black soldier in middle of group. From Photographic History of the Civil War, Pub. by Review of Reviews Co., Patriot Pub. Co. 1910, 10" x 12" b/w halftone.
$65.00–75.00

Print: "The Dandy Charger." Man dressed in long coat and top hat riding bicycle. 7" x 8½" color lithograph, framed, ca. 1832.
$200.00–250.00

Carte De Visite: Shabbily dressed male with patch over left eye, umbrella in left hand/fan in right, a very unusual looking character.
$65.00–75.00

Trade Cards: Series of three 4¼" x 6½" cards advertising "Cole & Burt, One Price Clothiers and Furnishers, 39 Main St., Bennington, Vt.," color lithograph.
$20.00–25.00 each

Calendar: Complete 12 months of humorous situations, gold/color lithograph, issued by Clarence Brooks & Co., Manufacters of Fine Coach & Railway Varnishes, Cor. West & W. 12th Sts. New York," 5" x 6¼" (once pasted in scrapbook) 1894, suitable for framing. $75.00–95.00

Print: "Savandali an Erumango Boy", "Man of Erumango." 6" x 10" color lithograph (dual vigs, one plate). Ca. 1840, framed. $200.00–250.00

Print: Currier & Ives. "A Change of Base - I jist done got a call to anodder congregation!" Vig. (parson with turkey under arm being chased by congregation, winter scene). Thos. Worth, on stone, unframed. 15" x 20" color lithograph. $500.00–575.00

Postcard: Small group of b/w and color views depicting Blacks working and in group (family) situations. 42 different views, most rare. Pre-1915, us/uns. $20.00–30.00 each

Cigar Box Label: "Sweet Repose." Man sitting on bales of cotton with gun under leg/dog with head resting on leg - smoking cigar. Color lithograph, Heppenheimer & Harris & Maurer, N.Y. 7½" x 5". $20.00–25.00

Imperial Cartes: Nine different babies, ca. 1890.
$20.00–25.00 each

Print: "The Secession Bubble. It Must Burst!" Young girl blowing bubbles with pipe while dog watches. Pub. by J.H. Bufford, Boston, 1862, color lithograph. 12" x 18"; framed 17" x 21". $300.00–375.00

Print: Currier & Ives. "Won by a Foot." Kemble, del. Man with big feet winning race, vig., 1883, color lithograph, 15" x 20", unframed. $450.00–500.00

Print: Currier & Ives. "The Darktown Fire Brigade – Investigating a Smoke." (Parson - No Sah De Meeting Hose Aint Afire, but de Congregation am taking a Smoke of de World's best terbakker.") #13 Joseph Koehler, Publ. N.Y. color lithograph, 15" x 20" unframed.
$400.00–500.00

Print: Currier & Ives. "Goin for a Shine." ("He kin knock de stuffin outen a mule!") A group of men following one who is about to box, with his seconds walking beside him with gloves/pail, 1888, color lithograph. 15" x 20" unframed. $400.00–500.00

Print: "Photographing the Bridal Party Before the Christmas Wedding at Blackville." 10" x 14", b/w.
$75.00–95.00

Book: *Slavery Defended: The Views of the Old South.* Edited by Eric L. McKitrick, Assoc. Prof. of History at Columbia Univ., A Spectrum Book, Prentice Hall, Inc., N.J., 1963. $65.00–75.00

Print: "Life in Philadelphia." Well-dressed male asking consent of well-dressed lady to dance. "Hall I hab de honour to dance de next quadrille wid you, Miss Mint?" "Tank you Mr. Dato, wid much pleasure, only I'm engaged for de nine next sets!" 7" x 8" hand tinted eng., frontispiece, framed, slightly stained, pub. by W. Sampson, No. 66 Chestnut St., Phila. 1828. $300.00–350.00

Photos: Four b/w 5" x 7" views depicting Greencove Springs, Florida scenes (depot, watermelon being loaded on box cars, etc.) ca. 1915–21. $45.00–65.00 each

Print: Young man/woman at what seems to be New Year's Eve party. Lithograph by Marion Greenwood, 11" x 14", b/w, ca. 1935, framed, signed in pencil. $350.00–425.00

Print: "Josh Educating a Pig." Man pouring hot water on pig while two others look on, on board ship. 6" x 8", b/w, ca. 1845, framed. $70.00–90.00

Photo: Ambrotype. Elegantly dressed man with book (Bible) in hand sitting at table (studio pose). 6th plate in case, ca. 1875. $200.00–275.00

Photos: Six beautiful 4½" x 6¼" sepia views of young boys acting as golf caddies on unknown golf course. All but one depicts woman and/or man golfer about to take stroke at ball (one depicts caddy in sailor suit placing ball on tee), ca. 1900. (An excellent lot) $50.00–60.00 each
Carte De Visite: Handsome middle-aged male with two young Caucasian boys - teacher or guardian? $45.00–55.00

Print: Top from game box - "The Game of Coon Hunt" by Milton Bradley Co., Springfield, Mass. Man with gun and dog hunting in moonlight, 12" x 16", matted (suitable for framing). $50.00–60.00

Print: "Revd. Richard Allen," founder and first bishop of the African Methodist Episcopal Church in the United States. Born 1760 - died March 26, 1831. Pub. by Wm. H. Jones, Baltimore, Md., E. Schnabel, Lith. P.S. Duval & Co. Steam Lith Press, Phila., 11" x 14", framed, with stain across bottom, b/w, extremely rare. $500.00–550.00

Engraving: "Burial of Latane." Group of women and children around grave with four male/female slaves to their side. 28" x 36", b/w, eng. by A.G. Campbell, ptd. to W.D. Washington, 1868, W.H. Chse (presented to every annual subscriber to the Southern magazine) foxed w/4" tear at top into print, 2" tear at bottom (no effect to overall quality of print), unframed. $350.00–450.00

Postcard: Actual photo of "Tup Lucas, Thurmont, Maryland Barber." Mr. Lucas standing in door with arm across chest, hat in hand, in salute to flag, in respect, by C.R.R. Bock Thurmont, unsigned. $45.00–55.00

Imperial Carte: Five children, studio pose by Westcott & Cummings, 302 Market St., Wilmington, Delaware.
$35.00–45.00

Poster: "Journee Coloniale," Sous Le haut Patronage de S.M. Le Roi. 2 Juilet 1922 Comite Central 34 Rue de Strassart, Bruxelles." (Native with spear vig. view in circle). 28½" x 43", color lithograph by Ed Peelaes, Affiches D'Art. Litho et Gouweloos fre & Sr., Bruxelles.
$350.00–400.00

Imperial Carte: Music trio with flute, guitar/violin. Kenyon and Son, New London, Conn. $55.00–65.00

Measuring Stick: Hardwood, hickory or oak. 81½" tall w/ 15" x 11" base/ 19½" overhanging bar that slides up and down pole with carved-in lines. Bar is held to pole by metal straps. Stick was found in tunnel beneath the Lankford House next to the Teakle Mansion, Princess Anne, Somerset County, Maryland. The tunnel led to the Minokin River Basin, supposedly used by Patty Cannon, abolitionist, to smuggle slaves. (Superb piece of folk art). With documentation. $575.00–650.00

Prints: Pair of color lithographs. "There's a time for disppearing," "Take a Header, Down You Go." Woman/ man who are reaching for bottle in boat that is about to capsize. Boat has capsized with woman holding to sides, while man's head has disappeared under water. Wm. Breens, 1882, 10" x 14", slightly foxed with few small holes in one. Unframed. (2) $250.00–300.00

Print: "Life in Philadelphia." Man/woman in millinery shop, where woman is trying on bonnet. "What do you think of my new poke bonnett Frederick Augustus." "I don't like him no how, case dey hide you Luby Face, so, you can't tell one She Nigger from anoder." Ca. 1836. 6¼" x 7½", tinted, trimmed, unframed. $125.00–175.00

Print: "Life in Philadelphia." Man scolding young boy, "What de debit you hurrah for General Jackson for? you Black Nigger - i'll larn you better - I'm a'ministration Man!!!" "Hurrah!! Hurrah for General Jackson!!!" in square with people in background dancing around May pole, boy with newspaper in foreground, 6" x 7", tinted, 1836, trimmed, unframed. $125.00–175.00

Print: "Dis Am de Fust of de Season." Young boy carrying watermelon. 7" x 9", halftone, framed. $85.00–95.00

Print: "Just Two Coons," Small boy with raccoon by Bernard Wall, 5" x 7" color lithograph in frame w/applied metal roosters. $125.00–150.00

Print: "You All can hab de Rine." Small child with doll and half of watermelon. By Bernard Wall, 5" x 7" color litho-

graph in frame w/two applied metal roosters.
$125.00–150.00

Print: "Deed, I didn't steal um!" Small child with duck. By Bernard Wall, 5" x 7" color lithograph in frame with applied watermelon slice (metal). $125.00–150.00

Pen and Ink Drawing: "Life Class." Young man leaning on fence. Oct. 4, '81, Sr. Rog. (init.) "C.L.F." 5" x 7", unframed. $125.00–150.00

Watercolor: Woman washing clothes in wooden tub beside cabin with people on porch, clothes hanging on line w/cabin in background, by John McGrath. 6" x 8", framed. $300.00–375.00

Pen and Ink Watercolor: Young girl with doll. 3½" x 4¾" framed behind glass, ca. 1890, unsigned. $350.00–425.00

Painting: Primitive. Young girl with ribbon in hair. 8½" x 12" unsigned, on board (break across bottom), framed, ca. 1890. $400.00–450.00

Watercolor: 7" x 9". Bare fist striking man's jaw, unsigned, ca. 1948, framed blue/white. $250.00–300.00

Watercolor: 8" x 11", signed "C.F. Gibson," ca. 1900, framed. $410.00–475.00

Print: "Pore Lil Mose - His Pet Monkey meets an Old Acquaintance." (Poor Lil Monkey.) Comic by R.F. Outcault, color litho, 10½" x 14". 1901. The New York Herald Co. $75.00–95.00

Print: "Pore Lil Mose's Pet Chicken." Comic by R.F. Outcault, color lithograph, 10½" x 14". 1901, The New York Herald Co. $75.00–95.00

Print: "Pore Lil Mose In Chinatown." Comic by R.F. Outcault, color lithograph, 10½" x 14". 1901, The New York Herald Co. (w/sl tears.) $75.00–95.00

Print: "Pore Lil Mose - He Tells his Mammy About The Football Game." Comic by R.F. Outcault, color lithograph, 10½" x 14". 1901, The New York Herald Co. $75.00–95.00

Print: Pore Lil Mose and His Hatchet." Comic by R.F. Outcault, color lithograph, 10½" x 14", The New York Hearald Co. $75.00–95.00

Watercolor: Young boy eating slice of watermelon. Unsigned, 5" x 7" in 12" x 14" gold frame. Ca. 1890.
$325.00–400.00

Photo: Elderly man in cart, being pulled by donkey on brick paved street. B/W, 7½" x 9½" taken by Grace Hooper (not signed). Ca. 1947. $70.00–80.00

Photos: Two views of street paving crew working on 33rd

Street, Baltimore, Maryland. (Blow-up: "Sunlight and Shadow - 10½" x 13") other not titled. 7¼" x 9½" b/w taken by Grace Hooper, ca. 1947. $70.00–80.00 each

Print: "Pore Lil Mose Talks to the Animals." Comic by R.F. Outcault, color lithograph. 10½" x 14". 1901. $75.00–95.00

Watercolor: Man fishing in river beside cabin with two people standing in door, palm trees growing along river bank. Signed "Waterbury," 11" x 21", framed. Ca. 1890. Frame needs repair. $500.00–650.00

Print: "Moses." Old gentleman in long coat and vest with stovepipe hat in right hand, selling newspapers, *Baltimore Gazette*. A. Hoen, Balto., original painting by T.W. Wood. (Hanging in the Maryland Historical Society center gallery). B/W lithograph, 14" x 22", framed w/sl. tears. An extremely rare print. $575.00–675.00

Painting: Three young boys sitting on orange crate with smiles on their faces. Unsigned, 12" x 15", canvas, framed. Ca. 1895. $500.00–600.00

Watercolor: Young boy seated on ladder w/hands clasped over right knee, wearing cap/short pants signed "E.H. Stewart, '99," 10" x 15", w/slight stains, framed, b/w. $500.00–600.00

Watercolor: Two babies boxing in ring; one has knocked the other down in corner of ring, w/caption "Who Am Champion Now?" Signed, dated "H. Macklin, '14." Orange background, framed. $525.00–600.00

Painting: 6½" x , unsigned, artist board, ca. 1880, framed. $500.00–600.00

Painting: Man w/bundle of wood across shoulders walking path beside stream, unsigned, ca. 1900, on artist board, 7¾" x 11¼", framed (needs repair). $300.00–350.00

Painting: "Voodoo Queen." Elderly woman. Signed "Steffi", ca. 1960, 20" x 24", unframed. $200.00–225.00

Print: "Pore Lil Mose entertains a visitor." Comic by R.F. Outcault, color lithograph, 10½" x 14", 1901, NY Herald Co. $75.00–95.00

Print: "Pore Lil Mose Still in New York" (writes his weekly letter), comic by R.F. Outcault, color lithograph, 10½" x 14", 1901, The New York Herald Co. $75.00–95.00

Print: "Happy Lil Sal as the Queen of the May." Comic by R.F. Outcault, color lithograph. 10½" x 14". 1901, The New York Herald Co. $75.00–95.00

Ceramic Box (salve): Very colorful transfer print "The Battle of the Nile." Young boy, elderly couple in window and Negro male watching peg-leg male and gentleman playing game; dog and rooster in foreground with man walking and ship in background on lid. 4" dia. x 2½" tall, ca. 1870. Excellent condition, rare. $550.00–600.00

Stereoptic Views: Five Keystone View Co. views depicting Blacks at work (#6952 "Gathering Peaches, Delaware;" #13722 "Rosin on the Docks, Savannah, Ga;" #13747 "A Turpentine Farm - Dippers and Chippers at Work, Savannah, Ga"; #13751 "Hoeing Rice, South Carolina" and #16738 "Mining Phosphate and Loading Cars near Columbia, Tenn." B/W photos. $30.00–40.00 each

Magic Lantern Slide: Mechanical. Couple sitting on grassy hill with umbrella - front/back view. 4" x 7", color. $85.00–110.00

Movie Poster: One sheet. Joe Louis in "The Fight Never Ends" with one of Ruby Dee's earliest appearances. The Mills Brothers, red and black on white background. Some damage from folding. $75.00–100.00

Plastic Clock: Joe Louis photograph in the center. 10–11". $125.00–150.00

Metal/Tin Button: Joe Louis photograph. 1-3". $65.00–75.00

Watercolor: Woman with small boy in cart pulled by bull, with basket on back of cart. Signed "Edith Clarke," b/w, ca. 1890, 14" x 19", framed. $500.00–600.00

Watercolor: Woman out for stroll with parasol across shoulder, wearing yellow dress and hat with red shoes. Artist unknown, ca. 1900, 12" x 18", framed (slightly stained). $425.00–500.00

Engraving: Shakespeare's *Othello,* Act V, Scene II - "A Bedchamber. Desdemona in Bed, Asleep." Painted by J. Graham, eng. by W. Leney, published Sept. 29, 1799 by J & J Biydell at the Shakespeare Gallery, Pall Mall; No. 90, Cheapside, London, 18" x 24" (foxed) unframed. $175.00–250.00

Postcards: Four "Bernard Wall" cards of young boy with chicken, goose, watermelon/coon (w/ethnic sayings) and one view "A Horseless Carriage" (young man on pig's back), used. $25.00–35.00 each

Painting: Young boy in tattered clothes sitting behind harvested cornstalk stack eating watermelon, farmer with rake on shoulders peering from behind stack, dog in background; boy is barefooted. 21" x 30", unsigned, unframed. Ca. 1895. $500.00–600.00

Painting: 2 young children eating watermelon with quarter sliced from melon on plate. 6" x 12" (walnut wood), ca. 1900, unsigned, unframed. $400.00–500.00

Painting: Young girl sitting on bench with cat looking over her back, cabin in background, fashioned after "Clapsaddle" picture of girl on bench, 4½" x 12¼", artist board, unsigned, framed. $400.00–500.00

Watercolor: Woman walking toward cabin. Signed "Seth C. Jones, '80". 2½" x 5", framed (Jones 1853 - ?) b/w.
$475.00–525.00

Original Calendar Art: Man in contraption wagon with dog lagging behind. 8" x 11" pen/ink and watercolor, ca. 1930.
$350.00–400.00

Postcards: 17 different views/comic PC. $11.00–16.00 each

Milk Glass: Satin Finish. 14" plate depicting young boy, titled "Honey," ca. 1885.
$500.00–550.00

Prints: 5½" x 7½" hand-colored lithographs by F. Lecomte, "Negre domestique," "(Kistar age) Eunuque gardien de la porte du Serail." Ca. 1840.
$125.00–150.00 each

Photo: Comedian, Bert Draper, black face minstel (Br'o Jazz) inscribed in pencil - "Here's to Carl Miller who I love like anything." Signed, 7" x 9".
$100.00–125.00

Scrapbook: Forty-six pages of prints, ads (Gold Dust Twins, Cream of Wheat, etc.) stories, music, etc. w/loose music.
$150.00–200.00 set

Bookmark: Sterling silver. Woman with basket on head, 3½".
$125.00–150.00

Vending Machine Cards: 3½" x 5½", sepia tones (Elston Howard, Hank Aaron, Larry Doby, Don Newcombe, Willie Mays and Orestes Minoso), ca. 1950. (6 items)
$13.00–17.00 each

Watercolor: 15" x 22". Woman carrying watermelon from field. Signed "E.N. Lusk," ca. 1900, framed. $400.00–525.00

Handpainted Plate: 9½". Two small children in bed under red/yellow blanket with caption "Two Lil Darkies Lyin in Bed, One was Sick and de Odder Mos' Ded, Called fo' de Doctor and de Doctor sed, Fed dem Chillun on Shortnin Bread!" New Orleans, La.
$200.00–225.00

Print: 9¾" x 14¼". "A Base Hit" by Thomas Worth. Gentleman with umbrella hit by baseball while three players converge on ball and another player is running bases. Color lithograph, unframed.
$150.00–185.00

Glass Slides: Three different b/w photo slides, 3¼" x 4", natives, ca. 1920.
$45.00–65.00 each

Photo: 16" x 20" reprint b/w photo of three men playing cards. One man is reaching for card between toes of another player while the other (older man) who has spied the action is looking over table watching them cheat. Framed.
$65.00–85.00

Pencil Sketch: Elderly gentleman in bowler with mustache and goatee. Ca. 1900-10, 9" x 12", unsigned.
$125.00–200.00

Photo: Matthew Henson, 4" x 6½", b/w by Sullivan, Phila., 1937.
$45.00–65.00

Photo: Matthew Henson, Snow Baby and others, six identified, standing in front of Peary Statue, dedication of Peary Memorial. 3" x 5", b/w 1937. $75.00–85.00

Postcard: Sepia illustrating 2 babies kissing in hooded wicker beach chair with black crow watching (Gluck and Winkel), ca. 1921. "African Bridge." Party game box for game combining bridge and dice with directions and score books. Buzza Co. ca. 1945. Game - $75.00–125.00
Postcard - $20.00–25.00 each

Movie Poster: "Cabin in the Sky" starring Ethel Waters, Eddie "Rochester" Anderson, Lena Horne, Louis Armstrong, etc. 1943 pasted on board. $200.00–250.00

Movie Poster: "Stormy Weather" starring Bill Robinson, Lena Horne, Cab Calloway. Bright red borders and large red lettering. Pasted on board. 43" x 28". $200.00–250.00

Painting: "Little Lad." A very fine oil painting of young boy in straw hat holding black kitten under his right arm with his left hand up thumbing his nose, ¾ length figure, snubbing with artist's caption painted lower border, "Tain't Your Cat." On canvas, unsigned, n.d. (ca. 1890). 17" x 13".
$2,000.00–2,200.00

Painting: Old Man. Interesting subject, oil painting of elderly gentleman with can leaning against door in open doorway of a log cabin peering up and pointing at bright stars in sky, with painted caption in lower border "I wonder of ef dat could be de same ole' star." Background has shadowy figures of others watching celestial phenomenon. Initialed l.r. "HMD," ca. 1890. Oil on canvas, 18" x 13".
$700.00–800.00

Watercolor: Woman carrying basket with flower basket on head. Signed with initials "ARHS," 7¼" x 12", ca. 1900.
$350.00–450.00

Watercolor: Young boy with watermelon in hand and basket with eggs, flower/birds on ground. Signed w/ initials "ARHS," 7¼" x 12", ca. 1900. $350.00–475.00

Watercolor: Young boy playing with baby girl in sand with wagon, and hat is laying on ground. Signed with initials "ARHS", 7¼" x 12", ca. 1900. $375.00–475.00

Painting: 51" x 63". Man walking up path toward village, at a distance in upper right corner of painting signed "John R. Johnston," ca. 1880. Damaged with holes and needs cleaning, framed. $5,000.00–6,500.00

Photo: (Negative). "Zip Black," member of the Wellsboro, Pa. Military Band during the 1890's. (Extremely rare situation to find Negro being allowed to participate in non-Black community projects.) 5" x 7". $225.00–275.00

Photo: (Negative) "Farman Black & Sister." Probably children of Zip Black. 5" x 7", taken on April 7, 1891.
$225.00–275.00

Photo: Ambrotype. Full plate of Mr. Henry Mengee (man of perhaps 65 years of age with receding hairline, mustache and beard), ca. 1879. (no case) $375.00–400.00

Watercolor: Primitive drawing of Black male trying to kiss Caucasian male. Caption: "Take, O' Take those lips away." Signed w/initials "H.S.S." 2½" x 3", ca. 1830, framed.
$550.00–625.00

Painting: 9" x 12". Young boy. $275.00–325.00

Print: "Ye Abolitionist in Council - Ye Orator of Ye Day Denouncing Ye Union." B/W simple single line sketch. (R) *Harper's Weekly,* May 28, 1859. 9¼" x 14", plus margins.
$75.00–95.00

Christmas Cards: Beautiful Black Greetings. Box of 15 cards and envelopes. Olympicards #321-325 (3 each) including Black Santa, Black Virgin and Child, Black Holy Family, Black Country Store, Black Angels. $75.00–95.00

Comic Cards: Set of 3 sepia cards, "I'm Granpa at Last" series. Each card announcing another arrival of quintuplets. (1882, John McGreer, Chicago). Plus 2 color postcards. (1) Four children on mule. (2) Alligator after boy up palm tree. (7 items) $20.00–25.00 each

Cards: Greeting. Six (6) valentine cards - four different (w/two duplicates) and 1 birthday card, ca. 1940. (Used) (7 cards) $20.00–25.00 each

Imperial Carte: Young man in local fireman's band uniform. Kenyon & Son, New London, Conn. $75.00–95.00

Painting: Rail Birds. Two men b/w at rail watching horses at race track with collage (paste-on) of parimutuel stubs (torn losers) spread about their feet. Unsigned, n.d., oil on canvas, 30" x 24". $200.00–225.00

Painting: 4 men b/w seated on a park bench passing a bottle of wine from hand to hand. Man left center holding newspaper with murder headline. Signed l.r. "W.F. Boddington, 1958." Oil on pressed board, 22" x 28". Titled on reverse "The Cocktail Hour" with signature and address of artist. $250.00–300.00

Photo: Dancers. Studio photograph of young couple doing an intricate dance step. Inked across top "Johnie Peters & Ethel Williams - Waltz Tango - Turkey Trot & Texas Tommie." She is dressed in long shoe-top length gown, he is in white long-tailed tuxedo trimmed in black and striped pants. Possibly vaudeville team. Girl's name and message, ink smeared. 10" x 12½", laid down. n.p., n.d. (ca. 1900–1910). $125.00–150.00

Print: "Dat Possum Smell Powerful Good." B/W print from drawing by T. Hovington depicting an elderly gentleman seated before an iron kitchen stove savoring the fumes from a pot cooking on the stove. 9½" x 14". (R) Harper's Franklin Square Library Christmas Number, 1888.
$75.00–95.00

Postcards: Comic. 35 comic postcards from pre-1920's to mid-1940's, regular and on linen, used and unused. (1 duplicate) all in color. $13.00–17.00 each

Postcards: 4 postcards of cotton industry, two of turpentine industry; all different pre-1920 views depicting Blacks working (used and unused) plus Old Slaves Market, St. Augustine. (7 items) $13.00–17.00 each

Postcards: 8 different color linen cards. 6 comic cartoons plus "Listening to the Master's Word, The Old Folks at Home." Unused. (8 pieces) $13.00–17.00 each

Poster: Prize Fighters. "World Champions and Post Greats of the Prize Ring." Numerous photos in boxing poses showing each champion and four past greats in seven different weight classes (ca. 1940). Centered around Joe Louis are Sugar Ray Robinson, Henry Armstrong, George Dixon, Ike Willams, Joe Gans, Sam Langford and (the original) Joe Wolcott. 22½" x 28". $110.00–135.00

Stereo Card: Black School. Rare cabinet-size stereograph card by S.T. Blessing, ca. 1870. "Louisiana Scenery - Negro's School - sold by S.T. Blessing #87 Canal St., New Orleans" with approximately 32 children of varying ages and colors with books in hand with their male teacher photographed outside little clapboard schoolhouse. 4" x 4".
$65.00–85.00

Stereo Cards: Roots. 4 standard stereograph cards of Chief Kapuzi. (1) With two sons. (2) With two daughters. (3) His wives and children (3 wives and 13 tiny tots.) (4) Seven favorites of the Kraal. All published by N.E. Wright, ca. 1890 (part of Excelsion Stereoscopic Tours Series).
$55.00–65.00

Photo: 10" x 14". Minstrel group depicting 25 men (black face/costume). $55.00–65.00

Photograph: Jackie Robinson on the front of a glass candy container. 5"-6". $65.00–75.00

Lithograph: Midgets. Gold bordered card with 2 oval portraits, lithograph by Sarony & Major of "Bartola" (age 10). 17" W, 29½" H & Maximo (age 20), 20" W, 33¾" H. Written on back "Azteck Children. Exhibition in Phila." Ca. 1875. $65.00–85.00

Lithograph: Fine color lithograph by G. Baxter with impressed title on lower margin of mat "Me Warm Now" depicting charming young lad sitting on barrel in front of fireplace with bellows in hand, dated 1853. 4¼" x 6", plus original mat, 7½" x 10". $300.00–400.00

Lithograph: Currier & Ives, Boxing. Color print, after Thomas Worth's cartoon caricature "De Fust Knock Down," 1882. Tear on left side of print. 10½" x 13" plus wide margins. 13" x 17" overall. $350.00–450.00

Letter Box: Lincoln Freeing the Slaves. Wooden letter/document box, approx. 9" x 12" x 4" D. with lacquered fine print on cover of "Abraham Lincoln Freeing the Slaves," print showing bowing slave, his shackles broken, kissing the left hand of President Lincoln, who stands with one foot on the broken chain and right hand aloft proclaiming emancipation. Cracked left corner with brittle, fragile edges somewhat chipped. $250.00–300.00

Commemorative Plate: M.L. King Nobel Prize Winner - Toleware plate with photo on cardboard attached to front with rim marked "I Have a Dream - Freedom for All my People." Reverse imprinted with biography of Dr. King "Youngest to ever win the Nobel Peace Prize." (1964) 8¼" overall dia. with attachment for wall plaque. Maker "Fabcraft, Frenchtown, N.J." $150.00–200.00

Diorama: Wood carved, polychromed, three-dimensional scene of 13 Black men in conversation, lolling in foreground about the dock, seated on cotton bales and barrels, looking out at the four-decked river boat tied to the dock. Painted panorama backdrop of the river, the opposite shore and a huge setting sun. 28½" L x 19" H x 13" D. $575.00–675.00

Postcards: Includes Tonsorial Artist in Fla., Braddock's Spring, Braddock Heights, Md., Out in the Woods, Fla. (playing cards), Giant Crop of Irish Potatoes, in Fla., Monday in "Coon Town" (hanging the wash). 4 in color, 1 b/w. (5 cards) $13.00–17.00 each

Postcards: Color photo postcards including 3 watermelon scenes, 2 cotton picking, Monday in Coon Town, Race Suicide down South, Alligator Bait, A Coon Trees a Possum, Thanksgiving Morning in the South, etc. 11 different views, all published by Leighton, used and unused (1905–10). (11 cards) $13.00–17.00 each

Drawing: Comic Cartoon. Pen/Ink/Crayon Drawing. 10" x 13½" of young man holding rope with a snorting bull on the other end, looking the bull straight in the eye, with brick in opposite hand with penned legend below "Now Start Something - Go Ahead Start Something - So I Kin Rub Dis Ground Apple Over Your Head." Signed "G. Williams." $225.00–325.00

Drawing: Pencil Sketch. Nude Black man carressing woman-headed plant (rowboat in near background). Signed "J. Fayson (Balto., 1960)." 4½" x 6". $95.00–125.00

Drawing: Half-length charcoal portrait of an elderly well-dressed gentleman (facing half-right) with beard, wearing bowtie, 14" x 18", ca. 1895. $150.00–195.00

Drawing: Pastel drawing of pretty, young woman wearing a scarf-turban and looking at a bowl in her hands. Signed lower right, (John) Fayson, (Balto.) ca. 1960. 20" x 14" (bowl and hands unfinished). $325.00–425.00

Print: Colored lithograph. Small child in bright yellow hat waving party favors above her head. Signed Jean Charlot. 6½" x 8". $75.00–95.00

The following color lithos are all from the charming "Pore Lil Mose" comic series by R.F. Outcault. Each 10½" x 14", N.Y. Herald Co., 1901, printed on white stock, has a lengthy poem (center) and colored cartoon vignettes and illustrations completely around each border adding a visual delight to each section of the humorous poems of this series.

Comic Lithograph: "Ef I Wuz a Millionaire." $65.00–75.00

Comic Lithograph: "Pore Lil' Mose on the Speedway." $65.00–75.00

End: "Pore Lil' Mose Series

Print: Centennial Expo, Freedom - The Freed Slave. B/W print of the statue exhibited at Memorial Hall, Centennial Exposition, Phila. depicted being viewed by numerous Black museum goers. 9½" x 11" (R) cover *Frank Leslie's Illustrated Newspaper,* Aug. 5, 1876. $65.00–75.00

Print: Kurz & Allison. Spanish-Amer. War Black Cavalry Charge. "The Battle of Quasimas near Santiago, June 24, 1898 The 9th and 10th Colored Cavalry in Support of Rough Riders Kurz & Allison, Chicago, 1899. Color litho. 20" x 28". Minor damage to right edge, stained center top. $225.00–275.00

Print: Kurz & Allison. As above. Brown stain on top of print, lesser stain left edge. $200.00–250.00

Print: Theatre. "The English Mania for Private Theatricals Invades Blackville." B/W print from drawing by Sol Eytinge, Jr. depicting theatrical group performing in costume. 9½" x 14" (4) *Harper's Weekly,* Nov. 1, 1883. $65.00–75.00

Silhouette: Uncle Tom and Little Eva. A very early cut-out silhouette enhanced by penned-in detail features. Unsigned. Mid-19th century art. 3½" x 5¼". $300.00–325.00

Sculpture: Roots. African head sculpted from brown clay with tribal beaded style head dress, scarified face and wide snake neckpiece. 8". $125.00–150.00

Sketch: Charcoal drawing of a Black man wearing a straw hat, kneeling and playing a long-necked banjo. Marked on back of frame "Anna Cassatt, Mt. Pleasant, Ohio. By Anna

Cassatt 1906 to Nanna Moser/Calendonia/Ohio. 8" x 11½".
$200.00–250.00

Watercolor: Still Life. Bust of smiling youth wearing old hat behind five-string banjo and tattered page of sheet music on table. Unsigned. Ca. 1890, 16" x 22½". $375.00–425.00

Watercolor: Street Vendors. Well-done watercolor street scene of two women at street vendors carts pulled to curbside in front of a lunchroom. First woman with vendor at cart marked "Fish Man," and second woman is approaching a vendor at second cart marked "Fresh Oysters" with third woman watching from second story window above the lunchroom. Signed D. Thrash, Ca. 1935. 15" x 10" plus margins. $375.00–425.00

Sketch: Ink drawing of two Blacks wearing derby hats looking at each other, other one has cigar. 5" x 5", signed "Paj" in upper left corner with typewritten identification and address of artist on lower margin, "Philippe A. Judd, 2600–½ N. High Street, Columbus, Ohio. $75.00–95.00

Lantern Slides: Three b/w glass lantern slides with comic scenes: (1) "Dar! I knew mischeif was Breeding" (painter falling off ladder and through window); (2) "If dese am yourn boss, you can hab 'um (thief with chickens caught red-handed by armed farmer); (3) "Castigation" (mother spanking child, father kicking dog through window, etc.) One slide marked "W.J.A. Lieder successor to A.J. Fisher - N.Y." Ca. 1900 (3 slides). $45.00–65.00 each

Photo Exhibit Advt.: King, Mary Elizabeth, photographer. Photo-print advertising an exhibit of photographs by Mary Elizabeth King (3/10 - 3/17/1968) at the Church of the Redeemer, Balto., of photos taken throughout Mississippi in 1965. This photo titled "Under the Shadow" depicting a mother with her 2 children. 18" x 12". $65.00–75.00

Photo: Ambrotype. Young woman in beautiful brocade gown, wearing gold earrings, brooch and ring and seated by table with fine tablecloth. ⅙ plate (3¼" x 2¾") with brass ornate mat (no case). Ca. 1860. $200.00–225.00

Photos: Blacks depicted working in cotton/rice industries. (1) Cotton market (exterior), Montgomery, Alabama; (2) Cotton Gins, Arkansas; (3) Picking Cotton, Arkansas; (4) Baling Cotton, Arkansas; (5) Harvesting Rice, Louisiana. Each 7" x 9" published. The Philadelphia Museums. On 9¾" x 12" boards with full description of each scene. Ca. 1915. (5 photos) $40.00–45.00 each

Photos: Lot of twelve photos depicting Blacks (men, women, children), ca. 1895 including 4 cartes de visite, (2) J.W. Watson and (1) Swift (Raleigh, N.C.); other studio pictures from Norfolk, Philadelphia and Baltimore. $30.00–35.00 each

Photos: Three photos of adults - two of long-gowned women carrying purses, third of an elderly male sporting

fancy beard. Two with D.C. photographer's stamp: D. Freeman and Paul Tralles. Ca. 1890–1910. (3 items) $30.00–35.00 each

Photo: Ethel Waters. Vintage ¾ length silver print portrait of Ethel Waters by Crain of Detroit, ca. 1928. Approximately 13½" x 10½" plus narrow margins, credit in negative; nice condition. Very nice studio portrait of Miss Waters, shown in right profile. She is shown seated in pensive mood, her head slightly arched forward. $125.00–175.00

Photo: Musician. Publicity photo in color of Dizzie Gillespie, with big smile and hand wave, his horn in hand. Signed in print; tinted, ca. 1950. 14" x 25". $75.00–95.00

Photo: Nurse Companions. (1) Tin types of Black nanny posing with white infant and family; (2) Photo of Black nurse/companion with elderly white woman. (2 pieces) $100.00–125.00 each

Print: "St. Valentine's Day - Colored Valentines - The Favored Young Lady - I'll Just be ye Sont Dis Yere One, Yous Did, Mister Johnsing!" B/W print from drawing by W.L. Sheppard depicting young maiden and her admiring swains with mother ironing ruffled petticoat in background. 9½" x 14" (R) *Frank Leslie's Illustrated Newspaper,* Feb. 26, 1870. $65.00–75.00

Print: "Scene in the Military Market at Beaufort, S.C." B/W print depicting large crowd with soldiers and sailors (mainly supply officers) dickering for vegetables, poultry and meat with the Black civilians. Center of interest is a sailor pulling away a large pig by its hind leg. 10" x 15" (R) *Harper's Weekly,* ca. 1863-64. $65.00–85.00

Print: "Solution of the Labor Question in the South," B/W print from sketch done for *Harper's Weekly,* Dec. 2, 1865, depicting "Inquiring Stranger," center foreground, on horseback, group of "ex-slaves" (to left) and group of "ex-dominant race" (to right). Stranger asking, "Well, now that the war is over, what are you people going to do?" The "ex-slave" responds, "We's gwine to draw - draw rations." The ex-dom. race responds, "We'll run - for office…congress, legislature, constable." (R) 9½" x 14". $65.00–85.00

Print: "Their Pride." B/W print from painting by Thomas Hovenden of standing young woman checking her just completed oufit (hat and dress) in a small hand mirror while mother seated at right pridefully watches; father, seated left, smokes and rocks contentedly and little brother by dropleaf table, grins admiringly. 12" x 9½" (R) Dec. 8, 1888, *Harper's Weekly.* $65.00–85.00

Print: T.W. Strong, N.Y. colored lithograph. "First Meeting of Uncle Tom and Eva" in lower margin; "Scenes from Uncle Tom's Cabin No. 2" in upper margin. 12" x 9" plus margins. Ca. 1860. Clean fresh antique print depicting Uncle Tom seated on crate reading to Eva, seated on bale of cotton with 3 young slaves and boat's smokestack in background. $200.00–225.00

Print: "Uncle Tom and His Grandchild." B/W print from sketch by W. Jewett showing "Uncle Tom" seated outside log cabin reading to a young girl seated at his side. 9½" x 11½". (R) *Harper's Weekly,* Nov. 3, 1866. $65.00–85.00

Print: "Waiting For An Offer." B/W print from sketch by W.L. Sheppard depicting a young woman (with her children nearby) dickering with a junk dealer for the old rifle, bottles and broken pan she has offered while an older woman is counting on her fingers what she has to sell and what she'll want for it. 9½" x 10½" (R) Harper's Weekly, Jan. 31, 1874. $65.00–85.00

Print: "Water-Millions is Ripe," b/w print from drawing by Sol Eytinge, Jr. showing two young men carrying watermelons from a moonlit field, the larger boy (foreground) has a melon under each arm and a huge melon balanced on his head. 9½" x 11½" (R) Harper's Weekly, Aug. 23, 1879. $65.00–85.00

Photo: Preacher. Large photo of solemn, dignified, white-haired reverend in black robes seated in high-back turn-of-century chair. (Unmarked). 15¾" x 13". $65.00–85.00

Photos: Wash., D.C. Two cabinet photos. (1) Woman in waist coat, fitted bodice, long draped gown (Davis, 723 - 7th St., D.C.) (2) Man with knee-length jacket, vest, gold watch chain and fob. (Geo. Prince, Penna. & 11th St., D.C.) Each 6½" x 4¼" (two photos) $45.00–65.00

Photos: Tin types. Fourteen tin types of adult females and males, ca. 1890. (14 items) $75.00–95.00 each

Stereo Cards: Seven stereopticon cards of (1) comic card, new series "Trubble in de Church"; (2) "Cotton is King - Plantation Scene, Georgia." 4 cards are variants by Underwood & Underwood, Keystone and Stromeyer & Wyman and 1 duplicate. (3) Florida Series - 15th Amendment or the Darkey's Millennium. (7 cards) $20.00–30.00 each

Print: Oilette from a Harry Roseland painting (titled "A Penny Short") signed in print upper left hand corner, depicts an elderly Black couple seated at dining table worriedly counting out their money. 18½" x 13½" plus margins. $125.00–150.00

Print: "Running the Rapids of New River, Virginia." B/W print from sketch by M.J. Boyd showing seven men in an overloaded flatboat threading the treacherous rocks of the rapids. 9½" x 14" (R) *Harper's Weekly,* Feb. 21, 1874. $65.00–85.00

Print: "Who Struck De Fustest." B/W print from drawing by Sol Eytinge, Jr. depicting top-hatted teacher (?) seated with pointer in hand, trying to settle fight by two young'uns with other kids on fence enjoying situation. 9½" x 14". (R) *Harper's Weekly,* June 13, 1874. $65.00–85.00

Print: Civil Rights. Large Sachse colored lithograph "The Shackle Broken - By The Genius of Freedom." E. Sachse & Co. - Balto., 1874, with two large center scenes and six smaller border panels. Central theme (top center) "Hon. Robert B. Elliott of South Carolina Delivering His Great Speech on Civil Rights in the House of Representatives, Jan. 6, 1874." Lower center: Farm scene with farmer and family. "American Slave Labour Is of the Past – Free Labour is of the Present – We Toil for Our Children and not for Those of Others." Top left: Black Cavalry Charge. Top right: Black Infantry assault. Left center: Statue of A. Lincoln with Proclamation. Right center: Statue of Charles Summer. Lower left: Black officer on horseback with Black infantrymen. "Of those who were slaves – 100,000 are now in the U.S. Service." Lower right: Black sailors on ship's deck. "So far as tested...they are as good soldiers as any." – A. Lincoln. Plus marginal quotes from Robt. Elliot. Large print 21" x 26". Bright colors, water stained left margin, chemical stain in center. Minor top marginal tears. Very rare. $600.00–700.00

Photos: Tintypes. Two unusual tintypes: (1) Black male drummer (salesman) of hats. (2) Men dressed in military uniforms in boxing pose. (2 photos) $125.00–150.00 each

Print: Cartoon Comic. Little story illustrated with four b/w cartoons. (1) Dog lying in middle of street with bicyclist approaching (I'll jes' make dat dorg wih he done took a reef in his tail."); (2) cyclist runs over dog's tail ("De Reef's Done Took."); (3) Bike is wrecked (no comment); (4) Dog bites cyclist ("De Dorg Comes to Fust & Takes a Reef.") Ca. 1900, (R) $65.00–75.00

Print: Cleveland, Grover. "One of the First Fruits of the Victory." President-elect Cleveland directing the Negro and Southern White Democrat to "Shake Heartily, Boys!" Cover of *Harper's Weekly* for Nov. 22, 1884, 11½" x 16¼". $65.00–85.00

Print: "Close of the War – Babylon is Fallen, 1865." B/W print depicting a couple in their kitchen quietly dancing at the news of the surrender. 9½" x 14" (R) *Frank Leslie's Illustrated Newspaper,* Dec. 16, 1865. $75.00–95.00

Print: Comic "Wash-Day in Coonville" by E.W. Kemble. Print of four b/w drawings on 2 pp. (1) Little girl bending over large wooden wash tub to wash her own clothing; (2) falls in tub; (3) decides to take off clothes and wash them as well; (4) shyly request reader not to look - "I'se fru. Please tur turn de page, so's I kin git out er de tub." 9½" x 6 (R) *Cosmopolitan Magazine,* Nov. 1913. $55.00–65.00

Print: Cotton. Large print from drawings by H. Linton - "American Cotton. Its Cultivation and Preparation in Mississippi" with large center scene "Picking Cotton" and nine border scenes showing "Planting," "Hoeing," "Packing," "Levee at New Orleans," etc. Approximately 14" x 19" plus mat. (R) *Illus. London News,* Sept. 1881. Later hand tinted. $75.00–95.00

Print: Currier & Ives cartoon lithograph. "Wound Up" - Black man carrying tall case (grandfather) clock fleeing from Keystone-like cop. "Run Down" - Black man and policeman with wrecked clock after violent collision with fire plug. Each 10½" x 14" plus margins, 12" x 17" overall. King & Murphy, del.; publ. 1884. Colored comic caricatures. (Together, 2 Currier & Ives) $325.00–400.00 each

Print: "Gathering the Mistletoe for Christmas in the South – A Country Scene in Virigina;" large b/w print from original painting by Horace T. Carpenter. Depicts Black children and man helping white women gathering mistletoe and putting it into an oxen wagon. Removed centerfold from *Mail and Express Illus. Saturday Magazine.* (Dec. 1903) 16" x 22". $55.00–65.00

Print: Fugitive Slaves. "Morning Mustering of The Contraband at Fortress Monroe on Their Way to Their Day's Work, Under the Pay & Direction of the U.S." B/W, removed from *Leslie's,* Nov. 1861, 10" x 15". $55.00–65.00

Print: "Ignorance is Bliss." B/W print of painting by E.W. Kemble depicting a bundled-up white bearded old man with cane walking through snow unaware that wicker-covered jug he is carrying is leaking out its precious contents. 12½" x 9" plus margins. $45.00–65.00

Print: "A Letter From De Ole Man." B/W print from drawing by S.C. McCutcheon depicting woman seated between stove and high-poster bed examining an unopened envelope while a boy awaits the word and a tiny baby sitting on the bed eats and watches. 9" x 11½", (R) *Harper's Weekly*, Feb. 15, 1879. $45.00–65.00

Print: "The Long Suffering & Patient Race." B/W print from sketch by H. Murhman showing two seated men, the visitor, a politican trying to sell his candidate to his host. 9½" x 14". (R) *Harper's Weekly,* Sept. 25, 1880. $45.00–65.00

Print: "Negroes Escaping Out of Slavery." B/W print from sketch by A.R. Waud depicting a large band of refugees traveling after dark, fleeing the South (after the Emancipation Proclamation) by carriage, wagon, horseback and many on foot. (R) *Harper's Weekly,* May 7, 1864. (Note: Sketch by famous artist illustrates success of E.P. in depleting southern manpower reserve of slaves.) $45.00–65.00

Painting: Elderly Black man. Large oil painting on pressed board (36" x 48"), ca. 1950. Elderly man with closed eyes or lowered eyelids, wearing floppy straw hat. $200.00–225.00

Painting: "Florrie," oil portrait on canvas of young Black girl wearing daisies in her hair, seated half-right. Signed on back "Lilyan King 1942." 24" x 18". $225.00–275.00

Painting: Portrait. "Young Woman With Fan." Signed lower right, "H. Johnson." Oil on canvas, half-length portrait of girl wearing green dress facing half-left with open orange floral decoration fan held to her chin. 18" x 22". $500.00–600.00

Painting: Voodoo Man. Depicts a seated white-bearded elderly Black man holding a mystical ring before him with a skull perched behind his left shoulder and a devil figure partially shown behind his right shoulder. Oil on canvas, signed upper right, "J. Fayson" (Baltimore black artist), ca. 1955, 31½" x 16½". $300.00–400.00

Poster: Munich Olympic Games, marked "Olympische Spiele, Munchen - 1972" with full-length color print of painting by Jacob Lawrence depicting five Black runners with batons in hands making curve on track in relay race. Printed by Editions Olympics GmbH 1972 in Germany for Kennedy Graphics, Inc. Such items are often destroyed after the events and thus become scarce. (Note: Jacob Lawrence, world renowned Black primitive artist.) $75.00–95.00

Poster: Satchmo. Louis Armstrong poster marked "Les Artiste Associates, presentent/Louis Satchmo Armstrong/ Ambassadeur Du Jazz." with 2 photos of Armstrong - one, blowing trumpet; the other, a laughing Louie. Also marked "Louis Armstrong & Edward R. Murrow avec Leonard Bernstein et W.C. Handy." Red and black colors on white, 14" x 21" n.d. (ca. 1958) Brussels, J. Lichtertert Fils, printers. $75.00–95.00

Print: "A Question of Colour." Large color print of a painting by W. Small, 1896, depicting two pretty little girls (b/w) happily gazing down at their two dolls lying together on a pillow (with background left of natives unloading a British riverboat and background right of the planter reading a paper). 15" plus bottom margin and 19¾" (3 other margins cut to print.) $125.00–150.00

Print: Large b/w print "Onward." Abraham Lincoln (u.l.), Fred. Douglass (u.r.) and Booker T. Washington (l.c.) with 4 paragraphs on Lincoln and Douglass (top border) and The Tuskegee Institute and Booker T. Washington (lower margin), with left vignettes of house where Lincoln was born, Tuskegee drawing room, Tuskegee Laboratory and general view of Tuskegee; right vignettes of Fred. Douglass learning to read, Tuskegee machine shop and house where B.T.W. was born. Printer, W.L. Haskell, 1903. 20" x 16"; linen-backed. $75.00–95.00

Print: "The Captain (sic) of a Trading Sloop Bargaining with Negroes for a Cargo of Pineapple at Nassau." Matted (R) *Monumental City Balto. Advertiser.* 5" x 7". $45.00–65.00

Toys

Marx, Amos n' Andy wind-up tin taxi. The open car is lithographed - black and orange, 8" L. $450.00–500.00

"Rolo Chair," tin lithographed toy, three-wheeled cart pushed by walking Black man, original box, 6½" H. $550.00–700.00

Mechanical Bank: "Jolly Nigger Bank," 5½" H, blue tie w/ stamp, "Beacon Products, S&M Ltd." on back, iron. $550.00–700.00

Mechanical Bank: "Jolly Nigger Bank," 5½ H, blue tie, aluminum. $650.00–750.00

Mechanical Bank: "Little Joe Bank" in a top hat, red tie, aluminum, 6½" H. $650.00–750.00

Mechanical Bank: Iron "Jolly Nigger Bank, Mar. 14 '82." 6½" H, original paint (flaking), no bottom, w/arm replaced (brass). As is - $300.00–350.00

Mechanical Bank: "Jolly Nigger Bank." "Starkies Patent No." incised on the back, blue tie, ears move, aluminum, 6½" H. $700.00–800.00 mint

Mechanical Bank: "Jolly Nigger Bank" - "Bamboula" painted red and black, w/unusual trap, 6½" H, iron. $750.00–900.00

Still Bank: Mammy, ceramic, head has been glued, red and white dress, 6¾" H. $300.00–350.00

Optical Game: Stereoptics. "Ten Little Nigger Boys" (10 cards, complete set) depicting brown illustrations starting with ten Negroes and ending with one, who takes himself a wife, numbered 1 through 10, published by Theodore Hamblin, Ltd., Opticians, London, W.I., ca. 1920. $275.00–375.00

Mechanical Toy Head: A colorful German-made animated tin head, with pinback, eyes move when the string is pulled. 2½" x 2½", ca. 1915. $500.00–550.00

Card Game: "1118 In Dixie-land." B/W half-tone views depicting Blacks in the South, original box, one card is missing w/a few broken, box is also broken, 1897, The Cincinnati Game Co. $200.00–225.00

Game: "The Game of Ten Little Niggers" (card game similar to "Old Maid", with 21 cards depicting Negroes). Parker Bros.; Salem, Mass., ca. 1895. $225.00–325.00

Toy: Painted sheet metal kazoo. When metal lever is depressed, wooden figure of male tap dancer (6½" H) with loose pinned arms and legs moves in a tap-like dance to the music of the kazoo. Ca. 1920–30. $200.00–225.00

Toy: "Topsy" marionette, 14" airplane control marionette dressed in red floral print dress, manufactured by "Hazell's Popular Marionettes," Kansas City, Mo. (in original box), ca. 1940. $325.00–375.00

Toy: Sheet metal shooting gallery with spring loaded "cannon" to shoot marbles at two rows of numbered "heads" to give score of 5 or 10 points when struck and spun by marble. Marked "#900 Baby Rack Mfg. by The Brinkman Engineering Co., Dayton, Ohio." 14½" L x 5½" W x 6½" H. (Supply your own marbles.) $300.00–325.00

Toy: Skill Game. "Jolly Nigger Puzzle." Grinning face in iron with mouth open wide, 1½" long. Polished steel ball fits into mouth. Object of puzzle is to pick ball from mouth without overturning puzzle, turning over face, or using extra long fingernails. $300.00–350.00

Toy: "Bojangles" String Puppet. Composition head straw-hatted island man wearing green and black print pullover blouse, yellow and white striped pants and holding a maraca in each hand. Wooden feet. 14" H (strung and ready for your puppet show.) $150.00–175.00

Toy: Tinker/Pull. Two painted wooden toys. (1) Turned wood "Mammy Tinker." Tinker Toys, Evanston, Ill. 7" H. (2) Boy on wheeled cart, horsedrawn Hustler Toy Corp., painted wood 11½" L x 5" H x 4¼" W.
$110.00–125.00 each

"Darktown Battery", cast iron mechanical bank, depiction of three Black baseball players, 10" L, ca. 1875. $1,100.00–1,300.00

Toy: Nodder. Mechanical man, 8" tall, pressed paper, yellow coat/white pants, Made in Germany, ca. 1950, portion of right hand missing, otherwise in excellent condition. $110.00–125.00

String Puppet: "Lucifer." 14" tall w/original brochure - "Clippo" presents "Lucifer," manufactured by Fleischaker and Baum, 45 Greene St., New York City, 1938, excellent condition. $250.00–300.00

Game: Bowling Set. Four lithograph Black faces w/numbers, "5, 2, 3, 5" that pop up when hitting pin w/ball - lithograph paste on wood, 14" long, 1914. Rough condition w/no bowling ball. $300.00–350.00

String Puppet: "New Puppinette" made by American Crayon Co., Sandusky, Ohio/N.Y. #16764, 14½" H, in original box, w/red and white suit and white top hat. $225.00–275.00

Mechanical Bank: Little Joe Bank, original paint w/no bottom. As is - $300.00–350.00

Mechanical Bank: Jolly Nigger w/top hat, original paint. $550.00–700.00

Mechanical Bank: Jolly Nigger Bank, original paint. $550.00–700.00

Mechanical Bank: Jolly Nigger aluminum, original paint w/straw hat, ears move along w/arm. $550.00–700.00

Mechanical Bank: Jolly Nigger Bank, repainted.
$300.00–325.00

Mechanical Bank: Little Joe Bank, excellent condition.
$350.00–425.00

"Jazzbo Jim" window displaybox (without figure and works) in shape of log cabin, 7½" H x 9½" W x 14" L, w/tin cover lithograph on all four sides, w/hole in box for crank.
$475.00–600.00

Toy: Noise Maker. Colorful tin toy with photo print of singing man wearing straw hat and big bowtie. U.S. Metal Toy Mfg. Co. 2¼" x 4½". Ratchet makes noise when turned/spun by small wood handle.
$75.00–95.00

Marionette: Stuffed male minstrel marionette dressed in green top hat, shoes, polka-dot shirt, red vest, black velvet pants, red socks. Sewn eyes, mouth and nose. 13" H.
$175.00–225.00

Skill Game: Round glass-covered case with colorful head of woman and 5 white beads. Object of game is to see how quickly one can get all 5 beads into woman's mouth (to represent teeth). Marked "Made in Germany D.R.G.M. No. 116769." Ca. 1890–1910. 1⅞" dia.
$75.00–95.00

"Always Did 'Spise A Mule," a cast iron mechanical bank, depicting a Black jockey being bucked off a mule, 10" L.
$550.00–650.00

Game Board: "The Game of Little Black Sambo," published by Saalfield Publ. Co., Akron. Folding checkerboard-type board, 17½" x 18" (open), 4 different illustrations of Sambo in corners, center and cover picture.
$300.00–350.00

Puppet: Wooden jointed puppet or marionette with large turned wood head, painted face, wood body, arms and feet, but metal hands. 12" H.
$300.00–350.00

Skill Game: Ball Throwing. "Alabama Coon." A cardboard ball-toss game. Object to toss balls into open mouth of laughing minstrel man. 10¾" x 5½" x 1½" deep within original box with cover illustration of 3 children playing the game.
$250.00–300.00

Skill Toy: Tap Dancing Sambo. Wooden figural toy with flat cut-out body, arms and feet but with dowel leg; w/ painted face, shirt and fez. Jointed at hips, arms and knees which when maneuvered on the end of a pliable stick will jump, jive dance, and tap especially when used on a rebounding board.
$125.00–150.00

Toy: Walking Sam. Wooden cut-out figure of man, ca. 1930's with jointed knees and oversized feet so that figure will appear to walk when used with a small dowel stick placed in hole in back. Painted features, clothing painted red, yellow and blue. 7½" H, excellent condition.
$125.00–150.00

Game: "The Adventures of Little Black Sambo" w/beautiful game board. Cadaco-Ellis, Merchandise Mart, Chicago, Ill., 1945, original box, excellent condition.
$300.00–350.00

Squeeze Toy: Acrobat. Cut-out wooden flat figure on high bar who does amazing acrobatic tricks when the lower portion of the uprights are squeezed. 11" H. Japan.
$95.00–125.00

Still Bank: Bowling. Figural pottery still bank of grinning, freckled, seated pinboy holding a large bowling ball in his hands, with a bowling ball behind him. Brightly colored, high glazed, 6½" H.
$75.00–95.00

Still Bank: Mammy figural china bank with hands on waist and hips, base painted brown with red lips. Semi-vitreous china, 6" H.
$125.00–150.00

Still Bank: Iron. Aunt Jemima figural iron still bank, 8" H, painted red, white and black, ca. 1940.
$250.00–325.00

Still Bank: Iron Aunt Jemima figural iron still back, 8" H, unpainted, ca. 1970.
$75.00–100.00

Still Bank: Iron. Aunt Jemima iron figural still bank, 8" H painted red dress and head covering with white apron and shawl.
$250.00–325.00

Brower's Automatic Dancer Clockwork Toy: American, patented Sept. 23, 1873, in the form of a carved wood Black man dancing in front of a cabin (lithographed paper on wood) when clockwork mechanism at back is wound. 9" H.
$4,500.00–4,800.00

Weeden's "Plantation Darky Saving Bank." American, patented August 7, 1888. Painted tin clockwork mechanism, 5½" H. Fair condition, operative.
$750.00–850.00

French musical automaton of a Black banjo player, Vichy or D'Camps, late 19th century. Well-molded composition head, turns and nods while blinking its eyes, right hand strums the banjo, right leg crossing and uncrossing. The works contained in the chair-formed base, with an acorn-formed stop/start finial, 22½" H.
$10,000.00–12,000.00

French musical automaton of a mandolin player, late 19th century. The painted black bisque-head figure nods slightly while strumming his (replaced) mandolin. The works are contained within the base, 12" H.
$4,000.00–5,000.00

Japanese lithographed tin clockwork "Louis Armstrong" toy. The figure is holding plastic trumpet, leaning back and forth while playing, 10" H.
$375.00–425.00

Wind-up tin waiter, lithographed, Japan. 6" H.
$300.00–350.00

Wind-up tin "Mammy-type," (USA), 8" H, lithographed.
$325.00–375.00

Lithographed tin Sparkler Toy, depicting a Black man's head with glass eyes wearing a fedora and smoking a cigar. $625.00–725.00

Lithograph tin Sparkler toy, depicting a Black man's head w/glass eyes wearing a taxi driver's cap. $625.00–725.00

Lithograph tin Black saxophone player squeeze toy with cymbals on his ankles. $800.00–850.00

Clockwork tin Black waltzing couple, the lady is wearing red and yellow gown, lifting her partner (male is shorter) above the ground as they dance. $1,500.00–2,000.00

Lithograph tin seesaw toy with a Black and a White boy on the rolling platform toy. $950.00–1,100.00

Clockwork tin Black figure w/cigar in mouth, carrying a cane. Head turns as he walks. $1,200.00–1,500.00

Jointed Black figure w/cast iron head and trunk. Moving jaw causes his jointed wooden legs to dance. Dressed in a velvet jacket and satin knickers. $4,000.00–4,200.00

Clockwork tin hand-painted figure of Black boy being bitten in seat of his pants by dog. $1,100.00–1,500.00

Jigger Penny toy w/hand-wound crank. $300.00–350.00

Still Bank: Iron two-faced bank, cast face on front and back of cast bank, man wearing hat, painted black and gold, 3¼" H. $500.00–600.00

Mechanical Bank: "Bad Accident." Iron, 10" L, good condition. $4,000.00–4,200.00

Mechanical Bank: "Mammy and Child," cast iron, 8" H, fair/good condition. $3,500.00–4,000.00

Clock depicting a Black organ grinder with moving arms. $300.00–350.00

Clockwork tin toy with French patent marks, hand-painted, jointed Black figure on the front of an apple cart pusing it backwards. $1,000.00–1,200.00

Marx Black drummer: Lithograph tin musician with key wound drumming arms and cymbals on his feet. $1,000.00–1,200.00

Lithograph tin of a Black laughing figure, flat jointed face with a key-wound mechanism moving his jaw and tongue in a laughing gesture. $1,200.00–1,500.00

Lithograph laughing figures. (1) Black man wearing a top hat. (2) Manually operated Black clown. Both figures have moveable jointed faces. $500.00–600.00 each

Clockwork walking Black figure, carrying a cane, wear-

ing a checkered cloth suit. $500.00–600.00

Gunthermann musical tin toy, depicting two Black clowns, one playing the accordion, the other has clarinet in his hands and cymbals on feet. $3,000.00–3,300.00

Gunthermann mechanical tin musical toy, depicting Black banjo player and dancer. $3,000.00–3,300.00

Cast iron cigar cutter in the form of Black man. Cuts cigar tip in his mouth when arm is pressed. $950.00–1,100.00

Jointed wood Jigger Toy, depicting two Black female dancers dressed in cloth costumes with hats, dancing on wooded box. $600.00–700.00

Jointed wood Jigger Toy, the key-wound dressed Black figure dancing on wooden box. $600.00–700.00

Lithographed tin key-wound dancing Black figure, dressed in top hat, tailcoat and striped trousers, German. $350.00–450.00

German lithographed tin clockwork figure. Black woman, fitted with wheels beneath her long skirt, moveable. $400.00–450.00

"Unique Art" Jazzbo Jim. Key-wound lithographed tin banjo player dancing on the roof of log cabin. Patented Oct. 1921. $1,200.00–1,700.00

"Strauss" Alabama Coon Jigger, key-wound lithographed tin dancer on platform stage. $700.00–800.00

"Lehmann" lithographed tin wagon, drawn by ostrich and driven by uniformed Black man. The key-wound cart has "Africa" printed on it (firm's trademark). $700.00–800.00

"Dinah" cast iron mechanical bank, depicting Black woman tossing a coin into her mouth. $1,100.00–1,500.00

"Strauss" clockwork tin toy, depicting a Black man pushing a wheelbarrow. $550.00–700.00

Key-wound dancing Black male figure. Felt clothing and celluloid head and hat, standing at Hollywood and Vine Street sign. $450.00–525.00

Jolly Nigger "High Hat" cast iron mechanical bank. The figure is wearing white top hat, 8½" H. $550.00–700.00

"Stump Speaker" cast iron mechanical bank. The Black man drops a coin into his briefcase as his mouth moves, pat'd Nov. 1866, 10" H. $1,200.00–1,500.00

Painted Black figure, depicting boy wearing short green trousers and rust shirt, seated with one arm extended, possibly to hold fishing pole. 12½" H. $200.00–250.00

Toy Bank: Shimmy/Nodder. Ceramic nude Kewpie-type baby holding slice of watermelon, wearing only pearl earrings, seated on brown/white ceramic box of tissues or diapers (?). Neck set with springs; baby shakes her head with movement upon insertion of coin in slot atop box. Box - 3½" x 2¾" x 3¼". Overall height - 7¼".

$75.00–100.00

"Lehmann" felt tin Black figure. When the hat is pressed down it causes his eyes, mouth and limbs to move.

$400.00–500.00

Afro-American Museums

AAMRP
Northeastern University
360 Huntington Avenue
Boston, MA 02117

African American Cultural Center
2429 S. 8th Street
Minneapolis, MN 55454

African American Cultural Heritage
Center
Nolan Estes Ed Plaza
3434 S.R.L. Thornton Freeway
Dallas, TX 75224

African American Family Historical
Association
2077 Bent Creek Way
Atlanta, GA 30311

African Arts Museum
S.M.A. Fathers
23 Bliss Avenue
Tenafly, NJ 07670

African Studies and Research
Howard University
P.O. Box 231
Washington, DC 20059

Afro-American Cultural Center
30 Concord Terrace
Springfield, MA 01109

Afro-American Cultural Center
2191 7th Avenue
New York, NY 10027

Afro-American Cultural Center
Cleveland State University
1983 E. 24th Street
Cleveland, OH 44115

Afro-American Cultural and Historical
Society
1839 E. 81st Street
Cleveland, OH 44103

Afro-American Cultural Foundation
Westchester Community College
75 Grasslands Road
Valahalla, NY 10595

Afro-American Historical and
Cultural Museum
7th and Arch Streets
Philadelphia, PA 19106

Afro-American Historical Society of
the Niagra Frontier
P.O. Box 1663
Buffalo, NY 14216

Afro-American Museum of Detroit
1553 W. Grand Boulevard
Detroit, MI 48208

Amistad Research Center
400 Esplanade Avenue
New Orleans, LA 70116

Anacostia Neighborhood Museum
Smithsonian Institution
2405 Martin Luther King, Jr. Avenue, S.E
Washington, DC 20020

Arts N Artifacts Gallery
531 1st Avenue
Columbus, GA 31901

Avery Institute
P.O. Box 2807
Charleston, SC 29403

Aunt Len's Doll and Toy House
6 Hamilton Terrace
New York, NY 10031

Beck Cultural Exchange Center
1297 Dandridge Avenue
Knoxville, TN 37915

Bethune Historical Development
Project
National Council of Negro Women
1318 Vermont Avenue, NW
Washington, DC 20005

Bethune-Cookman College
Carl S. Swisher Library
640 2nd Avenue
Daytona Beach, FL 32015

Black American West Foundation
P.O. Box 717
Denver, CO 80207

Black Archives
Research Center and Museum
Florida A&M University
P.O. Box 809
Tallahassee, FL 32307

Black Archives of Mid-America
2033 Vine Street
Kansas City, MO 64108

Black Fashion Museum
Harlem Institute of Fashion
157 W. 126th Street
New York, NY 10027

Black History Exhibition Center
106 N. Main Street
Hempstead, NY 11550

Black Studies Division
Western Reserve Historical Society
10825 East Boulevard
Cleveland, OH 44106

California Museum of Afro-American
History and Culture
700 State Drive
Los Angeles, CA 90037

Carter G. Woodson Foundation
P.O. Box 1025
Newark, NJ 07102

Carver Public Museum
1165 Angelina
Austion, TX 78702

Collections of Life and Heritage
171 Ashby Street, SW
Atlanta, GA 30314

College Museum
Hampton Institute
Hampton, VA 23368

Community Folk Art Museum
2024 S. Salina Street
Syracuse, NY 13205

Connecticut Afro-American Society
444 Orchard Street
New Haven, CT 06511

Crispus Attucks Community Center
605 S. Duke Street
York, PA 17403

Dunbar Hotel Cultural and Historical
Museum
4225 S. Central Avenue
Los Angeles, CA 90011

Dunbar House
219 Summitt Street
Dayton, OH 45407

DuSable Museum
740 E. 56th Place
Chicago, IL 60637

East Bay Negro Historical Society
5606 San Pablo Avenue
Oakland, CA 94608

Ebony Museum
582 14th Street
Oakland, CA 94612

First National Black Historical
of Kansas
601 N. Water
Wichita, KS 67203

Frederick Douglass Memorial and
  Historical Association
14th and WaStreets, SW
Washington, DC 20020

Gallery Ligon
P.O. Box 1105
Columbia, MD 21044

Gallery of Art
Morgan State University
Baltimore, MD 21239

Genesis II
509 Cathedral Parkway
New York, NY 10025

George Washington Carver Museum
Tuskegee, AL 36088

Great Plains Black Museum
2213 Lake Street
Omaha, NE 68110

Harriet Tubman Museum
566 Columbus Avenue
Boston, MA 02118

Howard Tilton Library
Tulane University
Freret and Newcomb Place
New Orleans, LA 70118

Howard University Gallery of Art
2455 6th Street, NW
Washington, DC 20059

I.P Stanback Museum
South Carolina State College
Orangeburg, SC 29117

Joseph E. Zee Memorial Library and
  Museum
Jacksonville Public Library
122 N. Ocean Street
Jacksonville, FL 32202

Karamu House
2355 E. 89th Street
Cleveland, OH 44106

Laney Walker Museum
938 Wrightsboro Road
Augusta, GA 30901

Mann Simon's Cottage
1403 Richland Street
Columbia, SC 29201

Martin Luther King, Jr. Center for
  Social Change
503 Auburn Avenue, NE
Atlanta, GA 30312

Martin Luther King Museum of Black
  Culture
511 N. Henry Street
Eden, NC 27288

Maryland Community of Afro-American
History and Culture
Department of Economics, Room 304
1623 Forest Drive
Annapolis, MD 21403

Merabash Museum
P.O. Box 752
Willingboro, NJ 08046

Michigan Ethnic Heritage Studies
  Center
71 E. Perry Street
Detroit, MI 48202

Moorland-Spingarn Research Center
Howard University
Washington, DC 20059

Museum National Center of Afro-
  American Artists
300 Walnut Avenue
Boston, MA 02119

Museum of African American Art
2617 Lincoln Boulevard, Suite 207
Santa Monica, CA 90405

Museum of African and African-
  American Art and Antiquities
11 E. Utica Street
Buffalo, NY 14209

Museum of African Art
316 A Street, NE
Washington, DC 20002

Museum of Afro-American Life and
  Culture
P.O. Box 41511
Dallas, TX 75241

Museum of Afro-American History
Box 5
Roxbury, MA 02119

NAACP Historical and Cultural Project
441 Bergen Avenue
Jersey City, NJ 07304

National Afro-American Museum and
  Cultural Center
Ohio Historical Society
1982 Velma Avenue
Columbus, OH 43211

National Minority Military Museum
  Foundation
459 Kerr Hall
University of California
Davis, CA 95616

New Muse
1530 Bedford Avenue
Brooklyn, NY 11216

North Carolina Central University
  Gallery
1805 Fayetteville Street
Durham, NC 27707

Ntu Art Association
2100 NE 52nd Street
Oklahoma City, OK 73111

Old Slave Mart Museum
P.O. Box 446
Sullivan's Island, SC 29482

Parting Ways
Museum of Afro-American Ethnohistory
130 Court Street
P.O. Box 1776
Plymouth, MA 02360

Penn Center
Fogmore
P.O. Box 126
St. Helena Island, SC 29920

Resident Art and Humanities Consortium
Black History Museum
1515 Linn Street
Cincinnati, OH 45214

Rhode Island Black Heritage Society
1 Hilton Street
Providence, RI 02907

San Francisco African-American
  Historical and Cultural Society
Fort Mason Center, Bldg. C
San Francisco, CA 94123

Schomburg Center for Research in
  Black Culture
New York Public Library
515 Lenox Avenue
New York, NY 10037

Selma Burke Art Center
6118 Penn Circle S.
Pittsburgh, PA 15206

Smith Robertson Black Cultural Center
Marino Branch YMCA
527 N. Furish Street
Jackson, MS

Smith-Mason Gallery
1207 Rhode Island Avenue, NW
Washington, DC 20005

Society for Preservation of Weeksville
and Bedford
P.O. Box 120
St. John Station
Brooklin, NY 11216

South Side Center
3831 S. Michigan Avenue
Chicago, IL 60653

Southeastern Center for Afro-American
Architecture
Tuskegee Institute
308 Gregory Street
Tuskegee, AL 36088

Store Front Museum
162-02 Liberty Avenue
Jamaica, NY 11433

Studio Museum in Harlem
144 W. 125th Street
New York, NY 10027

Sutton's Black Heritage Gallery
5003 San Jacinto
Houston, TX 77004

Vaughn Cultural Center
1408 N. Kings Highway
St. Louis, MO 63113

Waddell Gallery
Trevor Arnett Library
Atlanta University
Chestnut Street, SW
Atlanta, GA 30314

YMI Cultural Center
47 Eagle Street
Asheville, NC 28801

Your Heritage House
110 E. Ferry Street
Detroit, MI 48202

319 Gallery
319 W. 108th Street
New York, NY 10025

Schroeder's ANTIQUES Price Guide

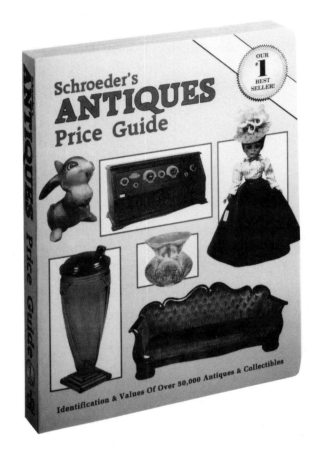

Schroeder's Antiques Price Guide is the #1 best-selling antiques & collectibles value guide on the market today, and here's why . . . More than 300 authors, well-known dealers, and top-notch collectors work together with our editors to bring you accurate information regarding pricing and identification. More than 45,000 items in almost 500 categories are listed along with hundreds of sharp original photos that illustrate not only the rare and unusual, but the common, popular collectibles as well. Each large close-up shot shows important details clearly. Every subject is represented with histories and background information, a feature not found in any of our competitors' publications. Our editors keep abreast of newly-developing trends, often adding several new categories a year as the need arises. If it merits the interest of today's collector, you'll find it in Schroeder's. And you can feel confident that the information we publish is up to date and accurate. Our advisors thoroughly check each category to spot inconsistencies, listings that may not be entirely reflective of market dealings, and lines too vague to be of merit. Only the best of the lot remains for publication. Without doubt, you'll find Schroeder's Antiques Price Guide the only one to buy for reliable information and values.

8½ x 11", 608 Pages   **$12.95**

COLLECTOR BOOKS
A Division of Schroeder Publishing Co., Inc.